Josh McDowell's
One Year® Book of
Youth Devotions

Josh McDowell's

BOOK OF

YOUTH DEVOTIONS

BY Bob Hostetler

Tyndale House Publishers, Inc.
WHEATON, ILLINOIS

Visit Tyndale's exciting Web site at www.tyndale.com

Edited by Betty Free and Linda Washington.
Designed by Catherine Bergstrom.

The One Year is a registered trademark of Tyndale House Publishers, Inc.

Library of Congress Cataloging-in-Publication Data

McDowell, Josh.
    [One year book of youth devotions]
    Josh McDowell's one year book of youth devotions / Bob Hostetler.
      p. cm.
    Summary: Presents Scripture verses and readings for each day of the year, designed to help young people make good choices in their daily lives.
    ISBN 0-8423-4301-6 (alk. paper)
    1. Teenagers—Prayer-books and devotions—English. 2. Preteens—Prayer-books and devotions—English. 3. Devotional calendars—Juvenile literature. [1. Prayer books and devotions. 2. Devotional calendars.] I. Hostetler, Bob, date. II. Title
BV4850.M2837   1997   97-17458
242'.63—dc21   AC

Printed in the United States of America

03 02 01 00 99 98 97
7   6   5   4   3   2

March

April

May

June

July

August

September

October

November

December

Your Daily Adventure in Making Right Choices

DINOSAURS AND MOVIE STARS.

A game show.

A brother and sister named Muck and Mire.

Full moons and streaking comets.

A network newscast the day after the Battle of Jericho.

Devils and angels. Stories, games, and jokes. Scientists and farmers. A crow and a canary. Quizzes and polls. Even an Erobian Mickatoo lizard. You'll find all these things—and more—in the pages of this book. *Josh McDowell's One Year Book of Youth Devotions* is a daily adventure in making right choices. From "Ike's Bike" (the first day's reading) to "Positive Daydreaming" (the reading for December 31), you will enjoy a wild ride of 366 gripping and captivating readings that will help you know right from wrong—and equip you to choose right.

Each daily adventure is accompanied by a short Bible reading, a key verse, a few questions or suggestions to help you apply the truth of that day's reading, and a brief prayer. Yet all of the daily adventures are different. Some are stories, some are quizzes; some will make you laugh, others might make you cry; some are fiction, and some are stranger than fiction. But each daily adventure is designed to make you think—and live—as "children of God without fault in a crooked and depraved generation, in which you shine like stars in the universe" (Philippians 2:15, NIV).

Josh McDowell's One Year Book of Youth Devotions can also be used with *Josh McDowell's One Year Book of Family Devotions,* as well as many other "Right from Wrong" resources.

1 Ike's Bike

Bible Reading: Judges 17:1-6

In those days Israel had no king, so the people did whatever seemed right in their own eyes. Judges 17:6

"WELCOME TO THE latest episode of *Current Culture!* My name is Geraldo Winfrey-Raphael, and I'm your host. Today we're talking to ordinary people about morals and values and whose version of right and wrong is . . . well, right . . . or wrong. Our first guest is Ike, a high school student."

Geraldo nods seriously into the camera, then turns and thrusts a microphone toward a teenage boy dressed in black. Geraldo tries to keep up with Ike's purposeful stride as they walk across the school quad.

"You look like an intelligent high school student," Geraldo says. "How do you choose between right and wrong?"

Ike stops walking and looks straight into the camera.

"Right and wrong?" the student says. "There *is* no 'right' and 'wrong'! Read your Nietzsche, man! Get a grip on Machiavelli! Those words are nothing but the wishful thinking of a society too weak to face the prospect of a godless world and the lack of moral absolutes! That's what Nietzsche said, man! Look it up!"

Ike begins walking again. Geraldo starts jogging to keep up with the young man. Finally, Ike stops abruptly in front of a bike rack, an expression of shock on his face.

"Is something wrong?" Geraldo says. "Are you all right?"

"My bike! It's gone! Somebody stole my bike!"

Ike throws his arms in the air and begins pacing in front of the bike rack.

"Oh, dude, this is wrong! This is totally wrong!"

"But I thought Nietzsche said . . ."

"Aw, shut up, man! Like, Nietzsche never had a Trek 950 with titanium hubs and alloy rims and all kinds of really cool stuff! Oh, this is *so* wrong!"

Another student approaches, then stops.

"I thought your mom drove you to school this morning," the other student says.

Ike suddenly stops his pacing and looks at the camera.

"Oh," he says. "Yeah. That's right." He shrugs. "Cool."

Ike and his friend walk away. Geraldo faces the camera, then draws a single finger across his throat in a slicing motion.

 REFLECT: In the above script, Ike quoted Nietzsche and Machiavelli. These were two philosophers who said that there is no such thing as right and wrong. Their writings had a significant influence on Adolph Hitler and other dictators of the twentieth century. Do you think that Ike really believed what he said about right and wrong? Why or why not? What do you believe about right and wrong?

 PRAY: "God, I admit that sometimes I act like there's no such thing as right and wrong. But I don't want to do what's right in my *own* eyes; I want to do what's right in *your* eyes. Help me especially in the area of_____."

2 Which Way Do 1 Go?

Bible Reading: Proverbs 14:12

> There is a way that seems right to a person, but its end is the way to death. *Proverbs 14:12*, NRSV

HOW DO YOU usually decide whether a certain belief or behavior is right or wrong? Do you:

(a) toss a coin: Heads it's right, tails it's wrong?
(b) weigh it carefully, considering whether it *feels* right?
(c) measure it against what the majority thinks? (If it's pretty much accepted in your school, church, or community, it's probably OK.)
(d) none of the above?

If you answered (a), you've got a lot of company. Many people today make decisions this way. They may not actually flip a coin, but they don't lose any sleep over such a decision. They put more thought into what kind of dog food to buy Ol' Yeller than whether a certain action would be right or wrong.

If you answered (b), you chose an extremely popular model for determining right and wrong. People who choose this usually try to decide what's right or wrong based on their own opinions or feelings. They're likely to say, "I think it's wrong to hurt another person," or "I feel it's OK to get mad as long as you have a good reason."

If you answered (c), you're with a number of people who make decisions about right and wrong the way you do. They try to decide what's right or wrong depending on what everyone else is doing. If they see other people cheating or breaking the law, they think it's OK for them to do it too.

If you answered (d), you'll probably find yourself in the minority most of the time. But the truth is, we can't make right choices based on how we feel or on what everyone else is doing. Right and wrong are not determined by an individual's opinions or feelings or by what the government or society accepts or rejects. Right and wrong are determined by God, who is the original, the universal, the absolute standard for everything that is good and right.

For example, lying is wrong because God is true. Stealing is wrong because God is just. Hatred is wrong because God is love. These things are wrong no matter what you may think or feel. These things are wrong, not because the majority thinks so or because society frowns on them, but because *God* thinks so.

REFLECT: Proverbs 14:12 says: "There is a way that seems right to a person, but its end is the way to death." How might choices (a), (b), and (c) (above) have the same consequence? Think back on how you usually make decisions about whether a belief or behavior is right or wrong. Now think about Proverbs 14:12. To what consequence will your method of deciding lead you?

PRAY: "God, help me consider your desires in every choice I make, especially when it's hard to do the right thing, like when I have to_____."

Recipe for Right

Bible Reading: Deuteronomy 32:1-4

*He is the Rock; his work is perfect. Everything he does is just and fair.
He is a faithful God who does no wrong; how just and upright he is!
Deuteronomy 32:4*

YOU'RE PLANNING A surprise birthday party for your mom. You invite your little sister to help you bake the cake.

"Let's make a chocolate cake!" Sis squeals.

"OK," you agree and pull out a box of chocolate cake mix from the cupboard. "This says we need a half cup of water, a half cup of vegetable oil, and two eggs."

Sis says, "I wanna do that!"

You shrug. "Sure, OK," you say. You pour the cake mix into a large mixing bowl. Then you see that Sis is putting water into a doll cup.

"Sis," you say, "we need to use a measuring cup."

"This is a cup," she says, pointing to the miniature teacup holding the water.

"But we need to use *this* cup," you say. You grab a glass measuring cup.

"But I wanna use *my* cup!" Sis's face wrinkles up as though she's just swallowed a lemon whole. She's about to cry.

What should you do? If you use Sis's doll cups, your cake will be a disaster, of course. Why? Because the recipe relies on a standard measurement. You can't just use any size cup. You know that when a recipe says to use a *cup* of flour or a *teaspoon* of cinnamon, you must measure those quantities against a standard.

It's the same way with knowing whether something is right or wrong. A lot of people try to "measure" whether it's right to do something by how they feel or what they think or what other people might say. But the recipe for right and wrong relies on a measurement just like the recipe for a cake does. Only the standard measurement of right and wrong isn't a cup or a teaspoon; it's God.

In other words, God is the measurement of whether something is right or wrong. "He is a faithful God who does no wrong," Deuteronomy says. Whatever is like God is right. Whatever is not like God is wrong. For example, telling the truth is right and lying is wrong because God is true and trustworthy.

If you want to figure out whether something is right or wrong, all you need to do is follow the recipe: Measure it against our God, "a faithful God who does no wrong."

REFLECT: Think about the statements "Whatever is like God is right" and "Whatever is not like God is wrong." Can you think of any examples (like the example of telling the truth and lying that was given above) that agree with either statement?

ACT: To remind yourself that God's Word is the standard of "measurement" for right and wrong, you could carry a small measuring spoon around with you in your pocket, purse, or backpack today. Or you could keep a measuring tape in your locker.

PRAY: "Thank you, God, for being perfect and fair and faithful. Show me how to be more like you, especially when I_____."

4 Shell Talk

Bible Reading: John 8:31-32
And you will know the truth, and the truth will set you free. John 8:32

HERMAN THE CRAB stormed across the sea floor and under the family rock.

"I want to be free!" he screamed at his father. "I don't see how you can expect me to wear this stupid shell twenty-four hours a day! It's confining! It cramps my style!"

His father, Fred, inhaled deeply and draped a heavy claw on Herman's shoulder. "Son," he said, "let me tell you a story."

Herman rolled his eyes. "Dad, not another . . ."

"It's about Humphrey the human, who insisted on going barefoot to school. He complained that his shoes were too confining. They cramped his style, he said. He longed to be free to run barefoot through fields and streams. Finally, his mother gave in to him. He skipped out of the house barefoot. Do you know what happened?"

Herman opened his mouth, but his father continued before he could answer.

"Humphrey the human stepped on pieces of a broken bottle. His foot required twenty stitches, and some other guy took his girl to the prom while Humphrey sat home watching reruns of *Flipper.*"

"That's a pretty lame story, Dad," Herman said.

"Maybe, Son, but the point is this: Every crab has felt this way at one time or another, thinking life would be better if he could be completely shell-free. But that's like a sailor getting tired of the confinement of a ship and jumping to freedom in the sea. He may think that's freedom, but if he doesn't get back to ship or shore, he'll drown and end up as crab food. What kind of freedom is that?"

Herman pondered his father's words.

"Soon you will shed your shell, Son," Fred said, thinking how hard it would be to say that five times fast. "It's called *molting,* and all crabs do it as they grow up. But," he said with warning in his eyes, "when that happens, you will be more vulnerable than at any other time in your life. Until your new shell hardens like this one—" he tapped his son's armored back—"you'll have to be much more careful and watchful than usual. You'll be *less* free without this shell, not more free."

"That's weird, Dad," Herman said. "I never thought of it that way. You mean that some things may seem to limit freedom but really make greater freedom possible?"

Fred smiled broadly and patted his son on the back with a mammoth claw. "How'd you get to be so smart, Son?" he asked.

 REFLECT: What, according to John 8:31, must happen before you can know the truth? Think of John 8:31-32 like a math problem: Obeying Jesus' teachings + knowing the truth = FREEDOM.

 PRAY: "Lord, I really do want to be free. Help me to learn all about your teachings so that I can obey them."

5 First Knight

Bible Reading: Ephesians 6:11-18

Put on all of God's armor so that you will be able to stand firm against all strategies and tricks of the Devil. Ephesians 6:11

PICTURE TWO KNIGHTS sitting on sparkling white horses. They face a gleaming castle surrounded by mammoth stone walls, which in turn are circled by a wide moat. Archers line the battlements, awaiting the signal to launch their deadly arrows at the pair below.

The first knight wears a shining suit of armor. A heavy helmet protects his head. His body is encased in a massive iron suit; his arms and legs are enclosed by hinged pieces of metal. His armor is completed by heavy "boots" and rigid "gloves."

The second knight sits astride his charger like the first knight, but the only metal he's wearing are the braces on his teeth. A backward baseball hat and sunglasses protect his head from the glare of the sun. His shirt bears a picture of Ren and Stimpy. A pair of shorts, socks, and Reebok shoes complete his attire.

The first knight looks at the second. He says, "We shall charge yon castle on my signal and bring honor to our families this fair day." He raises the broadsword he holds in his right hand and points it in the direction of the castle.

"OK, dude," the second knight says as he lifts a baseball bat. "Whatever!"

Which knight would you rather be? The first knight is rather confined, of course—it gets stuffy and sweaty inside his unwieldy suit, and it's hard to scratch your back or wipe your nose. The second knight is totally free of such restrictive dress. He's got it made, right? Wrong! The first knight may feel restricted by his armor, but he wears it for his own good. The second knight may be more comfortable, more "free," but he's unprotected.

God's commands work like a suit of armor. They're designed to protect you from the "fiery arrows aimed at you by Satan" (Ephesians 6:16). His command not to steal, for example, protects you from the guilt and fear of punishment—and the shame, embarrassment, and real punishment that would result if you got caught! His command not to lie protects you from being trapped by a web of your own lies, spun from having to invent new lies to cover up the old ones. It also keeps you from losing the trust of your friends and family. His command to forgive those who have hurt you protects you from becoming a bitter, resentful person.

God's commands are not designed to cramp your style or spoil your fun; they're intended—like a suit of armor—to protect you from harm.

 REFLECT: Do you ever feel cramped by God's commands? Do you ever feel like they limit your freedom? How can you become more aware of the ways in which God's commands protect you from the Devil? Remember that he "prowls around like a roaring lion, looking for some victim to devour" (1 Peter 5:8).

 PRAY: "God, thank you for your love and for the way you protect me by demanding my obedience to your commandments. Please help me with the weakest part of my armor right now, which is_____."

6 Truth and Consequences

Bible Reading: Hebrews 11:24-28

It was by faith that Moses, when he grew up, refused to be treated as the son of Pharaoh's daughter. He chose to share the oppression of God's people instead of enjoying the fleeting pleasures of sin. Hebrews 11:24-25

"WELCOME TO TV'S most popular game show! And now, the host of *Truth and Consequences,* Tom Foolery!" *Wild shouts and applause as the handsome host jogs down the center aisle and leaps onto the stage.*

"Thank you! Let's welcome our first contestants, Paul and Susan!"

Two teenagers leap from their seats and jog down the aisle to join Foolery.

"Let's play *Truth and Consequences.* For our first game, you may choose the prize behind the red door or the one behind the blue door. I'll even tell you what they are."

The sound of a drum roll enters the studio through the loudspeakers.

"Behind the red door are two free tickets to next Saturday's Counting Cannibals concert. You want to go with your friends, but you don't have the money—am I right?"

Paul and Susan nod. The audience applauds.

"Behind the blue door is a night with Mom and Dad watching a rerun of *Matlock.*"

"I choose the red door!" *Paul and Susan shout their response in unison.*

Foolery flashes a toothy smile.

"Not so fast. To open the red door, you must agree to 'borrow' sixty dollars from your mother's purse. After all, you didn't think *we'd* buy the tickets, did you? And, of course, you can always repay the money later. To open the blue door, simply don't 'borrow' the money. What'll it be, the concert with your friends . . . or *Matlock* with Mom and Dad?"

Tough choice, huh? Many times, trying to do the right thing is really tough because the wrong thing could be so much fun, while the right choice seems like a drag! Take Moses, for example. He faced a tough choice: turn his back on God and his people to live his life in the lap of luxury, *or* hang out with a bunch of complainers in the desert. Pretty clear choice, wouldn't you say? But Moses chose the longer-lasting rewards of obeying God instead of the immediate gratification of sin.

That's the way it goes. Many wrong choices offer immediate "gain," while right choices often seem to involve short-term "pain." To be honest, if we make moral choices simply on the basis of what will bring immediate pain or gain, we will very often make the wrong choice. But if we're willing to choose right, we'll be much better off in the long run. That's the truth.

 REFLECT: Note that Hebrews 11:24 says Moses managed to make the right decision by faith. How can someone use faith to make a decision?

Think about the recent choices you've made between right and wrong. Did you base your choice on which way was easiest or on which way was right? How do you know?

 PRAY: "God, help me choose right even when it seems easier to choose wrong."

7 A Sure Foundation

Bible Reading: Psalm 111:1-10

Reverence for the Lord is the foundation of true wisdom. The rewards of wisdom come to all who obey him. Praise his name forever!
Psalm 111:10

IT LOOKS LIKE a failed science fair experiment. It took 199 years to build, from start to finish. It's already crooked and gets more and more crooked every year. Some day (unless preventive measures are taken) it will lean so far out of line that its eight stories, three hundred steps, and church bells will topple to the ground in a pile of rubble.

What is it? You've already figured it out, haven't you? "It" is the famous leaning Tower of Pisa, a famous bell tower in Pisa, Italy. It was begun in 1173. By the time the first three stories were completed, the tower had begun to pitch to one side. Why? Because the ground beneath it began to sink. Its foundation was unstable.

Imagine that—a masterpiece of architecture threatened because of a faulty foundation.

Same thing happens every day. People go to school, devour books, pass exams, earn degrees, graduate with honors. Yet, in spite of all their learning, in spite of all their knowledge, they do all kinds of stupid things, make poor choices, and mess up their lives *big time!* Why? Because of a faulty foundation. They may have knowledge. They may have learning. They may have education. But they don't have wisdom. Because "reverence for the Lord is the foundation of true wisdom. The rewards of wisdom come to all who obey him" (Psalm 111:10).

"Reverence for the Lord" has traditionally been referred to as "the fear of the Lord." The word *fear* in that phrase doesn't mean fearing God the way we might fear Freddie Krueger or Frankenstein, the kind of fear that churns your stomach or keeps you awake at night. It means respect for God, for his power and for his love.

If you *really* want to be wise and make good choices, you need to begin with reverence for the Lord. Reverence for God means developing a profound awareness of him. It means respecting him for who he is and what he can do. It means obeying him. It means not taking his gifts or his grace for granted. It means remembering that he is the judge of good and evil, of right and wrong.

True wisdom is like a magnificent bell tower—a structure of power, beauty, and grace. And, like all sound structures, it has a sure foundation: reverence for God.

 REFLECT: How firm is your foundation? Do you respect and obey God, or are you trying to become wise without that foundation?

 ACT: Hang one of your favorite posters or pictures slightly crooked to remind yourself over the next few days of the importance of a sure foundation.

 PRAY: "God, sometimes I feel like my foundation is pretty shaky. I don't have a lot of wisdom, but I'm glad that you do. Help me to stay close to you so that I don't topple to the ground when_____."

Because of Love

Bible Reading: 1 John 5:1-5

Loving God means keeping his commandments, and really, that isn't difficult. For every child of God defeats this evil world by trusting Christ to give the victory. 1 John 5:3-4

THOUGH FIFTEEN-YEAR-OLD Shannon Miller won a silver medal in the 1992 Olympics in Barcelona, Spain, she returned home disappointed—she had not won a single gold medal. Four years later, however, at the age of nineteen, Shannon captured two gold medals in Atlanta for her effort in the team gymnastics competition and for her performance on the balance beam.

A few days after her thrilling victory on the balance beam, she was asked by a television reporter how hard it had been to keep practicing and working in the years between the Olympics.

Shannon shrugged in response to the question and answered that she loved gymnastics. Because she loved it so much, she hadn't minded the toil of training for the Olympics. The work that might have seemed hard and unpleasant to someone else was not so hard for Shannon because of her love for the sport.

It's kind of the same with obeying God's commands. People who don't know God or his Son, Jesus, often look at the commands he has given to his people and think, *Thou shalt not this!* and *Thou shalt not that!* They may say, "There are too many 'thou shalt nots'! I don't see how you Christians can stand all the rules and stuff you have to obey. That's too hard for me." Or they may say, "I could never keep all those commands."

But such thoughts and statements show that they don't really understand how the Christian life works. Like Shannon Miller, who trained hard because of her love for gymnastics, Christians obey God's commands because of their love for God. God's commands are not burdensome to his children. Obeying him isn't torture. It's not even difficult for those who rely on the Holy Spirit's power because the Spirit does all the work—we just have to trust him moment by moment.

 REFLECT: Compare the ways the following translations phrase 1 John 5:3:

For this is the love of God, that we keep his commandments: and his commandments are not grievous (KJV).

This is love for God: to obey his commands. And his commands are not burdensome (NIV).

Loving God means keeping his commandments, and really, that isn't difficult (NLT).

How does your love for God make you more willing to obey him? How does your love for God make you more able to obey him?

 PRAY: "Loving God, help me to show my love for you today by_____."

9 Rules, Rules, Rules!

Bible Reading: Exodus 20:1-17

You must worship the Lord your God; serve only him. Matthew 4:10

"DON'T PLAY WITH matches."

"Look both ways before you cross the street."

"Don't touch a hot stove."

"Say please and thank you."

"Don't sit too close to the TV."

"Don't cross your eyes."

"Don't dye your little sister's hair green."

Rules, rules, rules! Sometimes it seems like you're not allowed to do *anything*, doesn't it? "Do this," your parents say. "Don't do that." "Eat your vegetables." "Brush your teeth." "Fasten your seat belt."

It can get to you sometimes. But think about it: Why do you think your parents have rules like "Don't run with scissors"? Most of their rules are for your protection. If they hadn't told you not to play with matches as a little kid, you might have been your own science fair project. If they hadn't prevented you from dyeing your little sister's hair green—well, OK, that would have been totally fun and would have been worth whatever happened. But you get the idea.

Think about this, too. Why do you think God has rules like "Do not lie" and "Do not murder"? Do you think he gave those commands because he was having a bad day? Do you think he issued the Ten Commandments because he liked the way they sounded? Do you think he laid down the law to throw his weight around or to be a party pooper? Of course not. God gave commandments to us because he wanted to protect us and provide for us. He knows the surest, safest path to pleasure and fulfillment, and his commands are intended to help us get there.

Look at what Moses said about God's commands:

And the Lord our God commanded us to obey all these laws and to fear him *for our own prosperity and well-being,* as is now the case. . . . And now, Israel, what does the Lord your God require of you? He requires you to fear him, to live according to his will, to love and worship him with all your heart and soul, and to obey the Lord's commands and laws that I am giving you today *for your own good.* (Deuteronomy 6:24; 10:12-13; emphasis added)

 REFLECT: According to Deuteronomy 6:24 and 10:12-13, why did God make rules? Our parents usually try to do the best they can to protect and provide for us based on what they know. God, of course, knows everything—even the future—and his commands are the result of his knowledge and wisdom. Can you think of ways his rules protect you?

 PRAY: "God, I praise you because you're a wise and loving God, and you give your commandments for my own good."

10 A Detective Story

Bible Reading: Exodus 33:7-13

Moses said to the Lord, . . . "If you are pleased with me, teach me your ways so I may know you and continue to find favor with you."
Exodus 33:12-13, NIV

DR. WATSON HAD not told the great detective Sherlock Holmes that he had recently gotten married. He was surprised, therefore, when Holmes greeted him, acting as if he'd known it all along.

"Wedlock suits you," he remarked. "And I see you're in practice again."

Watson expressed his shock. How did Holmes know?

"It is simplicity itself," Holmes answered. "You have gained seven and a half pounds since I last saw you."

"Seven," Watson corrected.

"Indeed, I should think more. And you walk into my rooms smelling of iodoform, with a black mark of nitrate of silver on your right forefinger and a bulge on the side of your top hat to show where you have tucked your stethoscope. I would be dull indeed not to notice that you have both taken a wife and once again become an active member of the medical profession."

"My dear Holmes," Watson cried, "you are truly amazing!" *

Amazing or not, you don't have to be Sherlock Holmes to perform similar deductions of your own. Did you know you can tell a lot about your parents just by the rules they set for you? Really!

Your parents' rules show what sort of people they are. For example, if they expect you to say "please" and "thank you," that reveals they value manners. If your parents require you to help keep the house clean, that shows they value cleanliness. If they insist that you tell the truth at all times, that means they value honesty.

The same thing is true of God. His commands reveal his character. That's why Moses, who received the law on Mount Sinai, asked God, "If you are pleased with me, teach me your ways *so I may know you*" (Exodus 33:13, NIV, emphasis added). Moses recognized that learning God's ways—understanding his commands—would acquaint him with the character of God himself.

His character is written in his commands. And it doesn't take a Sherlock Holmes to deduce that! It's elementary!

REFLECT: Clues to God's character can be found in his commands. What clues have you found? Think about one of God's commands and consider how it reflects God's character.

PRAY: "Like Moses, I pray that you will teach me your ways, God, so that I may really know you."

*Based upon "A Scandal in Bohemia." Arthur Conan Doyle, *The Adventures of Sherlock Holmes* (London, Wis.: Octopus Books, Ltd., 1981, 15–16).

11 A One-of-a-Kind God

Bible Reading: Exodus 20:1-3

Then God instructed the people as follows: "I am the Lord your God, who rescued you from slavery in Egypt. Do not worship any other gods besides me." Exodus 20:1-3

WHAT'S THE MOST famous painting in the world? Probably the *Mona Lisa*.

Leonardo da Vinci painted a portrait of Lisa del Giocondo, the young wife of a wealthy merchant, around 1503 in Florence, Italy. The smile he captured on the woman's face has mystified people ever since its creation. Is she happy? Is she sad? Is her smile appearing? Is it disappearing? Or does she just have a little indigestion?

You've seen the picture, right? Probably not. You've seen *copies*. You've seen it reproduced in encyclopedias, classrooms, textbooks, television shows—but unless you've visited the Louvre Museum in Paris, you've never seen the actual *Mona Lisa*.

The *Mona Lisa* is unique. It's one of a kind. There is no other painting like it.

What is true of the *Mona Lisa* is true, in a much greater and deeper way, of our God. He is unique. He's one of a kind. There is no one like him. When Moses ascended the slopes of Mount Sinai many years ago, God delivered the Ten Commandments:

> Then God instructed the people as follows: "I am the Lord your God, who rescued you from slavery in Egypt. Do not worship any other gods besides me" (Exodus 20:1-3).

The first commandment God gave to Moses revealed that he is unique. There is no one like him. But his uniqueness exceeds the uniqueness of the *Mona Lisa*. There is only one *Mona Lisa* in the world, but there are many paintings. There is only one God in the universe, and there is none other. He's not only *unique* in his class, he's *alone* in his class! He alone is God. He says, "Let all the world look to me for salvation! For I am God; there is no other" (Isaiah 45:22).

That is why God tells us to worship no one but him. And that's why we will never be satisfied worshiping someone—or something—else.

 REFLECT: Do you worship only God? Are you devoted to anyone or anything else? How do you know? What other things in the world can be truly called unique? Are any of those things unique in the way that God is unique?

 ACT: Look for a picture of the *Mona Lisa*. (Try looking in an encyclopedia.) If possible, keep a copy of the painting posted on your bedroom door or bathroom mirror. Every time you see it this week, take a moment to think about God's uniqueness.

 PRAY: "God, I'm really glad that I don't need to look anywhere else for salvation. I praise you for being the only God there is."

12 A Spirit God

Bible Reading: Exodus 20:4-6
Do not make idols of any kind. Exodus 20:4

"WHAT'S THE BIG deal?" Omri asked his friend Levi. The pair sat beside Omri's family tent in the desert; the great Mount Sinai loomed in the distance.

"Huh?" Levi adjusted his striped headgear to shield his face from the sand.

Omri pointed to the front page headline of the local newspaper, *The Sinai Grumbler:* "Moses returns from mountain, reports Ten Commandments given to him by God."

"I just don't see what the big deal is," Omri explained, kicking the pebbles on the ground with his sandaled feet. "I mean, some of these commandments make sense. But listen to number two: 'Do not make idols of any kind, whether in the shape of birds or animals or fish. You must never worship or bow down to them,' it says."

"Yeah, so?" Levi asked.

"I don't get it," Omri explained. He pointed to the sky. "Why should he care if we use a little carving of a bird or a cow to imagine what he might be like?"

"Is he a bird or a cow?" Levi's face showed his confusion.

"Well . . . no."

"Is he a fish?"

"No," Omri answered.

"What is he, then?"

"He's the God of Abraham, Isaac, and Jacob! He's the God of all our people."

"But what does he look like?" Levi asked.

"How am I supposed to know?" Omri answered. "I've never seen him."

Levi shrugged. "Neither have I. And Moses says he can be anywhere and everywhere all at the same time. I don't know any fish or birds that can do that. So maybe making pictures or statues would distort our worship."

Omri looked thoughtful but unconvinced.

"Look at it this way," Levi suggested. "How would you like for me to make a statue of a goat and say it looks like you?"

"Yeah, right," Omri countered. "Me, a goat?"

"Yeah, you're right. You don't smell quite that nice," Levi said, as he jumped to his feet and ran away to avoid the pebbles Omri threw in his direction.

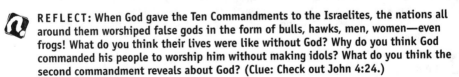

REFLECT: When God gave the Ten Commandments to the Israelites, the nations all around them worshiped false gods in the form of bulls, hawks, men, women—even frogs! What do you think their lives were like without God? Why do you think God commanded his people to worship him without making idols? What do you think the second commandment reveals about God? (Clue: Check out John 4:24.)

PRAY: "God, I may not be able to see and touch you the way I might see and touch a statue or a picture, but I thank you that I can learn about you and know you in other ways, like_____."

13 A Holy God

Bible Reading: Exodus 20:7
Do not misuse the name of the Lord your God. Exodus 20:7

BASKETBALL GREAT CHARLES Barkley, after signing a new million-dollar contract, once responded to reporters' questions by saying, "I'm so tired of talking about money, money, money. I just want to play basketball, drink Pepsi, and wear Reeboks!"

Barkley was joking, of course. Not only does his basketball playing earn him millions of dollars, he is also paid a lot of money for his endorsement of products like Pepsi-Cola and Reeboks. These companies pay Barkley, and other celebrities and athletes like him, to endorse their products because they want that star's name to be associated with their drink, shoe, car, or long-distance phone company.

Of course, celebrities want their name to be linked with good products, too. Charles Barkley probably wouldn't have endorsed Dirty Joe's Puke Juice, even if they'd offered him more money than PepsiCo. He probably would have turned down an offer from Ugly-Shoes-That-Don't-Fit 'R' Us, even if they could have paid him more than Reebok, Inc. Why? Because who wants his or her name to be associated with something crummy, shoddy, or "uncool"?

You can understand that, can't you?

If you can, then maybe you can see why God is so concerned about how his name is used. You can see why, in the Ten Commandments, God told his people not to misuse his name. And you can see why, in Leviticus 19:12, God said, "Do not use my name to swear a falsehood and so profane the name of your God. I am the Lord."

See, God is a holy God. He is perfectly pure, good, and righteous. And because he's holy, he doesn't want his name to be associated with anything evil or false or frivolous (anything unimportant, silly, or careless). That's why it's wrong to use God's name in a profane expression. That's why it's wrong to use God's name thoughtlessly, even in popular expressions such as "omigod." That's why it's wrong to use God's name to cover up a lie or swear to something that's false. Because doing those kinds of things offends God's holiness.

If Charles Barkley and other famous people like him have good reasons to protect their names, God has infinitely better reasons.

 REFLECT: When God gave the Ten Commandments to the Israelites, the common practice was to swear an oath with the name of a god in an effort to make the oath more believable. Some people follow similar practices even today. Think of an example.
Do you ever tie God's name to anything evil or false or frivolous? Think about the commandment in Exodus 20:7. How can you change this behavior?

 ACT: Place a soft-drink bottle (or your name-brand tennis shoes) in a prominent place in your room or school locker to remind you to honor God's name today.

 PRAY: "God, I know that your name is misused a lot. The next time I hear that happen, whether it's a friend or me doing it, help me remember to_____."

14 TGFS
(Thank God for Sunday)

Bible Reading: Mark 2:23-27

Remember to observe the Sabbath day by keeping it holy. Exodus 20:8

"And on the seventh day God rested from all his work." Hebrews 4:4, NIV

THE FINAL BELL rang. Jesse slammed his locker door shut and started toward the school doors. He saw Steven in the jostling crowd ahead and pushed forward until he was walking beside his friend.

"What are you doing this weekend?" Jesse asked.

Steven shrugged. "I don't know. Nothing, I guess. How about you?"

"I'm gonna be pretty busy down at church. Our youth group is helping with worship on Sunday, so . . ."

"You sound like you enjoy that stuff," Steven said.

"I do! Sunday mornings are great. And then we (my family, I mean) usually spend Sunday afternoons doing stuff together. Even if we just play Monopoly, it's kinda cool because it's different from any other day in the week. And Sunday dinner is always the best meal of the week."

"Your Sunday is sure different from mine. The only way I know it's Sunday is that there's more newspaper lying around the house."

Jesse shrugged as he and Steven boarded the school bus together. "My parents say that Sunday shows us God's grace, because he gives us a day not to work. It reminds us that he gives us things, not because we deserve them, but just because that's the way God is!"

Is your Sunday any different from the rest of the week? Jesus said the Sabbath was made for man; that means it's a special day with a special meaning. We are to use it as God's day to understand more about him, especially about his graciousness toward us.

It's not always easy to know how to make and keep Sunday special. Even in Jesus' time there was disagreement over how people should spend the Sabbath (as today's reading shows). But from the beginning, God wanted us to enjoy a special day of rest and *re*-creation.

 REFLECT: *Sabbath* is a Hebrew word that means "to stop doing something." What do you stop doing on your Sabbath? What do you start doing? How is your Sunday different from other days? What can you do to make it more special?

 PRAY: "God, sometimes I forget what Sunday is all about. Help me to remember your graciousness for your sake and for mine."

15 Learning Respect

Bible Reading: Exodus 20:12

Honor your father and mother. Then you will live a long, full life in the land the Lord your God will give you. Exodus 20:12

SOMEONE TOLD ME that when he was very young, his grandfather showed him how to use a hand saw. (That's the one about six inches wide with sharp teeth and no electrical power.)

"First," he said, "carefully make a pencil line showing exactly where you want to cut. Then check your measurement again to make sure you marked it right. Measure twice, cut once."

He continued, "Make sure the piece of wood you are cutting is on a smooth, steady surface. If it isn't, the wood could shift and throw you off the mark. Then, holding the piece of wood as securely as possible with your knee or hand or both, begin *slowly* to saw. Start the cut so you have a guide rut for the saw.

"And above all, keep your hand away from the saw!" As he said this, he held up his hand; two fingers were half as long as the others, fingers that had been cut off at the knuckle. My friend said his eyes must have widened as he absorbed the message of his grandfather's experience.

One of the reasons God gave us parents, grandparents, and guardians is that he wants us to learn from their experience. It may be hard to believe, but your parents used to be kids—a *million* years ago! They've done a lot of stuff, and they've even made mistakes. Not all their mistakes cost them a finger or two, but they have made your parents a little smarter and wiser than they once were.

That's why God commands us to honor our parents or guardians. He knows that their experience has taught them a few things, and he wants us to learn from them, without losing any digits or limbs! But there's another reason God wants us to honor our parents. Like all his commandments, his commandment to honor our parents reveals something about his nature. The fifth commandment reveals that he is a God who values respect.

Respect is important to God because it's a part of who he is. It's also important to him because a healthy respect for our parents (and grandparents) can provide for us and protect us, just like the grandfather's bad experience with a saw helped his grandson reach adulthood with all of his fingers intact!

REFLECT: Think back on the instructions and correction a parent has given you in the past couple of days. Have you honored him or her by taking those instructions to heart? How can you honor your parent or parents better in the future?

ACT: Wear a string or draw a line around the middle of one of your fingers today to remind you of the value of honoring your parents or guardians and learning from them.

PRAY: "God, you know it's hard for me to honor my parents when _____. Help me to remember that they've had experiences I haven't had. And help me to show that I want to honor them by_____."

16 Run, Rabbit, Run

Bible Reading: Genesis 4:1-10

And while they were in the field, Cain attacked his brother Abel and killed him. Genesis 4:8, NIV

Do not murder. Exodus 20:13

POOR WILE E. COYOTE. Even with all the help of ACME technology, he has been unable to kill the Roadrunner (meep, meep)! Slingshots, rockets, nets, bear traps, holes in the ground, trains, cars, and snares have been used to try and catch Roadrunner; anvils, bombs, guns, special bow-and-arrow sets, missiles, fighter planes, and a variety of other weapons have been used to try to kill Roadrunner. But Roadrunner just pauses long enough to wag his tongue, say "meep meep," and speed away in a cloud of dust.

And Elmer Fudd has yet to have "Bugs Bunny Stew." He's used more shotgun shells than anyone on television, yet that "wascally wabbit" is still kicking, still chewing carrots, and still asking, "What's up, Doc?"

We root for Roadrunner and Bugs; we love it when Tweety outwits Sylvester, when Jerry outruns Tom. We pull for them to escape the murderous intentions of their enemies. They're just cartoon characters, but we naturally want to see them escape harm. Why do we care what happens to cartoon critters? Why would we be horrified if Wile E. Coyote finally succeeded in his aim to end Roadrunner's life?

Two reasons: We know, deep in our heart, that life is beautiful, and we know that murder is ugly.

We know it because God has planted that awareness in us, and it's reflected in his command, "Do not murder" (Exodus 20:13). That's why murder is wrong. But there's more to it than that. Murder is wrong not just because it has something to do with God's commands. It is wrong because it reflects God himself—his nature and character.

God commanded us not to murder because his very nature is offended by murder. He is a living God, the author of life itself, and he commands us to be like him in our respect for human life, for all those created in the image of God.

 REFLECT: Some ancient rabbis taught that the name God gave himself—"I AM" (Exodus 3:14)—revealed God as *pure being, pure life,* the source of all being. Can you think of any form of life that does not owe its existence to God? Why or why not?

Does respecting human life *only* mean not committing murder? What are some other ways to show respect for human life?

As you pass people in the halls at school or church or elsewhere today, try to look at each person as someone infinitely valuable, created in the image of God.

 PRAY: "Thanks, God, for life! Thank you for creating me in your image. Thanks for creating_____, too."

17 1 + 1 = 1

Bible Reading: Genesis 2:15-24

This explains why a man leaves his father and mother and is joined to his wife, and the two are united into one. Genesis 2:24

Do not commit adultery. Exodus 20:14

ALEX USUALLY HATED science class, so he hardly paid attention when Mr. Brooks started the demonstration. Mr. Brooks was saying something about "sodium" and "unstable" or something when suddenly there was a loud *POP.* Alex jumped a little more than the students paying attention and heard Mr. Brooks say, "And that is how violent just a small amount of pure sodium can be."

Cool! thought Alex, who was now paying close attention to the science teacher.

"Then there is chlorine. In its pure form, it is a poisonous gas, and only a small amount would kill all of us."

Wow, thought Alex. *Explosions and poison gas. This is cool.*

"When we combine the two . . ."

Here it comes! It'll blow your guts out while it poisons you!

"We get plain old, everyday table salt." Mr. Brooks held up a glass saltshaker. "The salt you sprinkle on your popcorn and French fries is sodium chloride, a combination of these two elements. Combining the two makes each much more useful to our everyday life."

Alex stared at the saltshaker in Mr. Brooks's hand and soon imagined what it would be like to sprinkle pure sodium on his popcorn. *The popcorn would* really *go* POP! he thought. Before long he was daydreaming again, as if Mr. Brooks and the whole science class had never existed.

God intended marriage to be something like that combination of sodium and chlorine Mr. Brooks talked about. Marriage brings together two very different entities—a male and a female—and unites them in a relationship that makes them both more useful than each one individually would be. And God also intends for that relationship to reflect his nature and character. That's why he gave his people the seventh commandment, "Do not commit adultery" (Exodus 20:14). God is pure and faithful, and he wants the relationship between a husband and wife to be the same way.

When impurities like unfaithfulness and mistrust enter the relationship between a husband and wife, the results can be more explosive than sodium and more poisonous than chloride. God knows that. And because he loves us, he wants to protect us all from the tragedy that comes with impurities in a marriage. He wants to provide for us the blessings that characterize a marriage that is pure and faithful like he is.

 REFLECT: Who is the happiest married couple you know? What do you think makes them happy? Do you plan to get married? What kind of marriage do you want?

 PRAY: "God, remove any impurities that are affecting my relationships now. Prepare me for my adult life, whether your plans are for me to be single or married."

18 Meat Loaf, the Mother Ship, and God

Bible Reading: Ephesians 4:22-24, 28
Do not steal. Exodus 20:15

YOU GO TO a friend's house for dinner. When it's time to eat, you head for the bathroom to wash up, but your friend says, "Skip it. We never wash our hands before eating." Your friend's behavior would probably make you think:

(a) Your own family is weird for washing up before every meal.
(b) Your friend's family must keep their hands really clean between meals.
(c) You'd better not eat the meat loaf.

You sit beside a lady on the bus. She hands you a roll of aluminum foil and whispers, "The alien invasion starts at noon tomorrow. Use this to signal the Mother Ship." Her statement prompts you to conclude:

(a) You should skip school and wait for the Mother Ship.
(b) She's probably a spy and mistook you for her "contact."
(c) This lady is a few fries short of a Happy Meal.

You ascend a great big mountain in a vast desert. God meets you there and gives you ten commandments, one of which says: "You shall not steal." You figure that

(a) God needs a better speech writer;
(b) God's making this stuff up off the top of his head;
(c) God values trustworthiness.

If you didn't answer (c) for each of the above, we need to have a talk, especially about the third scenario. You see, a lot of people understand that God said, "You shall not steal." But they *don't* understand *why* God said that. They know stealing is wrong, but they don't understand *why* it's wrong. They know God's not so keen on the idea of swiping a few dollars from your brother's dresser drawer, but they don't know *why* God has such a problem with it.

The eighth commandment, "Do not steal," was not just thrown into the Ten Commandments because God thought, *Hey, that's a good one, let's throw it in there.* He included that one because it communicates something very important: God wants us to be trustworthy because he values trustworthiness. He values trustworthiness because *he is trustworthy.* The eighth commandment reveals an important truth about God: He is a trustworthy God, and he wants us to reflect his nature and character.

REFLECT: The eighth commandment reveals God as a trustworthy God. Can you think of other reasons to believe that he is trustworthy? Do you trust him? Why or why not?

PRAY: "God, I thank you for being trustworthy. Help me place my trust in you. And enable me to be trustworthy, too, especially when I_____."

19 Nothing But the Truth

Bible Reading: Acts 5:1-11

You shall not give false testimony against your neighbor.
Exodus 20:16, NIV

HAVE YOU EVER noticed the headlines of some of the newspapers in the racks beside the grocery store checkout lines?

"Alien spaceship found in New Mexico!" (It was a four-seat plane from Mexico.)

"Baby born with treasure map on its back!" (It was a birthmark.)

"I gave birth to Elvis's two-headed alien love child!" (Yeah, right.)

"Vince Foster's ghost haunts White House!" (The floor in the west wing creaks.)

Do people really believe this stuff? They certainly buy it. Supermarket tabloids sell millions of newspapers every week, so somebody out there must be reading it, liking it, and maybe even believing it.

Of course, those newspapers aren't the only ones to "embellish" the truth or even to stretch it to its breaking point. You and I do it all the time. We may not claim to have seen Elvis at the local Wal-Mart, but we do stretch the truth sometimes. After all, what's the harm of a "little white lie"?

A lot. God has another word for "stretching the truth" or "embellishing the truth." He calls it *lying*. He says, "Do not testify falsely against your neighbor" (Exodus 20:16), and "Do not lie" (Leviticus 19:11). But lying, whether it's a little white lie or a big fat one, is wrong not just because God says it is. The ninth commandment reveals God as a God who values truth because he himself is true.

Another reason God tells us to avoid lying and to speak the truth is that lying is destructive. Ananias and Sapphira found that out in one deadly lesson! Lying separates us from God. It erodes our character and destroys our reputation. It makes us less like God.

God wants to save us from all that by showing us, through his commandments, what he is like. When we reflect *his* nature, we also make things a lot easier on ourselves.

REFLECT: The ninth commandment tells us not to lie. What does that reveal about what God is like? Do you think God ever lies? Why or why not?

Finish this statement: "I reflected God's nature this week when I_____."

If you can't finish the statement, what could you do now to reflect God's nature?

ACT: Cut out letters from news headlines to form the words "Do not lie." Arrange them on a piece of paper. Then attach the paper to your mirror, bulletin board, or refrigerator as a reminder to always speak the truth.

PRAY: "I'm sorry, God, that it's hard for me to tell the truth when_____. Help me to be more like you."

20 Gotta Have It

Bible Reading: Exodus 20:17
Do not covet. Exodus 20:17

SOFT DRINK COMPANIES wage a constant battle with new slogans and clever commercials in their efforts to get you to buy their brand instead of their competitors' brands. See if you can match the following slogans and soft drinks.

1. GOTTA HAVE IT!		A. COCA-COLA
2. DO THE DEW		B. SPRITE
3. OBEY YOUR THIRST		C. 7UP
4. UH-HUH!		D. PEPSI-COLA
5. SQUIRT YOUR THIRST		E. MUG ROOT BEER
6. JUST WHAT THE DR. ORDERED		F. DR. PEPPER
7. IT'S AN UP THING		G. DIET PEPSI
8. THE FOAM GOES STRAIGHT TO YOUR BRAIN		H. MOUNTAIN DEW
9. IT'S THE REAL THING		I. SQUIRT

Some of those soft drink slogans are more well known than others, but Pepsi's "Gotta Have It!" is among the most appropriate—and not just for a cola. Have you ever seen a friend wearing a cool hat or pair of shoes and thought, *Gotta have it?* Have you ever seen a classmate's science fair project and thought, *Gotta have it?*

That's the kind of feeling God was talking about when he commanded us not to covet. But the tenth commandment does more than tell us what God doesn't want us to do. It also reveals something important about God. It reveals that God values contentment. And God values contentment because he never *wants;* he has everything he needs because he *is* everything he needs. And he wants us to be content with what he gives us. When we are content, instead of constantly wanting or demanding more, we reflect what God is like.

Francis Schaeffer, a Christian philosopher, wrote, "The climax of the Ten Commandments is the Tenth Commandment. . . . Any time that we break one of the other commandments of God, it means that we have already broken this commandment, in coveting."* Think about it. When a person steals, he first covets what he steals; when a person lies, she first covets what will be gained by lying, and so on. In that way, the sin of coveting is at the root of all sin.

 REFLECT: How does God want us to look at possessions? Is it wrong to admire what someone else has? When does admiration become coveting?

 PRAY: "God, help me appreciate what I have, to enjoy the beautiful things around me, and to be content with you and all you have given me."

*Francis Schaeffer, *True Spirituality* (Wheaton, Ill.: Tyndale House Publishers, 1971), p. 7.

ANSWERS: 1D; 2H; 3B; 4G; 5I; 6F; 7E; 8E; 9A.

21 A Snake in the Grass

Bible Reading: Genesis 3:1-6

You will be like God, knowing good and evil. Genesis 3:5, NIV

THE SERPENT SLOWLY approached the woman.

"Yo, mama," he said.

The woman sighed and rolled her eyes. She knew this snake; he'd once offered to take her for a ride in his convertible. But she was too smart for him; she knew snakes couldn't drive.

"Take a look at this," he whispered. He showed her a shiny, emerald-green fruit. The morning dew still glistened on its soft skin. "It's tastier than all the fruits in the Garden," he told her, locking gazes with her. "It's sweet and juicy and feels warm and cool all at the same time." He pushed the fruit under the woman's nose. "Here, mama, give it a sniff."

"I know where you got that," she said accusingly. "You got it from the tree in the middle of the Garden."

"So what if I did? Who says you can't eat from any ol' tree you want?"

"You know," she answered slowly. She was sure she'd had this same conversation with the serpent many times before. Yet now she could scarcely remember what she'd said, what he'd said, even what God had said.

"Oh, come on now." He moved closer to her until his head was almost resting on her shoulder. "God doesn't want you eating this fruit because he just wants to control you." He flashed a charming smile. "But *I* think you're old enough to make those decisions yourself, don't you?"

He watched as she blinked. "Of course," he continued, his voice as smooth as dew rolling off a leaf, "I can always eat it myself."

She stared at the fruit in silence.

Finally, he jerked the fruit away. "Never mind," he said sharply. "Later, mama."

"No, wait!" she shouted. She covered her mouth with a hand, shocked at the volume of her own voice. "Wait," she repeated softly. "I want to taste it."

"Now you're talking, mama." He watched with grinning satisfaction as her slender fingers grasped the fruit and lifted it to her mouth. Juice dripped down her chin as she bit into the fruit. Her eyes widened as she chewed, and her face blushed red for the first time. She felt an odd pleasure and something else, something new, something she could not name. She didn't know what to call it, but it scared her. And it hurt.

The serpent smiled wickedly. "Now, mama," he said, "let me show you some designer fig leaves that I can sell you real cheap."

REFLECT: The woman not only took a piece of fruit from the serpent; she also tried to take something that belonged only to God—the power to decide good and evil. Her husband, Adam, later did the same thing. What disastrous results occurred?

PRAY: "Give me your strength, God, to resist temptation. I especially need your help to flee from_____."

22 It's Not **What** You Know, It's **Who** You Know

Bible Reading: Proverbs 9:10-12

Fear of the Lord is the beginning of wisdom. Knowledge of the Holy One results in understanding. Proverbs 9:10

EDDIE WAS DOING his homework on the computer when his dad came into his room.

"It's almost time for dinner," Dad said. He watched the computer screen for a few moments. "What are you doing?" he asked.

Eddie shrugged. "Math homework. I surfed the Web looking for data and specs on adding memory cards," Eddie answered. "We're supposed to come up with ways in which numbers are used in modern technology."

Dad laughed. "I have no idea what you just said." He paused. "You've been learning quite a bit about computers since you started hanging around with Jordan, haven't you?"

Eddie spun in his chair and faced his dad. "Yeah, Dad, he's really cool. It's like, I can learn so much just by hanging out with him and talking to him. I feel like I didn't know anything about computers until I got to know Jordan." He snapped his fingers. "Now I feel like I know what I'm doing. It's easy."

Eddie didn't take a class in binary code to become an adept computer user. He didn't have to struggle through Computer Science 101. Those things might not have hurt, of course, but Eddie learned a lot about computers simply because his friend Jordan knew computers; by getting to know Jordan, Eddie got to know computers.

Knowing right from wrong and making right choices works in much the same way. Proverbs 9:10 says, "Fear of the Lord is the beginning of wisdom. Knowledge of the Holy One results in understanding." In other words, the key to *knowing* right from wrong is knowing God. If you know God, you know the one who is always right. If an attitude or action agrees with God's Word, it's right; if not, it's wrong.

But if you don't know God, you can't know what he likes or what he doesn't like. If you know him only by what others say about him or by what you read about him, you'll have a very limited knowledge of what's right or wrong. But if you know him personally—if you and he are close friends, if you talk to him every day, and if he talks to you through his Word—that knowledge will result in understanding. And the better you know him, the easier it will be to know and do the right thing.

 REFLECT: If you want to get to know someone at school or church, how do you go about doing it? How did you first get to know your best friend? If you want to get to know God better, how would you do it?

 PRAY: "God, I want to know you better, but I'll need your help. Help me to pray and read my Bible every day and to learn more and more from you as I get to know you better."

23 Smooth Landings

Bible Reading: Psalm 25:4-9

Show me your ways, O Lord, teach me your paths. Psalm 25:4, NIV

IT WAS WILLIAM'S first airplane flight, and since his uncle was one of the pilots, William got to visit the cockpit.

"How high up are we?" William asked.

William's uncle pointed to the instrument panel. "Well, this gauge shows how high we are. Each number represents a thousand feet, so we're about 25,000 feet. We'll eventually reach 36,000 feet."

For the next hour William was full of questions. "How do you steer?" "How fast can you go?" Each time the pilot flipped a switch or turned a dial, William wanted to know what was happening. "What's he doing now?"

"We're changing to a new radio frequency because we're getting close to the airport. He'll be talking with people in the control tower who will direct him in."

"But I can't see a thing! How do they know where we are? How do you know where to go?"

William's uncle smiled. "We're in the clouds right now." He pointed to the instrument panel again. "But we have instruments that show us any other planes in the area. Plus, we're in constant touch with the control tower. The people there use radar, which helps them see everything a lot better than we can. They know which runway we should land on, what other planes are coming in to land, whether there are any storms in the area, and stuff like that. Even if we can't see because of clouds or fog, the people in the control tower can tell us exactly what we need to know to arrive safely at our destination."

Sometimes we become confused in life, and we have a hard time knowing which way is right and which way is wrong. Like William, we can't always see things clearly. Our friends tell us one thing, teachers say another thing, our parents say something else, and we end up not knowing what's right and what's wrong. Right and wrong get all fuzzy and foggy, and we feel like we're flying through a cloud.

At such times we need to be in constant touch with the "control tower." God can see everything a lot better than we can. We need to rely on his Word and his wisdom. We need to listen to him and follow what he says. If we do that, he will tell us exactly what we need to know to arrive safely at our destinations.

REFLECT: When do you feel as if you're "flying through a cloud"? What do you usually do when you can't "see your way clearly"? What part does faith play in your actions?

God is like the person in the control tower, and you are like the pilot. God says, "Whether you turn to the right or to the left, your ears will hear a voice behind you, saying, 'This is the way; walk in it'" (Isaiah 30:21, NIV).

PRAY: "God, show me the way you want me to go."

24 Tracing the Truth

Bible Reading: Ephesians 4:14-15

Hold to the truth in love, becoming more and more in every way like Christ. Ephesians 4:15

DON'T WALK.
Merge right.
No right turn on red.

You see those phrases all the time, don't you? These are just a few examples of the precepts (instructions and commands) that we follow, often without even thinking.

Refrigerate after opening.
Shake before using.
Tear here to open.
Watch your step.
Place first-class postage here.

Precepts are all around us. They're a part of our life. They help us function more easily and more comfortably in life. And most of the time, they're pretty painless.

God has given us precepts as well. We usually call them commandments. He has told us, "Do not worship any other gods besides me. Do not steal. Do not lie. Love one another." These precepts are just a few of the commands God gives in the Bible. Jewish tradition maintains that God gave 624 specific commands!

God has communicated a lot about himself through precepts. His commands reveal what he likes, what he doesn't like, what he says is good or bad. But the precepts of the Lord are not just a bunch of do's and don'ts; they also show us important *principles* God values.

Principles help explain the why behind a command. A concern for safety is one of the principles behind a mother's command to look both ways before crossing the street. Reverence for life is the principle behind the command "Do not kill." A principle behind the command "Do not give false testimony" is honesty. Learning to identify the principles behind God's precepts will help us see the overarching truth that applies, even when a specific command doesn't seem to apply.

But if you really want to know right from wrong, you must look beyond the precept, beyond the principle, to the *person* of God. His nature defines right and wrong. The reason honesty is right and lying is wrong is that God is truth. The reason love is right and hatred is wrong is that God is love. The reason mercy is right and cruelty is wrong is that God is merciful.

 REFLECT: Choose a virtue (for example: purity, love, honesty, justice). See if you can explain *why* it is right by tracing it through precept and principle to the person of God. Or think about the virtue you chose. Is it something you value? Why?

 PRAY: "Father God, when I don't know which way to turn, help me remember to rely on your principles for direction."

First Step, Second Step

Bible Reading: Galatians 5:16-18

> *The old sinful nature loves to do evil, which is just opposite from what the Holy Spirit wants. And the Spirit gives us desires that are opposite from what the sinful nature desires. These two forces are constantly fighting each other, and your choices are never free from this conflict.*
> Galatians 5:17

WALKED LATELY? Of course you have. You've probably walked a lot this week. You walk from your bed to the bathroom in the morning. You walk from class to class in school. You walk from the television to the refrigerator. You walk upstairs, you walk downstairs, you walk outside, you walk inside.

There was a time, however, when you couldn't walk.

You probably don't remember, but you didn't even crawl for the first few months of your life. One day you pulled yourself up in your crib or playpen and stood, hanging on to the sides. Then one day you took your first step. Then a second step. Before long, you were walking like a pro!

Making right choices is not much different. The *first* step is knowing right from wrong. A lot of people never even make it to this first step, and many others never progress beyond it. But you didn't stop walking after your first step, and you shouldn't stop after taking the first step in knowing right from wrong either.

The second step—and this is where a whole lot of people fall flat on their faces—is *doing* right. The problem is, of course, that doing what's right is sometimes hard. More than likely, we *want* to do wrong more than right. Read again (above) how Paul put it in Galatians 5:17.

Does that sound like you? You may *know* what's right, but *doing* it sure is a lot harder!

So how are you supposed to make right choices when it seems so much easier to do whatever comes naturally (which usually is the wrong choice)? Paul gives us the answer: "Live according to your new life in the Holy Spirit. . . . [W]hen the Holy Spirit controls [your life], he will produce this kind of fruit . . . love, joy, peace, patience, kindness, goodness, faithfulness, gentleness, and self-control" (Galatians 5:16, 22-23).

Letting the Holy Spirit control your life is the only sure way to do the right thing. That will mean submitting to his control every day, committing yourself to follow his leading, and then trying to stay in touch with him through prayer and obedience all through the day. Then you won't have to *try* to do the right thing; he'll do it for you.

 REFLECT: Do you struggle most with *knowing* what's right or with *doing* what's right? Can you do what's right if you don't know what's right? Can you know what's right and still do wrong?

 PRAY: "Dear God, I submit to your Holy Spirit's control, and I commit to following you throughout this day. Help me to trust you every time I'm faced with a choice between right and wrong. Thank you for the wisdom and the strength to do what's right."

26 The Umbrella of God's Protection

Bible Reading: Psalm 119:1-6

Happy are those who obey [God's] decrees. Psalm 119:2

TRY THIS EXPERIMENT the next time it's raining really hard outside:

1. Select two friends to help with the experiment; it helps if one of your friends is not too bright (the reason for that will become clear in a moment).
2. Send both friends out into the rainstorm. Equip one friend with a large umbrella, and send the other (the not-so-bright one) out into the rain without an umbrella or raincoat.
3. Tell your friends to walk around in the pouring rain; call them back inside after two minutes have elapsed.
4. See who gets wettest!

Now, this may not sound like much of an experiment. You can probably figure out how the experiment will turn out all by yourself, right? You don't have to be "Bill Nye the Science Guy" to figure out that the friend with the umbrella will stay pretty dry, while your other friend will get soaked, right?

That experiment, however simple (or stupid) it may seem, illustrates the value of umbrellas. When you put up an umbrella, it shields you from the rain. But if you choose to move out from under that umbrella during a storm, you're sure to get wet.

God's commandments are like an umbrella. As long as you stay under the umbrella of God's commands, you'll be shielded from many consequences. If you step out from under that protective cover, however, you should not be surprised if you suffer the consequences.

For example, if you obey God's commands to not steal, not cheat one another, and not lie (Leviticus 19:11), you'll be under the protective umbrella of his commands. But if you ignore those commands, you expose yourself to all sorts of unpleasant consequences. If you disobey his command not to steal, you might get caught stealing and end up in a chain gang. If you defy his command not to cheat, you might get kicked out of school, ending your hopes of a career in nuclear physics. If you ignore his command not to lie, you might lose the trust of your friends and family.

Seriously, disobeying God's commands can result in all sorts of bad things even when you don't get caught (things like guilt, shame, mistrust, broken relationships, unhealthy behaviors, and so on). That's why God gave you those commands in the first place—for your protection.

So next time you go out in the rain, don't forget your umbrella.

 REFLECT: Think of a time when you were protected by obeying God's commands. Name specific ways you can stay under the umbrella of his protection today.

 PRAY: "God, thank you for your commandments. Help me to understand how they protect me. Show me how to obey you today, especially when _____."

27 Missing the Goal

Bible Reading: 1 John 1:8-10

If we confess our sins to him, he is faithful and just to forgive us and to cleanse us from every wrong. 1 John 1:9

EMILY BROKE TOWARD the goal. If she could get past one more defender, she would have a shot at winning the game for the Golds, her team.

Time was running out. Emily sprinted toward the goal, and Ashley kicked the ball just above the heads of the defenders. Emily would catch up to it just fifteen yards from the goal. The Blues' goalie then would have to make a decision whether to stay home in the net or come out after the ball.

Emily sprinted around her defender to receive Ashley's pass. The ball hit the turf a split second before Emily's foot hit the ball. She put a little spin on it, hoping to curve it around the goalie's outstretched arms and into the upper right corner of the goal. As the ball left her foot, Emily was excited. A clear shot at the goal, under a minute to play, with the game on the line.

Emily watched the ball sail past the goalie's hands. Emily pumped her arms victoriously in the air, then froze. The ball continued, sailing up and over the top bar of the goal. Emily had missed!

"Oh no!" she yelled, and then uttered a foul word.

On the way home from the game, Emily apologized to her mother for her language. "I'm sorry. It just slipped out," she said, tears rimming her eyes. "I was so upset. But I shouldn't have said that, and I'm sorry. You must hate me. *God* must hate me."

"No, God still loves you," Emily's mother said, "and so do I." They drove in silence for a few moments until Emily's mom said, "Did your coach yell at you for missing that goal?"

Emily shook her head and shrugged. "No. I told him I was sorry I missed it, but he said—" Emily stopped suddenly. She smiled at her mom. "I see what you're trying to do."

Emily's mom smiled back at her daughter. "You did something wrong," she said, "but God doesn't hate you for that, any more than your coach hates you for missing that goal. God loves you, Emily, and he's willing to forgive you. All you have to do is admit your mistake to him, ask for his forgiveness, and trust him to help you make the right decision the next time."

"Thanks, Mom," Emily said. "I guess I need to practice a little more."

"We all do," Mom said.

 REFLECT: You can make an action a habit if you repeat it every day for twenty-one days. Try to make the following procedure a habit: When you make a wrong choice, *instantly* admit your sin, ask for forgiveness, and begin to trust God to help you make the right decision the next time. (But don't stop after twenty-one days!)

 PRAY: "God, I made a wrong choice when I_____. Forgive me, and help me make the right decision next time."

28 What's the Difference?

Bible Reading: 1 Corinthians 10:23-24, 31

> *Whatever you eat or drink or whatever you do, you must do all for the glory of God. 1 Corinthians 10:31*

Q: WHAT'S THE DIFFERENCE between boogers and broccoli?
A: You can't make kids eat broccoli.

Q: What's the difference between an elephant and spaghetti?
A: Elephants don't slip off the end of your fork.

Q: What's the difference between a mistake and a sin?
A: Good question!

OK, so the last one wasn't a joke. But it *is* a good question.

A lot of people confuse mistakes and sins. Some feel guilty for mistakes that aren't sins. Others shrug off sins as "honest mistakes."

It's possible to make a mistake and yet not sin. You may forget a person's name. You may hurt someone's feelings without meaning to. You may lose your permission slip for a school field trip. You may accidentally step on the dog's tail. None of those things are sins. They're mistakes.

It's also possible to sin without making a mistake. You may call somebody a name. You may *mean* to hurt someone's feelings. You may hide your permission slip from your parents because you don't want to go on the school field trip. You may step on the dog's tail *on purpose!* Those things aren't mistakes. They're *sins*.

It's important to know the difference between a mistake and a sin. Even more important is to react the right way to both. When you make a mistake, especially one that hurts someone else, it's natural to feel sorry. You may want to apologize for your mistake. But you don't need to feel guilty or ashamed.

When you sin, you *should* feel remorse. You should admit that it was a sin, ask God (and anyone your sin hurt) for forgiveness, correct any effects of your sin (like paying for the dog's tail to get fixed!), and try to make a better choice—the right choice—the next time.

God doesn't expect you to never make a mistake, but he does command you (and he will help you) to avoid sin.

 REFLECT: Think about the difference between a mistake and a wrong choice. Think about how you should feel if you made an honest mistake and how you should respond to sin.

   Have you made any mistakes for which you haven't yet apologized? Have you committed any sins for which you haven't received forgiveness? If you answered yes to either question, do the right thing now to correct your mistake or sin.

 PRAY: "God, help me to remember the difference between mistakes and sins, and help me to avoid sin, especially in situations where_____."

29 Way Out

Bible Reading: 1 Corinthians 10:12-13

But remember that the temptations that come into your life are no different from what others experience. And God is faithful. He will keep the temptation from becoming so strong that you can't stand up against it. When you are tempted, he will show you a way out so that you will not give in to it. 1 Corinthians 10:13

"THOSE GIRLS MAKE me sooooo mad!" Melanie stormed into the kitchen, close to tears. She found her mother preparing dinner.

"What happened?" Mom asked.

"Greta is having a party next week, but she and Phyllis say that if I'm going to be friends with Natalie, they don't want me coming," Melanie explained. "Natalie's a girl from Russia. She doesn't speak English very well, and she wears clothes that are a little different. Some of the girls make fun of her, so I've been trying to be her friend."

"That's a very good thing to do," Mom said as she chopped some onions. "In fact, it's the kind of thing Jesus would do."

"But I want to go to the party. Greta is one of the most popular girls in my grade, and this is the first party she's invited me to. Maybe I can just tell Natalie I have too many things to do and can't spend much time with her anymore, at least until after the party."

"Wouldn't that be lying?" Mom asked. She handed Melanie the cheese grater.

"I guess so," said Melanie as she started grating the cheese. "Isn't there some way to stay Natalie's friend and go to Greta's party?"

"If you gave in to Greta, do you think she'd stop trying to tell you what to do? Do you think other girls would start lining up to be your friend because you treated Natalie cruelly? Do you think you could stop grating the cheese before you grate your fingers?"

Melanie stopped. She hadn't realized how vigorously she'd been working. She popped the remaining nub of cheese into her mouth. "You're right," she said. "I'll do the right thing, even if it means I'll be unpopular."

"Oh, that's so nice," Mom said, sniffing. "It makes me cry."

Melanie turned and saw tears on her mother's cheeks. "You're not fooling me," she said. "That's the onion making you cry."

"Better me than Natalie," Mom said, winking.

 REFLECT: When you're tempted to do wrong, do you most often:
    a. have trouble recognizing the right choice?
    b. not like your choices?
    c. do what you feel like without even thinking about your choices?
How can you make better choices in the future?

 PRAY: "Lord God, when I'm tempted to do wrong, help me to see—and choose—the right way out."

30 Good Measure

Bible Reading: Deuteronomy 30:11-20

I have commanded you today to love the Lord your God and to keep his commands, laws, and regulations by walking in his ways. . . . Choose to love the Lord your God and to obey him and commit yourself to him, for he is your life. Deuteronomy 30:16, 20

A THERMOMETER
A tape measure
A yardstick
A speedometer
A pressure gauge
God

What do the above have in common? They're all standards of measurement.

"Wait a minute," you may respond. "What's God doing on the list?"

Well, like a thermometer or a yardstick or a pressure gauge, God himself is a standard of measurement. If you want to measure distance, you might use a yardstick. If you want to measure the speed your car is going, you might use a speedometer. And if you want to measure the rightness or wrongness of an attitude or action, you measure it against God's values.

Is something wrong or right? Compare it to God.

Is it OK to lie as long as you're not hurting anybody? Compare it to God. He says, "Do not lie" (Leviticus 19:11) because he values truth. He values truth because he is truth itself (John 14:6).

Is it right to hate somebody who has hurt you? Compare it to God. He says, "Love each other" (John 13:34) because he values love. He values love because he *is* love (1 John 4:8, 16).

Is it right to hold grudges? Is it right to keep something that doesn't belong to you? Is it right to give in to your passion or temper? Is it right to make fun of other people? Is it right to treat someone unfairly? Compare it to God. He is the standard for measuring right and wrong.

 REFLECT: Unfortunately, many people try to measure right and wrong according to their feelings, their desires, what their friends say, what their parents say, or what their communities or cultures tolerate. What standard have *you* been using to figure out what's right or wrong? Your feelings? Your desires? What your friends say? Something else?

 ACT: Place a tape measure, thermometer, or some other instrument of measurement in your pocket or on your desk or dresser today to remind you to measure your actions against God, the only true standard for measuring right and wrong.

 PRAY: "God, I really appreciate having your Word to help me know what you value. You're the best standard of measurement there is."

31 The Price Is Steep

Bible Reading: Jeremiah 29:11-13

"For I know the plans I have for you," says the Lord. "They are plans for good and not for disaster, to give you a future and a hope."
Jeremiah 29:11

HAVE YOU EVER seen the game show *The Price Is Right?* It's been on TV since Noah was a teenager. One of the games contestants play on the show involves matching different products with the correct prices. See if you can match the items in the column at left with the price tags in the column on the right:

1. NEWSPAPER	A.	$800,000
2. NEW MUSTANG CONVERTIBLE	B.	$1,500
3. BOTTLED WATER (16 OZ.)	C.	$400
4. ONE-MINUTE COMMERCIAL DURING MONDAY NIGHT FOOTBALL	D.	$1.75
5. POSTAGE STAMP	E.	$55
6. COMPUTER WITH MONITOR, PRINTER, CD-ROM	F.	$25,000
7. SCHOOL LUNCH	G.	35-50¢
8. 1910 HONUS WAGNER BASEBALL CARD	H.	$1.25
9. FAX MACHINE	I.	$451,000
10. VISIT TO THE DOCTOR'S OFFICE	J.	32¢

Now, the price of some of those items may seem steep, $451,000 for a baseball card? (That's what hockey great Wayne Gretzky and a partner paid for the rare card in 1991.) Others—like a postage stamp or a newspaper—may seem like bargains by comparison.

To be honest, sometimes the price of doing the right thing can be pretty steep, too. Sometimes doing the right thing can make you feel like a party pooper or a geek. It might cost you a friend. It might cost you money. It's even cost people their lives. It's enough to make you wonder why anybody would choose to do right.

There's no doubt about it, doing the right thing can be hard. It can seem dumb. But though it may seem hard at the time, the price of doing wrong is usually steeper—maybe not right away, but in the long run. Doing *wrong* can end up costing you friends. It can get you in really big trouble. It could even cost you your life . . . and your soul.

That's what God's trying to tell us in today's Scripture reading. He does not promise that we will be rewarded in this life for every right choice we make. But he *does* promise that obeying his commands will accomplish our good—maybe not right now, but in the long run, and certainly in eternity. As Proverbs 21:21 says, "Whoever pursues godliness and unfailing love will find life, godliness, and honor."

 REFLECT: Have you ever made the wrong choice because the cost of making the right choice seemed too high? Are you glad you made the choice you did? Would you do it differently if you could?

 PRAY: "God, help me to do the right thing, even when it's hard to_____."

ANSWERS: 1G; 2F; 3H; 4A; 5J; 6B; 7D; 8I; 9C; 10E.

1 Muck and Mire

Bible Reading: John 18:28-38

All who love the truth recognize that what I say is true. John 18:37

ONCE UPON A time, in a land far away, two young peasants—a brother and sister named Muck and Mire—left home together. They packed a lunch and skipped through the front door of their home.

"Where are you going?" their mother asked.

"We're off to see the king!" they answered. (They often talked in unison. They were very close, you see.) They pointed to the royal castle on the hillside.

Their mother smiled. "That's nice. Be sure you're home in time for dinner."

Muck and Mire just laughed. They planned to have dinner with the king and all his noblemen and servants at the palace. Before long, Muck and Mire met a woman washing clothes on the rocks by the river.

"Pray tell us," they said to the woman in unison, "how we mightest findeth the kingeth."

The old woman glared at them. "Whatcha talkin' all funny for?" she barked. "This ain't no fairy tale. Besides, there ain't no king. Now run along!"

Muck and Mire left the woman and continued on their journey. Before long they met a man carrying a large pig.

"Pray tell us," they said, "how we mightest findeth the kingeth."

"Forsooth," the man said. "Each of us must find the king himself. I cannot tell thee where to find the king." And he walked away.

Muck and Mire began to get discouraged. They hung their heads in disappointment and hardly noticed the man who approached them. He wore long, flowing robes of purple and scarlet, trimmed with white fur. A golden scepter was in his right hand, a jeweled crown of gold sat on his head, and a paper name tag was pasted over his heart. On the name tag was written, in magic marker, "King."

"Pray tell us," they said, "how we mightest findeth the kingeth."

The man smiled. "I that speak unto thee am he."

"No, really," they said. "We want to meet the king."

The man pointed a finger at his name tag. "See?" he said. He pointed to his crown and waved his scepter at them. "I'm the king."

Muck turned to Mire. "Let's go home," he said. "We'll never find the king."

"Yeah," Mire agreed. They shook their heads and turned away from the man with the crown and the scepter.

 REFLECT: How was Muck and Mire's mistake like Pilate's mistake in today's Bible reading? How were the reactions of the laundry woman and the pig farmer similar to how some people today think about right and wrong? Is either reaction similar to your own?

 PRAY: "Lord Jesus, you are my King. You are "the way, the truth, and the life." Help me to follow you, obey you, and live for you."

2 Double Fault

Bible Reading: James 4:11-12

God alone, who made the law, can rightly judge among us. James 4:12

YOU'RE A TENNIS player. You're playing a critical game in an important tournament. You're serving for the match; if you win this point, you're the champion. You toss the ball into the air and hit it with all your might, but your serve sails past the other player and lands on the grass outside the fence that surrounds the tennis court.

"Second serve," the umpire announces.

You get one more chance to serve for the match. You toss the ball into the air and hit it. This time your serve hits the net and bounces back into your court.

"Double fault," the umpire intones.

You shake your head in disappointment and prepare to serve again. But the umpire informs you that the score is now tied. You charge the umpire's chair.

"No way!" you protest. "I want to serve again!" You throw your racket to the ground and insist that *you* always take *three* serves, not two. You scream that you've been playing tennis for five years. "You have no right to tell me how the game is supposed to be played!" you howl. "I'll decide that for myself." Enraged, you throw your arms up in disgust and storm off the court.

You'd never act that way, of course. You're much too nice, right? Besides, everyone knows that two missed serves—a *double fault*, in tennis lingo—scores a point for the server's opponent. Those are the rules. That's the way the game is played.

Yet, surprisingly, a lot of people expect the rules of right and wrong to be different. They think they can make up their own rules as they go along, changing what's wrong or right to fit their mood or circumstance. But right and wrong are just as clear as the rules of tennis. Everyone knows that stealing is wrong and integrity is right; cruelty is wrong, and mercy is right; hate is wrong, and love is right. Those are the rules. And, like the Bible says, "You are not a judge who can decide whether the law is right or wrong. Your job is to obey it. God alone, who made the law, can rightly judge among us" (James 4:11-12).

Of course, as long as good and evil exist in the world, people will continue to try to make up their own rules. But not you. You're much too smart, right?

 REFLECT: Do you think tennis would be more fun or less fun if everyone could make up his or her own rules? Why? Do you think life is more fun or less fun when we obey God's rules? Why?

 ACT: Challenge a friend or family member to a set of tennis, and use that as an opportunity to share the point of today's reading with him or her. Or simply place a tennis ball or tennis racket in a prominent place in your room this week to remind you that your job is to obey God's rules, not to try to change them or challenge them.

 PRAY: "Creator God, you are much wiser than I am. Forgive me for questioning your rule about_____."

3 Fair Play

Bible Reading: Matthew 7:12

Do for others what you would like them to do for you.   Matthew 7:12

CLIVE STAPLES (C. S.) Lewis, a famous twentieth century British writer, wrote the Chronicles of Narnia. You may have read these books. They describe the adventures of Peter, Edmund, Susan, and Lucy, who discovered a magic wardrobe that took them to the land of Narnia. Lewis also authored a series of science fiction novels about a distant planet called Perelandra. Then he created a famous exchange of letters between two devils named Screwtape and Wormwood in his book *The Screwtape Letters.*

One of Lewis's most influential books is *Mere Christianity.* In that book, he had a number of things to say about fair play. He wrote:

> Everyone has heard people quarreling. Sometimes it sounds funny and some-times it sounds merely unpleasant; but however it sounds, I believe we can learn something very important from listening to the kind of things they say. They say things like this: "How'd you like it if anyone did the same to you?"–"That's my seat, I was there first"–"Leave him alone, he isn't doing you any harm"–"Why should you shove in first?"–"Give me a bit of your orange, I gave you a bit of mine"–"Come on, you promised." People say things like that every day, educated people as well as uneducated, and children as well as grown-ups.
>
> Now what interests me about all these remarks is that the man who makes them is not merely saying that the other man's behavior does not happen to please him. He is appealing to some kind of standard of behaviour which he expects the other man to know about. . . . It looks, in fact, very much as if both parties had in mind some kind of Law or Rule of fair play or decent behaviour or morality or whatever you like to call it, about which they really agreed. And they have. If they had not, they might, of course, fight like animals, but they could not *quarrel* in the human sense of the word. Quarrelling means trying to show that the other man is in the wrong. And there would be no sense in trying to do that unless you and he had some sort of agreement as to what Right and Wrong are. . . .
>
> It seems, then, we are forced to believe in a real Right and Wrong. People may sometimes be mistaken about them, just as people sometimes get their sums wrong; but they are not a mere matter of taste and opinion any more than the multiplication table [C. S. Lewis, *Mere Christianity* (New York: Macmillan Publishing Company, 1943, 1945, 1952), pp. 3–4, 6].

 REFLECT: If C. S. Lewis attended your school, what phrases appealing to a sense of justice or fairness would he hear most often?

 PRAY: "I like to be treated fairly, God. Help me to treat others that way this week."

4 Super Powers

Bible Reading: Deuteronomy 32:1-4

How glorious is our God! He is the Rock; his work is perfect. Everything he does is just and fair. He is a faithful God who does no wrong; how just and upright he is! Deuteronomy 32:3-4

DO YOU THINK Superman and Batman became superheroes by accident? Do you think they just woke up one morning in a cape and tights? No, sir. Like all superheroes, they had to pass the SAT first (Superhero Aptitude Test). Would *you* like to be a superhero, too? Take the following test and see if you qualify:

1. If you could be a superhero, who would you choose to be?

☐ Superman   ☐ Spider-Man
☐ Batman   ☐ A Power Ranger
☐ The Tick   ☐ Other _____

2. If you could have your own super powers, which ones would you choose?

☐ ability to fly   ☐ ability to shoot lasers
☐ super strength   ☐ ability to shrink or grow
☐ ability to shoot spider webs   ☐ ability to_____

3. If you could use your super powers any way you wanted, would you

☐ defend the oppressed and downtrodden?
☐ go all over the world doing good?
☐ use your powers to steal all the money in the world?
☐ use your powers to become really popular?
☐ fight for truth and justice?
☐ fight for better school lunches?
☐ other_____

Now, simply mail your completed Superhero Aptitude Test to the Planet XR37 and allow eighteen thousand light years for delivery of the results.

Actually, the Superhero Aptitude Test won't get you a gig as the next comic book hero; but it may reveal a thing or two about you, just as God's super powers—and the ways he uses them—reveal something about him. He uses his powers to promote justice, because he is just and fair. And because he is just, it is always right for us to be just.

 REFLECT: While you don't have super powers, do you use the powers you *do* possess (intelligence, for example, or physical health) to accomplish good things (like justice)? Or do you use your "powers" mostly for selfish purposes? Does the use of your "powers" reveal anything about your character?

 PRAY: Use the Scripture reading above as the basis for a prayer of praise. (For example, "O God, how glorious you are! You are my Rock.")

5 What Makes Justice Right?

Bible Reading: Isaiah 45:18-23

There is no other God but me—a just God and a Savior—no, not one! Let all the world look to me for salvation! For I am God; there is no other. Isaiah 45:21-22

HOW DO YOU react when Mom blames you for something your brother or sister did?

How do you react when a girl ahead of you in the lunch line lets three of her friends into the line you've been waiting in for ten minutes?

How do you act when a teacher deducts points from your test for an "incomplete answer" but gives Melvin Sheldon full credit for the same answer?

If you're like most people, you react to such situations by saying, "Hey! Wait a minute. That's not fair!"

Everyone seems to know instinctively that justice is right and injustice is wrong. But *why?* What makes it right to be fair and wrong to be unfair?

Well, a lot of people would answer that question, "Because the Bible says so." They're right, in a way; the Bible has all kinds of precepts, such as "Give fair judgment to the poor and the orphan" (Psalm 82:3); "Give to everyone what you owe them" (Romans 13:7); and "You slave owners must be just and fair to your slaves" (Colossians 4:1). The law of Moses contained detailed commands to treat strangers and foreigners fairly, to provide for orphans and widows, and even to return stray animals to one's enemies. Those precepts can be summed up in what has been called "the Golden Rule": "Do for others what you would like them to do for you" (Matthew 7:12).

But those precepts are more than just a list of do's and don'ts; they reveal the fact that God values justice. But *why* does God value justice? Because he is just.

You see, justice is not right only because God commands it or even because God values it; it is right because it reflects the qualities of God himself. Justice is not something God does; it is something he *is*. "God is just," Paul wrote (2 Thessalonians 1:6, NIV). Moses sang, "Everything he does is just and fair" (Deuteronomy 32:4).

Then why should we be fair? Not just because Mom says so or because our friends say so or even because the pastor says so. We should be fair because justice is a reflection of God's character. Treating everyone fairly is right—for all people, for all times, and in all places.

 REFLECT: You've probably heard people say, "Life isn't fair." Are there some unfair circumstances that we all have to accept in life? If so, what unfair circumstances do you think you have to accept?

 ACT: Place a ruler on your desk or in your locker or on the dining room table to remind you to follow the Golden Rule this week.

 PRAY: "God, everything you do is 'just and fair.' I know that doesn't mean life will always seem fair. But it does mean I should *be* fair because I want to be like you."

6 Know It and Show It

Bible Reading: Micah 6:1-8

He has showed you, O man, what is good. And what does the Lord require of you? To act justly and to love mercy and to walk humbly with your God. Micah 6:8, NIV

IMAGINE GETTING YOUR driver's license the day after your sixteenth birthday—and choosing not to drive.

Imagine learning your ABCs but never reading a single word in your life.

Imagine discovering a cure for the common cold but choosing not to take it when you're sniffing and sneezing like a banshee.

Why would anyone do something like that? We do it all the time, especially when it comes to choosing between right and wrong.

For example, we know that justice is right and injustice is wrong. Yet we don't always choose to act justly, do we? We may *know* it, but we don't always *show* it. We butt in ahead of people in cafeteria lines. We treat some people better than others. We "play favorites." We take advantage of people. We accuse people or dislike people without really knowing the whole story.

But if we know it's wrong to act unfairly, why do we do it anyway?

Well, part of the answer to that question is that we're all sinners. We tend to do the wrong thing more than we tend to do the right thing.

Another part of the answer to that question is that we act unjustly because sometimes it seems more beneficial to us than acting justly. (Who wants to wait longer than necessary in a cafeteria line, right?)

A third reason we act unjustly is that we don't make a conscious decision to do otherwise. Since acting unjustly seems to come more naturally (because of our sinful nature), we tend to do that *unless* we've made a commitment to follow God's way of justice instead of doing what comes naturally.

You can make such a commitment by determining in your heart that when you're faced with a choice between a right action and a wrong action, you will choose what's right—even when it's inconvenient. But that's not all; you then need to ask God for the strength to choose justice over injustice and trust the Holy Spirit to enable you to keep your commitment.

That won't guarantee that you'll always act justly, but it will help you the next time you're tempted.

 REFLECT: *Knowing* what's right and *doing* what's right are two different things. Sometimes we do wrong when we're not sure what's right. Other times we know what's right, but we do what's wrong anyway. Which is a bigger problem for you: *knowing* what's right or *doing* what's right?

 PRAY: "Lord, I commit to your way. I commit to acting fairly when I'm faced with the chance to do something unfair. Help me especially to_____."

7 Maria's Mistake

Bible Reading: Psalm 112:1-9

All goes well for those who are generous, who lend freely and conduct their business fairly. Such people will not be overcome by evil circumstances. Psalm 112:5-6

MR. LUNDSTROM ADJUSTED his tie in the mirror. "Who's baby-sitting the kids tonight?" he asked. He and his wife were going to a neighbor's anniversary party.

"I finally got Kelly Kenton," Mrs. Lundstrom said. "But it took forever. I didn't think I was going to find anyone."

"Whatever happened to Maria from down the street?" Mr. Lundstrom asked. "She hasn't watched the kids in a long time."

His wife stood beside her husband and brushed her hair. "The last two times she stayed with the kids, she overcharged me; she expected almost twice as much as the Vanovers pay her." She shrugged and set the brush down on the counter. "I just decided I wouldn't ask her to baby-sit anymore."

Maria may never know why she lost her regular baby-sitting job with the Lundstroms. She may never discover that Mrs. Lundstrom stopped calling her because she felt that Maria had treated her unfairly. But then, few people realize the cost of acting unfairly or the reward of acting justly.

You see, God's commands are not intended to spoil our fun or to make our life more difficult. God didn't command us to "do justly" because he wanted to be a pain in the neck; he gave us that command—and all his commands—to protect us and provide for us. And his command to act justly toward each other can protect us from dishonor and disappointment, providing honor and fulfillment for us.

Take Maria, for example; if she had not overcharged the Lundstroms but had treated them the same way she treated the Vanovers, she probably would have kept her job baby-sitting the Lundstrom kids. Even if she never fully realized how acting justly benefited her, she would have enjoyed the rewards.

You may never completely realize all the ways that acting justly benefits you, either, but if you treat everyone fairly, you will nonetheless experience the protection and provision that come as a result of obeying God's commands.

 REFLECT: Have you or your parents ever stopped going to a store (such as a grocery store or drugstore) or business (such as a doctor or auto mechanic) because you thought you were being cheated or treated unfairly? If you answered yes, do you think the business owner knew about losing your business?

Obeying God's commands to treat other people fairly can protect you from dishonor and provide honor for you. That does not mean that people will always recognize or appreciate your fairness; it does mean, however, that over the course of time, you will more likely be highly regarded and respected.

 PRAY: "Lord, I don't often consciously think about being fair until someone treats me unfairly. Help me make fairness a way of life."

8 The Hatfields and the McCoys

Bible Reading: Deuteronomy 16:18-20

Follow justice and justice alone, so that you may live and possess the land the Lord your God is giving you. Deuteronomy 16:20, NIV

NOBODY KNOWS FOR sure how it started.

Maybe Jethro Hatfield hornswoggled Abner McCoy out of his favorite goat. Maybe Clem McCoy failed to tip his hat to Betty Jo Hatfield. Maybe Homer Hatfield cheated Milo McCoy out of the Eastern Kentucky Horseshoe Championship.

No matter how it got started, the feud between the Hatfield family and the McCoy clan of the Appalachian area of eastern Kentucky became one of the bloodiest and most famous feuds of modern times. Over the course of about thirty years, from 1860 to 1890, at least twenty people were killed by one side or the other. By the time the animosity faded, no one was really sure how and why it all started.

The tragic feud between the Hatfields and McCoys illustrates one way God's commands are intended to protect us. You see, back when God first issued the Ten Commandments to his people on Mount Sinai, feuds like the one between the Hatfields and the McCoys were fairly commonplace. An injustice committed by one person would often be avenged against his entire family, resulting in a bitter and deadly blood feud. If Abib accused Ibrahim of selling spoiled goat cheese, Ibrahim might have sought revenge by slaughtering Abib's entire flock. If Gad's ox gored Laban's son, Laban might have descended on Gad's tents some night and killed every male in his family.

God's commands to his people to treat others justly not only helped people understand what God was like but also protected them from revenge and provided for more peaceful relationships. God's commands protected his people from a cycle of wrongdoing, resentment, and revenge.

Following justice still protects us and provides for us. Treating other people fairly still promotes peace in our life and protects us from the destructive cycle of revenge. The teacher who treats his or her students fairly will more likely be rewarded with appreciative and achieving students. The Burger Heaven employee who treats her coworkers fairly will more likely be promoted to supervisor later on.

God's concern for justice reflects his nature and character and his love for us, because he knows that treating people fairly will protect and provide for us.

 REFLECT: You may already have enjoyed God's protection and provision in your life as a result of treating someone fairly. Can you think of any instance when you might have avoided resentment and revenge by treating someone fairly? Have you witnessed any vengeful situation (at school, for example) that might have been avoided if one person had acted justly?

 PRAY: "Lord, thank you for your protection and provision. Help me to treat others fairly, even when it's difficult or tempting to do otherwise."

9 Hidden Treasure

Bible Reading: Proverbs 2:6-11

For the Lord grants wisdom! From his mouth come knowledge and under-standing. He grants a treasure of good sense to the godly. He is their shield, protecting those who walk with integrity. He guards the paths of justice and protects those who are faithful to him. Proverbs 2:6-8

YOU'RE DREAMING. You're not sure how you know it's a dream. Maybe it's because you're seven years old again and God is standing before you wearing a pair of Reeboks and blue jeans. God has told you to make a wish and he'll make it come true.

You wish for riches. Of course. Who wouldn't?

The next moment in your dream, you're old—like maybe fifty. And you're not rich. In fact, you're upset with God for not making your wish come true as he had promised.

"I asked you to make me rich," you complain to God.

"I did," God answers softly.

"Nuh-uh," you protest. You turn your pockets inside out, revealing nothing but pocket lint and six cents, all in pennies.

"Remember when I gave you my commandment to 'act justly and to love mercy and to walk humbly with your God'? And remember when I told you to 'follow justice' and 'do for others what you would like them to do for you'?"

"Yeah," you say, nodding.

"Well, that alone was worth a fortune to you," God says.

"What?" you say. "How do you figure?"

"Well," says God, "let's just take one example. Obeying those commands protected you from the guilt of cheating people and treating them unfairly, right?"

"Well, yeah," you say, "I guess so."

"That saved you the $27,410 you would have paid to a therapist to try to overcome your guilt. That doesn't even count the money you saved from not buying sleeping pills and antacids to combat the sleeplessness and indigestion that would have resulted if you had ignored my commands."

"Wow," you say, suddenly feeling very sheepish. "I guess I never thought about it that way before."

"So you see," God says, putting the calculator into the pocket of his jeans, "I really did grant you your wish. I made you rich—in more ways than one."

And you remind yourself that it's a dream, because in real life God wouldn't wear jeans—or would he?

 REFLECT: Why do you think obeying God's commands protects us from guilt and provides us with a clear conscience?

 PRAY: "God, sometimes I wish for things that you know aren't right for me. Thanks for saying no. Now give me the 'treasure of good sense' today as I get ready to
_____."

10 The Absolute Truth

Bible Reading: Genesis 2:1-17

You may freely eat any fruit in the garden except fruit from the tree of the knowledge of good and evil. Genesis 2:16-17

1. WHICH FLAVOR ICE cream is best?

chocolate	butter pecan	vanilla
rocky road	strawberry	mint chocolate chip

2. Who was the greatest baseball player?

Babe Ruth	Whitey Ford	Ted Williams
Willie Mays	Henry Aaron	Leroy "Satchel" Paige

3. Which of these actions is wrong?

eating meat	kissing	singing
water-skiing	lying	sleeping

Now, those questions may seem pretty dumb to you. But I ask them for a reason.

Some people think there is no difference between questions #1 and #2 and question #3. But there is a huge difference.

The first question asks you to make a choice based on your taste. You may like chocolate ice cream, but your sister or friend may like vanilla ice cream best. So who's right? Both of you, because it's a matter of taste. Whether you're talking about ice cream, favorite colors, or favorite songs, different people have different tastes.

The second question asks you to make a choice based on opinion. You may have an opinion about who was the greatest ballplayer ever, but someone else who is equally informed may have a different opinion.

But the third question is a different kind of question entirely, because it asks you to make a choice involving, not taste or opinion, but right and wrong. You see, some things are a matter of taste, some things are a matter of opinion, and others are true beyond a shadow of a doubt. Some things are *absolute* truths—that means they are true for all people, for all places, and for all time. Those things are true no matter what you like or don't like; they're true no matter what your opinion is; they're true *absolutely*.

Now, there are some people today who claim that right and wrong are just a matter of taste or a matter of opinion. But God has already revealed to us in his Word what is absolutely right and what is absolutely wrong.

 REFLECT: Some things are a matter of taste, some things are a matter of opinion, and others are true beyond a shadow of a doubt. Can you think of two actions or attitudes that belong to each category?

 PRAY: "Thanks, God, for the way your Word makes the absolute truth absolutely clear."

11 Dances with Angels

Bible Reading: Matthew 5:43-48

You have heard that the law of Moses says, "Love your neighbor" and hate your enemy. But I say, love your enemies! Pray for those who persecute you! In that way, you will be acting as true children of your Father in heaven. Matthew 5:43-45

RAYBANN AND SOLOPLEX, two of heaven's angels, exchanged high fives. "Yyyyyesss!" Raybann shouted. He grabbed Soloplex and started twirling him around and around in a dizzying dance of celebration in the thin air above the earth.

"Did you see that?" Soloplex shouted. "Whoosh!"

They turned and peered together at the scene below them. The Israelites stood, high and dry, on the banks of the Red Sea. They had just crossed to freedom and safety as Raybann and Soloplex, under instructions from God, had rolled back the waters of the sea. The Israelites had hurried across the channel on the miraculously dry ground, while the armies of Egypt pursued them on horses and chariots. Once God's chosen people had safely reached the opposite shore, Raybann and Soloplex released the water, and the entire Egyptian army had been drowned in the returning waters of the sea, prompting the delirious celebration of the two angels.

Upon their return to heaven, however, Raybann and Soloplex were summoned into the presence of God. They were shocked to find the blinding light of his face dimmed and his expression sad.

"Is the Holy One not pleased with our success?" Raybann asked, bowing before God's throne with his face to the ground.

"You rejoice," God said. It was not a question.

"Your people are delivered, and their enemies are dashed to pieces," Soloplex reported.

God looked at his two messengers, and the sorrow in his expression turned their white robes to gray. "The work of my hands is sunk in the sea, and you rejoice!"

That story is a variation on a tale that has been told by rabbis for centuries to illustrate the love of God. Although Pharaoh and his armies sought to enslave—even destroy—God's chosen people, God loved them as he loves all his creation. And he makes it clear that he wants his children to display that same kind of love, even to those who are mean and hateful. He didn't say it would be easy to do those things, but he did say it is right.

 REFLECT: Have you ever rejoiced at the fall of an enemy? How do you feel about that person now? Do you think Jesus' command to "love your enemies" instead of hating them means you have to *feel* love toward everyone? Does it mean *acting* in loving ways? Both? Neither?

 PRAY: "God, thank you for your love and for reminding me that love is always right. Help me especially to love_____ today so that I may act as a true child of my Father in heaven."

12 Your So-Called Life

Bible Reading: Matthew 22:34-40

Jesus replied, "'You must love the Lord your God with all your heart, all your soul, and all your mind.' This is the first and greatest commandment. A second is equally important: 'Love your neighbor as yourself.' All the other commandments and all the demands of the prophets are based on these two commandments." Matthew 22:37-40

IF YOUR LIFE were a television show, what would it be like? *Friends? Baywatch? My So-Called Life? The Brady Bunch?* Or maybe *3rd Rock from the Sun?*

If your life had a theme song, what would it be titled? Maybe something like "Insensitive"? Or "Jealousy"? Or maybe "The Great Adventure"? How about "I Get By with a Little Help from My Friends"? Or "Nobody Loves Me But My Mother (and She Could Be Jivin' Too)"?

If your life were a cable TV channel, would it be more like the Disney Channel, MTV, the Sports Channel, the Comedy Channel, or the boring Documentary Channel?

While it may be fun to come up with answers to those questions, the answers are probably not particularly revealing. But you know what? If Jesus' life were a television show, it could have only one title—*Love*. If a hit song were written about his life, it would be called "Love." In fact, if his life were a tennis game, every point would be love.

Jesus commanded us to love. He said,

A new command I give you: Love one another. As I have loved you, so you must love one another. By this all men will know that you are my disciples, if you love one another (John 13:34-35, NIV).

Jesus commanded us to love because he values love. The single greatest characteristic of Jesus' life, his most important theme, the center of everything he did and said, was love. He left heaven because of love. He became a man because of love. He went around doing good because of love. He even died—and was resurrected—because of love.

Jesus' words and life made it clear that love is always right. It is right for all people, for all places, and for all times. It is right not only because he commands love and values love, but also because he ultimately *is* love. Love is a part of his nature and character as God (1 John 4:8, 16). When we love others, even our enemies, we are "acting as true children of [our] Father in heaven" (Matthew 5:45).

 REFLECT: The paragraphs above refer to the three "steps" in discerning right from wrong (precept, principle, Person). Look back over today's reading and identify the precept, the principle, and the person.

 ACT: The next time you hear a television theme song, remember the theme of Jesus' life: *love.*

 PRAY: "Father, I want to love you as your Son, Jesus, has commanded me to do. I want to love the people around me, too. This week help me to show love to_____."

13 Loving When It's Hard

Bible Reading: 1 John 4:7-11

Dear friends, let us continue to love one another, for love comes from God. 1 John 4:7

A LEAGUE OF THEIR OWN is a film about the women's professional baseball league that existed during World War II. At one point in the movie, the star catcher for the Rockford Peaches, Dottie Hinson (played by Geena Davis), tells the manager, Jimmy Dugan (Tom Hanks), that she's quitting the team to go home.

"It just got too hard," she says.

"It's supposed to be hard," Dugan says. "If it weren't hard, everyone would do it. The *hard* is what makes it great."

Jesus spoke similar words to his disciples when he said,

If you love only those who love you, what good is that? Even corrupt tax collectors do that much. If you are kind only to your friends, how are you different from anyone else? Even pagans do that. But you are to be perfect, even as your Father in heaven is perfect (Matthew 5:46-48).

Dugan was talking about baseball, of course, and Jesus was talking about loving those who are hard to love. But the message is strikingly similar.

Are you having trouble loving that kid who's made fun of you ever since you were both in third grade? *It's supposed to be hard. If it weren't hard, everyone would do it. The* hard *is what makes it great.*

Having a hard time loving that teacher who gives you homework every night, even on weekends? *It's supposed to be hard. If it weren't hard, everyone would do it. The* hard *is what makes it great.*

Finding it tough to love the coach who won't play you, the neighbor who yells at you, the former friend who stabbed you in the back? *It's supposed to be hard. If it weren't hard, everyone would do it. The* hard *is what makes it great.*

Our tendency, of course, is to excuse or explain away our unloving attitudes and actions toward such people because *it's so hard.* But love isn't right only when it's easy; it's right when it's hard, too. In fact, loving such people—the ones who are hardest to love—is not only hard, it's impossible without God's help. And God knows that. That is why "he has given us the Holy Spirit to fill our hearts with his love" (Romans 5:5). As we spend time with him and rely on him, he will help us do the right thing and love even those who are hard to love.

 REFLECT: Whom do you find easy to love? Whom do you find hard to love? Think of something you can do this week to act in love toward these people, both those you find easy to love and those whom you have a hard time loving.

 PRAY: "Thanks, God, for your Holy Spirit, who makes it possible for me to love others."

14 Love Can Make You Happy

Bible Reading: 2 Peter 1:1-5

Make every effort to apply the benefits of these promises to your life.
2 Peter 1:5

IF ONE OF your teachers gave you an assignment to list the happiest people in the history of the world, who would be on the list?

Adolph Hitler, the leader of Nazi Germany?

Joseph Stalin, the communist dictator of Russia in the 1940s?

Nero, the Roman emperor who supposedly fiddled while Rome burned?

Herod the Great, who ordered the slaughter of all babies in his kingdom when he heard reports that a new king had been born somewhere around Bethlehem? (See Matthew 2:16-18.)

How about Haman, the guy in the biblical book of Esther who tried to engineer the destruction of Persia's Jewish population? (See Esther 3-4.)

What about Queen Jezebel, who was married to Ahab? She had a man killed just to take his land. (See 1 Kings 21.)

You mean *none* of those famous people would be on your list of the happiest people in the history of the world? Why not? They had it all—power, prestige, wealth. Why don't you think of them as happy people? For one very good reason: Their lives were characterized by hate, and a hateful person is never a happy person.

Think about it. The happiest people you know are those who love other people, lots of people. The happiest people are the lovingest people. That's the way it works.

And God knows that's how it works. That's one reason he commands us to love one another, because he knows that hate hurts us and love enriches us. He knows that people who act in love toward all those around them experience love twice—when they give it away to another person and when they receive it back again.

A sixties singing group sang, "Love can make you happy." It's true. Obeying God's command to love one another provides for your health and happiness, because love really can make you happy.

 REFLECT: Who *would* be on your list of the happiest people in the history of the world? Who are the happiest people you know? Think about those people who have come to mind. Are their lives characterized by hate or love?

 ACT: Give a valentine to the most loving person you know. Then perform a loving act for a friend or family member.

 PRAY: "Your love for me makes me happy, God. It makes me so happy that I want to be loving and act loving, too."

15 The Difference Love Makes

Bible Reading: 2 Peter 1:5-11

Godliness leads to love for other Christians, and finally you will grow to have genuine love for everyone. The more you grow like this, the more you will become productive and useful in your knowledge of our Lord Jesus Christ. 2 Peter 1:7-8

EARLY IN WORLD War II, as Paris was being bombed mercilessly by Nazi planes, a French doctor named Rene Spitz made a remarkable discovery. He was appalled by the high death rate among babies in shelters and orphanages. Upon closer examination, he discovered that babies who received regular affection fared better than others. Intrigued, he conducted a brief experiment, dividing the babies into two groups. Both groups of infants were cared for physically; they were fed identical diets, bathed regularly, and their diapers were changed at regular intervals. There was only one difference between the two groups. One group of babies received hugs and kisses from their caretakers; they were cradled and held and rocked and patted. The other group received no affection from their caretakers but were cared for and provided for in every other way.

You can probably guess what happened. The babies who were cuddled and loved not only grew but thrived. The other babies, who had all their needs met except their need for love and affection, did not grow as fast; they cried more and succumbed to more illnesses than the opposite group. Their development was measurably stunted until the study was discontinued.

Those two groups of babies were different only in the amount of love and affection they received. But what a difference that made in their health and development! The study revealed that children who are not treated with affection do not develop properly, even though they may be well nourished otherwise. It also shows how much human beings need to receive and give love in order to thrive.

That need doesn't change as we get older. Neither does the effect of love on a person's life. Obeying God's commands to love others can bring you love in return, which can actually make you healthier and happier. Obeying God's commands to love one another can help you "become productive and useful in your knowledge of our Lord Jesus Christ." Obeying God's commands to love others can make a huge difference in your health and development. That's just part of the difference love makes—in your life and in the lives of those around you.

 REFLECT: Through today's Scripture reading we learn that godliness will lead to love for other Christians and then to an even wider kind of love. What is that wider love? Do you think it happens overnight? How do you think it happens?

How have you been blessed (made happier and healthier) by loving others? How have others been blessed by your love?

 PRAY: "Thank you, God, for the way I feel when I let others know that I love them. Show me someone who needs my love this week."

16 Say It, Show It

Bible Reading: 1 John 3:18–20

> *Dear children, let us stop just saying we love each other; let us really show it by our actions. It is by our actions that we know we are living in the truth.* 1 John 3:18-19

WOULD YOU BELIEVE a person who claims to be a famous race car driver but can't back his car out of his garage?

Would you believe a person who tells you she is a trapeze artist in a world-famous circus but is afraid to climb a ladder to change a light bulb?

Would you believe a person who claims to be the world's greatest psychic and then asks you what time it is?

Probably not, right? Why not? Because their actions don't support their claims.

It's no different when people say they love someone but don't show it by their actions. Such claims are hard to believe because there's no evidence to support their claims.

You see, it's one thing to *talk* about love, to say we love each other. It's something else entirely to really show we love each other by our actions. For example, you might *say* you love others, but when's the last time you did something to help Mrs. McCready, the old lady who looks like she's about three hundred years old and lives alone down the street and has to shovel the snow off her sidewalk and mow the lawn herself? You might *say* you love pretty much everybody, but how long has it been since you *showed* your love for someone with your actions and not only with words?

"It is by our actions," the apostle John said, "that we know we are living in the truth." Do your actions show your love for others?

 REFLECT: Today's Scripture reading doesn't say that we should stop saying "I love you" to our parents, siblings, friends, and others we love; it says we should "stop *just* saying we love each other." In other words, we should say it *and* show it. Is there someone who needs to be reminded of your love? How can you do a better job of *showing* your love to others?

 ACT: Suggest a family "project" to your parents to show God's love to someone outside your family (bake cookies for a shut-in, take the family pet to visit nursing home patients, send a card to a prisoner, baby-sit for a single parent, shovel snow for an elderly couple, or whatever).

 PRAY: "God, I know that love comes from you. So please help me find a way to show love to_____ this week."

17 The Scream Machine

Bible Reading: Deuteronomy 6:20-24

The Lord commanded us to observe all these statutes, to fear the Lord our God for our good always and for our survival, as it is today.
Deuteronomy 6:24, NASB

"LET ME SHOW you something," Kyle said to his friend Jason as they climbed into the front car on the roller coaster. He gripped the safety bar and pulled it toward his lap, but not all the way. He leaned over to whisper to Jason. "I know how to keep it from locking into position."

As the ride jerked into motion, Kyle turned to Jason. "See?" he said, lifting the safety bar.

"Are you crazy?" Jason said.

"Pretty cool, isn't it?" Kyle said.

"I'm serious, Kyle." The train jerked again as it started up the huge hill that would send them plummeting down the other side.

Kyle shrugged. "Don't worry, I've done this before."

Jason gripped the bar and yanked it downward. Both boys heard it lock in place. "What'd you do that for?" Kyle asked.

"Look, they put these bars here for a reason," Jason answered.

"Yeah, because they're wimps."

"No, because they don't want to peel your face off the ground after you fall!"

"We're not going to fall out," Kyle insisted.

"Right," Jason said as they reached the crest of the hill. He patted the safety bar, locked in place across his lap, then lifted his arms high into the air over his head.

Some people react to God's laws about right and wrong the way Kyle felt about the safety bar on the roller coaster. They think that God's commands (like "Do not lie," "Honor your father and your mother," and "Flee sexual immorality") are intended to cramp their style and spoil their fun. They think that rules are meant to be broken and that people who break the most rules have the most fun.

But God's commands—like the safety bar on a roller coaster—are given to us for good reasons. They're not intended to spoil anyone's fun; they're intended for our own good, for our safety and protection. The people who break those rules may sometimes *look* like they're having the most fun, but looks can be deceiving.

Obeying God's commands doesn't just keep you safe while you're riding; it can also make the ride more fun.

 REFLECT: How are God's commands like a safety bar on a roller coaster? How are they different? Do you think a safety bar does any good if it's not used? Do you think God's commands do you any good if you ignore them?

 PRAY: "Thank you, Lord, for all your commands. Thank you for protecting me with your commands. Help me to obey your commands, especially when_____."

18 The Truth about Truth

Bible Reading: Psalm 146:1-10

He is the one who made heaven and earth, the sea, and everything in them. He is the one who keeps every promise forever. Psalm 146:6

GOD DID NOT create *everything.*

Does that statement surprise you? It's true.

Oh, he created the universe, with its countless galaxies of stars and planets, asteroids, and black holes.

He created this earth and all its rivers and oceans, mountains and valleys, rocks and grass and trees.

He created all the fish and creatures in the sea. He created dolphins, whales, swordfish, and tuna. He created the glassy eyes of the shark. He created the spoon-shaped tail of the manatee. He created the poisonous fins of the lionfish and the eerie sleekness of the manta ray.

He created the broad wings of the condor and the rapid, darting flight of the hummingbird. He created the tufted ears of the Canada lynx and the long neck of the giraffe. He created the odd waddle of the armadillo, the grace of the antelope, the powerful jaws of a crocodile, and the purr of a kitten.

But God did not create everything. He didn't create truth because he is truth. Truth is a part of his nature.

Of course, there are some people who believe that there is no such thing as truth. "Truth is relative," they say. "It is different for each person." But even those who say such things believe that their own statement is *true,* or they would not say it.

But truth does not only exist, it is eternal and unchanging because it is a part of the nature of God. As Moses said, "He is . . . a God of truth" (Deuteronomy 32:4, KJV). Truth also can be our guide, for we can pray as the psalmist did: "Lead me by your truth and teach me, for you are the God who saves me" (Psalm 25:5).

 REFLECT: Why does today's reading say that God did not create truth? How is truth related to God? Do you think it makes sense for someone to say that there is no such thing as truth? Why or why not?

 PRAY: Look up Jesus' prayer for his disciples in John 17:17. Pray that verse aloud, making it your own prayer by saying *me* every time you see the word *them.*

19 The First Epidemic

Bible Reading: Romans 5:12-17

When Adam sinned, sin entered the entire human race. Adam's sin brought death, so death spread to everyone, for everyone sinned.
Romans 5:12

THEY CALLED IT the "Black Death." It started in China around the year 1334 and quickly spread to India, Persia, Russia, and then to Europe. People started getting sick. They would become sick, sometimes quite suddenly, with a high fever. Then their throats would swell, and they would break out in a rash and a hacking cough; black spots would appear on their faces and, within a few days, they would die. In just a few years, 60 million people died of the plague. In fact, the plague was so widespread in Europe that almost one of every four Europeans died. In the late nineteenth century, the plague reappeared in Hong Kong and then in other places, particularly India, where 10 million people died over the next twenty years.

An epidemic of influenza—the "flu"—started among soldiers who fought in northern France late in World War I, around 1918. Thousands of soldiers experienced the fever, chills, and nausea associated with the virus. The epidemic spread around the world as some of those soldiers left France. Hundreds of millions of people became sick. An estimated 20 million died—a greater number than those who were killed by bullets and bombs in the war.

A plague of a different kind, far more deadly than the bubonic plague (as "the Black Death" has become known) or influenza, has spread throughout the world today. It threatens close to 5 *billion* people—the inhabitants of every nation and household in the world. It's called *sin*.

Ever since the first man and woman sinned by disobeying God (check out Genesis 3), we've all been born with a sinful nature. That means we're all infected with a condition that makes it *natural* for us to do what's wrong. We may sometimes make poor choices because we're confused about what's right or wrong. We may sometimes give in to pressure from friends. Or we may do wrong things because we've developed bad habits. But the ultimate reason we make wrong choices is because we are sinners.

That doesn't mean we *have* to make wrong choices. There is a cure for this plague: the sacrifice of Jesus Christ on the cross. He not only paid the penalty for our sins, he also conquered sin and death so that we can stop making wrong choices. By praying to him and trusting him, we can start making right choices.

 REFLECT: Do you think a person can stop making wrong choices without God's help? Why or why not?

 PRAY: Have you accepted Jesus' sacrifice as payment for your sins, asked God to forgive you, and trusted Christ to save you from sin and its punishment? If not, why not do so right now? If you've already done this, thank him for his "generous gift of forgiveness" (Romans 5:15).

20 What It Takes

Bible Reading: Galatians 5:16-22

> *When the Holy Spirit controls our lives, he will produce this kind of fruit in us: love, joy, peace, patience, kindness, goodness, faithfulness, gentleness, and self-control.* Galatians 5:22-23

HERE'S A QUICK little test for you. See if you can match up the trees listed in the column on the left with the fruit those trees bear listed in the column on the right:

apple tree	pecans
oak tree	pears
banana tree	hickory nuts
pear tree	acorns
peach tree	cherries
hickory tree	apples
walnut tree	walnuts
cherry tree	peaches
pecan tree	bananas

Pretty dumb test, huh? *Everybody* knows that apples come from apple trees and walnuts come from walnut trees. No matter how hard it tries, a cherry tree could never produce apples; a pecan tree couldn't squeeze out a single banana. Why not? Because neither tree has what it takes to produce that kind of fruit.

Making right choices works the same way. None of us can make right choices all the time. Some days it seems as if we can't make right choices *at all!* Because we're sinners we don't have what it takes to produce that kind of fruit—not by ourselves, at least. We might as well try to squeeze pears out of our ears!

So, does that mean we should just give up? No, but it does mean that the only way we can consistently make right choices is through the Spirit of Christ living in us. His Spirit lives in everyone who has trusted Christ for salvation. It's only by relying on him every day—through prayer and Bible reading—that we can consistently make right choices. In fact, you might say that making right choices is the fruit that the Holy Spirit produces in our lives when we trust God day by day.

 REFLECT: What kind of choices have you been making recently? Have they been sort of prickly, like a pineapple? nutty, like an acorn? sweet, like a cherry? sour, like a crabapple? something else? What kind of choices do you want to make from now on?

 ACT: Try making a simple song or poem out of Galatians 5:22 and 23.

 PRAY: Here is an example of a prayer you may want to say the first thing every morning: "God, I praise you for this day that you have made. I give your Holy Spirit complete control of everything I do today. Help me to make right choices all day long. In Jesus' name. Amen."

21 The Saint of the Gutters

Bible Reading: Zechariah 7:8-10

This is what the Lord Almighty says: Judge fairly and honestly, and show mercy and kindness to one another. Zechariah 7:9

SHE'S BEEN CALLED "the saint of the gutters."

She was eighteen years old when she joined a religious order and went to India. She began teaching in Calcutta. There she saw more poor people than she'd ever seen in her life. Her heart overflowed with mercy and compassion for them, so she asked—and received—permission to leave her sheltered life as a nun and start working among some of the poorest, hungriest, neediest people in the world.

She started scraping food together for the hungry. She began taking in children, orphans who had nowhere else to go. Eventually, the group she started, called the Missionaries of Charity, operated food kitchens, hospitals, schools, orphanages, and shelters for lepers and those who were dying.

She worked in obscurity for years before the world began to learn of her work of mercy. Then, in 1979, the Nobel Peace Prize was awarded to this "saint of the gutters," Mother Teresa. With the award came international recognition.

Today, it seems that everyone agrees that the mercy displayed by Mother Teresa is a good thing. Even when a lot of people claim that everyone has to "decide" what's right or wrong for himself or herself, no one would argue that what Mother Teresa does is wrong. It's easy to see that she is doing good, not evil. That judgment has nothing to do with what *you* think or what your *culture* thinks; what she does is good and admirable because it reflects what *is* good and admirable.

You see, it's not up to any one of us—or even all of us put together—to *decide* whether mercy is right or wrong. God made it clear long ago that mercy is right, that acting mercifully toward others is good. Just about everybody in the world knows, in his heart of hearts, that mercy is right. That's why we admire Mother Teresa; not because we have *decided* that mercy is a virtue, but because we *recognize* that which God has already called good, because she models what God has told us is right.

REFLECT: Mother Teresa is a model of mercy in many ways. Can you think of someone else who shows mercy to other people?

You may not know any lepers or starving people to show mercy to, but there are people in your life who need mercy and compassion. How can you practice showing mercy and kindness to others this week?

PRAY: "God, help me not to go through a single day this week without showing mercy to at least one person."

22 Off the Hook

Bible Reading: Zechariah 7:8-10

Where is another God like you, who pardons the sins of the survivors among his people? You cannot stay angry with your people forever, because you delight in showing mercy. Micah 7:18

IN THE MOVIE *Hook,* a Steven Spielberg retelling of the Peter Pan story, Peter (played by Robin Williams) and Captain Hook (Dustin Hoffman) engage in an epic sword fight as the children of Neverland—and the adult Peter's two children, Jack and Maggie—look on. Finally, after a fierce fight, Peter knocks Hook's sword from his hands, and the pirate falls to one knee. Peter levels his sword and points it at the neck of the man who killed his friend.

"You killed Rufio, you kidnapped my children, you deserve to die," Peter says.

But Peter's children approach and his daughter, Maggie, lays a hand on Peter's arm. "Let's go home," she says. "Please. He's just a mean old man without a mommy."

"Yeah, Dad," Jack agrees. "Let's go home."

Peter lowers his sword. "Take your ship and go," he tells Hook. He puts away his sword in his belt and turns toward home, holding Jack and Maggie by the hand.

In the end, Hook meets his end anyway—but not at the hands of Peter Pan.

Peter's action in sparing his enemy is heroic. He would have certainly been less heroic if he had executed Hook, even though Hook had tried to kill him. But why? Why do we feel that way?

Because mercy is right.

Mercy is right because God commands us to be merciful. The Bible says, "The Lord has already told you what is good, and this is what he requires: to do what is right, to love mercy, and to walk humbly with your God" (Micah 6:8).

But mercy is not right only because God *commands* mercy; it is right also because God *values* mercy. His commands show what kind of attitude and behavior he values.

But mercy is not right only because God *values* mercy; it is right also because God *is* merciful. Mercy is a part of who God is. The Bible describes God as "a merciful God" (Deuteronomy 4:31; Nehemiah 9:31). The Bible also says he delights in showing mercy (Micah 7:18). Mercy is right, then, not because we *think* it's right or because we *feel* it's right or even because everybody *says* it's right. Showing mercy is right because it reflects God's nature and character. And refusing to show mercy is wrong because it's not like God.

 REFLECT: What makes an action or an attitude right? What makes an action or an attitude wrong?

How do you know that God is merciful? How has God shown his mercy to you? to others you know?

 PRAY: "God, you are merciful, and I thank you for your mercy. Help me to show mercy to others, especially when_____."

23 70 x 7

Bible Reading: Luke 6:36-38

> *Be merciful, just as your Father is merciful. Do not judge, and you will not be judged. Do not condemn, and you will not be condemned. Forgive, and you will be forgiven.* Luke 6:36-37, NIV

THE CHARACTERS ON the children's television show *Sesame Street* often sang a song that went something like, "One of these things is not like the others, one of these things just doesn't belong." Viewers were supposed to pick out which item didn't belong in the group. Well, Big Bird's not here to sing for you (this is a pretty low-budget devotional), but let's play the game anyway. Ready?

One of these things is not like the others, one of these things just doesn't belong. Which one is it?

| Cake | Pie | Pudding | Motor oil |

One of these things is not like the others, one of these things just doesn't belong. Which one is it?

| Moses | Hootie & the Blowfish | Daniel | King David |

One of these things is not like the others, one of these things just doesn't belong. Which one is it?

| Mercy | Kindness | Compassion | Unforgivingness |

OK, so it's not as good as *Sesame Street*. But if you answered "unforgivingness" to that last question, you get the point: one of the main ways people fail to show mercy to each other is by refusing to forgive each other.

Peter, one of Jesus' disciples, once asked Jesus, "How often should I forgive someone who sins against me? Seven times?" Jesus probably shocked Peter with his answer. "No!" Jesus replied, "seventy times seven!" (Matthew 18:21-22). The rabbis of Jesus' day taught that a person should be forgiven three times. But Jesus made it clear that we should never stop forgiving people.

In many ways, mercy begins with forgiveness. If you refuse to forgive someone, then you are not showing mercy. Mercy means loving someone even when he or she has wronged you. Mercy means letting that person "off the hook." Mercy means letting go of your "right" to be mad or resentful. It's not always easy to forgive, of course. It's not always easy to show mercy. But it's always right.

 REFLECT: Do you have a "forgiveness limit"? Is there someone you need to forgive? Perhaps there is someone you need to ask for forgiveness.

 PRAY: "Lord, I'm sorry that I've had a hard time forgiving_____. Help me to show your mercy by_____."

24 Andy and the Lion

Bible Reading: Matthew 5:1-10

> *One day as the crowds were gathering, Jesus went up the mountainside with his disciples and sat down to teach them. This is what he taught them. . . . God blesses those who are merciful, for they will be shown mercy. Matthew 5:1-2, 7*

THE PEOPLE OF ancient Rome told the story of Androcles, a slave whose master was cruel. Androcles ran away and hid in the woods for a long time. He was happy to be free but had a hard time finding food, so he began to get hungry and weak. Finally, convinced that he was dying, Androcles crawled into a dark cave and lay down to sleep.

He was awakened by the loud roar of a lion that had entered the cave. Androcles thought the lion was going to eat him, but he watched in fascination as the lion limped in circles around the cave, constantly whimpering and occasionally roaring in pain.

When the great creature finally lay down, Androcles approached the lion carefully. To his surprise, the lion allowed him to gingerly lift the injured paw. Androcles discovered that a long, sharp thorn had lodged itself in the lion's paw. With one quick motion, he pulled the thorn out. The lion licked the tender paw while Androcles still held it in his hand, and soon both man and animal fell asleep.

The next morning the lion brought food to Androcles, and it continued to do so every day until a band of soldiers came into the cave and recognized Androcles as an escaped slave. The soldiers arrested him and took him to Rome.

In those days runaway slaves were forced to fight wild animals in the Colosseum for the entertainment of the people. After a few days in prison, Androcles was taken to the Colosseum. His guards dragged him out into a dirt arena and left him alone. He trembled as he heard the roars of a hungry beast.

Finally, a gate was opened at the other end of the arena, and a mighty lion raced in, roaring and baring his teeth. The creature leaped upon Androcles in a single bound as the crowd watched in astonishment to see Androcles and the lion he had befriended roll over and over in the dirt in a happy reunion. When the crowd heard the slave's story, they cried out for Androcles and the lion to be set free, and they were.

This fable illustrates an important truth. Jesus put it this way: "Blessed are the merciful, for they will be shown mercy" (Matthew 5:7, NIV). The person who shows mercy to others often receives mercy back, while the person who refuses mercy to others is cheated out of many good things.

It's just another way that obeying God's commands protects us and provides for us.

 REFLECT: Have you ever been blessed by someone who has shown you mercy? Have you returned that blessing? Have you ever been blessed by being merciful to someone else?

 PRAY: "Thank you, God, for the mercy you have shown to me. This week, help me think of a way to show mercy to one of your creatures."

25 Shadowman

Bible Reading: Matthew 18:21-35
Shouldn't you have mercy . . . just as I had mercy on you?
Matthew 18:33

A SHADOWY IMAGE appears on the television screen. His voice warbles oddly, and a line of type scrolls across the bottom of the screen: *Manny (not his real name) is speaking on condition of anonymity. His image and voice have been altered to protect his identity.*

"I had it made. Money, car, apartment in town, house in the suburbs. I'd gotten into a little debt—OK, so it was a lot. Millions. I'd kinda 'borrowed' it from the company, if you know what I mean."

The shadowy figure shifts in his chair. "My boss found out, told *his* boss. Eventually it got all the way to the top. So the owner of the company called me in, told me he wanted the money I took. I says, 'I ain't got it right now. But I'll pay it back, honest.'

"Then he tells me he could send me away for a very long time and have my family thrown out into the street. I told him, 'Look, I'll do anything. I'll pay back every cent—with interest. All's I need is a little time.'

"The big boss stared at me for a long time, not sayin' nothin'. Finally he says, 'Tell you what. I'll give you a break. I'll forget all about the money. You walk outta here a free man. Just don't try somethin' like that again.'

"I couldn't believe it! He let me off the hook—" *the man snapped his fingers*—"just like that! I walked outta his office like I was walkin' on air!

"When I got out into the boss's reception area, I saw Mike Kennedy, a guy I used to work with. I says to Kennedy, 'I want the two thousand you owe me,' and he says, 'I can give you some now and the rest in a few weeks.' I says to Kennedy, 'That ain't good enough.' I told him if he didn't get all the money to me by the end of the day, I'd ruin him. I figured he had it—he was just holdin' out on me, you know?

"Well, it turns out the boss's secretary heard me talkin' to Kennedy, and next thing I know, the boss calls me back into his office. He says, 'Didn't I give you a break? a *million-dollar* break? But after I show mercy to you, you go out and refuse to have a little mercy on Kennedy. Well,' he says to me, 'the deal is off.' Next thing I know"—*the camera pans out to show a background of prison bars behind the anonymous storyteller*—"I'm wearin' an orange jumpsuit and makin' license plates.

"Wanna know the funny part?" the man asks without a trace of humor in his voice. "Kennedy got my old job!"

REFLECT: What do you think the story above and Jesus' parable teach about the benefits of showing mercy to others?

PRAY: "God, you have forgiven me for so many sins. I ask you now to help me forgive_____ for_____."

26 What's Your Rep?

Bible Reading: Proverbs 3:1-4

Never let loyalty and kindness get away from you! Wear them like a necklace; write them deep within your heart. Then you will find favor with both God and people, and you will gain a good reputation.
Proverbs 3:3-4

IN THE LEFT column below are the names of fictional and factual people who have become identified with a certain reputation. See if you can match each name with the corresponding reputation:

1.	Benedict Arnold	A.	barbaric
2.	Midas	B.	brave
3.	Ebenezer Scrooge	C.	artistic
4.	Michael Jordan	D.	miserly
5.	Attila the Hun	E.	romantic
6.	Pocahontas	F.	smart
7.	Hercules	G.	traitorous
8.	Albert Einstein	H.	rich
9.	Michelangelo	I.	athletic
10.	Romeo	J.	strong

How'd you do? If you got less than half right, don't sweat it; it's only for fun. If you got all of them right, substitute your name for Albert Einstein's!

More important than how many you got right is this question: If *your* name were on that list, what sort of reputation would your friends, family, and others identify with you? If the words *kind* and *merciful* were in the right-hand column, would anyone associate those words with you? If so, then you have already begun to establish a reputation for kindness and mercy. That should not only make you feel good, but it can also protect you and provide for you. A reputation for kindness and mercy will tend to make other people want to hang around you. It will often prompt people to be understanding toward you. It may open doors of opportunity for you to help others and, perhaps, be helped yourself.

If the words *kind* and *merciful* would *not* be associated with you, it's not too late to begin cultivating kindness and loyalty. Then, as today's Bible reading says, "you will find favor with both God and people, and you will gain a good reputation" as you begin to reap the rewards of showing mercy to others.

 REFLECT: Proverbs 22:1 says: "Choose a good reputation over great riches, for being held in high esteem is better than having silver or gold." Why do you think this is true?

 PRAY: "God, I really want both you and people to think well of me. Today I'm going to be especially kind to_____ by doing this:_____."

ANSWERS: 1G; 2H; 3D; 4I; 5A; 6B; 7J; 8F; 9C; 10E.

27 The Lord's Own Reward

Bible Reading: 1 Samuel 26:1-25
The Lord gives his own reward for doing good. 1 Samuel 26:23

POOR JOSEPH. He was minding his own business, working for a man named Potiphar, when the boss's wife started getting fresh. She said, "Yo, Joe, come to bed with me" (Genesis 39:7, loose translation). So what did Joseph do? He made a quick dash for the exit! Joseph did the right thing, and you know what? He ended up in prison for it!

Poor Elijah. He was minding his own business, doing his thing as a prophet of God in Israel, when God told him to summon to Mount Carmel all the people of Israel, including 850 false prophets. So what did Elijah do? He prayed and won a mighty contest against the enemies of God! Elijah did the right thing, and you know what? He had to run for his life from an angry Queen Jezebel (see 1 Kings 18:1-19:9).

Poor Daniel. He was minding his own business, praying to God three times a day in his own room, when the king decreed that for thirty days no one could pray to anyone except the king (see Daniel 6:1-18). So what did Daniel do? He prayed to God, just as he had always done. Daniel did the right thing, and you know what? He got thrown into a den of lions!

"Whoa, now!" you might say. "Are you telling me that those guys all did the right thing, and they ended up worse than before?"

Yup.

"But," you might ask, "I thought right choices were supposed to protect us and provide for us."

Yup.

"So how come," you might wonder, "all those bad things happened to Joseph, Elijah, and Daniel? It doesn't sound like they were better off for making right choices."

Actually, they were. But their experiences—and the experiences of many people since—show that right choices aren't always rewarded. There's no guarantee that doing the right thing will bring immediate benefits; in fact, much of the time, doing the right thing doesn't seem to bring any good results at all.

When David was being chased by King Saul (1 Samuel 26), he chose to show mercy toward the king God had anointed. But sparing Saul's life made things *worse* for David, not better. His actions didn't promise immediate benefits, but David did the right thing anyway. And eventually God made David the king in Saul's place.

Doing the right thing may not always be rewarded immediately—perhaps never. But whether it's rewarded or not, doing the right thing will please God. As David himself said, "The Lord gives his own reward for doing good" (1 Samuel 26:23).

 REFLECT: Have you ever been sorry for doing the right thing? Why or why not?

 PRAY: "Lord, help me to do the right thing, even when I may not be rewarded. Right now I most need your help doing the right thing in the area of_____."

28 Beyond Mildew and Tassels

Bible Reading: Romans 14:21-23

Anyone who believes that something he wants to do is wrong shouldn't do it. Romans 14:23, TSLB

GOD HAS GIVEN a lot of direction and instruction about what is right and what is wrong. He has made it pretty clear: "Don't lie," "Don't steal," "Honor your father and mother," and so on.

In fact, God has been really specific with some of his commands. For example, his commands to Israel actually included such details as

- what priests should wear (Exodus 28:1-43)
- which kinds of animals, fish, and birds could be eaten (Leviticus 11:1-19)
- how to rid a house of an "infectious mildew" (Leviticus 14:33-53)
- how tassels were to be worn (Numbers 15:37-41)
- which vows made by wives or daughters were binding (Numbers 30)
- what to do if you found a bird's nest on the ground (Deuteronomy 22:6-7)

Isn't that great? If your house ever has an "infectious mildew," or you wonder just how you ought to wear the tassels your great-grandmother gave you for Christmas, you'll know what to do!

Unfortunately, it's not always that easy to know what's right and what's wrong. Oh, there's no doubt about the "big" things, like murder and stealing and love and mercy. But sometimes it can be hard to know if a choice is right or wrong. A lot of the choices kids face can be pretty hard to figure out. If you're not sure something is wrong, should you go ahead and do it anyway? Or should you never do anything unless you're absolutely positive it's right? What if you get stuck between two choices and you *have* to choose one, but you don't know if either one is right?

Well, it's not necessarily a sin to do something that we don't know is wrong—or right. We can't know everything, and we don't have to assume that everything we don't know about is wrong. On the other hand, if you have doubts and think it *might* be wrong, you'd better make sure by doing these four things first: (1) Put off doing it; (2) pray about it; (3) search the Bible for direction; and (4) ask for advice from your parents or from a Christian friend you trust. If you still can't determine what's wrong or right, steer clear of it. It's better to *not do* something that would have been OK than to *do* something that is wrong.

Remember, too, that God wants you to choose what is best, not just avoid what is wrong.

 REFLECT: Have you ever had trouble figuring out whether something is right or wrong? What did you end up doing in that situation? Ask your parents what they think about the decision you made.

 PRAY: "Lord, help me to choose what is best and not just avoid what is wrong."

29 The Farmer and the Snake

Bible Reading: Proverbs 19:2-3

Zeal without knowledge is not good; a person who moves too quickly may go the wrong way. People ruin their lives by their own foolishness and then are angry at the Lord. Proverbs 19:2-3

AESOP, A GREEK slave who lived about six hundred years before Christ, recorded many fables—short stories that were intended to teach an important truth. One of Aesop's fables was the story of the farmer and the snake.

One winter a farmer was walking down the dirt road near his farm when he saw a snake lying across the road, stiff and frozen from the cold.

The farmer felt sorry for the snake and picked it up. He cradled the poisonous creature against his chest, and before long the warmth of the man's body began to revive the snake. Immediately upon gaining the use of its muscles, the snake coiled and bit the farmer, inflicting a deadly wound.

The farmer was foolish, of course. He should have known better. He should not have taken a chance with a poisonous snake.

Many people make the same mistake today. Oh, they may not pick up snakes from the road, but they do something that is infinitely more dangerous. They play with sin. They flirt with temptation. They make wrong choices. And they wonder why they can't seem to find happiness and fulfillment. Sometimes their wrong choices have tragic consequences, and they look at their ruined lives and ask, "How could God do this to me?"

"People ruin their lives by their own foolishness," Solomon said, "and then are angry at the Lord" (Proverbs 19:3). But it's not God's fault if people who disobey him suffer the consequences of their disobedience. People who play with snakes should expect to be bitten.

REFLECT: Today's reading compares sin to a snake. In what ways do you think sin is like a snake? In what ways is it different?

Are you "playing" with any sin or "flirting" with any temptations in your life? God can help you steer clear of that sin or temptation if you let him.

PRAY: "Father God, I don't want to ruin my life by making a foolish choice. Help me to steer clear of sin and temptation, especially in the area of_____."

Thinking in New Ways

Bible Reading: Ephesians 4:17-23

Instead, there must be a spiritual renewal of your thoughts and attitudes.
Ephesians 4:23

LOOK AT THE arrangement of dots below. Without lifting your pencil, can you draw four straight lines in such a way that at least one line goes through each dot?

•   •   •

•   •   •

•   •   •

How'd you do? It's impossible, you say? Can't be done? Think again. It can be done, but it requires breaking out of your usual way of thinking. Did you consider starting your straight lines only on one of the dots, or did you consider the possibility that the straight lines could extend beyond the figure of nine dots?

Try it this way: Beginning with the dot in the lower left corner, draw a straight line diagonally to the top right corner. Next, draw a straight line down from the top right corner, *continuing past* the dot in the bottom right corner. Then, beginning below the dot at the bottom right, draw a straight line diagonally through the dot in the middle of the bottom row and the far-left dot in the middle row (piercing only two dots) and again *continuing past* that dot into the space to the left of the top row. Then draw your fourth straight line across the top row of the figure. Phew! You did it!

What's the point of this exercise? Well, the more you learn about God and his ways, the more you will begin to think in ways that other people just can't understand. As you learn more and more about God and accept him as the authority over right and wrong, your thoughts and attitudes will begin to change. When others react one way to a certain situation or temptation, you will act and react in a totally different way. When others choose wrong, you will be able to choose right because you know some things that they don't understand.

If something seems impossible, people think, "Hey, it can't be done." Let's face it—as humans we can be pretty limited in our thinking. But just like the dot exercise, we can be trained to go beyond our limitations. How? By thinking like Christ. First Corinthians 2:16 tells us, "We can understand [spiritual and other truths], for we have the mind of Christ." With his limitless thinking, the possibilities are endless!

 REFLECT: Do your friends ever express surprise about the way you think or the things you do? Do they think differently from you about right and wrong? If so, why? If not, why not?

 PRAY: "God, how great it is that you give us a new way of thinking. Help me to develop the same mind as Christ and to act—and react—like he would?"

2 In Control?

Bible Reading: Ephesians 4:24-27

You must display a new nature because you are a new person, created in God's likeness—righteous, holy, and true. Ephesians 4:24

DOESN'T IT JUST make you mad when

- you take the dog for a walk and he "walks" on your pant leg or shoe?
- you call a friend to talk about how much you like this "total fox" in your class and you realize—too late—that you dialed the wrong number and spilled your guts to the "fox"?
- you forget your lunch and have to eat the food your friends don't want, like carrot sticks, Spam, and something mushy and gray?
- you turn on the television to watch your favorite show and it's being preempted so the president can talk about meeting with people you've never heard of in some place you've never heard of to discuss something you don't care about?
- you realize at noon that you forgot to take off your pajama top before getting dressed for school?

Lots of things can make you mad. Sometimes it can seem like the whole world is just waiting for a chance to get on your nerves. But it's not.

What is happening, though, is that every day you face a lot of choices that challenge your self-control. Self-control is your ability to control your temper and your actions. It's not like being double-jointed, though, in that "some people are and some people ain't." It's like any choice between right and wrong: Sometimes you make the right choice (and exercise self-control), and sometimes you don't.

No matter how many times something or someone gets on your "last nerve," no matter how often you're tempted to lose your cool, no matter how much you'd like to blow off some steam, you need to recognize that being self-controlled is a *choice* you make. And, with God's help, you'll be able to choose self-control more and more often.

Self-control is one of the fruits of the Holy Spirit. (See Galatians 5:22-23.) If you're controlled by God's Spirit, you'll have self-control. Does that make you a robot? Hardly! You still have the freedom to choose self-control or to blow your cool. Someone won't "leggo your Eggo"? You can choose what to do: get mad or use self-control. You can heed or ignore the psalmist's warning, "Don't sin by letting anger gain control over you. Think about it overnight and remain silent" (Psalm 4:4).

 REFLECT: Reread Ephesians 4:24. What do you think it means to be a "new person"? How can that affect your actions?

What was the last thing that got you really upset? How did you respond? How could you have responded differently?

 PRAY: "Lord, stop me when I start to get angry. Help me to see my choices. And give me the strength to make the right choice."

3 Villains 'R' Us

Bible Reading: Ephesians 4:28-32

> *Get rid of all bitterness, rage, anger, harsh words, and slander, as well as all types of malicious behavior. Ephesians 4:31*

CRUELLA DE VIL
Scar
Jafar
Captain Hook
Fauna and Flora
Shere Khan

Recognize any of those names? Cruella De Vil, of course, was the totally mean and nasty villainess in Disney's *101 Dalmatians*. Scar was little Simba's evil uncle in *The Lion King*. Jafar? He plotted against Aladdin, the Genie, and Jasmine in Disney's *Aladdin*. Captain Hook was out to get Peter Pan. Fauna and Flora, Cinderella's wicked stepsisters, treated her like dirt. And Shere Khan, the tiger in *The Jungle Book*, wanted to eat poor Mowgli! Anybody who has seen those animated classics would agree that characters such as Scar and Jafar are evil. But why?

A lot of people today claim that right and wrong don't exist, that everybody has to decide for himself or herself what's good or bad. "You're old enough to know what's right for you," they might say. "Don't let anybody tell you what's right or wrong. That's up to you."

But *everybody* would agree that wanting to steal and to slaughter innocent little puppies to make fur coats (like Cruella De Vil) is downright nasty, and that engineering your brother's death and blaming it on your nephew (like Scar in *The Lion King*) isn't very nice, either. Those villains are despicable characters because *anyone* can recognize that their actions and attitudes are evil. Why? Because right and wrong is not up to you or me; it's already been decided—and decreed—by God himself. He alone has the authority to decide right from wrong, and he has said that murder and hatred and bitterness and rage and anger—and all types of malicious behavior—are wrong.

"Instead," God says, we are to be self-controlled, "kind to each other, tenderhearted, forgiving one another, just as God through Christ has forgiven you" (Ephesians 4:32). No matter what anyone else may tell you, that's what's right!

 REFLECT: Do you ever find yourself justifying bitterness, rage, or anger toward someone else? Do you ever say, "I didn't do anything wrong," when you really did? Do you tend to be "self-controlled" or "uncontrolled"?

 ACT: Suggest that your family rent one of the movies mentioned above. As you watch it, notice the traits of the villains and how much they reflect the things God has called evil.

 PRAY: "God, I'm glad that you love me and want to help me even when I feel like a villain. Show me today how to get rid of anything bad I may want to say or do."

4 Follow the Leader

Bible Reading: Ephesians 5:1-4

The keynote of your conversation should not be coarseness or silliness or flippancy—which are quite out of place, but a sense of all that we owe to God. Ephesians 5:4, Phillips

HAVE YOU EVER worked with someone and sewed something from a pattern? Or have you ever used a plan to make something from wood? Have you ever followed the directions to make a model car or plane, put together a new toy or bike, or used a recipe to bake a cake "from scratch" (where do you buy "scratch," anyway)?

To do any of those things correctly you have to follow some type of plan, whether it be a sewing pattern, a construction plan, assembly instructions, or a recipe. Think what the cake would be like if you put spinach in it instead of flour. Yuck! Or how would the bike look if you tried to put both wheels on the back or left the seat off? Not much fun to ride! Or if you decided to ignore the pattern and put sleeves wherever you wanted or left out the neck hole?

It may be a hassle at times to follow instructions, recipes, and patterns, but the outcome is sure better if you do. And the creator of the plan knows things will work out properly if you follow the instructions.

Well, when it comes to living our life, we have a pattern, too. Jesus is our pattern. As God's Son, he came to show us what God is like. He is the ultimate example for us.

When God tells us, in his Word, to be self-controlled, he's not just making a new rule off the top of his head. He's telling us, "Be like me," because *he* is self-controlled. When God says, "These are the things I will do" (Isaiah 42:16, NIV), he does them. He never lies, never gets carried away.

Some people seem to be controlled by their temper; yet God never loses control of his temper. Some people's tongues seem to be out of control; yet God never loses control of his tongue. Some people seem to be victims of their passions; yet God is never controlled by anything except his own perfect, holy nature and will.

And because God is self-controlled, he wants us to be self-controlled and to follow the example he sets for us.

 REFLECT: Do you think God ever has to exercise his self-control with you? Can you ever be perfectly self-controlled, as God is? Can you reflect his self-control in your behavior? How?

 ACT: Carry a carpenter's pencil or a recipe card in your pocket or purse to remind you to follow God's example and be self-controlled today. Or memorize Ephesians 5:1.

 PRAY: "God, thank you for providing an example of how I should live my life. Help me to closely follow your plan for me."

5 Your True Colors

Bible Reading: Ephesians 5:5-9

Live life, then, with a due sense of responsibility, not as men who do not know the meaning of life but as those who do. Ephesians 5:15, Phillips

SOME SPORTS TEAMS' emblems or logos make sense. For example, the symbol for the New York Yankees is Uncle Sam's top hat on the end of a baseball bat. The Chicago Bulls' mascot is a red bull. The Dallas Cowboys have a lone star (Texas is the Lone Star State) on their helmets.

Other team traditions seem strange, to say the least. Penn State University's colors are blue and white, but Nitanny Lions—their teams' names—are neither blue nor white. The Detroit Red Wings? Their emblem is a red automobile tire with wings. And what does a Los Angeles Dodger dodge?

And, of course, some teams have strange mascots. You'll find everything from a gorilla in Utah (the only one not in a zoo) to a fish in Florida to a creature known as a "Phanatic" in Philadelphia.

But the most interesting thing about many sports teams is not their names, emblems, or mascots, but their fans. They wear hats, wigs, and jerseys. They carry towels and Styrofoam hands with upraised index fingers indicating, "We're number one." (How many "Number Ones" can there be?) They paint their faces and their bodies. They wave team pennants. They wear team pins. They sing team songs. They are clearly identified with the team they cheer for, the team they follow closely.

How closely are you identified with God? How do people know you love and serve him? After all, he doesn't have "team colors" or a team mascot. Oh, you might wear a T-shirt. You may listen to Christian music. You might even carry this book around. (Buy a hundred copies for your friends!)

Those things are OK, but they're not the main way God wants us to identify with him. He wants us to show we worship him, not by waving pennants or painting our faces, but by the way we live. He wants our behavior to show that we worship him.

That's why self-control is important to God. When we exercise self-control instead of getting angry, we admit that some things are more important than our petty resentments. When we exercise self-control instead of using profanity, we show that we submit to an authority that's higher than ourselves. When we exercise self-control instead of using drugs or drinking alcohol or pursuing sexual immorality, we show that we worship God, not our own desires.

That doesn't mean a Christian T-shirt isn't OK; it just means that the person *inside* the T-shirt is what really matters to God.

 REFLECT: How closely are you identified with God? How do people know you love and serve him? Do you show, by your self-control, that you're on his team?

 PRAY: "God, let me show I worship you by demonstrating self-control, especially in_____."

6 Fruitless Activities

Bible Reading: Ephesians 5:10-14

Steer clear of the fruitless activities of darkness; let your lives expose their futility. Ephesians 5:11, Phillips

CHOOSE HOW YOU would respond in each situation.

You're stranded on a desert island, and you're desperate to escape. Suddenly a small plane appears, far away on the horizon. You

(a) hide in the bushes;
(b) cross your fingers and wish the plane to land on your island;
(c) start tapping out SOS in Morse code on your teeth;
(d) do none of the above.

You want to become a famous singer, touring around the world and performing music for throngs of adoring fans. You

(a) quit taking voice lessons;
(b) take a vow of silence and live in isolation in Pago Pago;
(c) listen to nothing but Yoko Ono records;
(d) do none of the above.

You want to develop self-control, knowing that will please God and protect you. You

(a) experiment with drugs;
(b) get drunk every once in a while;
(c) take up cigarette smoking;
(d) do none of the above.

Wait a minute! What's the deal? Why *wouldn't* you hide in the bushes or tap out SOS on your teeth if you wanted to be rescued from a desert island? Why *wouldn't* you take a vow of silence if you wanted to become a singing sensation or mess around with drugs if you wanted to obey God and develop self-control?

Simple. All of the above would be fruitless. Doing any of those things would accomplish exactly the *opposite* of what you were shooting for.

That's right. One of the big problems with drugs, alcohol, or tobacco is that they accomplish the exact opposite of self-control. Those substances tend to take control *away* from you so that after you've begun using drugs, for example, you're no longer self-controlled, you're drug-controlled. If you drink too much alcohol, you're no longer self-controlled, you're alcohol-controlled. And once you make tobacco use a habit, you're no longer self-controlled, you're nicotine-controlled.

That's what makes those things so dangerous and so undesirable. They're fruitless activities; they accomplish the opposite of what God commands: self-control.

 REFLECT: Some things are wrong because they hinder self-control. What things besides drugs, alcohol, and tobacco hinder self-control? How can you resist or avoid surrendering control of yourself to anything or anyone other than God?

 PRAY: "God, show me those things that threaten to take control away from me, and help me, by your Spirit, to avoid them."

7 Mission: Control

Bible Reading: Ephesians 5:15-18
Let the Holy Spirit fill and control you. Ephesians 5:18

SOME THINGS COME naturally, things like breathing, blinking, sleeping, navel lint, and—if you're a teenager—zits.

Other things require a little effort—like learning to stand or walk. Like hitting a baseball. Or singing a solo in front of your entire school. Or growing potatoes in your sock drawer (actually, that probably comes naturally to most of us).

Still other things are completely beyond our abilities no matter who we are or how hard we try—like leaping tall buildings in a single bound (only Superman can do that). Like understanding the opposite sex. Like exhibiting self-control.

"Wait a minute," you say. "What was that? You mean I can't exhibit self-control no matter how hard I try?"

Yup.

"Well then," you say, "what's the point? Why am I reading all these Bible verses that say, 'Be self-controlled' and that talk about controlling my anger or my language or my this or my that? If being self-controlled is beyond my ability, I might as well give up, right?"

Right. Oh, you can control yourself from time to time. Every once in a while, you can wrestle your temper under control and bite your tongue and not give in to your passions by using a little willpower. But you can't be self-controlled all the time. Nobody can.

"Wha—?" you say. "Well then, I mean, what . . . how . . . uh . . . ?" Take it easy. Don't blow a brain cell. It's true, you'll never succeed in being self-controlled all the time. It's just not possible. Just like you can't succeed in being totally pure or loving or righteous all the time. So you might as well give up.

That's the bad news. But the good news is, you don't have to. It's not *your* job to obey God's commandments totally under your own power. It's your job to surrender to the power of the Holy Spirit and, day by day, let *him* fill you and control you. Then you *will* obey God's commands—including his command to be self-controlled. But it won't be you doing all the work—it'll be him.

"Oh," you say. "So I can only be *self*-controlled if I'm *Spirit*-controlled."

To which I would say, "Hey! You're pretty smart!"

REFLECT: When it comes to self-control, what's your job and what's the Holy Spirit's job? How can you submit—every day, every moment—to God's Spirit?

PRAY: Begin right now—this moment—to let the Holy Spirit control you by praying this simple prayer: "God, I know I cannot control myself or my passions. I need you to take control of my life through your Holy Spirit. I trust you for salvation and believe that your Spirit fills me. Please remind me to submit every day to his control and, moment by moment, to trust him to live a holy and self-controlled life in me. In Jesus' name, Amen."

8 Now and Later

Bible Reading: 1 Thessalonians 5:6-11
Let us be alert and self-controlled. 1 Thessalonians 5:6, NIV

SIX-YEAR-OLD Lauren helped her mom and dad with odd jobs around the house for months until she had saved enough money to buy a doll she'd admired.

Four-year-old Andrew saved money and cereal box tops for weeks to buy four tiny toy cars. He had to wait almost six *more* weeks for the cars to arrive in the mail.

Jenita's mom gave her a choice between a nice restaurant dinner with her family on her thirteenth birthday and waiting almost two weeks for a larger party that would include her friends from church and school. It wasn't easy, but Jenita chose to wait. She later said she had "the best birthday party ever!"

It may not seem like much, but Lauren, Andrew, and Jenita all did something that few kids (or adults) seem able to do anymore. They *delayed gratification.*

Huh? "Delayed gratification?" What's that mean?

Well, gratification means enjoyment. Pleasure. Satisfaction. Reward. Fun. Something that tastes good or feels good. Something desirable or pleasing.

One of the marks of maturity is the ability to delay gratification, the ability to postpone pleasure *until later.* Like Andrew did when he put that money and those box tops in the mail and had to wait *six weeks* to get his cars even though it would have been easier to buy something *right then!* Like Jenita did when she waited almost two weeks for her birthday party. Like Lauren did when she saved for months to buy a doll she wanted—a lot of us would have given up after three days (or hours!) and spent the money on some candy or gum.

There's another term for this ability to delay gratification—it's called *self-control.* It can be hard to control our wants and wishes and put off getting everything we want. That's why some kids get in trouble for stealing stuff. That's why some kids get into drugs. That's why some kids get pregnant or get a girlfriend pregnant. They have trouble delaying gratification because that takes self-control.

To tell the truth, it can be painful to wait for something you really want. (Ask any Chicago Cubs fan!) But if we don't learn to control ourselves, we can really get into big, big trouble—no matter how old we are. Not only that, but we'll end up missing out on a lot of important things. Like the respect of others. Like the trust of our parents. Like a good education. True love. And all kinds of really neat stuff.

 REFLECT: Think of a time when you couldn't wait for something good. Think of a time you delayed gratification. Did one have better results than the other? If so, which one and why?

 ACT: Be alert for chances to delay gratification today.

 PRAY: "Thank you, God, for all the good things you have planned for me—if I'm willing to wait."

9 Gladiators, Aliens, and You

Bible Reading: Proverbs 25:28

A person without self-control is as defenseless as a city with broken-down walls. Proverbs 25:28

YOU'RE ABOUT TO appear on an episode of *American Gladiators*. The show's producer explains that you're going to get into a ring with two iron-pumping, steroid-gulping athletes named "Slicer" and "Dicer." Your task is to carry a ball the size of your head, dash by Slicer and Dicer, and drop the ball into a barrel. Oh, yeah, Slicer and Dicer will be swinging twenty-pound mallets at you. And you have to do it six times. The producer asks, "Oh, by the way, do you want to wear any protective gear?"

Duh!

Or let's say you're the new captain of the starship *Enterprise*. You command your navigator, VoCal Solo, to steer toward the planet Blendor. Suddenly the ship starts to pitch violently back and forth, tossing crew members around like croutons in a salad. Suddenly your first mate, Vanna, shouts, "We're under attack, Cap'n!" You look at the giant screen before you, and a bazillion enemy ships and missiles are speeding toward your craft. Over the deafening screams and explosions occurring all around you, Vanna cries, "Should we turn on the defensive force field, Cap'n?"

Duh!

OK, then, say you're a Christian kid who wants to please God but who also wants to squeeze the greatest possible enjoyment and satisfaction out of life. You know God loves you, and you love him, too. But it's not always easy. Your parents expect so much. Your friends put pressure on you to do certain things. You even feel like giving up sometimes. In the midst of all that, the Bible says, "Be self-controlled."

Huh?

Actually, those three cases aren't so different from each other. If you're under attack from a couple of American Gladiators, you need some protective gear. If you're under attack from alien ships and missiles, you need a defensive force field. And if you're under attack from the temptations and traps of the world, you need self-control.

The Bible says, "A person without self-control is as defenseless as a city with broken-down walls" (Proverbs 25:28). In other words, self-control protects you, just like a tall stone wall encircling an ancient city or a safety belt that can hold you back at just the right time. It can protect you from saying the wrong thing. It can prevent you from doing something you'll regret later. Like all godly virtues, it can protect and provide for you. So don't leave home without it!

 REFLECT: How is self-control like each of the "defenses" in the above reading? Are there any areas of your life where you seem to have good self-control? Are there any areas in which you need to show more self-control?

 PRAY: "God, I need the defense of your armor, especially when_____."

10 The Road to Godliness

Bible Reading: 2 Peter 1:6-11

Knowing God leads to self-control. Self-control leads to patient endurance, and patient endurance leads to godliness. 2 Peter 1:6

"WANT TO GET to Jolly?" a Texan might say to you. "Simple. Just go to Wichita Falls and turn east, like you were going to Gainesville or Sherman." That's right, the road to Sherman, Texas, goes through Jolly.

The road to Elizabethtown, Kentucky, goes through Beaver Dam, Horse Branch, and Spring Lick. That's from the west. If you're coming from the east, you could go by way of Stamping Ground.

And if you're going to Saskatoon, you could get there through Prince Albert. (No jokes, please!) You could also go by way of Moose Jaw or Indian Head. You could even get there by going through Elbow and Eyebrow, but that would be out of your way.

But you may not be going to Jolly or Saskatoon (though Moose Jaw sounds like a fun place to visit). If you're a Christian, you should be heading toward godliness. And the road to godliness goes through self-control.

That's what the apostle Peter, one of Jesus' original twelve disciples, meant when he wrote, "Self-control leads to patient endurance, and patient endurance leads to godliness" (2 Peter 1:6). Self-control is the ability to say no to things that are harmful to you. It is the ability to put off things that you want to do but can't—or shouldn't—do right now. It's also the ability to discipline yourself to do the things God, in his Word, tells you to do. Paul, in his letter to Titus, said this: "We should live in this evil world with self-control, right conduct, and devotion to God" (Titus 2:12).

If you want to become more like God, then the way to get there is to develop self-control, because self-control helps you resist temptation and gives you the patience to develop some of the habits necessary for growth in godliness, like prayer and Bible reading. Self-control isn't the only stop on the road to godliness, but it's a main interchange.

 REFLECT: Self-control is the ability to (1) say no to things that are harmful to you; (2) put off things that you want to do but can't—or shouldn't—do right now; and (3) discipline yourself to do the things God tells you to do. Do you show self-control in any of these areas? Do you struggle with self-control in any of these areas?

 ACT: Cover one of your schoolbooks or your Bible with a road map. Using a magic marker, mark two dots on one of the major roads on the map. Mark one "Godliness" and the other "Self-control" as a reminder that the road to godliness leads through self-control.

 PRAY: "God, today's Bible reading says that knowing you leads to self-control. Help me to know you more. Help me to learn more self-control from you, especially in the area of_____, and lead me on the road to godliness."

Too Much of a Good Thing

Bible Reading: 1 Peter 5:8-9

Be self-controlled and alert. Your enemy the devil prowls around like a roaring lion looking for someone to devour. 1 Peter 5:8, NIV

CIRCLE T or F to indicate which statements you think are true or false:

1.	Drinking water can kill you.	T	F
2.	Taking a shower can be fatal.	T	F
3.	A bee sting isn't that dangerous.	T	F
4.	Flying in an airplane is the safest way to travel.	T	F
5.	Playing with guns is dangerous.	T	F
6.	Smoking causes lung cancer.	T	F
7.	Sunshine is dangerous.	T	F
8.	Sugar is bad for you.	T	F
9.	Spending too much time on the Internet or playing video games can hurt you.	T	F
10.	Dishrags have more germs than anything else in the house.	T	F

Compare your answers to the ones below:

1. True. Swallowing water down your windpipe can kill you if you are unable to clear the throat and breathe freely.
2. True. Many people slip and fall in the shower; some even die from their injuries.
3. False. People allergic to bee stings can die from a sting in seconds.
4. True. More people travel safely for more miles on a plane than any other way.
5. True (Duh!)
6. True (Ditto duh!)
7. True. Too much sun can cause skin cancer or sun poisoning.
8. True and False. In moderation, sugar is OK. But in great quantities, it can lead to cavities. If you're diabetic, sugar is a no-no.
9. True. Excessive use of a keyboard or joystick can cause carpal tunnel syndrome, which causes damage to the nerves in your wrist.
10. True (yuck!)

Some of the things in the list above are good things, but they can still be harmful to you if you're not careful and self-controlled. So self-control can protect you from excesses and extremes. This is starting to sound like your parents, isn't it? OK, OK. Just remember this: The devil wants to eat you up. And he'll use anything–even good things, if he can –to hurt you. So be alert. Be self-controlled. Don't be devoured.

 REFLECT: Have you allowed any "good things" or "harmless things" to enter your life that would be dangerous if you're not careful? Should you ask your parents, friends, or pastor to help you learn to control any of those areas?

 PRAY: "God, you know that I sometimes go to the extreme in the area of_____. Make me alert today so that I won't be devoured."

12 Tom and Becky's Excellent Adventure

Bible Reading: Psalm 119:97-101

I have more insight than all my teachers, for I meditate on your statutes.
Psalm 119:99, NIV

TOM SAWYER AND Becky Thatcher were trapped. They had wandered around in the cave for three days. They had eaten the last little bit of food Tom had saved from the picnic, and they had only a stub of wax left to use for a candle. They had nearly given up hope of ever being found or escaping from the dark, winding passages of the cave when Tom had an idea.

He pulled a wad of kite string out of his pocket and tied one end to a projection in the walls of the cave. Then, unwinding the kite string in his hand, he inched down one dark passageway, continuing only until the end of the string. He tried this again down another passage but reached the end of the string in darkness.

Tom tried a third time, following the string down a cave corridor until he reached the farthest he could go without letting go of the string. He was about to turn back when he glimpsed a far-off speck that looked like daylight. Dropping the line, he groped down the dark passage until he reached the hole, poked his head through it, and saw the familiar shores of the Mississippi River below.

Returning to Becky as fast as he could, he took her with him and retraced his way along the kite line until they both emerged from the cave into the warmth and freedom of daylight!

That story is from *The Adventures of Tom Sawyer*—a classic of American literature—by Mark Twain. It also illustrates what the Bible does for us.

You see, a lot of people get lost in life, just like Tom and Becky got lost in the cave. People lose the ability to know which way to go, which way is right. They spend their time wandering and guessing, hoping that they're right, but not really knowing.

But God's Word can act for us like the kite string did for Tom and Becky. The psalmist said in Psalm 119:105, "Your word is a lamp for my feet and a light for my path." The Bible shows the right direction because it points us to God. We may still feel lost sometimes and uncertain about what is right or wrong. But if we rely on the Bible, it will be much easier to find—and keep to—the right way.

 REFLECT: Would Tom and Becky have escaped the cave if Tom had left the kite string in his pocket? What if he had only used the kite string to find his way down one passage? How might those questions apply to your use of the Bible to find the right way?

 ACT: Carry a length of string in your pocket today to remind you how the Bible shows us the right direction.

 PRAY: "God, the area of my life that seems most uncertain right now is_____. Don't let me forget to keep talking to you about it and reading your Word to get the insight I need."

13 God Is 4 Us

Bible Reading: Jeremiah 32:38-41

I will make an everlasting covenant with them, promising not to stop doing good for them. Jeremiah 32:40

PETE HAS A pretty skewed picture of God. Why? Because Pete's dad is a top executive with a Fortune 500 company. He travels a lot and doesn't spend much time with his family. Pete thinks God is like his dad: distant and unreachable.

Melissa has a pretty skewed picture of God, too. Her dad is an alcoholic, whose violent rages make the family run for cover whenever he starts drinking. Melissa thinks God is like her dad: angry and unloving.

Lisha's picture of God is skewed for different reasons. Her dad buys her everything from the latest compact discs to the trendiest clothes. Lisha thinks God is like her dad: someone who'll give her whatever she asks for.

Erick's picture of God is also skewed. He never even knew his father. His parents weren't married when he was born. His father never wanted anything to do with his son. Erick thinks God also has abandoned him.

What Pete, Melissa, Lisha, and Erick are doing is pretty common. They're basing their ideas about God on what their earthly fathers are like. A lot of people do that. But such pictures of God are often pretty messed up.

No matter what Pete's dad does, God promises to be with us always (Hebrews 13:5). No matter how Melissa's dad acts, our heavenly Father loves us tenderly and unconditionally (Isaiah 54:10). No matter what Lisha's earthly dad may do, her heavenly Father may not always give her everything she wants, but he *will* give her what's good for her (Jeremiah 32:40). And even though Erick doesn't have a father in his life, God promises to be a "father to the fatherless" (Psalm 68:5).

Your relationship with your earthly father may be good, or it may be poor. Your relationship with your dad may be stable, or it may change from time to time. And it may be hard to separate your image of your heavenly Father from your experience with your earthly father. But no matter how good or bad your relationship with your parents may be, remember that your heavenly Father only wants to do good to you. And he will—if you let him.

REFLECT: Has God ever done something good for you through something that you *thought* was bad or negative? Does God always reveal how he plans to work things out? Do you trust him to do what's best for you? Do you trust him enough to obey him, no matter what the immediate results might be?

PRAY: "Lord, I know you don't give me everything I ask for, but help me to trust you to give me everything that's good for me."

14 The Tolerance Zone

Bible Reading: Isaiah 5:20-21

Woe to those who call evil good and good evil. Isaiah 5:20, NIV

"SUBMITTED FOR YOUR approval," says the black-and-white image of the man on the television, "is the story of a middle school student—we'll call him Brad. When his grandmother died, Brad wanted to make a small tribute to her in shop class. He carefully drew the dimensions of the pieces of wood that were to be assembled. The shop teacher allowed him to cut and sand the pieces in class but would not allow him to assemble them at school because it might be offensive, even illegal, to do so. Brad completed his project—a wooden cross—at home."

Does Brad's story seem odd to you? Maybe even a little spooky? Like something out of *The Twilight Zone?* Well, unfortunately, it's true. Brad was not allowed to craft a simple wooden cross as a tribute to his grandmother because someone—the teacher, the school, or the school district—thought it would be "intolerant" of other people's beliefs.

That sort of thing is happening more and more in our society, especially to Christians. Christian kids are often told that they should keep their beliefs to themselves, that to talk about Christ or to wear a Christian T-shirt or to take a biblical stand on certain issues is to be "intolerant," even bigoted or hateful.

A few years ago tolerance meant respecting everyone's right to his or her opinion. Today, however, tolerance means believing and teaching that everybody's ideas and opinions are right. There's a big difference between those two views. There's nothing wrong with the first, but there's everything wrong with the second.

God does command his people to respect others and to treat others with love and dignity. He calls us to be loving and to act justly (Micah 6:8). His Word says, "Try to live in peace with everyone" (Hebrews 12:14). But that doesn't mean that we should call evil "good," and good "evil." It doesn't mean that we should act as if there were no such things as right and wrong.

God's Word has not changed. It still gives this command: "Be ready to speak up and tell anyone who asks you why you're living the way you are, and always with the utmost courtesy" (1 Peter 3:15, *The Message*).

 REFLECT: What's the difference between respecting everyone's right to his or her opinion and believing that everybody's ideas and opinions are right? Can you do the first without doing the second?

What views do you tolerate? What are you intolerant of?

 PRAY: Turn to 1 Peter 3:15 and pray the words of verses 15-17 (for example, you might pray, "God, help me always to be ready to speak up . . . and remind me that _____."

15 Where's Waldo?

Bible Reading: Hebrews 12:1-2

Keep your eyes on Jesus, who both began and finished this race we're in.
Hebrews 12:2, The Message

DO YOU KNOW where Waldo is? How about Beverly, Martin, Murray, or Stanley? You can even find Elvas if you know where to look.

We're not talking about the Waldo you look for in picture books. This Waldo is a "where," not a "who." So are Beverly, Martin, Murray, and Stanley. Those aren't the names of people but of places. Waldo is located in the state of Kansas. Beverly is in Massachusetts, Martin is in Czechoslovakia, and Murray is in Utah. You'll find Stanley in the Falkland Islands and Elvas (not Elvis Presley but the town of Elvas) in Portugal.

If you tried to find those places by trial and error, by roaming around, or even by searching for them on a road map, you'd be looking a long time—and probably wouldn't ever find some of them! But with a little help from something called a GPS, it would be a snap.

A GPS (Global Positioning System) is an electronic device used by pilots, navigators, and others. A GPS sends a signal to a satellite, which stays in position in space above the earth. The satellite determines where the signal is coming from and reports that information back to the GPS. This whole process is called "getting a fix" on your position. It's a really handy tool if you're ever lost in the sky or on the ocean.

Of course, most of us don't have much need for a GPS. After all, we don't usually go wandering around in strange places in the Pacific Ocean. But we do need a kind of GPS for our soul. We get kind of lost in all the choices we face and all the decisions we have to make. Sometimes we may lose sight of what's right and what's wrong. We end up coming up with bad ideas and making bad decisions.

The answer is to keep our eyes on Jesus, our GPS. He's been through all this before, and he not only *knows* what's right and wrong, he *is* right because he's God! If we just keep our eyes on him—by spending time talking to him in prayer, worshiping him alone and with others, and reading his Word every day—a lot of those tough decisions and confusing choices tend to get straightened out. This is not because we're so smart but because he is.

 REFLECT: Spending time with Jesus can sort out a lot of the confusion kids and teens (and adults) go through. When is the best time for you to spend time alone in prayer and Bible reading? Morning? Evening? Some other time?

 PRAY: "Jesus, I need your direction every day. Remind me to keep my eyes fixed on you so that I will be less likely to get lost or confused."

16 Keep Yourself Pure

Bible Reading: 1 Timothy 5:21-22
Keep yourself pure. 1 Timothy 5:22

"PURE CHEWING SATISFACTION"
"99 and 44/100ths percent pure"
"100% pure mountain spring water"
"Pure cane sugar"
"100% pure Michigan honey"

Whether you're talking about chewing gum, soap, sugar, or honey, people value purity. They want pure air, pure water, pure enjoyment, pure excitement! They won't settle for anything less than pure spring water, pure Colombian coffee, pure cotton briefs, pure everything.

We're all that way. We love purity. We admire it. We desire it.

The word *pure* means "clean," "spotless," "free from contamination," "unmixed with any foreign substance." To say that water is pure means it has no dirt or chemicals in it. To say that cotton is pure means it has no wool or synthetic materials mixed in. To say that the air is pure means that it's free of pollution.

As you can see, purity's a good thing. But purity isn't just good for water or food or fabric. It's good for people, too. You see, it's like this: When God made water, he didn't put detergents and dyes and chemicals and crud in it—he put water in it! That's why 100 percent pure mountain spring water is so good; it's the way God wanted water to look, feel, and taste. Similarly, when he created humans and planted them on this planet, he made it clear to us what our life should contain—not only to please him but to make our life better, too.

Living a pure life means keeping out of your life all the things God didn't intend to go in there, like foul language, filthy thoughts, and sinful acts. A pure life is pleasing to God. And, like pure sugar or pure water, it's a lot healthier for you and more impressive to others as well.

 REFLECT: Nearly everyone agrees that purity in water or air is a good thing; many of us have trouble admitting that purity in life is even more valuable. What do you find valuable in life? Have you allowed any impurity to enter your life? If not, how have you kept yourself pure?

 ACT: See how many products (sugar, bottled water, soap, and so on) you can find in your house that claim to be "pure." You might even want to have a competitive scavenger hunt with a brother, sister, or friend to see who can assemble the most "pure" items.

 PRAY: Thank God for being there to help you keep yourself pure. If you've allowed any impurity to enter your life, take a few moments to ask God's forgiveness and seek his cleansing. Reading Psalm 51 might help you put your feelings into words.

17 Mountain Do's and Don'ts

Bible Reading: Exodus 34:27-34

The Lord said to Moses, "Write down all these instructions."
Exodus 34:27

MOSES SET HIS chisel down on the table and wiped the sweat from his forehead. A large slab of stone sat on the wobbly wooden table, and another stone, already chiseled in great detail, sat beside it.

"Is there a problem, Moses?" The voice of God could be heard in the thin mountain air inside the tent, though Moses sat alone.

"Well, it's . . . just . . . it's all these instructions for building the tabernacle."

"Yes," God answered, his tone urging Moses to go on.

"Well," Moses ventured, "you say the ark of the covenant has to be overlaid with pure gold, and the utensils on the table have to be pure gold, and the lampstand has to be pure gold. The bells on the priests' robes have to be pure gold, and the incense has to be pure . . ."

"Go on," God said.

"And the olive oil has to be pure, and the gemstones for the high priest's breastplate have to be flawless . . ."

"Yes," God said. "You've listened very well, Moses."

"But—," Moses began.

"You think I'm being too picky," God said.

"No!" Moses blurted out. "I would never say that!" Then he remembered that God knew everything. "Well," he said slowly, holding up his thumb and forefinger just a hair's width apart, "maybe just a little."

"Moses," God said, "I am glad you noticed. I am not being picky, but I do want to communicate something to my people through all these rules and requirements. One of the things I want them to understand is that I require purity. I want my tabernacle to show that I require purity. I want my priests to show that I require purity. In fact, much of the law I am giving through you is intended to make it clear that I require purity, from the robes of the priests to the lives of my people." The voice fell silent, but only for a moment. "Do you understand now, Moses?"

Moses answered quickly. "Oh, yes, Holy One. I understand, really I do."

"You wish to ask something else?" God asked.

"Yes, Holy One," Moses answered. He raised his hand timidly in the air, like a schoolboy. "I feel like I should wash my hands before I continue," he said.

 REFLECT: While the conversation above is fictional, it's a fact that God commands purity. What do God's commands reveal to you about what matters to God? Are the same things important to you? Why or why not?

 PRAY: "Lord, keep me pure as you are pure."

18 Big Shoes to Fill

Bible Reading: Habakkuk 1:12-13

O Lord . . . your eyes are too pure to look on evil; you cannot tolerate wrong. Habakkuk 1:12-13, NIV

BASEBALL'S KEN GRIFFEY JR.
Actress Tori Spelling
Singer Natalie Cole
Actor George Clooney
Congressman Joe Kennedy
Race car driver Michael Andretti
Singer Whitney Houston

What do all those people have in common? OK, OK, they're all famous. Yeah, yeah, their names all begin with capital letters. Anything else?

Here are a few hints: Ken Griffey Jr.'s father played baseball for the Reds, Mariners, and other teams. Tori Spelling's father is a television producer. Natalie Cole's dad was a famous singer. Joe Kennedy is the son of the late Senator Robert F. Kennedy. Whitney Houston's mother is Cissy Houston, a gospel singer. George Clooney comes from a show business family—his dad, Nick Clooney, and his aunt Rosemary Clooney.

All the people listed above are the sons or daughters of someone who achieved success and fame in sports, politics, or entertainment. If you talked to them, some would probably say their parents pressured them to "follow in their footsteps." Others probably pursued their careers in spite of Mom's and Dad's objections. Still others might have learned so much from Dad that it was only natural for them to excel in the same field. Probably most—if not all—of their parents were pleased when their sons and daughters chose to follow in their footsteps.

Which kind of brings us to God. God, as our heavenly Father, is different in a lot of ways from most earthly fathers. But in one way he's quite similar: He's pleased when we follow in his footsteps. That's why he commands us to be pure, because he himself is pure. He's so pure, in fact, that he can't even *look* at evil. Because he's pure, he values purity. And because he values purity, he wants us to be pure.

Whether we become famous athletes, singers, actors, or something else entirely, God wants us to be just like him in the purity of our life. He's even willing to help us, through the work of his Holy Spirit, who lives inside us.

 REFLECT: Has anyone in your family followed in his or her parents' footsteps? Are you following in God's footsteps? If so, in what ways? If not, how can you do so?

 ACT: Place a pair of your mom's or dad's shoes somewhere in your room as a reminder to follow in your heavenly Father's footsteps today.

 PRAY: "God, I'm really glad to have you, the Creator of the whole universe, as my heavenly Father. Teach me how to follow in your footsteps."

19 Pureblood

Bible Reading: 1 Thessalonians 4:3-8

It is God's will . . . that each of you should learn to control his own body in a way that is holy and honorable. 1 Thessalonians 4:3-4, NIV

BAILEY IS A thirteen-year-old girl who has had diabetes for two years. Diabetes occurs when something called an endocrine gland quits making insulin, which the body uses to break down food. While in most ways you would never know she has diabetes, Bailey has to watch closely what she eats (and how much). Like most kids, she loves sweets, but she can't eat as much sugar as her friends.

But sometimes she forgets. Other times she just can't resist, and she eats a few more cookies than she should (like half a bag!), followed by milk and maybe a bowl of ice cream. That doesn't hurt too much—she just gets "high blood sugar" and sometimes begins to act a little strange. (Her friends might say it's not always easy to tell when she's acting strange because she acts strange normally.)

Unfortunately, if Bailey has blood sugars that are too high for too many days, her body can't clean the blood of all the sugar she's dumped into her system. As a result, it gets kind of like the stuff that clogs up sinks—real gucky (that's not the medical term). Eventually, she will develop a condition called *ketoacidosis,* when there are so many ketones in her blood that she wants to throw up but can't. It zaps her energy and makes her stomach hurt. All she's allowed to have is water and lots of it. Once the water "flushes" out the ketones, she begins to feel better. It's possible, though, that after ten or twenty years of having *ketoacidosis,* Bailey will start to suffer real drastic problems, like losing toes or not being able to feel anything in her fingers.

Come to think of it, all of us are a little like Bailey. We don't all have diabetes, of course, but we all struggle with impurities that enter our life. And if we don't keep the impurities out of our life (like "dirty" thoughts and bad language, for example), we'll suffer both short-term and long-term consequences.

That's one reason why God commands us to be pure. He doesn't want us to suffer the consequences of impurity in our spirits, just as he doesn't want Bailey to lose her toes because of her physical condition.

 REFLECT: The consequences of impurity are sometimes immediate, sometimes long-term, but both kinds of consequences are worth avoiding. When any kind of impurity enters our spiritual lives, what short- and long-term consequences can it have? Have any of these happened to you? What steps can you take to make sure they don't happen again?

 PRAY: "God, search me and see if there is anything in me that is impure. Remove it, and guide me so that it will not get back into my life."

"Insulinating" Yourself

Bible Reading: Psalm 119:9-11

I have hidden your word in my heart that I might not sin against you.
Psalm 119:11, NIV

IF YOU READ yesterday's devotional reading, you learned about a thirteen-year-old diabetic named Bailey. When Bailey first discovered that she had diabetes, she learned that because her body was no longer producing insulin, she would have to give herself shots of insulin. Without the insulin, her body could not convert her food into the energy she needs to do the things thirteen-year-olds like to do.

Every morning before she eats breakfast, she gets a needle and puts first one kind of insulin into the needle (the kind of insulin that acts quickly) and then another kind (which acts slowly). Then she pokes the needle into either her arm or leg. Then, in the evening, before supper, she has to do the same thing again.

If she forgets or injects too little insulin into her system, it will not be long before she will begin to feel the effects. She will begin to lose energy, and eventually her health will be affected. If she gives herself too much insulin, she'll become weak and shaky, and eventually dizzy and confused. If something isn't done, she could go into a coma and even die.

Every day for the rest of her life (unless a cure is discovered), she will have to spend some time in the morning and evening to make sure she has in her system the insulin necessary to be healthy and active. It's not fun, but as long as she watches her diet and gives herself shots every morning and evening, she'll live a pretty normal life.

Once more Bailey's routine isn't much different from what it means to live the Christian life. There are certain things we must do if we want to obey God's commands and live a pure life. Just as Bailey must give herself a shot of insulin every morning and evening, we'll be better able to live a pure life if we give ourself daily shots of God's Word, reading it every day, studying it, and hiding it in our heart as a sort of "spiritual insulin" to keep us from sinning against God.

"How can a young person stay pure? By obeying your word and following its rules" (Psalm 119:9). Obeying God's Word is the only way a young person—any person, for that matter—can stay pure.

 REFLECT: God has a prescription for living a healthy Christian life. Read the first sixteen verses of Psalm 119, and underline the prescriptions (directions) God gives for being a healthy Christian. Then begin today to read God's Word every day. (Reading a psalm a day might be a good way to start.) Remember that a daily dose of God's Word is a good way to vaccinate yourself against impurities.

 PRAY: "Thank you, God, for providing the 'spiritual insulin' I need to keep from sinning against you. Help me to develop the habit of reading your Word each day."

21 Off the Path

Bible Reading: 1 Samuel 12:20-24

Serve the Lord with all your heart. And you must not turn aside, for then you would go after futile things which can not profit or deliver, because they are futile. 1 Samuel 12:20-21, NASB

YOU REMEMBER THE story. You heard it first when you were just a little kid—the story of Little Red Riding Hood.

Remember, she's the girl who disobeyed her mom (bad choice!), listened to the wolf (even worse choice!), and left the path to pick some flowers to take to her sick Grandma (dum da dum dum!). While Red Riding Hood was off picking posies, the wolf ran ahead, ate Grandma, and slipped into Grandma's bed. When Red came along, the wolf fooled her into thinking *he* was her loving Grandma. (Little Red Riding Hood obviously needed contact lenses.) After a few moments of dialogue, the wolf pounced on Red and ate her, too. Happily, however, a woodsman happened along, found the wolf sleeping, killed him, and cut him open, saving Grandma and Little Red Riding Hood. (OK, so it's not *The Lion King,* but you can't have everything!)

That classic (and somewhat gruesome) fairy tale is a great illustration of what happens when you make the wrong choice by turning aside from the right path (the one to Grandma's) to pursue useless things (picking a bouquet of flowers—although this is not always a bad choice).

For us as Christians, the evil that lurks off the godly path is just as dangerous as the fate that awaited Red Riding Hood. Every wrong choice we make—every bad decision, every moral slip—leads us off the path of righteousness and toward a lifestyle of sin and death. Yet, for all our confidence that by following the crowd we're going in the right direction, things never seem to work out that way.

Using bad language to feel grown up, taking drugs to feel cool, telling off-color jokes to feel popular—all of these things are sin, and they will all lead you on a dangerous and destructive path.

Believe this: Sin never delivers what it promises. Never. Never ever. It won't make you grow up, it won't make you cool, it won't make you popular. Sin just gets you into trouble.

Believe this, too: God will never disappoint you; he wants to do good things for you.

Just keep your feet on the right path.

 REFLECT: What steps do you take when you find yourself following the crowd and turning away from God? Remember that a "wolf" can disguise itself in many ways— like in the proverbial "sheep's clothing"—in an attempt to make the evil it does seem harmless. Keep your eyes open for sin's many disguises.

 PRAY: "Lord, day by day help me choose the path you chose for me. I want to turn from sin and look toward you. Guide my feet on your path."

22 Rock Candy

Bible Reading: Galatians 5:22-23

May you always be filled with the fruit of your salvation—those good things that are produced in your life by Jesus Christ. Philippians 1:11

HERE'S SOMETHING YOU can try at home, with sweet results! Fill a glass halfway with water and stir as much sugar into it as you can get, or about four tablespoons. Stir it until the sugar dissolves in the water. (This may take awhile.) Once you've dissolved as much of the sugar into the water as you can, get a piece of string and tie it to a spoon. Lay the spoon across the top of the glass with the string hanging down almost to the bottom of the glass (but not touching the bottom) in the middle of the sugar water. Cover the spoon and glass with a napkin or paper towel and set it out of the way, where it won't accidentally get knocked over and cause your parents to ground you from ever reading this book again!

Leave the string in the water for nine days. You'll see the sugar crystals that were dissolved in the water begin to attach themselves to the string, gradually forming what appear to be rocks of sugar. You will then be able to remove the rock candy from the glass and eat it. (Be prepared for your parents to claim that when they were kids, rock candy was the only candy they could afford.)

Now, what's the point? Just this: The glass involved in that little experiment doesn't produce the rock candy, does it? The ingredients *inside* the glass actually create those beautiful, tasty crystals. The glass was filled with sugar water; *that's* what produced the rock candy on the string.

You and I are kind of like that glass. We can't produce beautiful things out of our life. We can't be consistently pure and loving and patient and kind. We may *try;* most Christians do. But no matter how hard we try, the best we can produce is pretty bad.

But as Christians, we're *filled* with the Holy Spirit. As we learn to spend time with him and trust him every moment of our life, some of the qualities of the Holy Spirit will be produced in our life. Without him, we can only produce things like impurity, hatred, and jealousy (Galatians 5:19-21); but when we are filled with the Spirit, we will—like the string of rock candy in the glass of sugar water—take on the characteristics of the Holy Spirit. Sweet, eh?

REFLECT: If you never put the string in the sugar water, but only placed it near the glass, do you think rock candy would ever form on the string? Why or why not? How is that similar to you and your relationship with the Holy Spirit?

PRAY: For the next nine days, watch your rock candy forming in the glass of water. Pray briefly each time you check it (and especially as you eat it) that the Holy Spirit will produce his sweet fruit in your life.

23 Go Figure!

Bible Reading: Romans 13:8-10

When you love others, you complete what the law has been after all along. Romans 13:8, The Message

IN THE MOOD to amaze your friends and astound your family? Well, then, try this simple (but cool) trick:

1. Choose a number—any number.
2. Double it.
3. Add twelve to that number.
4. Divide your new number by two, then subtract your original number.
5. Now add one.

What answer did you come up with? Seven, right? If you followed the instructions at every step, your answer will be seven. It will always be seven. Whether you start with 1 or 500 million, you'll always come out with the number seven. Always. Every time. That's how the problem is designed. You can't miss as long as you do the math right. Go ahead, try it with another number!

Other than being a fun way to dazzle your friends with your intellect, what's the point? Well, it's this: You can do almost the same thing with God's commands. But you don't have to remember five steps, just one. Here it is. Ready?

1. Love others.

There. That's it! If you always do the loving thing, you will automatically do the right thing. The Bible says, "If you love your neighbor, you will fulfill all the requirements of God's law" (Romans 13:8). That's because you can't love someone else and steal from him at the same time. You can't lovingly murder someone (no matter what you may see on daytime talk shows!). You can't love someone and cheat him.

The right choice can become a lot clearer if you always remember to love others. If you do that, you will "fulfill all the requirements of God's law." And you don't even have to worry about getting the math right!

REFLECT: Name all the steps it takes to obey every commandment. (Sorry. That was a trick question. There's only one step—remember it?)
How does love fulfill God's law? Whom do you love? Whom do you not love? Can you obey God without acting in love toward someone? Why or why not?

ACT: Try the math puzzle with your friends, and use it to remind yourself that loving others fulfills all of God's other commandments.

PRAY: "God, thanks for making it simple, so I only have to remember one thing if I want to obey your commands. Please show me how to do the loving thing today when I'm with_____."

24 The Cosmic Killjoy?

Bible Reading: Nehemiah 8:1-10
The joy of the Lord is your strength. Nehemiah 8:10

MANY PEOPLE IMAGINE God as a cosmic cop standing in the center of the galaxies like a police officer directing traffic.

"Hey, you! Yeah, you. You look like you're having fun over there. Well, cut it out!"

"And you, with the videotape. What's it rated? R? PG-13? Hand it over, slow and easy like!"

"And who's that couple lip-locked in the corner? That you, Cindy? And Robert—I shoulda known! We'll have no more of that! Not while I'm patrolling this beat!"

God. The Cosmic Killjoy. All we want to do is have a little fun. God just wants to spoil it for us.

But that's not true at all. God is not out to spoil your fun. In fact, he wants you to enjoy life. He wants you to have a blast! He wants you to experience a full and *joy*ful life. He thinks it's cool when you laugh. He enjoys it when you're having fun. He wants your life to be full of joy—complete, full, incredible.

That kind of joy is what the Bible calls "the joy of the Lord," because true joy—like all good things—comes from God. The way puppies bounce around comically, tongues lolling out of their mouths—that was his idea. The way someone laughing really hard makes you want to laugh also, even if you don't know why he or she is laughing—that was his idea, too. The way you feel when you first experience the forgiveness of sin and the gift of salvation in Christ, as if you could jump high enough to slam dunk the moon through the rings of Saturn—his idea again!

Only a God who is joyful himself could come up with such terrific ideas. That's the kind of God our God is! And he wants you to experience that kind of joy, too. That's why he gave his commandments. That's why he sent his Son. That's why he spoke his Word—so that you could get downright giddy with joy as a result of knowing him, following him, and having his Spirit living inside you. Joy from God's Spirit dwells so deep within you that it doesn't depend on circumstances. Loving and serving God doesn't spoil your fun; it opens the door to "an inexpressible and glorious joy" (1 Peter 1:8, NIV).

Oh, and one more thing—the face babies make when they taste something sour or bitter? That was God's idea, too.

 REFLECT: Are you more joyful when you've done something wrong or when you've done something really good? How can you experience more of "the joy of the Lord"?

 ACT: Sing the chorus "The Joy of the Lord Is My Strength" as loudly as you can. Try singing it while jumping up and down or while patting your head and rubbing your belly. Or sing it while tickling a friend (or being tickled).

 PRAY: "God, you're not a killjoy. You're the one who brings joy to my life!"

25 Peace Out

Bible Reading: Colossians 3:13-15
I am leaving you with a gift—peace. John 14:27

YOU'RE ABOUT TO travel back in time to visit some war protesters of the ancient past. Fasten your seatbelts!

DATELINE: 1970 (A group of teenagers is milling around a Volkswagen van. One of them is talking.)

"It was far out, man! Me and my old lady hitched a ride down to Berkeley for this really happenin' sit-in to protest the war, you know?

"When we got there, the place was jumpin', man. Everybody was groovin' to the music and just peacin' out! We were, like, all together as one, you know what I mean? We were there to protest the war against our brothers and sisters in 'Nam, you know? We sang 'Give Peace a Chance.' We were just trying to say the world needs to make love, not war, man. Peace is where it's at, man.

"Of course, then I saw a cop watching us, and I said, 'Hey, Pig, what are you lookin' at?' I picked up a brick off the sidewalk and threw it at him, and he went *down!* It was far out! Some brothers around me started clappin', and I stood up and said, 'Down with the Establishment! Peace out, man!' Groovy, huh?"

BACK TO THE PRESENT: Everybody—past or present—agrees that peace is worthwhile, but most of us have trouble truly living in peace with others—little brothers, big sisters, parents, neighbors, classmates, not to mention the annoying little kid who lives down the block.

That's because true peace—like all good things—comes only from God, through his Holy Spirit. No matter how much you *want* to live in peace, no matter how sincerely you *believe* in "world peace," no matter how hard you try, you can't achieve true and lasting peace without God.

But if Jesus Christ, through the Holy Spirit, lives in you, then *his* peace can rule in your heart. As you surrender to him and trust him day by day, he will overcome the part of you that always insists on having your own way, the part that has trouble getting along with others or that wants to fight with others instead of trying to understand them. It doesn't happen all at once, but as the Holy Spirit controls more and more of you, you'll know more and more of his peace.

The civil rights anthem "Let there be peace on earth, and let it begin with me" had it right. Peace begins with you—your heart surrendered to God and filled with the Holy Spirit.

Otherwise, peace doesn't have a chance.

 REFLECT: Are you struggling to live in peace with anyone right now? How can you try to promote peace in your family this week? among your friends? at church?

 PRAY: "God, I really want to know you so I can know peace."

26 Playing the Waiting Game

Bible Reading: Ephesians 4:1-2

Accept life with humility and patience, generously making allowances for each other because you love each other. Ephesians 4:2, Phillips

THE LITTLE TYKE shuffled to his bed, his pajama-clad feet making only the slightest noise on the hardwood floor. He knelt beside the bed and closed his eyes tight, his fingers squeezed together in a tight clasp.

"Dear God," the youngster said, "I'm sorry. I didn't mean to get in trouble." He paused. "Mommy says I need patience. She says I need to ask you to help me. So God, please give me patience so I won't pester Mommy so much."

The boy paused again. Then he opened his eyes and looked upward, as if he were looking at the ceiling. "Well, God," he said, "I'm *waiting!*"

It can be hard to be patient. It doesn't come naturally, does it? After all, that's why we have fast food; instant coffee; express lanes; rapid tax returns; quick-drying paint, nail polish, and correction fluid; "speedy" printing; overnight delivery services; "Zip" Drives; and Jiffy Lubes. We hate to wait. And sometimes our impatience annoys other people and gets us in trouble. Like when you try to move a big school project before the glue dries. Or when you cut in front of someone in line. Or when you yell at your best friend and hurt his or her feelings because you wanted to be first in line when tickets to the Counting Cannibals concert went on sale, and because your friend just *had* to have an emergency appendectomy, you ended up fourth in line!

But no matter how hard it is, no matter how few people seem to have it, patience is a virtue. It's a good thing to have. In fact, it's necessary if you want to do right and please God, because a person who is patient reflects the image of God, who is "slow to anger" (Exodus 34:6; Numbers 14:18; Psalm 86:15) and "patient with you" (2 Peter 3:9, NIV).

God also tells us to "Be patient with everyone" (1 Thessalonians 5:14). So what are you waiting for? Start being patient. And do it *right now!*

 REFLECT: When are you most patient? When are you most impatient? Do you need more patience? How can you develop more patience? Remember that patience is a virtue and a fruit of the Holy Spirit. If you have experienced salvation through Jesus Christ, the Holy Spirit lives in you, and patience will show in your life as you let the Spirit control you day by day.

 PRAY: "God, help me to accept life with humility and patience. Help me to patiently make allowances for others because of your love for them and my love for them, especially for_____."

27 Washing Feet

Bible Reading: John 13:1-5

[Jesus] poured water into a basin. Then he began to wash the disciples' feet and to wipe them with the towel he had around him. John 13:5

YOU'VE HEARD THE story before. They arrived in groups of two or three, talking loudly, laughing uproariously. They were Jesus' disciples: men of the sea, men of the soil, and a couple of men of the sword. They entered the second-floor room with the low ceiling, where they had occasionally met before.

By the time Jesus entered the room, they were already uncomfortable. Though no one spoke of it, everyone in the room faced the same problem: Who would wash their feet?

You see, the roads and alleys these men traveled on their way to this "upper room" were not paved. Their feet were caked with the mud, dirt, and sweat of their travels. Usually the host of a banquet would provide a slave—equipped with a pitcher of water, a pan, and a towel—at the door of his home to wash the feet of the guests as they arrived. Though no one said anything, all had noticed that there was no servant to wash their feet.

The table in the center of the room was surrounded by cushioned couches, and the head of each couch was pushed against the table, like spokes in a wheel. The table was spread with plates and cups, and the fragrance of roasted lamb and herbs and fresh bread mingled with the odor of their unwashed feet.

So Jesus started to wash the feet of his disciples. Tenderly, he washed the feet of James and John and the others. He even washed the feet of Judas.

Jesus knew that Judas had made arrangements to betray him. But he washed Judas's feet anyway. He treated Judas kindly and lovingly, even though he knew the terrible thing Judas planned to do to him.

It's easy to be kind to those who are kind to us. Everybody agrees that treating nice people kindly is a good thing. But kindness is right even when it isn't easy.

"If you are kind only to your friends," Jesus said, "how are you different from anyone else? Even the pagans do that" (Matthew 5:47). But Jesus said we are to be kind even when it's hard because kindness is right—whether it's easy or not.

 REFLECT: Have you missed any opportunities to be kind to someone recently? If so, is it too late to be kind to that person? Can you think of five different ways to show kindness to someone today? Remember that kindness has very little to do with the person you're being kind to and everything to do with what you are like.

 ACT: Keep a towel (like the towel Jesus used to wash the disciples' feet) in your backpack or school locker this week to remind you to be kind to everyone. Or go out of your way to be "a servant" to your family this week.

 PRAY: "God, thank you that you'll help me follow through on being kind to _____ today."

28 Goody Two-Shoes!

Bible Reading: Romans 15:13-14

I am fully convinced, dear friends, that you are full of goodness. You know these things so well that you are able to teach others all about them. Romans 15:14

EVERY SCHOOL HAS ONE.

You know, the teacher's pet, the guy or the girl who never gets into trouble. The kid who *likes* cleaning chalkboards and erasers. The kid who *volunteers* for stuff. The one who walks the first grader who fell on the playground to the nurse's office. The one who actually defends Old Man McCracken when the other kids start calling him names and talking about how mean he is. The one who shares his lunch with the hamster in the science room.

When this kid gets to high school, he or she might be on the yearbook staff or student council or the prom committee. This kid actually seems to *like* school! Does extra-credit work. Visits his or her grade-school teachers. Seems willing to do anything for anybody. Seems to be happy—*all* the time. The kind of kid who makes you want to throw up!

These kids usually get branded with names like "goody-goody," "goody two-shoes" (where'd *that* come from?), "teacher's pet," or "brownnoser." And although it's true that some kids do all that stuff just to try to earn points with teachers or other people, goodness is a *good* thing, not a bad thing. Goodness—whether it's sharing your lunch with a hamster or being nice to teachers—is a godly virtue, one of the fruits of the Spirit.

That's what the apostle Paul said of the Christians who lived in Rome. He praised them for being full of goodness. If they saw a chariot on the side of the road with a flat tire, they stopped to help. If they heard that a neighbor lost her job at the toga factory, they dropped by with a bag of groceries. They even had a cheerful word for those annoying camera-toting tourists from Crete! They had a positive attitude and took every opportunity to help others.

Of course, that kind of attitude doesn't come naturally for most people. It's easier for some people to act that way than it is for others. But it should be true of you, if you're a Christian, because goodness is a fruit of the Holy Spirit, who lives in every Christian's heart.

 REFLECT: Do you know anyone who is "full of goodness," as Paul said the Roman Christians were? What can you learn about goodness from them? Like any fruit, goodness needs certain things (like water, soil, and sun) to grow. What can you do to cultivate the growth of goodness in your heart and life?

 PRAY: If you're honest, you may want to tell God what Paul said in Romans 7:19. "When I want to do good, I don't." But you can also be glad with Paul, who knew the answer to the dilemma: "Thank God! The answer is in Jesus Christ our Lord" (verse 25).

29 Full-Moon Faithfulness

Bible Reading: Psalm 57:1-11

[God's] faithfulness reaches to the skies. Psalm 57:10, NIV

Great is his faithfulness; his mercies begin afresh each day.
Lamentations 3:23

DID THE SUN come up this morning?

"Don't be ridiculous," you answer. "Of course it did!"

Well, are the rivers still running to the sea today?

"What kind of question is that?" you might say.

Have you floated off into the atmosphere yet?

"Of course not!" is your likely response. "What is your problem?"

Those are pretty silly questions, aren't they? Crazy, right? Absurd! The sun rises every morning. The rivers run constantly to the sea. Gravity holds you firmly on the ground all the time. Nobody even has to think about such things.

Right. You can count on Halley's comet to streak across the heavens every seventy-seven years. You can count on the seasons coming and going every year. You can count on a full moon appearing in the sky every 27 days, 7 hours, and 43 minutes. Because faithfulness is built into God's creation. And faithfulness is built into God's creation because God is faithful. His creation reflects his nature.

We should reflect God's nature, too. God wants us to be faithful. He wants friends to be faithful to each other. He wants husbands and wives to be faithful to each other. He wants his children to be faithful to him because he knows that faithfulness is an important part of any good relationship.

Being faithful means keeping one's promises, being someone others can count on. That description fits God. Does it fit you, too?

REFLECT: Faithfulness is built into God's creation because God is faithful. Where can you see God's faithfulness reflected in his creation?

Who are your most faithful friends? Are you faithful in your relationship with God? with friends? with others? In what ways can you be more faithful?

ACT: After dark tonight go outside and notice what phase the moon is in. Is it full? half? just a sliver? Take a few minutes under the night sky (unless it's raining) to talk to God and thank him for his faithfulness to you. (You may even want to pray the words of Psalm 57.)

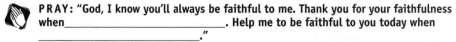

PRAY: "God, I know you'll always be faithful to me. Thank you for your faithfulness when_____. Help me to be faithful to you today when

_____."

30 Binti Saves the Day

Bible Reading: Philippians 4:4-5

Let your gentleness be evident to all. Philippians 4:5, NIV

When the Holy Spirit controls our lives, he will produce this kind of fruit in us: love, joy, peace, patience, kindness, goodness, faithfulness, gentleness, and self-control. Galatians 5:22-23, emphasis added

WHILE VISITING BROOKFIELD Zoo, in Brookfield, Illinois, with his family, a three-year-old boy climbed a railing and lost his balance. He fell eighteen feet into a rocky pit containing several gorillas. The impact of his fall knocked the boy unconscious, and he lay there, at the mercy of the apes.

Now, gorillas can be pretty rough customers—they don't exactly have a reputation for being particularly gentle. So everyone in the place screamed and ran around, trying to figure out how to prevent the boy from being attacked and mangled, perhaps killed, by the great apes.

Then an amazing thing happened. An eight-year-old female gorilla named Binti Jua, apparently sensing the boy was hurt, went over to the child and gently picked him up. Waving off the other animals, she toted him to the door of the enclosure, where eventually a zookeeper came and retrieved the boy, unharmed.

Binti's gentle heroism made newspaper and television news headlines for several days. People expressed astonishment. Crowds flocked to the zoo. Television crews from all over the world came to film the gentle gorilla. For a few days she became the most famous gorilla since King Kong.

Later news accounts revealed that the heroic gorilla had been nursed and raised by human caretakers in the zoo's infirmary. It was believed that she learned gentleness from those caregivers.

When a wild animal displays gentleness, that is considered "news," because everyone recognizes that gentleness is a moral behavior, something that's rare enough in humans! But it shouldn't be rare among God's people because it's a fruit of his Spirit. If God's Spirit lives inside you and controls you, he will show you that gentleness is right and cruelty and rudeness are wrong. He will give you a heart of gentleness and help you treat others with the gentleness that is part of his nature.

 REFLECT: Do your attitudes and actions show that you have learned gentleness? From whom? Have you thanked the person for teaching you gentleness?
Have you treated anyone cruelly or rudely in recent days or weeks? If so, have you sought forgiveness for your behavior? How can you allow God to produce gentleness in your heart and life today?

 PRAY: "God, thank you for being gentle with me. Help me to submit to your control every day and show your gentleness to others."

31 Your Invisible Fence

Bible Reading: Galatians 5:24-25

Since we live by the Spirit, let us keep in step with the Spirit.
Galatians 5:25, NIV

LET'S SAY THAT one day you noticed that your friend's gigantic dog is not kept on a chain or inside a fenced area.

"You let your dog run around loose?" you ask your friend.

"Naw," your friend answers. "We've got an invisible fence."

You roll your eyes. "Yeah, right. "Your imaginary friend installed it, right?"

"No, I'm serious," your friend says. "There's an electric wire buried under the ground. Brutus wears a collar that gives him a little shock if he gets too close to the wire."

"Really?" you say.

Your friend nods. "He hasn't gone anywhere near the wire since the first time he got shocked."

"Wow," you say. "That's a pretty smart dog."

"He just stays away from stuff he knows is going to hurt him, that's all."

Actually, you've probably heard of invisible fences. You may even use one to keep your pets in your yard. As a matter of fact, you have something like an invisible fence that's designed to keep you away from stuff that's going to hurt you, too. It's called self-control, which we learned a lot about earlier this month. But did you know that self-control is one of the fruits of the Spirit, too?

Suppose you're tempted to lose your temper because your little brother used your favorite baseball cap to protect his head from the orange and purple paint he used to paint his clubhouse. If the Holy Spirit controls your life, you'll probably feel a surge of strength in your spirit, helping you not to do it.

Or say you find yourself alone with your boyfriend or girlfriend, and your heart starts racing and you feel more in love than ever before and you want to do some things you know your parents would freak over. If you're controlled by God's Spirit, you'll have a fighting chance to say no to temptation and find somewhere else to be and something else to do.

The Holy Spirit already lives in you if you're a Christian. But you still need to submit to his control every day. One way to do that is by beginning each day with prayer and worship and Bible reading. Then, as the Holy Spirit controls your life, he will reproduce his own nature in you, and you'll begin to see his fruit or characteristics in your life: *love, joy, peace, patience, kindness, goodness, faithfulness, gentleness, self-control.*

 REFLECT: Do you think the Spirit produces his fruit in our lives *in order,* one at a time? Or do you think he produces the fruit of the Spirit all at the same time? Is he producing fruit in your life? If so, how? If not, why not?

 PRAY: Express your thanks to God for this promise from Jesus: "I am the vine; you are the branches. Those who remain in me, and I in them, will produce much fruit. For apart from me you can do nothing" (John 15:5).

1 April Fool

Bible Reading: Acts 4:36–5:5

> *How could you do a thing like this? You weren't lying to us but to God.*
> Acts 5:4

IT'S APRIL FOOL'S Day—time for twenty-four hours of nonstop pranks, plots, and practical jokes. There are the typical gags like "Your shoe's untied!" and—a favorite of brothers everywhere—"There's a spider crawling up your back!"

Then there are the more elaborate schemes, usually created by adults to try to "pull a fast one" on one of their friends. Take, for example, the two attorneys who take turns mailing each other the same sack of rotten, smelly garbage every year on April Fool's day. The joke is in coming up with creative ways to have it delivered so the other person has to accept the package.

Does God have a problem with April Fool's Day? Probably not. After all, God doesn't mind us having fun—he likes it when we laugh and play. Of course, he's probably not happy when practical jokes become mean or destructive. But a joke is a joke. Kidding can be fun. The problem is, some people play "April Fool" *every day.* They say something cruel and then add, "Just kidding." Or they get caught in a lie and say, "I was only fooling." They don't seem to understand—or they don't want to admit—that there's a difference between kidding and lying.

Kidding and joking are intended to produce fun and laughter. But lying is intended to hurt or to deceive another person. These words from Scripture explain it well: "Like a madman shooting firebrands or deadly arrows is a man whom deceives his neighbor and says, 'I was only joking!'" (Proverbs 26:18-19, NIV).

When you try to make someone believe something that isn't true, you're not only lying to that person, you're also sinning against God. And no matter who you may fool, you'll never fool God; he knows whether you're kidding—or lying.

So have fun on this April Fool's Day, but don't lie!

 REFLECT: Look back at today's Bible reading (Acts 4:36–5:5). What do you think Ananias hoped to gain through his lie? Did it work? What kinds of jokes do you play on April Fool's Day? Are there any that shouldn't be part of your bag of tricks?

 PRAY: "Lord, you are truth, and there is no deception in you. Help me to follow your ways closely."

2 Milk or More?

Bible Reading: Hebrews 5:12-14

> *You have been Christians a long time now, and you ought to be teaching others. Instead, you need someone to teach you again the basic things a beginner must learn about the Scriptures. You are like babies who drink only milk and cannot eat solid food. Hebrews 5:12*

MOST THINGS IN life go in a certain order. Babies crawl before they walk and drink milk before they eat solid food. Little kids ride a bike with training wheels before they take off on a two-wheeler. Teens get a temporary driver's permit that allows them to drive with an adult before they're allowed to drive on their own.

The Christian life goes in a certain order, too. When we're newborn Christians, we need to master the basics: knowing our own sinfulness; needing God's forgiveness and love through the gift of his Son, Jesus; desiring to forgive others. As we grow in Christ, the lessons we learn go deeper as we face the day-to-day decisions between right and wrong.

"Do I cheat on a test to get the grade I need so I can go on the youth group work project this weekend?"

"Do I lie to my parents and tell them my homework is finished so I can go to a concert tonight?"

"Do I throw food at my baby sister because she stuck out her tongue at me?"

OK, so maybe the last one's too easy. But the point is, all those opportunities to choose right or wrong are *more* than opportunities to choose right or wrong–they're opportunities to *train* yourself to make right choices. Not just now but when you get older. By making good decisions now (when the choice is "Do I stomp my kid brother into a bloody pulp because I'm in a bad mood or show him Christian love and mercy?"), you prepare yourself to make good decisions when the choices are tougher and more complex ("Do I control my raging hormones with my date or give in and see what happens?").

If you *don't* train yourself in making right choices, you will have a harder time of it later, when the stakes are higher and the consequences are greater! Every good decision you make now trains you for the harder decisions that are sure to come your way down the line. The more you train by making good choices, the more equipped you will be to make good decisions later on.

 REFLECT: Think back on the choices you've made this past week. Do you think they've equipped you to make right choices in the future? Have you made the right choice when the choices were easy? Have you made the right choice when the choices were hard? Which do you think "trains" you better for the future—hard choices or easy choices?

 PRAY: "Lord, with your help I know I can make good decisions. With your guidance, I know I can choose right over wrong. Be my strength, Lord, when I am weak."

3 A Clean Slate

Bible Reading: Acts 24:10-16

I always try to maintain a clear conscience before God and everyone else.
Acts 24:16

THE NEXT TIME your teacher erases the chalkboard at school, watch closely. That dark surface, once covered with math problems or vocabulary words or whatever else was up there, is suddenly wiped clean so that something new can be written. That's where we get the term "a clean slate," which means a chance to start over—a new beginning.

Your conscience is a lot like your classroom chalkboard. All your negative thoughts, actions, and feelings cause marks on your conscience, kind of like the chalk marks on the chalkboard. Yet your conscience is more than just a board that records those marks. A conscience can actually tell you if what you're thinking (or how you're feeling or what you're going to do) is right or wrong. It's sort of a self-correcting chalkboard. (Now, wouldn't *that* be nice in Algebra I?)

Your conscience "feels" dirty when you choose wrong—kind of like an unwashed chalkboard—and clean when you choose right—like a chalkboard that's been erased *and* washed. Your conscience is that part of your soul that sends messages to your spirit telling you right from wrong.

So what do you do when those "chalk marks" pile up on the chalkboard of your soul? No problem. Just call in the Great Eraser—God. Tell him that you desire a clean slate. Then ask him to forgive your sins. Ask for the strength and wisdom to make better decisions in the future. And thank him for giving you a conscience to know right from wrong.

Remember that "if we confess our sins, he is faithful and just to forgive us our sins, and to cleanse us from all unrighteousness" (1 John 1:9, KJV).

 REFLECT: What is the state of your conscience right now—full of dirty marks or a clean slate? What can you do if you have a "dirty conscience"?

 ACT: Offer to clean the chalkboard today for your favorite teacher—or maybe even for your *least* favorite teacher. Think about the clean slate the Lord offers to those who come to him for forgiveness.

 PRAY: "God, I need a clean slate in the area of_____.
Please forgive me for_____. Give me the wisdom I need to make a better decision next time when_____. Thanks for the conscience you've given me to help me know I needed to talk to you about this."

4 A Worthy Life

Bible Reading: Titus 1:15–2:1

Nothing is pure to those who are corrupt and unbelieving, because their minds and consciences are defiled. Such people claim they know God, but they deny him by the way they live. Titus 1:15-16

THE SCENE: Glamorous Los Angeles, California.

The place: The Academy Awards ceremony at the Dorothy Chandler Pavilion, where an Oscar is being handed out for best actor in a motion picture.

Thunderous applause breaks out as Howard Handsome wins the award for Best Actor. He climbs the steps to the platform, takes the Oscar, kisses it, and raises it over his head in victory.

"Thank you, Hollywood, for this fabulous tribute," Howard intones as the commotion dies. "I'd like to thank my fellow actors whom I treated like dirt as we worked together on this film; my director; my live-in girlfriend, Susie Stunning; and, most of all (Howard pauses for dramatic effect), I'd like to thank God for making all this happen."

Stop action! Wait a minute! What's wrong with this picture? A man who has just admitted to mean-spiritedness, lying, and immorality is thanking *God* for making all this happen? I don't think so. God does want to be part of our life, but he doesn't want to be part of our sin.

Statements like those made by the fictitious Howard Handsome are sometimes made by people who want to justify their actions by trying to put God's seal of approval on them. Sometimes they're made by people who have totally lost touch with their conscience because of the overwhelming number of bad decisions they've made. "They are despicable and disobedient," the Bible says, "worthless for doing anything good" (Titus 1:16).

Of course, movie stars and sports figures are not the only ones whose consciences can become dull and useless. That can happen with anyone's conscience. If you deny your conscience often enough and suppress its warnings, you could someday come to the point where you can no longer tell the difference between right and wrong.

That doesn't have to happen, though. The way to prevent it is to listen to God when he pricks your conscience. Obey him when he convicts you. Repent when you know you've done something wrong, and you'll keep your conscience clean—and sharp! Then you can say with Paul, "I always try to maintain a clear conscience before God and everyone else" (Acts 24:16).

REFLECT: What kinds of things do people do to dull their consciences? When was the last time you felt a pang of conscience? Did you heed its warning or ignore it? How can you be more sensitive to your conscience in the future?

PRAY: "Lord, keep my eyes open and my conscience sharp. I don't want to fall in the way of sin and live a life unworthy of you."

5 Spiritual Roulette

Bible Reading: 1 Timothy 4:1-5

Now the Holy Spirit tells us clearly that in the last times some will turn away from what we believe; they will follow lying spirits and teachings that come from demons. Those teachers are hypocrites and liars. They pretend to be religious, but their consciences are dead. 1 Timothy 4:1-2

A FEW YEARS ago in a suburban home in Cincinnati, Ohio, five boys played a game. Each took a turn with a handgun one of the boys had taken from a locked gun cabinet. Each spun the cylinder, placed the gun to his head, and pulled the trigger. They thought the gun was unloaded. They thought they were playing a harmless game. What the boys didn't realize was that the gun wasn't empty.

Within minutes, a fourteen-year-old boy lay fatally wounded as his friends frantically called 911 in an effort to save his life. Their efforts failed.

While most of us would never consider participating in a game of Russian roulette, there are some who play a form of spiritual roulette. Each time they make a bad decision, it's another spin of the cylinder. Each time they choose wrong over right, it's another pull of the trigger.

Too often we rationalize our behavior by telling ourselves, "If I do this *just once,* it won't hurt me." The second time we say, "Well, it didn't hurt the first time, so it must be OK to do it again." And so the sin repeats itself—over and over and over—until the sin we thought was harmless turns destructive, and our consciences die.

It is possible for a person's conscience to die. When you continually dismiss those stabs of regret, when you push aside the feeling that you're making the wrong choices, when you disobey God over and over again, your conscience begins to harden until finally it just shrivels up and dies.

God has given you a precious warning system—like a smoke alarm or an air raid siren—that's designed to protect you and help you make right choices. It's your conscience. Take good care of it.

 REFLECT: What is "spiritual roulette"? Have you ever played it with your conscience? What were the consequences? Perhaps there is a sin in your life that you keep committing over and over that has desensitized you or made you feel distant from God. How can you take care of your conscience and keep it sharp and useful?

 PRAY: "God, help me not to play 'spiritual roulette' with my conscience. Keep me alert to the voice of my conscience. Make me sensitive to sin. And help me repent when I disobey you."

6 Are You Old Enough?

Bible Reading: Isaiah 7:13-16

By the time this child is old enough to eat curds and honey, he will know enough to choose what is right and reject what is wrong.
Isaiah 7:15

HOW OLD ARE you? Is that "old enough"?

"Old enough to *what?*" you may ask. Ah, that's the question.

Say you want to drive a car. The law in most places says sixteen is "old enough," though your parents may disagree!

Say you want to vote. "Old enough" to vote is eighteen.

Say you want to collect Social Security. Sorry, you gotta wait until you're really ancient, like in your sixties.

So, when are you "old enough to know better"? If your mom and dad are like most parents, they've used that phrase about a gazillion times. But like most parents, your mom and dad have probably never explained just how old "old enough to know better" really is. Five? Ten? Sixteen? Somewhere in between?

Well, even the youngest child understands that some things are right and some things are wrong. Because we're created in the image of God, some of this knowledge is instinctive. That's why a two-year-old will scream, "No fair!" when another child tries to take a toy away from him or her.

As children grow older, of course, they begin adding to that basic knowledge of right and wrong. But the point is, you don't have to have gray hair—or even an eighth-grade education—to know right from wrong. Most of that is pretty basic stuff.

Oh, some choices and decisions can be complicated, like that lifeboat thing. You know the situation: You're one of eight people in a lifeboat in shark-infested waters; the boat will only safely hold seven people; one of you has to go. Do you all die or should you sacrifice one person for the sake of the other seven? That kind of thing. But when was the last time you were in a crowded lifeboat in shark-infested waters? Most people go through their lives without once being in a crowded lifeboat in shark-infested waters. So let's not waste too much time worrying about it, all right?

For most of us, most questions of right and wrong are pretty basic and straightforward. The question usually isn't, "Is this right or wrong?" That's usually fairly obvious. The question most often is, "Am I going to *do* right?" In other words, if you're "old enough to know better" (and if you're reading this book, trust me, you are), you're old enough to do right. That's what really matters.

 REFLECT: Most choices between right and wrong that you face in life are pretty basic and pretty obvious. But do you have any sincere questions about some action you don't know is right or wrong? If you do, talk it over as soon as possible with your parents, pastor, or some other trusted Christian adult.

 PRAY: "Lord, help me be alert today to the choices I need to make. Help me remember that I'm old enough to make right choices."

7 "Yessir, Drill Sergeant, Sir!"

Bible Reading: Deuteronomy 6:4-9

And you must commit yourselves wholeheartedly to these commands I am giving you today. Deuteronomy 6:6

Keep my commands and you will live; guard my teachings as the apple of your eye. Proverbs 7:2, NIV

HAVE YOU EVER seen the members of an army platoon going through their drills? At each command from their drill sergeant, the group moves as if they are one.

"Right face!" Everyone turns.

"Forward march!" Everyone marches.

"Company, halt!" No one moves—not a muscle.

After months of hard work, these men and women know that when their drill sergeant gives a command, they'd better respond—and quickly. Not only that, but many of them discover that their commitment to obedience pays off: They become stronger, faster, more agile, and more effective.

God has given commands to us, too. He doesn't shout in our ears like a drill sergeant. He doesn't make us run ten miles with forty-pound backpacks. He doesn't make us drop to the ground and do twenty push-ups if we make a mistake. But he has given commands for us to follow day after day.

So, what kind of soldier are you in the army of God? Are you as committed to following God's commands as the members of an army squad or platoon are to following their officer's commands? Are you as quick to respond as they are? Or do you look for another way that makes it look like you're doing what God's asking when you're really more committed to having your own way?

Being committed to God means spending time in prayer and reading God's commands (the Bible) each day. Being committed to God means memorizing his words to us, which makes his commands easy to remember and follow because they're written in our heart. Being committed to God means aligning our will with his.

Being committed to obeying God's commands will pay off for you, too, just as obeying the drill sergeant does for armed forces recruits. As you spend time with him and his Word, as you commit yourself to obeying him, you'll become stronger, better, quicker to do what's right.

 REFLECT: Being committed to something means giving it your wholehearted devotion. Are there things in your life that you're more devoted to than God? Which of God's commands are easy for you to follow? Which are difficult?

 PRAY: "Lord, I'm committed to building my relationship with you day by day. Help me to respond quickly and willingly to your commands, especially to your command to_____."

8 True Wisdom

Bible Reading: 1 Kings 3:5-10

Give me an understanding mind so that I can govern your people well and know the difference between right and wrong. 1 Kings 3:9

HOW WOULD YOU define *wisdom?*

One fifth grader defined wisdom as "being smarter than anybody else."

Another said that wisdom was something only "grandparents and old people have."

Still another said that wisdom was "knowing enough not to do stupid stuff."

And another called it "a little voice inside your head that tells you what to do when nobody else knows what to do."

Not bad, but what do *you* think wisdom is? Is it knowing more than anybody else? Is it the ability to avoid "stupid stuff"? Or is it something else?

King Solomon, who became famous in his time as a wise man, gives us a clue in the Bible. The third chapter of 1 Kings (in the Old Testament) tells the story of how God appeared to Solomon in a dream when Solomon became king. God asked him, "What do you want? Ask, and I will give it to you!"

Now, if God made that offer to us, most of us would say, "A million dollars!" or "My own computer!" or something like that. But not Solomon. He said, "Give me an understanding mind so that I can govern your people well and know the difference between right and wrong" (1 Kings 3:9).

Solomon's words show that a major part of wisdom is the ability to "know the difference between right and wrong." You may be well educated. You may be the top student in your class—maybe in your school. You may win thousands of dollars on *Jeopardy!* But if you want to be wise, you will seek "an understanding mind so that [you can] know the difference between right and wrong."

No matter what else you may know, if you don't know right from wrong, you're not wise.

 REFLECT: Based on Solomon's words in 1 Kings 3:9, from where (or from whom) does true wisdom come? Do you think a person has to be old to be wise? Do you think a person has to be educated to be wise? How does a person become wise? How can you increase in wisdom?

 PRAY: The Bible says, "If you need wisdom—if you want to know what God wants you to do—ask him, and he will gladly tell you" (James 1:5). Spend a few moments in prayer, asking God for wisdom in specific areas of your life. You may want to start by praying the words that Solomon used in 1 Kings 3:9 when he asked God for wisdom: "Give me an understanding mind so that I can . . . know the difference between right and wrong."

9 True to the Original

Bible Reading: Deuteronomy 7:6-9

Understand, therefore, that the Lord your God is indeed God. He is the faithful God who keeps his covenant for a thousand generations and constantly loves those who love him and obey his commands.
Deuteronomy 7:9

A COMMERCIAL APPEARED on television some years ago featuring a famous singer. She started singing an impressive operatic-style song and then let loose with a piercing high note. Suddenly, the focus of the camera shifted, and the singer's form was in the background while the camera focused on a fine crystal wine glass. As the singer hit the high note, the glass shattered.

Immediately, however, the camera angle widened to reveal a tape machine running, and an announcer's voice posed the question, "Is it live—or is it Memorex?"

The point of the commercial, of course, was that a Memorex cassette tape could duplicate a sound so accurately that even the recorded version might conceivably shatter glass. In other words, the recorded version was so true to the original that it was difficult to tell the difference.

That's a pretty fair description of what faithfulness means: to be true to the original.

God has shown us what faithfulness looks like. The Bible says that "he is the faithful God who keeps his covenant for a thousand generations and constantly loves those who love him and obey his commands" (Deuteronomy 7:9). He keeps his word—even for a *thousand* generations! He never stops loving those who love him. He never disappoints those who count on him. He never deserts those who need him.

We Christians are faithful when we are true to the original, to the example that God has given us. Faithfulness means keeping our word, never giving up on those we love, never withdrawing our love from those who love us, never consciously trying to disappoint those who count on us, never deserting those who need us. That's faithfulness—being true to the original, our faithful God. And being true to God has benefits: "A faithful man [or woman] will be richly blessed" (Proverbs 28:20, NIV).

 REFLECT: Faithfulness means being true to the original—obeying God's commands and being like him in our relationships with others. How true are you to the original? How good are you at keeping your word? How good are you at not giving up on those you love? at not withdrawing love from those who love you? at not disappointing those who count on you? at not deserting those who need you? If you need help, don't try to do it yourself; rely on God to do it in you through his Holy Spirit.

 ACT: Look up the dictionary definition of *faithful*. Copy it onto an index card or slip of paper and place it in one of your schoolbooks or in a prominent place where you'll be likely to see it often in the next few days.

 PRAY: "I want to be true to you today, God. Help me to be faithful, especially when I_____."

10 Faithfulness Is Good

Bible Reading: Hebrews 3:1-6

[Jesus] was faithful to God, who appointed him, just as Moses served faithfully and was entrusted with God's entire house. Hebrews 3:2

"HE'S NOTHIN' BUT a quitter."

"You'd better watch yourself; she'll think nothing about stabbing you in the back."

"He'd betray his own mother for a few bucks."

Ever heard these kinds of statements? Maybe not in real life, but maybe you've read them in books or heard them on television. Would you want to be the kind of person those statements describe? You wouldn't, would you? But think about it—why not? What is it about those statements that makes you not want someone to think such things about you?

Nobody wants to be known as a quitter or a backstabber. Nobody wants a reputation as someone who would betray his own mother. But why not? Because you seem to know, almost instinctively, that unfaithfulness—disloyalty, betrayal, unreliability—is a bad thing.

How much better it would be to have people say of you:

"He's a stand-up kind of guy."

"If she said she'll be here, she'll be here."

"You can count on him."

"She's never let me down before."

That's the kind of reputation you want, right? Why? Because you know that faithfulness is a good thing. And it's universally recognized as a good thing, even by people who claim that there's no such thing as right and wrong. Even those people don't want friends who will betray them or let them down.

That's because faithfulness is a godly virtue. Faithfulness is good, and unfaithfulness is evil. Faithfulness is right, and unfaithfulness is wrong.

But, then, you knew that already, didn't you?

 REFLECT: Today's Bible reading describes two people as faithful. Who were they? Does the reading speak about faithfulness as a good thing or a bad thing?

In the reading above, which set of statements comes closest to describing you? If a friend or family member were asked to rate your faithfulness, how do you think that person would score you: excellent, good, fair, or poor? Why?

 ACT: Be alert and listen this week for statements people make around you that indicate a person's faithfulness or unfaithfulness (such as, "He never showed up" or "She's a true friend").

 PRAY: Ask God to help you live so that the following description is true of you: "Dear friend, you are faithful in what you are doing" (3 John 5, NIV).

11 God Commands Faithfulness

Bible Reading: Revelation 2:8-10

Remain faithful even when facing death, and I will give you the crown of life. Revelation 2:10

GOD GAVE A lot of commands to us. Sometimes it can seem a little hard to keep them straight. For example, see if you can identify which of the following commands really came from God:

1. Did God say:
   (a) "You must not eat fruit from the tree that is in the middle of the garden, unless it's been inspected first" or
   (b) "The seventh day is a sabbath to the Lord your God. On it you shall not do any work"?

2. Did God say:
   (a) "You shall not steal" or
   (b) "You shall not play loud music after midnight"?

3. Did God say:
   (a) "Follow justice and justice alone" or
   (b) "Do not trample down the lawn of your neighbor, for he will surely turn and rend you to pieces"?

4. Did God say:
   (a) "Children, obey your parents in the Lord, for this is right" or
   (b) "Let everyone do that which is right in his own eyes"?

5. Did God say:
   (a) "Remain faithful" or
   (b) "Let him who is without sin gather no moss"?

If you answered (a) to every question except the first, then you got them all right! See, it's not so hard to remember and recognize God's commandments after all.

One of the above commandments, of course, is taken from today's Bible reading, in which God commands his people to be faithful—even when facing death! Yikes! That shows, of course, that faithfulness isn't just one of many options; it's commanded by God. Just as he wants us to be truthful, loving, merciful, and just, he also wants all of us to be faithful. In fact, he commands it.

 REFLECT: Why do you think faithfulness is emphasized in today's Scripture passage? Is God's command to be faithful less important because it's not one of the Ten Commandments? Do you think God commands us to do anything that he doesn't think is important? Do you think God commands us to do anything that isn't right or good?

 PRAY: "God, show me how to be faithful, and help me obey your command to be faithful."

12 God Values Faithfulness

Bible Reading: Proverbs 3:1-8

Let love and faithfulness never leave you. Proverbs 3:3, NIV

YOU KNOW WHAT a slam book is, right? It's a notebook in which kids jot down messages to each other—usually messages that "slam" or insult someone else. They're passed around a lot in some schools.

A kinder, gentler version of the slam book is a notebook in which friends and classmates are encouraged to answer questions about their favorite things. One page, for example, might be headed "Favorite Sport," and the entries below might include "Baseball—Joel Wannamaker" and "Synchronized swimming—Jan Tzen."

Let's try our own version. Try listing your favorite . . .

Song _____
Singer or group _____
TV show _____
Season of the year _____
Book of the Bible _____

Now let's try the opposite approach. List your *least* favorite . . .

Food _____
School subject _____
TV commercial _____
Day of the week _____
Thing your parents say _____

Believe it or not, God has a similar list. He's even written it down. According to his list, one of his favorite things in the world is faithfulness. He thinks faithfulness is totally cool. He loves being faithful, and he loves it when people are faithful—to him and to each other.

Think about this. Are there some foods and school subjects you absolutely hate—like maybe broccoli, cottage cheese, lima beans? P. E., math, English? Well, there are *some* things God hates, too. And one of the things he hates is *un*faithfulness.

That's why God commands us to be faithful. Because he values faithfulness. For that matter, we should, too.

 REFLECT: A "value" is something that a person considers important. Do you value faithfulness in your friends? in your family members? in yourself?

 ACT: Create your own "favorites" book to pass among your friends, making each page a different list of the things your friends like most. Which of your "favorites" are also God's?

 PRAY: "God, help me to value faithfulness just like you do."

13 Faithful in All He Does

Bible Reading: Psalm 33:1-4

For the word of the Lord is right and true; he is faithful in all he does.
Psalm 33:4, NIV

"THE COURT CALLS Abraham of Ur to the stand!"

A bearded figure leaning on a tall stick walks slowly to the front of the courtroom. The bailiff swears him in, and the man sits down.

"You are Abraham, originally of the city of Ur?" asks a lawyer in an expensive suit. The old man nods. "You did not always understand the defendant or agree with him, did you?" he asks, pointing to the defense table, where another attorney sits next to an empty chair.

Abraham shakes his head. "No. But there is no friend more faithful. I often let him down—in Egypt, and at Gerar, and many other times—but he never let *me* down."

The lawyer calls another witness. A man named Joseph, wearing a multicolored robe, takes the stand.

"You were in trouble a number of times because of the defendant, weren't you?" the lawyer asks.

"I was in trouble, all right—twice. I was sold as a slave because of my own arrogance. And I was imprisoned because I was wrongly accused of a crime. But he," Joseph says, nodding to the empty chair at the defense table, "stuck with me through thick and thin. He delivered me from these troubles—he didn't cause them."

The lawyer dismisses Joseph and calls a third witness, Jonah.

"Your so-called friend nearly made fish bait out of you, didn't he?" the lawyer asks.

Jonah answers. "I gave him every reason to give up on me. In fact, when the fish swallowed me, I thought that's exactly what had happened. But he didn't give up! He never gives up." Jonah stands. "My friend—my God—is faithful. Not sometimes. Not most of the time. *All* the time. He is faithful in all he does. And you wanna know why? Because that's just *who he is.* Faithfulness isn't something he *does.* It's *who he is!*"

Jonah gazes at the lawyer with a mixture of contempt and compassion. "And you, who have brought this case against the God of heaven and earth, cannot truly judge God's faithfulness, because it is his nature alone that shows you what faithfulness is. And his nature alone shows you that faithfulness is right and unfaithfulness is wrong."

The lawyer turns away, but Jonah is not done speaking. "If your actions had been like God, your soul would be at peace. But your actions *have always been* wrong, Judas Iscariot, because you are not like God, who is faithful in all he does."

 REFLECT: If you were called to testify in court about God's faithfulness to you, what would you say? What evidence would you give of God's faithfulness?

 PRAY: "Thank you, God, for your faithfulness to me."

14 Beyond Brains and Trains

Bible Reading: Matthew 25:14-23

Well done, my good and faithful servant. You have been faithful in handling this small amount, so now I will give you many more responsibilities. Matthew 25:23

"WHEN GOD WAS passing out brains, you thought he said *trains,* and asked for a slow one!"

"When God was giving out looks, you shouted, 'Gimme!' but he thought you said, 'Skip me!'"

"When God was handing out personality, you thought he said *abnormality,* so you asked for an invisible one!"

None of those statements is true of *you,* of course. After all, you've got a thing or two going for you, right?

Right. God has given you some good things, no matter how unattractive or untalented you may feel at times. Maybe he gave you a great family. Or he might have blessed you with athletic ability or at least a healthy body. Or a healthy mind. Or understanding parents. Or a better-than-average singing voice. Or a pleasant personality and a talent for making friends. Or good eyesight. Good posture. Straight teeth.

The point is, God has given you *something.* Maybe you don't think he gave you as much to work with as he gave "Crash" Helmut, the captain of the football team, or Heather Fields, the prettiest girl in the history of adolescence.

But whether God has given you little or much, it's important how you are using what he has given you. If he gave you a good mind, do you use it well, or do you use it to figure out how to fool your parents or lie to your teachers? If he gave you a nice voice, do you use it to sing and pray to God, or to curse your brothers and sisters?

Scripture says, "The Lord rewards every man for his righteousness and faithfulness" (1 Samuel 26:23, NIV). If you are faithful with what God has given you already, he may someday reward you with more blessings, more responsibilities, more advantages. But if you waste or misuse what he's given you, why should he trust you with more?

REFLECT: Faithfulness to God includes using his many good gifts wisely. Take a moment to list in your mind as many good things as you can think of that God has given you. Don't overlook the obvious (such as your five senses) or the material (such as a comfortable bed to sleep in). On a scale of one to ten (ten meaning "like Socrates or Solomon" and one meaning "needs immediate help"), how would you rate your wise use of God's good gifts?

PRAY: "Thank you, God, for the good things you've given to me, especially
_____."

15 Role Reversal

Bible Reading: Matthew 25:24-30

From those who are unfaithful, even what little they have will be taken away. Matthew 25:29

PUT YOURSELF IN your parents' shoes for a minute. OK, they're too big, they're ugly, and they smell funny (the shoes, not your parents). But try it anyway.

Suppose you're the parent. You decide to let your kid eat whatever he or she wants. A week later you realize that your child's diet has included a dozen Twinkies, twenty-three cans of Pepsi, two boxes of Fruit Roll-Ups, and a tub of ice cream the size of a foreign car—but not one bite of vegetable or protein. You decide

(a) to stop buying meat and vegetables;

(b) to start buying larger clothes for your kid;

(c) to cancel the deal and plan a steady diet of brussels sprouts and asparagus.

Or suppose your kid insists he or she is old enough to stay home alone, without a baby-sitter. You agree, and leave the child alone for a few hours while you and your spouse go shopping together. You return home to discover your kid having a food fight in the living room with Madonna and Dennis Rodman. You decide

(a) to take photos to sell to *The National Examiner;*

(b) to ask your kid to let you know the next time he or she plans a food fight, so you can cover the furniture in plastic wrap;

(c) never to leave your kid home alone until he or she is collecting Social Security.

Or suppose you give your kid the keys to the family Gremlin on his or her sixteenth birthday. Three days later your kid still has the keys but can't find the car. You decide

(a) to post pictures of your lost car around the neighborhood;

(b) to buy another Gremlin;

(c) to take the keys back.

Now, admit it—you'd probably choose (c) in each case. Why? It's obvious, right? Because as a parent you would want to reward faithfulness, not unfaithfulness.

That's pretty much how it goes. As Jesus said, "To those who use well what they are given [freedom, responsibility, friendship, etc.], even more will be given, and they will have an abundance. But from those who are unfaithful, even what little they have will be taken away" (Matthew 25:29).

In other words, those who are faithful—to God, to parents, to friends—tend to bring good things into their lives, while those who are unfaithful tend to lose out.

 REFLECT: Do you think it's easier to be faithful or unfaithful? Why? Do you think it's better to be faithful or unfaithful? Why?

 PRAY: "Lord, make me your faithful servant."

16 The Water Tank

Bible Reading: Psalm 18:24-28

To the faithful you show yourself faithful. Psalm 18:25

Let love and faithfulness never leave you. Proverbs 3:3, NIV

A STORY IS told of a village in a part of the world that is rainy for a small part of the year and dry throughout the rest of the year.

One year the village elders announced a plan: Everyone in the village was to bring a single cup of water to a large tank in the center of the town during the rainy season. Then, when the dry season came and water was scarce, the village would still have water, and they would all share equally the water in the tank.

The villagers all cheered the elders' plan, and it was agreed. The rainy season came and went; dust began to settle on the village, the ground began to crack from the dryness, and water became scarce.

Then the day arrived when the elders agreed that the tank should be opened and the precious water should be shared among the villagers. Everyone gathered around the tank with cups and bowls, and a spirit of celebration was in the air. With great ceremony, the elders opened the tank—and discovered that not a drop of water was to be found inside!

Only then was it learned that not one of the villagers who had agreed to the elders' plan had given a single cup of water. Each had assumed that his or her cup of water would not be missed, and so the water tank had sat empty throughout the rainy season. The village was without water.

It's easy to think that no one will notice our unfaithfulness. It's easy to skip church or not attend a club meeting at school or decide not to fulfill a promise we've made to a friend, thinking "no one will notice" or "it's no big deal."

But unfaithfulness doesn't hurt *only* those who are depending on us; it hurts us, too. If each of the villagers had brought his or her cup of water, that water would have been returned to them all. If you are faithful, you'll receive faithfulness back—from God and from others, many times over.

 REFLECT: What do you think would have happened if the villagers in the story above had kept their agreement? Do you ever act like those villagers, thinking no one will notice your irresponsibility or unfaithfulness? Have you ever been hurt or disappointed by someone's unfaithfulness? Have you ever been hurt or disappointed by your own unfaithfulness?

 PRAY: Read the words of Psalm 18:25-28 out loud, this time making them your prayer to God.

17 "I Knew You'd Come"

Bible Reading: Proverbs 17:17

A friend is always loyal, and a brother is born to help in time of need.
Proverbs 17:17

AN OLD BOY Scout manual told the story of two brothers who were fighting side by side in France. The brothers struggled to rejoin their unit, but only one made it back safely. He approached his commanding officer and asked permission to retrace his steps in an effort to find his brother.

The officer shook his head. "It's too dangerous," he said, not without pity. "Your brother is probably dead, and there's no use risking your life just to find him dead."

The brother persisted, however, and begged the officer to let him try. Finally, the man agreed, and the soldier dashed back toward the enemy fire to hunt for his brother. Some time later, he returned—with his brother draped across his shoulders. But just as he reached the safety of the bunker, his brother gasped and died in his arms.

"You see," said the officer. He clapped a hand on the soldier's shoulder and shook his head. "I let you risk your life for nothing."

"Oh no, sir," the brother answered respectfully. Tears welled in his eyes. "No, sir," he repeated emphatically. "You see, when I crawled up beside him where he lay, hurt and dying, and I took him in my arms, he said, 'I knew you'd come, Tom. I knew you'd come.'"

That soldier's faithfulness was rewarded by his brother's dying words. Can you imagine how Tom felt to know that his brother's last words were a testimony to his faithfulness?

Don't forget, "The Lord rewards every man for his righteousness and faithfulness" (1 Samuel 26:23, NIV). Your faithfulness may be rewarded immediately—and it may not. You may see the results of your faithfulness to a friend or family member in this lifetime, and you may not. But faithfulness is often its own reward, as it was for Tom.

 REFLECT: What do you think would have happened if Tom had not gone to look for his brother? Do you think Tom would have known of the blessing he had missed? Do you think you have missed any blessings by not being faithful to a friend or family member? Have you experienced any rewards for your faithfulness? If so, what?

 ACT: Be alert this week for a chance to be faithful to a friend or family member, especially "in time of need" as Proverbs 17:17 stresses.

 PRAY: "Lord, I don't want to miss the rewards and blessings you give for faithfulness."

18 Faithful God

Bible Reading: 2 Timothy 2:8-13

If we are unfaithful, he remains faithful, for he cannot deny himself.
2 Timothy 2:13

LOOK OVER THE following checklist, and check every circumstance in which you think God will be faithful to you or will still love you, still believe in you, and still expect the best from you:

- ☐ If I eat all my vegetables at dinnertime
- ☐ If I *don't* eat all my vegetables at dinnertime
- ☐ If I eat my brother's vegetables at dinnertime
- ☐ If I join the chess club
- ☐ If I join a motorcycle club
- ☐ If I join a CD, cassette tape, and videotape club
- ☐ If I sell everything I own and give the money to the poor
- ☐ If I sell everything my parents own and give the money to the poor
- ☐ If I sell everything my parents own and keep the money
- ☐ If I shave my sister's head while she sleeps
- ☐ If I shave my sister's head while she's awake
- ☐ If I'm kind to children and animals
- ☐ If I'm kind to children who act like animals

Now, score yourself: If you left any item on the list unchecked, you don't understand God's faithfulness. If, on the other hand, you checked *every single answer,* you probably know something about God's faithfulness that most people don't understand.

You see, God isn't like many of our friends and acquaintances. He isn't faithful to us only when we act a certain way. He isn't faithful to us only if we do what he wants. He is faithful to us no matter what, because faithfulness is a part of his nature; it's part of who he is.

That's what the Bible means when it says, "If we are unfaithful, he remains faithful, for he cannot deny himself" (2 Timothy 2:13). He can't stop being who he is, and since faithful is part of who he is, he can't stop being faithful.

That means he will always love you, always believe in you, and always expect the best of you. He will never leave you, he will never betray you, he will never let you down. No matter what you do, he remains faithful—because that's who he is.

 REFLECT: Have you ever failed God? Have you ever ignored him? Disappointed him? If so, did he leave you or forsake you then, or was he faithful to you? (Remember that faithfulness isn't just what God does; it's part of who he is.)

 PRAY: Look up the hymn "Great Is Thy Faithfulness," and read or sing it aloud as a prayer to God. (If you need help locating the hymn, ask your parents.)

19 More Gladness Than Anyone Else

Bible Reading: Psalm 45:1-7

You love what is good and hate what is wrong. Therefore God, your God, has given you more gladness than anyone else. Psalm 45:7, TLB

WHAT WOULD IT take to make you happy? Check any of the following that apply:

☐ A new bike or car
☐ Popularity
☐ One or two good friends
☐ No more school
☐ Fame as a rock star
☐ Good looks

☐ My own room
☐ A boyfriend/girlfriend
☐ A nice house
☐ A million dollars
☐ A trip to Disney World
☐ A pet python

It would be nice, wouldn't it? After all, who *wouldn't* want a million dollars? Who doesn't want to get out of school? Who doesn't want to look like some model or movie star?

But you know what? Chances are, if you're not happy now, you probably won't be happy when school lets out either. If you're not satisfied with life now, you probably *wouldn't* be satisfied with a million dollars.

Oh, things could get better, that's for sure. Things can always get better. But the path to happiness and satisfaction doesn't involve riches or fame; believe it or not, it involves right choices.

David, the psalmist, wrote, "You love what is good and hate what is wrong. Therefore God, your God, has given you more gladness than anyone else" (Psalm 45:7, TLB). That ancient songwriter said that loving what is good and hating what is wrong brings gladness into your life. God gives gladness—happiness—to those who love what's good and hate what's wrong.

That doesn't mean you'll never have a rotten day. It doesn't mean you'll never have to sit at home while others are out partying. But it does mean that over the long run (and sometimes even sooner), making right choices will tend to bring more happiness and satisfaction into your life than making wrong choices. It might not be a million dollars, but it's worth a whole lot more.

 REFLECT: Do you agree that those who love what is good are usually happier than those who make wrong choices? Why or why not?

 PRAY: Have you given God a chance to give you gladness as a result of right choices? If not, ask him to teach you to "love what is good and hate what is wrong" and to show you in the coming days and weeks how your right choices open the way to greater happiness and satisfaction in your life.

20 The Line between Good and Evil

Bible Reading: Romans 7:21-25

It seems to be a fact of life that when I want to do what is right, I inevitably do what is wrong. Romans 7:21

LOOK AT THIS LIST:

Adolf Hitler	Attila the Hun	Benedict Arnold
Josef Stalin	Jack the Ripper	Genghis Khan

Compare the above list with these names:

Mother Teresa	St. Nicholas	Francis of Assisi
Abraham Lincoln	Joan of Arc	Martin Luther

Most people would label the first list of names as "bad" people and the second list of names as "good" people. Ah, but there's a problem with those categories. The line between good and evil doesn't separate *us* (people like you, me, and Mother Teresa) from *them* (people like Hitler, Stalin, and your seventh grade P.E. teacher); as Aleksandr Solzhenitsyn, a famous author, once wrote:

> If only there were evil people somewhere insidiously committing evil deeds, and it were necessary only to separate them from the rest of us and destroy them. But the line dividing good and evil cuts through the heart of every human being.*

Like Paul in today's Bible reading, as much as we want to be "good people," all of us do wrong. Sometimes we do good. Sometimes we do evil. It's not that we *want* to be rotten people, but the evil that lived in Hitler's heart lives in our heart, too. Pretty crummy, huh? Paul would agree. He said, "Oh, what a miserable person I am! Who will free me from this life that is dominated by sin? Thank God! The answer is in Jesus Christ our Lord" (Romans 7:24-25).

In other words, we don't have to give in to our sinful natures. We don't have to keep sinning. God sent his Son, Jesus, to take the punishment for our sins; he sent his Spirit to live in us and deliver us from the power of sin, day by day, decision by decision. *He* can overcome the evil in our hearts and help us to do good.

REFLECT: Have you accepted Jesus' sacrifice on the cross as punishment for your sins? Do you trust his Spirit to deliver you from the power of sin, day by day, decision by decision? If not, why not do it today, right now?

PRAY: "Loving and righteous God, I need you. I admit that I'm a sinner and that evil lives in my heart. Please forgive me for the wrong things I've done. Thank you for forgiving my sins through Christ's death on the cross. Please take charge of my life through your Holy Spirit, who lives in me. Help me to trust him to deliver me from the power of sin, day by day, decision by decision. In Jesus' name. Amen."

*Aleksandr I. Solzhenitsyn, *The Gulag Archipelago* (New York: Harper and Row, 1973).

Family Feuds

Bible Reading: Psalm 133:1-3

How good and pleasant it is when brothers live together in unity!
Psalm 133:1, NIV

ANNOUNCER: Today on *Okra,* we will talk to three people whose sordid stories of family feuding have made them famous—or should I say infamous?

First Voice: Yeah, hi. See, it's like this: I didn't exactly get along with my brother. Well, OK, that's an understatement. I killed him.

Second Voice (clears his throat): My uncle and I were business partners. Everything had been going along fine, but our herds were gettin' too big for the land. Besides, my employees and his employees didn't see eye-to-eye on a lot of things. Neither did Uncle and I, really. We had to part company.

Third Voice: He never acted like he wanted it anyway. My brother, I mean. When I tricked his inheritance out of our father . . . well, my brother went crazy. He woulda killed me if I hadn't skipped town.

Announcer: Three tragic stories. Today on *Okra.* Stay tuned!

Well, maybe you've figured it out. Okra's first guest was Cain, who killed his brother, Abel, in a fit of jealousy. The second voice belonged to Lot, who separated from his godly uncle at a crucial time in his life. The third guest was Jacob, who cheated his brother, Esau, out of his inheritance and his father's blessing, and had to run for his life.

But do you know the rest of their stories? Cain (Genesis 4) was banished far from his parents and lived the rest of his life in exile. Lot (Genesis 13-14, 18-19) thought he got a great deal from his uncle; he chose the finest land in the area, moved his flocks into the plains of Zoar, and settled in a doomed place called Sodom. Jacob (Genesis 25, 27-33) ran to a strange place called Paddan Aram, where he spent fourteen years in servitude to a man as devious and deceitful as himself.

Each of these individuals paid a high price for his inability to live in harmony and unity with others. That's the way it usually goes. People who can't get along with others usually succeed only in making things more difficult for themselves. Such people's lives become full of anger, strife, revenge, and all sorts of unpleasant things.

How much better it is when people live together in unity and harmony! Such people often experience the appreciation, kindness, and cooperation of others. They may never appear on *Okra,* but they understand that unity is better, nonetheless.

 REFLECT: Do you agree that it's better when people live together in unity and harmony? Why or why not? Does the experience of Cain, Lot, or Jacob sound like any of your relationships? Why or why not?

 PRAY: "I need your help today to live in harmony with_____."

22 What God Has Joined Together

Bible Reading: Mark 10:1-9

They are no longer two but one. Matthew 19:6

GOD PATIENTLY EXPLAINED his plan to the archangel Michael. "I will cause the man to fall into a deep sleep," he said, "and then I will take a rib from his side and make a companion for him . . . a woman."

"Uh-huh." Michael blinked as if he'd just been told a joke that he didn't get.

"Don't you see, Michael?" God said. "The woman and the man will be husband and wife. They will become one."

Michael's mouth slowly dropped open. "Oh," he said, drawing the word out into a long expression of realization. "*You* will make them one," the angel repeated. "A unity. The man. The woman."

God smiled and nodded. "A unity. A reflection of my nature."

"So," Michael said breathlessly, "although they are two, they will be one. Just as you are three in one." His eyes sparkled with exhilaration. "You will allow them to experience unity, just as you are one! What a brilliant plan! A generous plan!"

God nodded again, and excitement shone in his eyes, too.

That conversation probably never took place. It is certainly not recorded in God's Word. It's just a fanciful representation of what might have taken place in the first days of human life, when God devised a wonderful plan for humanity. He created a man and a woman and designed that "for this reason a man will leave his father and mother and be united to his wife, and they will become one flesh" (Genesis 2:24, NIV).

Jesus, speaking specifically of the marriage commitment, added, "Since they are no longer two but one, let no one separate them" (Matthew 19:6). Why? Because God intended our marital and familial relationships to be strong, loving, and lasting relationships that reflect the unity of God himself (Deuteronomy 6:4).

Unity is part of God's nature and character. He is one. And he wants us to reflect that unity in our marriage and family relationships.

That doesn't always happen, of course. Tragically, marriages sometimes come to an end; families sometimes fall apart. And, if you've witnessed or experienced the breakup of a family, you probably understand why God wants to save us all the pain and heartbreak of such an experience. He can heal such hurts, but he prefers—with our cooperation—to prevent them.

 REFLECT: God commands unity in marriage. What do you think that means? Does it mean just staying married? Does it mean always agreeing? Never fighting? Something else?

 ACT: Write the equation "1 + 1 = 1" on an index card, and place it in a prominent place all this week (such as folded, tent-style, on the dinner table) to remind everyone in the family that God commands unity in marriage.

 PRAY: Ask God for unity in your family, and thank him for seeing you through times of disunity.

23 "O Come [Together], All Ye Faithful"

Bible Reading: 1 Corinthians 1:10-17

Let there be real harmony so there won't be divisions in the church.
1 Corinthians 1:10

THERE ARE MANY different kinds of churches.

There are Presbyterian churches, Episcopalian churches, and Lutheran churches. There are the Assemblies of God and the Church of God in Christ. There are Nazarene, Brethren, and Reformed churches.

There are even different kinds of Methodist churches (Free Methodist, United Methodist, Wesleyan Methodist) and different kinds of Baptist churches (Freewill Baptist, Southern Baptist, American Baptist, Regular Baptist, Primitive Baptist, even Two-Seed-in-the-Spirit Predestinarian Baptist!).

There are churches with long names (National Baptist Evangelical Life and Soul-Saving Assembly of the United States of America), short names (Congregational Church), and confusing names (Duck River & Kindred Association of Baptists).

A lot of non-Christians look at the different denominations and say, "Hey, you Christians are so divided! Look how many different denominations there are and how many churches split over disagreements. Why should the rest of the world listen to you when you can't even get your own act together?"

To some extent, they're right. There are a lot of unnecessary divisions and disagreements in the church today. But Jesus does not insist that we all worship in the same style. He doesn't command all of us to walk the same, talk the same, or look the same. He doesn't demand that we all call ourselves the same thing.

But he *does* command us to be one. His Word makes it clear that all true Christians should "stop arguing among yourselves." His Word does instruct us to "Let there be real harmony so there won't be divisions in the church." He does plead with us to "be of one mind, united in thought and purpose" (1 Corinthians 1:10).

God desires unity in the church. He *commands* unity in the church. We are commanded to live in unity with other Christians whether we feel like it or not, whether it comes easily or not. Why? Simple. God commands unity because God values unity. And if he values unity, we should, too.

REFLECT: God doesn't command us to make all churches the same, but he does command us to live and work in unity with all Christians. Is there anyone at your church with whom you're arguing or not getting along with right now? How can you "stop arguing" (1 Corinthians 1:10) and start living "in harmony with one another" (1 Peter 3:8, NIV)?

ACT: Ask your parents to plan a visit to a church that worships the Lord in a different place or style than what you're used to as a way of affirming your unity with all true Christian believers.

PRAY: "Thank you, God, for Christian believers everywhere. Help me to live in harmony with everyone in my church family, especially with_____."

24 All One

Bible Reading: Galatians 3:26-28

There is neither Jew nor Greek, slave nor free, male nor female, for you are all one in Christ Jesus. Galatians 3:28, NIV

WHAT DID JESUS look like?

We don't really know the answer to that question, but many Americans and Europeans picture Jesus of Nazareth with brown hair, brown eyes, handsome—and white. Caucasian. Suntanned, maybe, but definitely white. The kind of "white" you might meet in Minneapolis. Cincinnati. Or Peoria, Illinois.

But that's a myth. In all probability, Jesus was much darker in complexion than the average white American or European. He was born a Jew, he lived as a Jew, and he remained a Jew throughout his life. More importantly, even though he entered the stage of humanity at a specific place and time and possessed specific racial characteristics, in a larger sense Jesus transcends the barriers of race and color.

He was a Jew, yet he spoke freely and respectfully to a Samaritan woman. (See John 4.)

Custom prohibited Jesus, a Jew, from entering the home of a Gentile; yet when a Roman centurion pleaded on behalf of his servant, who lay sick at home, Jesus replied, "I will come and heal him." (See Matthew 8:5-13.)

When he was hounded by a Canaanite woman (Canaanites were historic enemies of the Jewish people), Jesus commended her faith and healed her daughter. (See Matthew 15:21-28.)

Jesus, though, was a victim of racial prejudice himself. On one trip through Samaria, he was rejected because the Samaritans guessed that he was a Jew bound for Jerusalem. (See Luke 9:51-56.)

The society that Jesus entered when he became a man drew three primary distinctions among people: They were divided by their race (Jew or Gentile), class (slave or free), and sex (male or female). The Good News that Jesus brought presented a radical departure from those class distinctions, however. Paul summarized it eloquently when he wrote, "You are all sons of God through faith in Christ Jesus. . . . There is neither Jew nor Greek, slave nor free, male nor female, for you are all one in Christ Jesus" (Galatians 3:26-28, NIV).

The followers of Jesus must be like him, not in their color or racial characteristics, but in accepting and loving and living in harmony with all people—regardless of sex, class, or race distinctions.

 REFLECT: God commands unity—or living in harmony—among all people. How do you usually treat people who are different from you? Are you living in harmony with all people—regardless of sex, class, or race distinctions?

 PRAY: Say a special prayer today for victims of discrimination, particularly among the people you know.

25 The Lord Is One

Bible Reading: John 17:1-11

Hear, O Israel: The Lord our God, the Lord is one. Deuteronomy 6:4, NIV

WHAT WOULD YOU think if you discovered that Dave Thomas, the founder and spokesman for the successful Wendy's hamburger chain, actually detested hamburgers? The news would be shocking, wouldn't it?

What if someone told you that Madonna, the outrageous singer and actress, hated to shock people? You would find that a little tough to swallow, a little hard to believe, wouldn't you?

What if you learned that Michael Jordan, the legendary forward for the Chicago Bulls, never really liked sports at all? That would be astonishing, wouldn't it?

Why would those things be surprising, even shocking? What makes you think Dave Thomas likes burgers? What makes you think Madonna likes to shock people? What makes you think Michael Jordan likes sports?

Seems pretty simple, doesn't it? You figure Dave Thomas likes hamburgers not only because he says he does on all those television commercials but also because he owns a chain of hamburger restaurants. Hamburgers seem to be part, not only of what he does, but of who he is. It's the same with Madonna and publicity. It's the same with Michael Jordan and basketball.

It's the same with God and unity.

God likes unity. He likes it when people live together in harmony. He likes it when people overcome their differences and become united in attitude and purpose. He likes it when people break down racial and cultural barriers, resolve disagreements, pitch in together, and share each other's sorrow and happiness.

Why is God so crazy about unity? Because he is *one.* Moses told the nation of Israel, "Hear, O Israel: The Lord our God, the Lord is one" (Deuteronomy 6:4, NIV). God is one; he is a unity. He is Father, Son, and Holy Spirit, yet he is—in his very nature and character—united.

That's why God values unity. That's why he wants us to value unity and to achieve unity: because when we do, we resemble our God.

 REFLECT: Since the time of Moses, Jews have recited Moses' words, "Hear, O Israel: The Lord our God, the Lord is one," twice daily as part of their morning and evening prayers. What did Moses mean when he told Israel, "The Lord is one" (Deuteronomy 6:4, NIV)?

 ACT: Try reciting Deuteronomy 6:4 as you brush your teeth these next few mornings and evenings. (It's easy to remember!)

 PRAY: "God, I'm glad I don't need to figure out which god will hear my prayers. You're the one Creator of the universe, the one heavenly Father, the one who loves the world—and that includes me. Thank you, God!"

26 United We Speak

Bible Reading: John 17:12-23

My prayer for all of them is that they will be one. John 17:21

DEMOCRAT OR REPUBLICAN?
Liberal or Conservative?
Pro-life or Pro-choice?
Israeli or Palestinian?
Muslim, Croat, or Serb?
Rich or poor?
Coke or Pepsi?
Chevy or Ford?

There are thousands of categories or choices that divide people. Some are incredibly important. Some are more polarizing than others. Some are just plain silly. (Just don't tell a Chevy truck owner that I said so.)

Many people are just plain sick and tired of all the division and disagreement and disunity that exists in the world. "Why can't we all just get along?" they cry. There ought to be some place where people aren't divided. There ought to be some way for people of different backgrounds, classes, customs, and temperaments to come together and get along.

There is. It's called *the church*.

God's will for the church is that it be the one place—the one *body,* actually—where people aren't divided along lines of race, nationality, gender, class, or denominational lines. He wants you and me and all Christians everywhere to be one with each other, just as the Father is one with the Son, and the Son is one with the Spirit, and the Spirit is one with the Father. Although the three members of the Godhead are different in some ways, they are one in nature, in purpose, in purity, in holiness.

Jesus, the Son, expressed his desire for unity among his followers. He said to God, the Father: "My prayer for all of them is that they will be one, just as you and I are one, Father—that just as you are in me and I am in you, so they will be in us, and the world will believe you sent me" (John 17:21).

The more you and I reflect God's standard of unity, the more people will believe that Jesus is the Christ, the Son of God. Our unity with each other—particularly because it's so rare in this sinful world—can be a testimony to the power of God.

 REFLECT: Why do you think unity among Christians will make non-Christians more likely to believe the gospel? When was the last time you spent time with a Christian of another race, culture, or denomination? How can you do so more often?

 ACT: Watch this week for the number "1" (on signs, advertisements, etc.), and use its appearance to remind you of the importance and benefit of unity.

 PRAY: "Thank you, God, that you are one with your Son, Jesus, and that Jesus is one with your Holy Spirit."

27 United We Stand?

Bible Reading: 2 Corinthians 13:7-11
We pray to God that you will not do anything wrong. 2 Corinthians 13:7

YOU'RE IN A hurry to catch your ride after school, so you stop Darla in the hall and hand her a slip of paper. "Would you do me a favor?" you ask her.

"Oh," she answers, almost clucking the word like a contented hen. "Of course!"

"Could you give this to Cindy Johnson?" you say, nodding to indicate the slip of paper. "She missed algebra class today, so I told her I'd write down the homework assignment for her."

"Oh," Darla answers. "I'm not talking to Cindy."

"Well," you say, still holding the slip toward Darla, "could you give it to Mike, her boyfriend? He can give it to Cindy."

Darla rolls her eyes. "Well," she says, "if I'm not talking to Cindy, I'm not talking to her boyfriend, either. Duh!"

"OK, OK," you say, still holding the slip and determined to think of something. "What about . . . could you, um, ask Joe Deters to give it to his brother Kyle, who works with Sylvia? Sylvia can give it to Cindy on her way home from work."

Darla's nose wrinkles as if she's just smelled a dead fish. "Joe Deters? Ugh! I can't be seen talking to Joe Deters! He's such a—such a—you know what I mean."

You nod, not totally sure whether you know what she means or not. But one thing you know for sure—you'll have to call Cindy with the homework assignment.

Darla may be extreme, but she's not too different from a lot of people who seem to divide the world into "the people I'm getting along with right now" and "the people I can't stand right now." Or they divide people into "my type" and "not my type." Or "friends" and "enemies." Or "cool" and "you gotta be kidding."

But that kind of behavior, believe it or not, often hurts the Darlas more than it hurts the Cindys or the Joes. You don't need to litter your life with broken friendships and burned-out relationships. You're not helping yourself if you hold on to old feuds and resentments.

Unity is so much better than disunity and division. Unity with others brings rewards; disunity only brings resentment. Living in harmony with others promotes peace; living in disharmony only brings about pain.

That's why God desires unity for his children. He knows unity brings much better results than division and disagreement.

 REFLECT: Is there anything in your life causing division between you and a friend? If so, what steps can you take to bring about harmony and unity with that friend?

 PRAY: Use Jesus' prayer for his disciples from John 17:21 to pray for yourself and your relationships with your friends and acquaintances. (For example, you may pray, "Father, my prayer for_____ is that we will be one.")

28 Ebenezer Stooge

Bible Reading: Ephesians 4:3-13
Always keep yourselves united in the Holy Spirit. Ephesians 4:3

EBENEZER STOOGE SAW a strange figure standing before his bed. Its hair was white, yet the spirit's face appeared as young and wrinkle-free as a skin cream commercial. It wore a long white gown and seemed to hang weightlessly in the air.

"Who the Dickens are you?" Stooge asked. "What are you doing here?"

The phantom said simply, "I have come to show you your past." The ghostly figure summoned Stooge to follow him. Stooge did, wearing only his oversized Xena, Warrior Princess T-shirt. They passed through Stooge's bedroom door and into a church, though none of the worshipers seemed to notice his sudden appearance.

"Look around," the phantom said.

Stooge looked around and recognized Carrie, a friend he'd made in Sunday school. Stooge had pretty much ended their friendship after a silly fight they had had in seventh grade. The phantom pointed at another figure. "Remember, in ninth grade you wanted to tell a friend about Christ, but you didn't know how?" Stooge nodded without looking at the figure; the memory was bitter because his friend had moved away soon after, and Stooge had never seen him again. "Carrie had the gift of evangelism, even at that young age. She could have helped you and your friend."

The phantom's bony finger next pointed to "Fish," one of Stooge's high school buddies, whom Stooge hadn't seen in years. Stooge had quit going to church because Fish had wanted him to join the choir. "Fish knows how to worship God in a way that few people do. He'd have been good for you, too."

Stooge began to feel a sinking sensation in his gut, when the strange figure pointed to the pastor. "You never did like him, did you? He just rubbed you the wrong way. But he could have taught you so much about the Bible."

"OK, OK!" Stooge shouted, grabbing the hand of the specter. "I've had enough, OK? I realize that if I hadn't separated myself from so many Christian brothers and sisters over the years, I'd be a much better Christian, a much better person than I am now, OK? If I had it to do all over again, I'd do it all differently."

Suddenly Stooge was back in his own bedroom. He no longer held the phantom's hand, but his fingers clasped his bedpost. The figure was gone, but Stooge heard a voice. "You have your wish," the voice said. "Do it differently."

 REFLECT: Ephesians 4:13 says that unity with other Christians can help us become mature and full grown in the Lord. How do you think unity with other Christians can help you in this way? Be as specific as you can.

 ACT: Reread Ephesians 4:3-13 in your Bible, circling every occurrence of the words *one* and *unity*.

 PRAY: "God, help me not to separate myself from other Christians. I want to become 'full grown in the Lord'."

29 Don't Copy the World

Bible Reading: Romans 12:1-2

Don't copy the behavior and customs of this world, but let God transform you into a new person by changing the way you think. Romans 12:2

YOU'RE IN SCHOOL, in the middle of a brutal math test. You know you've already missed three questions—and you're only on question 4! You look around the room, desperate for a morsel of hope, a little help. Then your eyes settle on the test paper of the kid who sits next to you. Working furiously, you erase your answers and copy the answers of Eugene Farklemeier, a student who's failing every class.

Or imagine this: You have no idea what to wear for homecoming, so you decide to go to the store. On the way to the door, you spy a magazine. "Ah!" you cry. You rip off the cover, take it to the mall, and buy an outfit similar to the one worn by the movie star on the cover—the movie star who topped the year's "worst dressed" list.

Or perhaps it happens like this: You're planning to try out for the school basketball team, and you notice that one of the kids in your gym class has managed to miss every shot he's taken. You approach him after gym class one day and explain, "I'm going to go out for basketball. Will you teach me how to shoot?"

Why would you try to copy test answers from a failing student? Why would you imitate the fashion choices of someone who was voted "worst dressed"? Why would you take basketball lessons from someone who couldn't shoot a basket with a camera?

That would be ridiculous, right? Right. But it's no less ridiculous for Christians to try to copy what the world does.

A lot of people in the world excuse sinful behavior by saying, "The way I figure, right and wrong are just relative, you know? What's right for you may not be right for me." Christians hear that, and before long they're copying the behavior and explaining away their own wrong choices.

You may watch movies or television shows you know are not pleasing to God, but you tell yourself, *Hey, I'm not the only one.* Or you may reason that *everybody* is drinking or dipping, using or abusing, so there's nothing wrong with your doing it.

But why would you want to copy what everybody is doing? Why copy something that doesn't work? If you want what the world wants and do what the world does, you'll end up like the world: sinful, miserable, and messed up. But if you let God transform you into a new person—one who by the power of his Spirit copies *God* instead of the world—you'll not only please God, you'll take your life to a whole new level of fulfillment and enjoyment.

REFLECT: What warning does Romans 12:1-2 give? What can you do to heed the warning?

PRAY: "God, I don't want to copy this sinful world; I want to be transformed into a new person. Please change the way I think, especially in the area of_____."

30 The Moral Laboratory

Bible Reading: 1 Timothy 5:1-4
Children or grandchildren . . . should learn first of all to put their religion into practice by caring for their own family. 1 Timothy 5:4, NIV

THE STRANGE CASE of Dr. Jekyll and Mr. Hyde is a classic story written by Robert Louis Stevenson. It tells the story of an odd scientist, Dr. Jekyll, who conducted strange, secret experiments in his house. These experiments produced great concern, even fear, among Dr. Jekyll's neighbors and friends and even threatened the doctor's own life. As a result of the research he conducted in his laboratory, Jekyll—a well-respected doctor—was enabled to transform himself into a man totally unlike himself: snarling, skulking, sinister.

It may surprise you to learn that you can do the same in a laboratory of your own. No, you don't call 1-800-B-A-GHOUL. You can't buy your own home laboratory on any infomercial. You don't need to; your home is already a laboratory. It's a moral laboratory, in which you can learn to make right choices and develop strong moral character or in which you can learn to make wrong choices and deaden your conscience.

In fact, your home and family is a virtual hothouse for growing strong moral convictions, like a greenhouse grows carnations.

When your parents are having a tough day, what better opportunity is there to practice doing good to others? When your sister screams at you for walking in front of the TV, what better environment is there to practice patience? When your brother feeds the last piece of your birthday cake to the dog, what better chance will you have to practice mercy?

The problem is, of course, that most of us tend to think that our own homes are the *last* places on earth where we need to be respectful and patient and merciful—we save all that good stuff for our friends. But home is the laboratory where we should be learning to make right choices and do the right thing. If we can start getting it right in our own families, we'll be a lot more likely to make the right choice when we're out in the world—when we have to face an impossible teacher, a girlfriend or boyfriend who wants to get physical, or a friend who's trying to tempt us to do wrong.

They say that "practice makes perfect." And the perfect place to practice doing right—being patient, being respectful, being loving, being merciful—is at home.

 REFLECT: Are you most like the good Dr. Jekyll or the sinister Mr. Hyde when you're home? When you're away from home? Think of one way you can put your religion into practice in your family this week. Make plans to practice that behavior each day this week.

 PRAY: "Father, it's hard to do the right thing at home when_____. Help me as I practice right behavior this week."

1 May Day

Bible Reading: Isaiah 40:6-8

The grass withers and the flowers fade, but the word of our God stands forever. Isaiah 40:8

TAKE THE MAY Day Challenge! See how many answers in the following quiz you can get right. Circle T for True and F for False.

The sun revolves around the earth.	T	F
Tomatoes are poisonous.	T	F
Sneezes are the body's way of getting rid of evil spirits.	T	F
Iron, lead, and other metals can be transformed into gold by a chemical process.	T	F
The world is flat.	T	F
Trees have souls.	T	F
The Black Death was caused by evil vapors.	T	F

So, how many did you mark false? How many did you identify as being true?

The truth is, all of the statements above are false. While all of those statements *were* once thought to be true, the truth is, they have always been false.

For thousands of years, many people thought the sun revolved around the earth. But what they *thought* did not change what was true. The sun was the center of the solar system the whole time! Similarly, the fact that people once considered tomatoes— or "love apples" as they called them—to be poisonous didn't change the truth. And no matter how many people agreed that the "Black Death," or bubonic plague, was caused by "evil vapors," the truth (that the deadly plague is spread by fleas from infected rats) never changed.

Truth doesn't change. People may be mistaken. Stories may be incorrect. Ideas may be wrong. But truth doesn't change.

A prophet named Isaiah once wrote that "the word of our God stands forever" (Isaiah 40:8). And Jesus once prayed to his Father, "Your word is truth" (John 17:17, NIV). No matter what textbooks or teachers may say, no matter what you read in the newspaper or hear on the evening news, no matter what new light may be shed on old mysteries, the truth will never change. We may deny it or acknowledge it. We may ignore it or recognize it, but whether we know it or admit that we know it, the truth is the truth. And it doesn't change.

REFLECT: Can you think of other things that were once thought to be true but never were? Can you change what's true by admitting it or denying it? Can anyone do that? Since Jesus said God's word is truth, do you think followers of Jesus should: *(a)* believe the Bible? *(b)* read the Bible? *(c)* memorize parts of the Bible? *(d)* obey the Bible? *(e)* do all of these? Which do you do? Which do you need to do more of?

PRAY: "Thank you, God, that your Word will always be true."

2 Pluto, Where Are You?

Bible Reading: Matthew 6:22-23
Your eye is a lamp for your body. A pure eye lets sunshine into your soul.
Matthew 6:22

EVER HEAR OF Pluto? No, not Mickey Mouse's dog. We're talking about the ninth planet in our solar system.

Did you know that there was no proof, until 1930, that the planet Pluto existed? People knew about Mercury, Venus, Mars, Jupiter, and Saturn. They had even discovered two "new" planets—Uranus and Neptune. But the solar system was still one player short of a baseball team.

A lot of scientists suspected—because of the way Uranus and Neptune traveled around the sun—that there was probably a ninth planet in the solar system. But they couldn't prove it; they couldn't see it. The telescopes way back then just weren't powerful enough. However, a scientist named Percival Lowell had predicted the existence of another planet. He tried hard to prove his suspicion, but he died in 1916 without doing so.

Then, in 1929 a special camera was built and installed at the Lowell Observatory in Flagstaff, Arizona, just to try to find the planet Percival Lowell predicted would be "out there." In January 1930 Clyde W. Tombaugh was taking photographs of the area where the unknown planet should be. As he compared the photographs from two different days he noticed a "dot" that moved in a way that could only be explained if it were the planet. Clyde Tombaugh had "discovered" Pluto, something Percival Lowell had never been able to do because he didn't have the right telescope.

A lot of people "suspect" that some things are right and other things are wrong. A lot of people figure that hating and hurting people are both wrong, for example. They have a "feeling"—at least most of the time—that dishonesty is bad and honesty is good. They have a "hunch" that "right" and "wrong" are out there somewhere, but they have trouble "finding" them and "proving" their existence. Proverbs 4:19 explains that "the way of the wicked is like complete darkness. Those who follow it have no idea what they are stumbling over."

When we believe God's Word and accept him as the standard for right and wrong, we're able to see things more clearly. And that makes our choices much easier. We don't have to "guess" or "suspect" what's right or wrong. We don't have to depend on our hunches. We just have to believe what God says.

 REFLECT: Do you think the fact that many people don't believe in the Bible affects whether or not it's true? Why or why not? Do you have trouble believing what God has said about right and wrong? Or do you tend to see choices between right and wrong more clearly than your friends or classmates who don't believe the Bible?

 PRAY: "Lord, be the lens through which I see everything, especially decisions about right and wrong. Make clear to me what is the right choice, and help me to discover and follow the right way."

3 That's the Truth, Ruth!

Bible Reading: 1 Kings 22:6, 13, 15-16
Tell me nothing but the truth. 1 Kings 22:16, NIV

WITNESSES IN A courtroom are told to lift their right hands and promise to tell the truth, the whole truth, and nothing but the truth. Have you ever wondered why they don't just promise to tell the truth and leave it at that? Well, it's because some people may tell the truth—but not the whole truth. Others may tell the truth but add a lie to it.

See if the following examples help you understand why truth must be pure and complete in order to be truth:

The Whole Truth	*Less Than the Truth*	*More Than the Truth*
Philo T. Farnsworth invented the technology that made television possible.	Philo T. Farnsworth invented television.	Philo T. Farnsworth invented television, radio, CD players, micro-waves, and laser guns.
In the 1700s, politicians like George Washington often wore powdered wigs.	George Washington wore a wig.	George Washington wore a wig and other sissy clothes.
Charles Lindbergh was the first person to fly alone across the Atlantic Ocean.	Charles Lindbergh was the first person to fly across the Atlantic Ocean.	Charles Lindbergh flew across the Atlantic to bring back Limburger cheese.
Jesus is the Christ, the Son of God.	Jesus was a great teacher.	Jesus, Muhammad, and Michael Jordan are all God.
I left my unfinished home-work at home.	I left my homework at home.	My dog ate my homework before I could finish it.

See the difference? Telling the truth (but not the whole truth) can be deceiving. And, of course, adding a lie to the truth is no better.

That's why the courts—and God, as a matter of fact—want us to tell the truth, the whole truth, and nothing but the truth. God wants us to be completely truthful in what we say and do because he is completely true in everything he says and does. He says, "I, the Lord, speak only what is true and right" (Isaiah 45:19).

 REFLECT: Which do you want your friends, family, teachers, and others to tell *you:*
a. the truth?
b. the whole truth?
c. nothing but the truth?
d. all of the above?
Which do you think your friends or parents would choose? Why?

 PRAY: "Lord, I want to be truthful in all I say. Help me not to add or subtract anything that will make what I say something other than the truth."

4 Pilgrim's Gladness

Bible Reading: Psalm 32:1-5

What joy for those whose record the Lord has cleared of sin, whose lives are lived in complete honesty! Psalm 32:2

JOHN BUNYAN'S FAMOUS book, *Pilgrim's Progress,* is the story of a young man named Christian, who carries a heavy burden on his back everywhere he goes.

Everyone Christian meets seems to have an opinion as to how he can get rid of his burden. "Forget it," says one. "Ignore it," says another. "Overcome it by doing good," says another. But nothing seems to relieve Christian of his burden until he arrives at a highway fenced on either side by a wall. Christian runs along that road, "but not without great difficulty," Bunyan writes, "because of the load on his back."

> He ran thus till he came at a place somewhat ascending; and upon that place stood a cross, and a little below, in the bottom, a sepulchre. So I saw in my dream, that just as Christian came up with the cross, his burden loosed from off his shoulders, and fell from off his back, and began to tumble, and so continued to do, till it came to the mouth of the sepulchre, where it fell in, and I saw it no more. . . . Then was Christian glad and lightsome, and said with a merry heart, "He hath given me rest by His sorrow, and Life by His Death." Then he stood still awhile to look and wonder; for it was very surprising to him, that the sight of the Cross should thus ease him of his burden. He looked therefore, and looked again, even till the springs that were in his head sent the waters down his cheeks. . . .

John Bunyan's words are old-fashioned, but Christian's experiences still happen to people. Nothing matches what a person feels when God forgives him or her of sin, rolls that burden of sin and guilt away, and brings his salvation to a human heart.

If you've never asked God to forgive your sin and make you a new person, if you've never repented of your wrongdoing and determined to follow Jesus for the rest of your life—do it now, and you'll know exactly what the psalmist sang about and what John Bunyan wrote about.

If you *have* experienced the forgiveness of your sins, remember that path you took to joy: It involved admitting that you had sinned, asking for God's forgiveness, and accepting that forgiveness. It's the same process you should follow whenever you make a wrong choice, even as a Christian: Admit the wrongness of your choice, ask for forgiveness, and accept God's forgiveness on the basis of his love and Jesus' sacrifice for your sins.

 REFLECT: In *Pilgrim's Progress,* what did Christian's burden represent? What did the cross and the sepulchre (tomb) stand for? Has God cleared your record of sin? If not, why not? Is there any sin you need to confess and seek forgiveness for right now?

 PRAY: Reread Psalm 32:1-5 out loud, changing the words, if necessary, to make it your own personal prayer to God.

5 One Who Is True

Bible Reading: John 7:28-29

Then Jesus, in the middle of his teaching, called out in the Temple, "So you know me and know where I have come from? But I have not come of my own accord; I am sent by One who is true and you do not know him!" John 7:28-29, Phillips

GEORGE BALANCHINE WAS a famous ballet teacher/choreographer.

Maury Wills was a baseball player, one of the speediest base runners of all time.

Fra Filippo Lippi was a great Italian painter in the fifteenth century.

Martin Luther King Jr. was an American civil rights leader of the sixties.

Christopher Wren was a renowned architect, who rebuilt much of London after the Great Fire of 1666.

Each of these individuals excelled at something—baseball, painting, statesmanship. But there is something else that each of them had in common with the others: They not only did something well, they taught others.

Balanchine's students seemed to dance like no one else; his style and genius was evident in the techniques of those who learned from him. Lippi was a great artist, but the fame of his students—such as Sandro Botticelli and his own son, Filippino Lippi—equaled or excelled his own. Martin Luther King Jr. changed the face of American politics; those who learned from him (such as Andrew Young and Jesse Jackson) extended his influence. Christopher Wren was a genius in the field of architecture, but many young architects since his time have been influenced by his work.

Those people were "masters," individuals who became so good at what they did that other people worked hard to learn from them and imitate them.

Well, when it comes to morality—knowing and doing what is right—there is only one Master, and that is God. Everyone else among us fumbles around, sometimes doing right but often doing wrong. Only God is good (Mark 10:18). And he is good all the time. He is the Master we must all learn from.

Not only that, unlike Balanchine, Lippi, King, and Wren, God is not only skilled in his "field," he is the Creator and originator of everything that is good. In other words, the reason honesty is right (for example), is because God is true. There is nothing false in him. And because God is always true, he wants us to tell the truth and to be honest in everything we do.

 REFLECT: How many schoolteachers (including Sunday school) do you think you've had? Which teacher do you think has had the most influence on you in the area of honesty?

Do you think people would describe you as real and truthful? Would you describe yourself that way? How can you be more like the "Master" in truthfulness?

 PRAY: "God, I need your help to be truthful to_____ today."

Great Kick

Bible Reading: 2 Timothy 4:7–8
Run in such a way that you will win. 1 Corinthians 9:24

ONE OF THE most exciting races in the Olympics took place in Munich, Germany, in 1972. The favorite in the men's 800-meter race was Evgeniy Arzhanov from the Soviet Union. He had not lost an 800-meter finals race in four years, and everyone expected that record to remain intact.

The American runner was David Wottle, an exciting runner who always wore a painter's hat when he ran, making it easy to find him in the pack. Wottle's strategy in most races was to stay near or at the back of the pack of runners, waiting until very near the end to "kick" into a fast run, catching up to and often passing all the other runners before the finish line. But Wottle had run his fastest time ever just to get to the Olympics, and some felt he couldn't run that fast again. Plus, he had been less than healthy in the days leading up to the Olympics.

The race began predictably. A couple runners from Kenya started out fast, taking the lead early. Wottle was way back in sixth place as Arzhanov took over the lead from the Kenyans. Then, in the last two hundred meters, Wottle thought he noticed Arzhanov begin to slow down. Knowing that the end of the race was his strongest part, Wottle continued to "kick," catching up to Arzhanov at the finish line.

The record books show both Arzhanov and Wottle with the same time (1:45.9), but they list David Wottle as the winner of the gold medal—by a "nose," Arzhanov said.

Obeying God and choosing right may seem like an Olympic race. A lot of times it's hard to be honest, for example. Friends may make fun of you for being honest. The truth may be embarrassing. Sometimes being truthful can even get you into trouble! In the short run, honesty may seem like a "losing" strategy.

But even if honesty is hard in the short run, it is better in the long run. You may feel as if you're making a mistake by being honest. You may wonder if you're losing out by doing the right thing. But even when it's hard, honesty really is the best policy. Because it's right. Because God "watches over the path of the godly" (Psalm 1:6). Because life is a race *to the finish* (1 Corinthians 9:24; 2 Timothy 4:7–8).

REFLECT: Do you think David Wottle would have won if he had tried to keep up with the Kenyan runners? Why or why not? If you decide to be honest only when it's in your best interests, how will you know when it's "better" to be honest? If you decide (and seek God's help) to be honest all the time, do you think your choices will be clearer? easier? right?

ACT: Challenge a friend or family member to a race. Use the race as an opportunity to share the message of today's reading.

PRAY: "God, sometimes I feel like I'm losing when I do the honest thing. Please help me to remember that I'm in the race to the finish."

The Shepherd and the Wolf

Bible Reading: 1 Peter 2:11-12

Be careful how you live among your unbelieving neighbors. Even if they accuse you of doing wrong, they will see your honorable behavior, and they will believe. 1 Peter 2:12

THERE ONCE WAS a shepherd boy who kept his flock not far from a little village. One day, while watching the sheep all by himself, he decided to play a little trick on the people in the village. He started running toward the village, shouting, "Wolf! Wolf! A wolf is attacking my sheep!"

The villagers all left their shops and homes and fields to help him, following him all the way out to the field where he kept his sheep. But when they arrived, there was no sign of any wolf. The boy laughed at his little joke, and the people returned to their village, shaking their heads at the boy's foolishness.

Some time later the shepherd boy got a little bored and decided to play his little trick again. Once more he ran to the village, once more the villagers came to help him, but once more they discovered there was no wolf.

Still later the shepherd boy got a little lonely in the fields by himself, so he tried his trick a third time, with the same results. The villagers came and discovered that they'd been fooled again.

Then one day a wolf really did break into the sheepfold and began killing the boy's lambs. He tried to chase the wolf away, but he could not. At last, he ran to the village, crying, "Wolf! Wolf! A wolf is attacking my sheep!"

The people in the village heard his cries for help, but no one paid any attention to the boy; they thought he was fooling them again. No matter how loudly or how insistently he cried, no one believed the boy, and he lost all his sheep that day.

This fable illustrates an important truth. The person who is dishonest not only hurts others, he hurts himself, too.

Dishonesty cuts both ways. That's part of the reason God commands honesty—he wants to protect us from the harm dishonesty will do to us. He wants to protect us from having a bad reputation. He wants us to enjoy the rewards that come from being trustworthy and from having people believe what we say. And he knows that the only way to truly achieve those rewards is by being honest.

 REFLECT: Have you ever had trouble getting someone to believe you were telling the truth? If so, what did it feel like? Did it make you feel good? bad? frustrated? insulted? What's the best way to avoid those kinds of feelings in the future?

 ACT: Write the slogan "Honesty is the best policy" on an index card and post it where it will remind you often of the benefits of being honest. (If you're artistic, you might want to add a drawing of a sheep or a shepherd's crook to remind you of the boy who cried wolf.)

 PRAY: "Help me never to tell a lie" (Proverbs 30:8).

The Sun, the Moon, and Caterpillar Cocoons

Bible Reading: James 1:17-18

Every good and perfect gift is from above, coming down from the Father of the heavenly lights, who does not change like shifting shadows.
James 1:17, NIV

DO YOU KNOW where glass comes from? How about rubber or penicillin? See if you can match each item in the left column with its source in the right column.

1. RUBBER	A. THE SUN
2. SILK	B. SEA ANIMALS
3. PENICILLIN	C. SAND, LIME, AND SODA
4. GLASS	D. SHEEP
5. MOONLIGHT	E. ELEPHANT TUSKS
6. SPONGES	F. MOLD
7. WOOL	G. TREES
8. WAX	H. CATERPILLAR COCOONS
9. LEATHER	I. ANIMAL, VEGETABLE, AND MINERAL OILS
10. IVORY	J. ANIMAL SKINS

So, how many did you get right? More important, what's the point? Well, how about this: Can you add one more answer in the column on the right that would be the source for every one of the things in the left-hand column?

If you answered, "God," congratulations! You're right. God is the source of *all* those things on the left. He is also the source of all those items listed on the right. In fact, God is the source of *all* good—not just good "things," like roses and kittens and chocolate and laughter. He is the source of everything that is good—like honesty, faithfulness, courage, respect, love, and life. "Good" comes from God because he is good. "Right" comes from God because he is righteous. The definition of what is "moral" comes from God, because he is holy.

 REFLECT: Based on today's reading, what title would you give God? (For example, he is called Jehovah-jireh, which means "my provider.") Come up with your own name.
Do you ever try to "get" good things by disobeying God? Do you think good can come from doing wrong? Why or why not?

 ACT: Cover up the right column of the list above, and quiz your parents to see if they know the source of each item in the left column. Then surprise them by informing them that one answer can be given for all of the items in the left column: God!

 PRAY: "Thanks, God, for being the source of all the good things that are mine, including_____."

9 A-Maze-ing!

Bible Reading: 1 Timothy 6:11-12

But you . . . belong to God; so run from all these evil things, and follow what is right and good. Pursue a godly life, along with faith, love, perseverance, and gentleness. 1 Timothy 6:11

HAVE YOU EVER tried to find your way through a maze? It can be fun, frustrating, tiring, easy, or hard. See if you can find your way through the maze below:

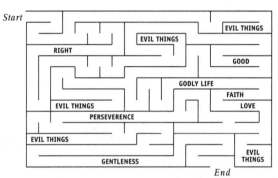

So how'd you do? Was it too easy? Too hard? What did you do when you realized you were headed into a passage that led to "evil things"? Did you keep going, or did you turn around and start again?

That maze symbolizes the many choices you face in life. There's no way you'll be able to go through life without ever facing—even making—a wrong choice. (You've already found that out, haven't you?) But two choices you can make in life—just like in mazes—are to look ahead and to avoid paths that lead to evil.

Even when you look ahead, though, sometimes you'll make the wrong choice and go down the wrong path. Sometimes you'll even do it on purpose. But when you realize you're headed down the wrong path, the safest—and smartest—course is to stop, admit you were wrong, and turn around. That's not always as easy in life as it is in mazes and puzzles, but it will save you a lot of trouble and sadness. It will also help you get through the maze of life instead of getting stuck in a dead end.

 REFLECT: How is your spiritual life like the maze? What should you do when you realize you are going the wrong way spiritually? Can you think of a time when you turned away from a wrong choice you made (or almost made)? Was the result of your decision good or bad? Do you regret any wrong choices you've made? Why or why not? Do you regret any right choices you've made? Why or why not?

 ACT: Draw your own maze sometime today or tomorrow (like during study hall at school) to remind yourself to turn away from wrong choices and follow what is right.

 PRAY: "God, help me to 'follow what is right and good.'"

Reflecting His Image

Bible Reading: 2 Corinthians 3:17-18

And all of us . . . can be mirrors that brightly reflect the glory of the Lord. And as the Spirit of the Lord works within us, we become more and more like him and reflect his glory even more. 2 Corinthians 3:18

LENNY GOT to spend the day at the bank with his father. They called it "Take Your Child to Work Day."

As his father showed him around behind the tellers' counter, he pointed out a neat machine that counted bills. The teller had just taken a wrapper off a stack of one-hundred-dollar bills and was putting them in the counting machine.

"Hey," Lenny said. "That money looks funny!"

His father took a couple bills from the machine and showed them to Lenny.

"They've just come out with a new one-hundred-dollar bill to make it more difficult to make fake ones. See, the picture is larger, they've moved it off-center, they've used a special kind of paper . . . and if you hold it up to the light, you can see a strip with writing on it. While it might be possible to make a good copy of most of what you see on the bill, it's supposed to be harder to copy everything."

Lenny was confused. "You mean whenever you get a hundred-dollar bill, you have to hold it up to the light?"

Lenny's father chuckled. "No," he said. "Bank tellers are trained to recognize counterfeit money by handling nothing but the real thing. They sort and stack and shuffle real money all day long, hour after hour. The more they see and handle the real thing, the easier it is for them to recognize a fake because something about it just won't feel right. When a counterfeit bill comes along, a teller's familiarity with the real thing will help him or her notice something different about the counterfeit. *That's* when he holds it up to the light or gets a magnifying glass or asks for the head teller to inspect it. But usually a teller is so familiar with real money, he can spot a fake pretty easily."

"That's neat," Lenny said. He smiled at his dad. "Think you could give me a bunch to practice on?"

"Sure," Dad said, "in your dreams."

 REFLECT: It's easier to know whether something is real—or "right"—by being familiar with the original. When it comes to choices between right and wrong, God is the original. How well do you know God? Does your relationship with God help you make right choices? How can you know God even better? How can you "reflect his glory" even more?

 PRAY: "Lord, make me willing to let your Spirit work within me so that I can become more like you and reflect your glory."

Shifting Sands

Bible Reading: Psalm 90:1-4

Before the mountains were created, before you made the earth and the world, you are God, without beginning or end. Psalm 90:2

THE SANDS OF a desert are constantly changing.

Sand dunes sometimes move across the desert like large, lumbering beasts; the wind blows against them, and they lose sand on one side and gain it on another—constantly shifting, changing, moving. A dune may grow to a height of five or six hundred feet and later disappear.

Sometimes the desert sands drift over farmlands, covering the fields and destroying crops. Sometimes the sands blow across a small city or town and fill its streets and alleys; some ancient towns have been buried beneath sand for hundreds of years.

The shifting sands of a desert can make travel difficult, even impossible. A cart or wagon cannot roll through the deep sands. Horses will soon become exhausted trying to step through shifting dunes, often sinking chest-deep. Humans trying to walk in desert sands often take a step or two forward before sliding a step or two back.

It is easy to get lost in a sandy desert, too, because the landscape is constantly changing. Dunes look different on one side than they do on the other, and the shape of the terrain can change in a matter of hours.

The shifting sands of a desert can be dangerous. The same is true of shifting opinions and ideas about what's right and what's wrong.

You see, some people think that they can decide what's right or wrong. "The way I see it," they say, "such-and-such is wrong." Or "*I* don't think it would be so wrong to do so-and-so." They may decide that a thing they thought was wrong last week is OK today. They may figure that something is OK for *them* to do, even though it would be wrong for someone else to do it to them.

But that kind of thinking is not only dangerous, it's wrong. It's not up to you and me to decide right from wrong. We can't rely on our own ideas or opinions; those things may change from week to week or day to day—even hour to hour, but right and wrong don't change according to what *we* think.

The only reliable standard of right and wrong is the unchanging God. He's the same yesterday, today, and forever. He doesn't change his mind. He doesn't forget stuff. He doesn't change the rules if he's in a bad mood. Our attitudes may vary, our moods may shift, our opinions may change, but God remains the same.

 REFLECT: Have you changed any of your opinions or ideas in the last few months? weeks? days? Has God changed during that time?

Do you make choices based on what you think or based on what others think? Or do you make choices based on what God thinks? Can you think of a time when you did each of the above?

 PRAY: "God, I praise you for your unchanging nature. Help me rely on you—not on myself or on my own ideas—for guidance, especially in the area of_____."

12 Bad Company

Bible Reading: 2 Corinthians 6:14–7:1
Don't team up with those who are unbelievers. 2 Corinthians 6:14

A GREAT STAG (an adult male deer), mighty and majestic, became sick and staggered off to a corner of the pasture, where he often fed. He chose a lush, green corner, where plant life abounded and where he could rest until he regained his strength.

His companions came to his resting place in great numbers to see him and to ask how he was doing. Each one, however, thinking only of himself, helped himself to the lush food that surrounded the ailing deer until the ground all around his bed was bare and the food was all gone.

Before long, the stag died, not from his sickness, but from the hunger and weakness his evil companions had caused.

That story, based on one of Aesop's fables, is an illustration of how bad company can hurt you. It's just one example of why the Bible says, "Don't team up with those who are unbelievers" (2 Corinthians 6:14).

That doesn't mean that God wants you to turn your back on people who don't know him. You can still follow God's command to treat everyone kindly and with respect. You should still witness to unbelievers and try to help them trust Christ for salvation.

However, if you're obeying God and growing closer to him, you'll find that you have less and less in common with unbelievers. After all, like the Bible says, "How can goodness be a partner with wickedness? How can light live with darkness? What harmony can there be between Christ and the Devil? How can a believer be a partner with an unbeliever?" (2 Corinthians 6:14-15).

Some people apply these verses mainly to dating relationships. However, the warning applies also to friendships, business partnerships, and so on.

Right now, it's important that you choose carefully the friends you spend the most time with. Seek out Christian friends who will help you grow in your faith. And think about these words from Scripture: "Do not be misled: 'Bad company corrupts good character'" (1 Corinthians 15:33, NIV). They're a good reminder that bad company—like the sick stag's companions—will do you more harm than good.

 REFLECT: Are your closest friends Christians or non-Christians? Do your closest friends influence you in good ways, or are they sometimes a bad influence? Do you need to seek out more Christian friends who will help you grow in your faith?

 ACT: Light a candle sometime today or tomorrow to remind you that light has no "fellowship" with darkness.

PRAY: "God, show me where I need to back off from friendships with non-Christians, such as_____, and help me to choose to spend more time with Christian friends, including_____."

Bible Reading: 2 Corinthians 7:2-4

We have not done wrong to anyone. We have not led anyone astray. We have not taken advantage of anyone. 2 Corinthians 7:2

YOU ARE SURROUNDED with warning systems.

Chances are, your family car has several warning systems that will alert you to the fact that your seat belt isn't fastened, the headlights are on, the keys are still in the ignition, the door is ajar. It's even possible to equip a car to emit a loud, annoying sound if the speed exceeds a certain level (say, fifty-five miles per hour).

There may be smoke detectors in your house that will beep loudly if their sensors detect the presence of smoke in the air. The electrical circuits in your house probably have fuses or circuit breakers that prevent the wires from getting too hot. Some homes have burglar alarms that will activate lights and sirens if a door or window is disturbed.

A school bus has more flashing lights than an alien spaceship. Railroad crossings are equipped with flashing lights, clanging bells, and barricades that block the road. Garbage trucks use loud beeps to warn you that the vehicle is backing up.

Such alarms and warning systems are all around you. And inside you.

That's right, inside you. You have a "personal warning system" of your own. Oh, it won't beep if you forget your homework, nor will it flash bright lights if you sit in Bruno the Bully's seat in the school cafeteria. But you do have one. Everyone does.

Your personal warning system is called a conscience. It emits a silent "beep" in your soul when you're thinking of doing wrong. Like any alarm, you can ignore it. But if you repeatedly do wrong in spite of its warnings, your conscience does you no more good than a disconnected burglar alarm or a smoke alarm without a battery. In fact, just like those things, it can even cause disastrous consequences.

But there's nothing better than a fully operational conscience—especially when it's clear. Scripture urges you to keep it that way: "Cling tightly to your faith in Christ, and always keep your conscience clear" (1 Timothy 1:19). A clear conscience will not only help you sleep better, it will help you enjoy life better, because a clear conscience is a source of joy to the soul.

REFLECT: In today's Bible reading, Paul told the Christians in Corinth that he had a clear conscience about his dealings with them. What kinds of good things resulted from his clear conscience?

Do you have a clear conscience? If not, confess whatever sin is on your heart, ask God to forgive you, and accept his forgiveness. You may also have to make restitution to anyone you've wronged.

ACT: The next time you pick up a glass of water to drink, notice how clear it is, and pray a silent prayer that God will help you keep your conscience clear.

PRAY: "God, I know my conscience won't be effective if I ignore its warning about _____. Help me cling to the faith I have in Christ and do my part to keep my conscience clear."

Bible Reading: 2 Corinthians 7:9-11

The result was to make you sorry as God would have had you sorry, and not to make you feel injured by what we said. The sorrow which God uses means a change of heart and leads to salvation without regret.
2 Corinthians 7:9-10, Phillips

RECENTLY, IN A big city the local police raided what they thought was a crack house. After searching for a few moments and finding nothing even remotely suspicious, the police realized they had the wrong house! The crack house was *next door*. By the time the police realized their mistake, the inhabitants of the real crack house had escaped, and the police had a lot of explaining to do.

In another town the local fire department scheduled a practice drill. Using a house they thought was scheduled for demolition, the fire department carefully set fire to it so they could practice their firefighting technique. Unfortunately, the condemned house was a block away! As you can imagine, the person who lived in the house was a little upset when he returned home to a pile of ashes.

Usually, our mistakes are a lot smaller than setting fire to the wrong house. But we all make mistakes. We can't avoid them—they're part of being human. The important thing is not whether we make mistakes, because everyone does; the important thing is how we respond when we make a mistake.

Now, sometimes our mistakes are sinful. Other times they're just mistakes. But whether our mistakes involve a wrong choice or just a poor choice, the way to respond is pretty much the same.

The first thing you can do when you make a mistake is *admit it*. That may seem pretty obvious, but it's surprising how many people have trouble doing that. The second part of a proper response to a mistake is to *apologize* to anyone your mistake hurt. (If your mistake was sinful, this would include God.) The third step is to try to *correct* the mistake. This isn't always possible (you can't "unburn" a house, for example), but you should do what you can to erase the effects of your mistake. Then, if your mistake was sinful, you should *accept* God's forgiveness and try (with his help) to do better the next time. Oh, yeah, one more thing—always remember to check (and double-check) the address of any house you intend to assault.

 REFLECT: What do you think is the difference between a mistake that's sinful and a mistake that's not sinful? Are there any recent mistakes you've made that you need to admit, apologize for, and try to make amends for? How will you do it? Do you think you'll ever stop making mistakes? Do you think you can (with God's help) make fewer wrong choices? Do you think you can (with God's help) do a better job of admitting and correcting your mistakes?

 PRAY: "Lord, I admit that I should (or shouldn't) have_____. I apologize for my sins. Show me how to correct the things I've done wrong, and help me not to do them again."

15 Strange But True

Bible Reading: Deuteronomy 11:1

Love the Lord your God and keep his requirements, his decrees, his laws and his commands always. Deuteronomy 11:1, NIV

BE CAREFUL WHEN you are in Kahoka, Missouri, especially if you are joining a procession lit by torches. You see, it is against the law in Kahoka to carry an open flame through the street. You can carry a lantern but not a candle (unless it's inside a glass case).

If you live in North Carolina, you should resist the urge to use an elephant to pull your plow through a cotton field. Otherwise, you could be fined; plowing with an elephant in a cotton field is against the law in North Carolina.

A Wisconsin law is still on the books requiring all train passengers to carry an axe and a handsaw with them.

Crazy laws, huh? They make no sense, right? Well, not exactly. They make a little more sense when you understand the reasons behind them.

For example, there was apparently a fire in Kahoka, Missouri, that could have been avoided if someone had been more careful in carrying an open flame (probably when houses were heated by wood stoves—if the fire went out, you'd borrow a light from a neighbor). North Carolina folks may have been bothered by a farmer who used an elephant to plow his fields. (Maybe the elephant just smelled too bad, or the animal might have gotten loose and hurt someone or damaged something. After all, elephants don't have brakes.) And a tragic fire on a train in Wisconsin (when fires were pretty common on trains) resulted in the law to carry axes and handsaws (so you could get out if the train caught on fire).

Makes sense, huh? The laws make a lot more sense when you understand something about why they were created in the first place. The same is true of God's commandments. We can't always understand God's laws, but we do know that his commands don't just arise out of nowhere. He gave his commandments to protect us and provide for us and to help us become more and more like him.

And even if we don't understand all of God's laws, they provide an opportunity to trust him and show how much we love him by obeying him, even when we don't understand.

REFLECT: Think about the laws or rules in your city, state, province, school, or family. Can you think of the reasons behind rules like "Obey the speed limit," "Don't run in the hallways," and "Eat all your vegetables"?

How do God's laws protect you? Do they protect you if you disobey them? Why or why not?

PRAY: "God, thank you for giving me your wise commands. Help me to obey you and make right choices, especially when_____."

You may also want to pray the psalmist's prayer from Psalm 119:35: "Make me walk along the path of your commands, for that is where my happiness is found."

16 True or False?

Bible Reading: Psalm 119:30-32

I have chosen the way of truth; I have set my heart on your laws.
Psalm 119:30, NIV

TESTS. YOU LIKE to take tests, right?

"Yeah, right," you say. "About as much as I like getting a tooth pulled . . . on my birthday . . . by a dentist using a pair of rusty pliers . . . with no anesthetic!"

OK, OK. But if you had to take a test, what *kind* of test would you choose? Essay?

"Yeah, right," you answer. "When donkeys fly."

Fill-in-the-blank?

"NOT! Fill-in-the-blank tests are better than essay, but . . ."

Multiple choice?

"Multiple choice isn't bad," you answer, "but . . ."

True/false?

"Bingo!" you answer. "Wouldn't *everybody* choose a true/false test?"

Well, maybe not everybody. But most people would. Why? Because there are only two possible answers to any question on a true/false test. True . . . or false.

"Duh," you say. "Tell me something I don't know."

OK, so it seems pretty simple, right? Some things are true and some things are false. That's just the way it is, right? Either "all deserts have sand," or they don't (they don't). Either John Wilkes Booth shot Abraham Lincoln or he didn't (he did). Either snakes are warm-blooded, or they're not (they're not).

The same thing is true when it comes to right and wrong. Not everybody admits it or recognizes it, but truth exists in moral and spiritual areas just like it does in science or geography or math. Hating other people is wrong (true). Respecting other people is right (true). Honesty is bad (false). Generosity is good (true).

Of course, some people say there is no such thing as truth. But that would mean every answer on a true/false test would have to be right. That might make it easier for you to get good grades. But it wouldn't make you any smarter, would it?

 REFLECT: What would life be like if things couldn't be proven "true" or "false"? Could you know whether to follow a friend's advice? Could you know how much a pizza really costs or how to build a model car? What would school be like? Could you learn how to do math problems or find out in which classroom your homeroom meets?

In Psalm 119:30, the psalmist says he has chosen "the way of truth." What do you think he means? What else does he say in that verse? How are those two things related? Have you "chosen the way of truth"? Have you set your heart on obeying God's laws (with his help)?

 ACT: The next time you take a true/false test, remember that truth exists in moral and spiritual areas just like it does in science, geography, or math.

 PRAY: "I have chosen the way of truth; I have set my heart on your laws."

17 Don't Be a Scrooge!

Bible Reading: Ecclesiastes 5:10-14
Whoever loves money never has money enough. Ecclesiastes 5:10, NIV

WHAT WOULD YOU think of

- a Texas billionaire who evicts his own mother from her two-room apartment in one of his many apartment buildings because she was three weeks late on her three-hundred-dollar rent payment?
- a preschooler who takes twelve cupcakes to his preschool classroom on his birthday and insists on eating every one himself?
- the owner of the largest cattle ranch in Oklahoma, who is found guilty of stealing cows from an adjoining ranch?
- the girl who has sung a solo in the church Christmas program for the last three years and throws a temper tantrum because someone else was asked to sing the solo this year?
- the kid who has been playing the *Savage Conquest* video game for three and a half hours—nonstop—and won't give anyone else a chance to play?

If you could think of one word that characterizes each of those people, would it be *cool? pleasant? likable? admirable?*

How about *greedy?* Or *stingy?*

That's it, isn't it? The people mentioned above aren't very pleasant, likable, or admirable at all, are they? Why? Because they're greedy or stingy.

Greed can be pretty unattractive and irritating. It's also wrong. Perhaps the main reason why most people dislike or disapprove of the behavior mentioned above is because it's wrong. What would be the right behavior? Generosity! "It is more blessed to give than to receive" (Acts 20:35, NIV).

Greed or miserliness is wrong; generosity is right. Most people seem to know that instinctively. That's why Scrooge is such a despicable character at the beginning of Dickens's *A Christmas Carol.* That's why Michael Douglass's character in the movie *Wall Street* was so outrageous. That's why the Grinch is such "a mean one" in *How the Grinch Stole Christmas.* Because greed is not only unattractive, it's wrong.

 REFLECT: Do you think greed is OK for some people, or is it wrong for everyone? Is generosity right for everyone? Do you think you need to be more generous?

 ACT: Rent one of the following movies (with your parents' permission) and watch it with your family. As you're watching it, think about how the movie depicts the vice (wrong choice) of greed and the virtue (right choice) of generosity: *A Christmas Carol* (starring George C. Scott), *A Simple Twist of Fate* (starring Steve Martin), *Greedy* (with Michael J. Fox), or *The Brothers Karamazov.*

 PRAY: "Lord, you are so generous, offering your love and your salvation to the whole world—including me! Give me the desire to be generous, too."

18 Give It Away

Bible Reading: 1 Timothy 6:17-19

Be rich in good works and . . . give generously to those in need.
1 Timothy 6:18

THE PHONE RANG late one night after the man, his wife, and their three small children had already gone to bed. The man rolled over, stretched an arm out of the tangle of sheets, snatched the phone receiver out of the cradle, and said a groggy hello.

It was an old friend calling from several time zones away. "I'm sorry for calling so late, old buddy, but I just had to give you something."

"Give me something?" The man lifted himself up on his elbows and sat back against the headboard of his bed. His wife sat up and turned on the light.

"Yes!" the caller explained. "Back when I was in college, I promised myself—and God, I guess—that I would give something away every single day of my life."

The man in the bed was awake now. "You what?"

"It's not always a big deal," the caller said. "Sometimes I give a quarter to a kid who lost his money in a candy machine, or I give a book I've enjoyed to someone I think will like it. But for the past fifteen years, I don't think I've missed a single day."

"You've given something away every day for the last fifteen years?"

"Yup! But I haven't given anything away yet today, so I thought I'd call you."

"What are you going to give me over the phone?"

"Well, old buddy, it may not be much, but it's something." The caller then read a short poem, explaining the godly influence his distant friend had had on him. When he stopped reading, silence hung between the two men.

"Thanks," his friend finally answered. His voice quivered with emotion. "That's the best gift I've been given in a long time."

Imagine giving something away every day for fifteen years! That's pretty cool, isn't it? You know what's even more amazing? That story is true.

When you hear about such people, does that kind of generosity fill you with respect and admiration? Of course it does, because you know, deep within your heart, that generosity is good. You're naturally drawn to people who are generous and repelled by people who are stingy or greedy.

It may not be easy to be generous, of course. It's part of our sinful nature to want to hang on to what we have. That tendency can be tough to overcome. But though it may not always be easy, it is good to be generous, especially to those in need.

 REFLECT: If you were charged with the "crime" of being generous, would there be enough evidence to convict you? How can you add to the evidence?

 ACT: Give something away today. You could give away a smile, a pat on the back, a helping hand, etc.

 PRAY: "God, I know someone who needs_____. Show me what I can share."

Bible Reading: Deuteronomy 15:10-11
Give freely without begrudging it. Deuteronomy 15:10

HAVE YOU EVER played the game "I've never"? It's a fun game to play at camp, at youth group meetings, or when a bunch of friends just get together. Here's how it's played: Someone makes a statement beginning with the words "I've never." Anyone who has done or experienced what the speaker says must stand. Then someone else makes another "I've never" statement, and the others must admit whether they've done such a thing by standing or sitting. The game ends when only one person is left sitting (or when everyone in the room turns eighty, whichever comes first).

How about playing a quick version of "I've never" right now? Check off any of the statements below that you could truthfully make:

- ☐ "I've never given my parents a Mother's Day or Father's Day gift."
- ☐ "I've never put any of my own money in a Salvation Army Christmas kettle."
- ☐ "I've never shared my favorite toys with other kids."
- ☐ "I've never bought something to share with someone else."
- ☐ "I've never volunteered my time to help a person or group."
- ☐ "I've never offered a favorite article of clothing to a friend."
- ☐ "I've never given a gift without expecting to get a gift in return."
- ☐ "I've never surprised anyone with a sincere compliment."
- ☐ "I've never visited anyone in a nursing home."
- ☐ "I've never put my own money in the offering plate at church."

How many did you check? Four? Five? Nine? Ten? In case you haven't noticed, all the "I've never" statements were about generosity. If you checked all ten, you really need to work on showing generosity to others. If you checked only one or two, you deserve a halo.

Maybe those things don't seem like a big deal to you. After all, a lot of people probably go through their whole lives without ever giving away clothes or tossing money into a Salvation Army kettle. But that doesn't mean generosity isn't important. It is. That's why God commanded it.

God says, "Give freely without begrudging it . . . share your resources freely with the poor and with [others] in need" (Deuteronomy 15:10-11). He commands us to be generous, not only because it helps others, but also because it's the right thing to do.

REFLECT: Are you usually generous with: money, time, possessions, toys, attention, or kind words? Can you be more generous in any of those areas?

ACT: Pick one of the "I've never" statements that you checked, and do it this week!

PRAY: "God, I need your help being generous with _____."

Bible Reading: Luke 21:1-4

"I assure you," [Jesus] said, "this poor widow has given more than all the rest of them. For they have given a tiny part of their surplus, but she, poor as she is, has given everything she has." Luke 21:3-4

YOU'RE WALKING ALONE down a dark, deserted street. Suddenly a dark form appears, seemingly out of nowhere, and points a gun at you.

"Hands up!" he says, in a gravelly voice. His face is hidden behind a ski mask.

You lift your hands in the air. Your eyes focus on the barrel of the pistol.

"Don't shoot," you say. "I'll give you all my money, just don't shoot!"

"Money?" the robber says. "Who said anything about money?"

You lift your eyes to the man's face. "You don't want my money?"

"No!" the man says. "I want your shoestrings!"

You're sure you must have heard wrong. "I'm sorry. What did you say?" you ask.

"Your shoestrings!" the man barks, waving the gun around in the air to indicate his impatience. "I want your shoestrings. Now, take 'em outta your shoes and hand 'em over . . . that's right . . . slow and easy like."

You untie your shoelaces and hand them to the robber, who snatches them from your hand and runs down the street, laughing and leaping in the air. "I'm rich, I'm rich!" he shouts. "Do you hear me? I'm rich!"

Yeah, right, you say. That's gonna happen. OK, so it is a little absurd. A command like "Hand over your shoestrings" sounds silly. Why? Because it reveals that the robber places an inordinate value on shoestrings.

His words reveal his values. Most robbers value money more than shoestrings; that's why they say, "Give me your wallet," or "Hand over the loot!" A person's words—especially his or her commands—often reveal what that person values.

The same thing is true of God. God commands us to be generous. "Therefore I command you to be openhanded toward your brothers and toward the poor and needy in your land" (Deuteronomy 15:11, NIV). God's commands show that he values generosity. That's why Jesus praised the poor widow who gave two tiny coins as an offering in the temple: because she was being really generous. Generosity is something God thinks is really, really valuable. And if he likes generosity so much, shouldn't we like it (and practice it), too?

 REFLECT: Do you value generosity? Do your words show that you value generosity? Why or why not? Do your actions show that you value generosity? Why or why not?

 ACT: Be alert for any opportunity today to show others that you value generosity.

 PRAY: "God, this is the day I'm going to be generous in the way I act toward _____."

21 Apples, Bees, and Cheddar Cheese

Bible Reading: Psalm 65:9-11

You crown the year with your bounty, and your carts overflow with abundance. Psalm 65:11, NIV

IF YOU WERE to make a list of the things God has given you, how long would it take you? An hour? Two hours? A day? A week?

It's easy to forget how generous God has been to us. He's given us family and friends and things like freedom and fun and food (and those are just some of the words that start with *f!*). In fact, God's generosity spans the whole alphabet:

Apples	Jelly Beans	Spectacular Sunsets
Bees	Kiwi Fruit	Teeth
Cheddar Cheese	Licorice	Ursa Major (The Big Dipper)
Dalmatians	Music	Vines
Eyesight	Noses	Winter Sunshine
Frothy Seas	Orchids	X rays
Ginkgo Trees	Playful Puppies	Yesterdays
Honeydew Melons	Quilts	Zucchini
Ice	Rivers	

When we stop just a moment to think about it, it's not hard to see that God's generosity is impossible to measure. His generosity is astounding. He didn't have to give us anything. He didn't have to bless us with apples, bees, and cheddar cheese! He could've stopped giving us good things after creating sunrises and summer breezes—but he kept going, all the way to zebras, zephyrs, zinc, zinnias, and zwieback—look it up; it's in the dictionary!

But that's the kind of God he is. Generosity is a part of God's nature. That's what makes generosity right: It's like God.

 REFLECT: A popular old gospel song says that God "giveth, and giveth, and giveth again." What do you think that means? What makes God so generous?

Generosity is right because it's like God. Can you ever be as generous as God? Why or why not? Can you be more generous than you are now? If not, why not? If so, how?

 ACT: Make your own list of God's generosity, using each letter of the alphabet. You might even try to make two lists: one of God's generosity to everyone and the second listing God's generosity to you specifically, including names of friends, family members, favorite songs, and so on.

 PRAY: Go through your list, from *A* to *Z*, praising God for his generosity.

22 Gift of the Magi

Bible Reading: Psalm 112:5-6

Good will come to him who is generous and lends freely.
Psalm 112:5, NIV

The generous prosper and are satisfied; those who refresh others will themselves be refreshed. Proverbs 11:25

O. HENRY wrote the famous tale "The Gift of the Magi," the story of Della and Jim, a young married couple who loved each other very much.

On Christmas Eve, Jim and Della had no gifts to give each other and no money to buy gifts. One dollar and eighty-seven cents was all they had. Well, not exactly all.

Jim had an expensive gold pocket watch that had belonged to his father and grandfather. Della had long, beautiful brown hair that would have been the envy of the wealthiest woman in the world. So Jim and Della secretly decided to sell their most prized possessions to buy a special gift for each other.

Della had her hair cut and sold to a wigmaker. When Jim came home from work, he looked upon Della's short hair with shock. Not only was her beautiful hair gone, but he had bought her an expensive set of decorative combs to use in her luxurious hair.

When Della unwrapped the combs, she turned her tearful eyes on Jim and smiled. "My hair grows so fast, Jim!" she said. Then she proudly produced the present she had bought him and held it out to him in her open palm. It was an expensive platinum chain for Jim's most precious possession—his watch.

Jim put his hands behind his head and smiled. "Let's put our presents away and keep 'em a while," he said. "They're too nice to use just at present." Then he explained. "I sold the watch to get the money to buy your combs."

Jim's and Della's gifts were motivated by unselfish sacrifice, by true generosity. By the time they gave their gifts to each other, the gifts themselves had lost their value. Yet their generosity was worth far more than any watch chain or hair comb because it showed how much they loved each other.

Most people think that generous people could be richer if they didn't give so much away. But that's not true. Generous people may give a lot away, but they often receive something worth far more than what they give away.

 REFLECT: In what ways do you think their generosity made Jim and Della, the characters in O. Henry's story, poorer or richer?
Have you ever been sorry for being generous? Have you ever been happy because you were generous? Why or why not?

 ACT: Anytime you comb your hair or look at your watch today, remember the blessings that can come from being generous.

 PRAY: "God, thank you for the happiness you bring to me when I'm generous."

Bible Reading: Ruth 2:1-3, 8-18

May the Lord, the God of Israel, under whose wings you have come to take refuge, reward you fully. Ruth 2:12

A LONG TIME ago, in a land far away, a famine occurred. Many people began to starve.

A woman named Naomi, her husband Elimelech, and her two sons decided to leave their home and go to a neighboring country where food wasn't so hard to find. There, in a country called Moab, the two sons met and married a couple of the local women—Ruth and Orpah. During their stay in Moab, Naomi's husband died. About ten years later, her sons also died, leaving Naomi in a strange land with no husband and no sons. Naomi decided to go back to the home she had left, to Judah.

She told Ruth and Orpah of her plans and said, "Go back to your mothers' homes instead of coming with me. And may the Lord reward you for your kindness to your husbands and to me" (Ruth 1:8). She kissed them good-bye, and the three women cried together. Orpah turned back to return to her mother's home, but Ruth did not. She insisted on staying with Naomi, even if it meant going to a strange land.

Ruth and Naomi were poor, and they arrived in Judah with nothing. But it was harvesttime, and God had commanded his people to allow those who needed food to go out to the fields after the harvest and gather whatever grain had been left on the ground. (See Leviticus 19:9-10; 23:22.) Ruth went to the field of a man named Boaz and picked up enough grain for her and Naomi.

Boaz noticed Ruth and, after asking around, learned her story. He told Ruth to help herself to the water from his well. He invited her to eat lunches with him and his field hands. He told his workers, "Leave extra grain on the ground for her to gather. Don't give her a hard time."

Ruth and Naomi were overwhelmed by the generosity of Boaz and, to make a long story short, Ruth and Boaz were later married. And they lived happily ever after.

A little generosity can go a long, long way. When we are generous, God can bless us in ways we would never imagine. Boaz's generosity to Ruth gained him her love and respect, which resulted in a successful marriage. But the story didn't end there. Ruth and Boaz had a son, and their son became the grandfather of King David, the second king of Israel. David had another famous descendant—Jesus, the Savior of the world.

It's amazing what a little generosity can do, don'tcha think?

 REFLECT: Do you think Boaz would have been happier if he had been greedy? Why or why not? How did God reward Boaz's generosity? Have you ever enjoyed the blessings of being generous?

 ACT: Why not start a generosity campaign by giving away unneeded or unused items? (Be sure to ask your parents' permission first.)

 PRAY: "God, thanks for Boaz's example. Thanks for the way you blessed Boaz and for the way you bless me."

24 Cecil's Secret

Bible Reading: Luke 12:13-15

Don't be greedy for what you don't have. Real life is not measured by how much we own. Luke 12:15

NINETY-THREE-YEAR-OLD Cecil Green climbed the stairs to the podium as the crowd watched. Cecil had already given away more money than most people ever see in their lifetimes. He had given millions of dollars to various organizations, and now he was being given an award for all the good things his generosity had accomplished.

As he reached the top of the wobbly steps to the podium, he shook loose from the people who supported his ninety-three-year-old form on either side and walked toward the podium. With each step he seemed to get more excited and energetic, until suddenly he stopped, looked at the crowd, and broke into a dance that looked something like an Irish jig.

"I am so excited," he said when he stepped to the podium after his little dance, "and I appreciate this award very much. But I don't understand why someone should be given such an award for doing something so enjoyable. Giving away my money is so much fun I wish everyone could do it. My goal is to be able to give everything away before I die."

Cecil Green had spent much of his life working hard to earn as much as he could. While he enjoyed making money, he didn't *really* start to have fun until he started giving it away! It seemed that the more he gave away, the more fun he had. He discovered how much fun it was to surprise people with generosity. He discovered how much fun it was to make a difference in other people's lives. He discovered that the greatest thing about making more money was being able to give more away!

That's one of the reasons God wants us to be generous. He wants us to find out Cecil's secret. He wants us to discover how much fun it is to surprise people with generosity. He wants us to experience how much fun it is to give to others. He wants us to learn that the greatest thing about having money, possessions, time, and talents is being able to give them away!

And once we *really* learn that, we'll discover that we can never outgive God.

 REFLECT: Do you think money makes people happy? Why or why not? What do you think Jesus meant when he said, "Real life is not measured by how much we own"? In what ways can generosity be fun?

 PRAY: "Lord, help me to learn Cecil's secret. I want to find out how much fun generosity can be, and I'll try to start by_____."

25 Tough Questions

Bible Reading: Isaiah 40:28-31

The Lord is the everlasting God, the Creator of the ends of the earth.
Isaiah 40:28, NIV

A YOUNG GIRL wanted to join the chess team at school. The teacher in charge of the team said, "I will ask you three questions. If you can answer at least two of them correctly, you will be on the team."

The teacher asked the first question: "Two people are cleaning a chimney. When they come out of the chimney, one has a dirty face and the other has a clean face. Which of them will wash his face?"

The girl answered, "The one with the dirty face."

"Not so," the teacher patiently replied. "The one with the clean face will wash because he sees his companion's face and assumes that his face is also dirty."

The girl looked disappointed but understood.

The teacher then repeated the first question word-for-word. The girl assumed the teacher was giving her a second chance and said, "The one with the clean face."

"Not so," the teacher said sadly. "The correct answer is *both,* for the man with the dirty face will ask why the other man is washing when his face is not dirty; then the first man will realize he needs to wash his *own* face."

"I've already missed two questions," the girl said, disappointment showing on her face. "I know I won't be on the team, but what is the third question?"

The teacher said, "The third question is one you should have asked yourself: If two men came out of a chimney, why would only one have had a dirty face?" The teacher smiled. "Don't miss the obvious, and you will be a successful player. Welcome to the team!"

Once that poor girl learned the answers to the teacher's questions, they seemed obvious. Choosing between right and wrong can be like that. The right answer may seem obvious when we're looking back, but that doesn't help us when we face a puzzling or difficult choice.

That's why it's so important to trust God and commit yourself to following his way—because he *does* know the answers. "He knows the way that I take," Job said (Job 23:10, NIV); he knows which choices are right, which are wrong, and which way is the best one for each of us to follow. He knows infinitely more than we do—which is why we're smart when we do what he commands.

 REFLECT: Christian philosopher Francis Schaeffer once said, "I would rather trust God's wisdom than mine." Do you agree? Why or why not?

 ACT: Spring the three questions above on a friend or family member. After you share the correct answers, share also the importance of following God's wisdom.

 PRAY: "Help me to trust your wisdom by obeying your commands."

26 The Image on the Card

Bible Reading: Genesis 1:26-28

God saw all that he had made, and it was very good. Genesis 1:31, NIV

YOU'RE WALKING DOWN the street, minding your own business, when you hear a voice. "Psst!" the voice says. You stop and turn. A thin man in dark glasses leans against the side of a building.

"Hey, Slick," the man says, casting furtive glances left and right. "You wanna make the smartest deal of your life?"

You start to turn and walk away, when the man hustles around in front of you and, after a quick glance up and down the sidewalk, opens one side of his coat. There, pinned to the inside of the fabric, is a row of . . . baseball cards.

"I got a 1953 Walt Zambrisky card for thirteen cents," the man says.

You shake your head and try to walk around the baseball card hawker.

"OK, OK," he says, as he backpedals up the sidewalk ahead of you. "I can tell you're a smart customer." He opens the coat again and points to a card. "A Bruno Gunderschmutz rookie card, mint condition, seventy-five cents." He wags his eyebrows as if they were battery operated.

You make a move to pass him again, but he holds up both hands. "OK, OK," he says. "You must want the good stuff." He steals a glance over your shoulder. "My last offer. Mickey Mantle. Rookie card. One thousand smackaroonies."

A thousand dollars? For a baseball card? Actually, yes. Some cards have sold for more than that. Sports cards have become a valuable commodity, an investment.

But what makes a Mickey Mantle rookie card worth a thousand dollars and a Bruno Gunderschmutz rookie card worth only seventy-five cents? After all, they're both made of nothing but cardboard and ink. What's the difference? Just one thing: the image on the card. A Mickey Mantle card bears the image of a New York Yankees slugger who broke Babe Ruth's record for World Series home runs and was later elected to the Baseball Hall of Fame. It's not what the card is made of that makes it valuable; it's the image that appears on the card.

It's sort of the same way with human life. Human life is valuable because of the image every person bears. No matter how tall or how old he or she is, no matter what color his or her skin or hair, no matter what language he or she speaks, every human being is unbelievably valuable because he or she is created in God's image. That's true of you. It's true of your friends and family. And it's true of people you've never met, and even people you don't really like. Their lives are precious because they're made in God's image.

 REFLECT: Do you act like you believe your life is unbelievably precious? If so, in what ways? If not, why not? Do you act like you believe the lives of others are unbelievably precious? If so, in what ways? If not, why not?

 PRAY: "God, I thank you that all human life is in your image and is valuable to you."

27 Your First Nine Months

Bible Reading: Psalm 139:13-16

You saw me before I was born. Every day of my life was recorded in your book. Every moment was laid out before a single day had passed.
Psalm 139:16

HERE ARE SOME things you probably never knew about yourself:

- The first moment—the very first nanosecond—of your life determined whether you would be a boy or a girl.
- In the first hours of your life, your eye color, hair color, and other features were decided.
- When your heart began beating, you were so small you would have fit on your mother or dad's fingernail—with room to spare!
- Before your mother even knew you were growing inside of her, you could hear and could even perform full flips inside her womb!
- About seven months *before* you were born, your fingers and toes looked much like they did at birth, though you were only two inches long!
- You started to grow hair in your fourth month of life (before birth) and may have even sucked your thumb!
- You first heard your mother's voice—and began kicking and stretching—three or four months before you were born!
- In the final two months before your birth, your weight tripled, you began sleeping and waking, and you used four of your five senses: sight, sound, taste, and touch—all before your mother went into labor.

You know what else? While all that was going on, God was watching you. He was forming you, day by day. The Bible says he was knitting you together in your mother's womb. He was *loving* you even before your mother knew she was pregnant. He knew how tall you would be, what color your eyes would be, whether you would have your dad's nose or your mother's cheekbones, and all sorts of other stuff that was going on from the first moment of your life.

Literally from Day One of your existence, you were precious in God's sight because you were already the best thing God ever created: human life.

 REFLECT: Today's reading calls human life "the best thing God ever created." How do you think we know that? If you're not sure, check out Genesis 1 and compare what God himself says about the various levels of his creation. How does it feel to know that you're "the best thing God ever created"?

 ACT: Do you have any baby pictures of yourself? If you do, place your favorite in your Bible as a bookmark at Psalm 139. If you don't, ask your parents if you can borrow one from their photo collection for that purpose.

 PRAY: Say the words of Psalm 139:14 as a prayer: "Thank you for making me so wonderfully complex! Your workmanship is marvelous—and how well I know it."

Bible Reading: Genesis 9:1, 5-6

And from each man, too, I will demand an accounting for the life of his fellow man. "Whoever sheds the blood of man, by man shall his blood be shed; for in the image of God has God made man." Genesis 9:5-6, NIV

TWO VERY DIFFERENT movies. Similar responses.

The movie *Schindler's List*, the story of a German man's efforts to redeem people from concentration camps during World War II, was shown in a high school. At one point in the movie, the commandant of the concentration camp walks onto a veranda with a rifle. For a moment he smokes his cigarette and watches the prisoners as they go about their forced labor. Then he raises the scope of the gun to his eye and spies a prisoner who had knelt to tie his shoe. The commandant squeezes the trigger, killing the woman. While the other prisoners quicken the pace of their activities in fear that they will be the next victim, the commandant continues his sport, shooting human beings like ducks in a shooting gallery. As this scene took place, the high school students watching the movie started to laugh.

Some time later, in a theater several thousand miles away, an updated version of William Shakespeare's *Romeo and Juliet* was on the screen. Romeo, who has fallen in love with young Juliet, sees one of his friends murdered by Juliet's cousin, Tybalt. Blinded by rage, Romeo chases Tybalt and—though he (and the whole audience) knows that this act must certainly doom the romance between him and Juliet—he guns down his friend's murderer. In the midst of what was intended to be a tragic scene, five or six teens in the theater laughed, clapped, and cheered Romeo's act.

How would you have responded if you had been in one of those theaters? Would you have laughed? Would you have cheered? Such scenes ought to make you hurt and cry. They are tragic because they portray the loss—the taking—of God's most precious gift: human life.

Whatever the reason for the reactions of the young people in these two instances, one thing seems to be obvious. Watching movies and television shows where violence and death occur every day has caused some people to view life and death as entertainment.

Every human life is precious: that of the elderly Alzheimer's victim no less than that of the handsome movie star; that of the prison inmate no less than that of the smiling child walking to her first day of kindergarten; that of the unborn no less than that of the newborn. God calls human life "good," and he has commanded us to value life, to preserve it, and to honor it.

REFLECT: What do you think of the way the young people responded to *Schindler's List* and *Romeo and Juliet*? Why do you feel that way? How do you show whether or not you value human life? How do you preserve it (or encourage its preservation)?

PRAY: "Lord, help me to feel about life the way you do and to respond to death as you do, especially when_____."

29 What Now?

Bible Reading: Genesis 2:4-7

And the Lord God formed a man's body from the dust of the ground and breathed into it the breath of life. And the man became a living person. Genesis 2:7

TWO ANGELS SAT in the heavens, their legs dangling over the edge of the firmament, as God began his work of creation.

They watched God create day and night. "Cool," said the first angel. "I love fireworks."

They watched God separate the waters into clouds and oceans. "Ooh," said the first angel. "Aah," said the second.

Then, as they watched, God caused dry land to arise out of the oceans. Next, the angelic observers saw the land sprout with grass, flowers, alalfa sprouts, cornstalks, bushes, and banana trees. Then, God flung the sun and the moon into place and spattered the sky with stars. The angels clapped and cheered.

The display in the heavens was hardly finished when the voice of God thundered, and the earth seemed to teem with life: geese flying, fish swimming, horses galloping, monkeys climbing, and bees buzzing.

Then God's voice thundered again, and the second angel pointed. The first angel's gaze followed the direction of the gesture. There, in the lush garden God had created, particles of dirt and dust were swirling together . . . into the form of a man.

Suddenly, the second angel bolted upright with a jolt. "Did you see that?"

"See what?" the first angel asked. "You were in my way!"

"He—he *breathed* into it! He breathed the breath of life into his new creation. He breathed his own life, his own spirit, into the man!"

The two angels looked at each other, eyes wide with amazement. The first angel swallowed loudly. "Wow," they said in unison.

It was pretty awesome. God gave to us humans something he gave to no other part of his creation: He made us in his image and gave us each a spirit that is like his own spirit. In fact, that's why God values our life so highly—because he is the source of the life that's in every human being on earth. And if God values your life—and all human life—so much, we should honor it and respect it, too.

 REFLECT: Do you think humans are different from the rest of God's creation? If not, why not? If so, why? How do you think God feels when people don't value the lives of others or even their own lives?

 ACT: Try to see others as special today—because they are. Go out of your way to treat others with respect.

 PRAY: "Thank you, God, for breathing your own life into us."

30 It's a Wonderful Life

Bible Reading: Matthew 10:28-31

Not even a sparrow, worth only half a penny, can fall to the ground without your Father knowing it. And the very hairs on your head are all numbered. So don't be afraid; you are more valuable to him than a whole flock of sparrows. Matthew 10:29-31

A SHOW ON The Learning Channel told the true story of a truck driver, traveling alone on the interstate highway one night, listening to his citizen's band (CB) radio.

Suddenly a call came over the radio that sent a chill through the truck driver. "Help me," the caller said. "I'm on Route 23 not too far north of the interstate and have just had an accident. Someone please help me."

The truck driver turned off the interstate and followed Route 23, deciding to answer the desperate call even though his detour would certainly make him late. As he drove slowly along Route 23, he noticed some headlights in the ditch at the side of the road. He stopped his rig and ran to the scene of the accident. No other traffic had passed; he was apparently the first to get to the scene. The man in the car looked pretty bad; he was covered with blood. The trucker searched in the man's car for the CB he had used to issue his plea for help. But though he looked high and low, he could find no radio.

He ran back to his truck and called for emergency help, which arrived soon afterward. The accident victim was taken to a nearby hospital, and the trucker was told that his chances of recovering were good.

The trucker was soon on the interstate again, happy that he had helped. He knew that if he hadn't responded to the radio call for help, the man might have died. Still, he puzzled over the absence of a CB in the man's car. *How had he called for help?* he wondered. He couldn't explain the incident, but he knew it would be forever etched on his memory.

Years later that same truck driver went on a fishing trip with some friends. While on the trip, he had a heart attack. One of his companions remembered that a nearby resident's father, who was a doctor, was visiting her. They carried the unconscious trucker to the house. The doctor worked skillfully to save the trucker's life, and soon the man opened his eyes. The first person he saw was the accident victim whose life he had helped save years before. The trucker, who had gone out of his way to save a stranger's life, had unknowingly saved his own!

REFLECT: Have you ever saved anyone's life? Do you know anyone who has saved a life? Do you know anyone whose life has been saved? Why is saving human lives a good thing? How do the lives of others benefit you? How does your life benefit others?

PRAY: "God, I thank you that you care so much about me. Help me see others the way you see them and to value others the way you value them. Help me also to recognize the many ways that my life is better because of those around me."

May 31

Miracle on the River Kwai

Bible Reading: John 15:9-13

Greater love has no one than this, that he lay down his life for his friends. John 15:13, NIV

THE SOLDIER BEGAN screaming and waving his arms at the grimy group of prisoners.

A group of POWs (Prisoners of War) were working on the infamous Burma Railway during World War II when one of the Japanese guards shouted that one of the shovels was missing. The soldier demanded to know which prisoner had stolen or hidden the shovel.

Ernest Gordon, author of *Miracle on the River Kwai,* tells the true story:

> He began to rant and rave, working himself up into a paranoid fury and ordered whoever was guilty to step forward. No one moved. "All die! All die!" he shrieked, cocking and aiming his rifle at the prisoners. At that moment one man stepped forward, and the guard clubbed him to death with his rifle while he stood silently to attention. When they returned to camp, the tools were counted again, and no shovel was missing.*

That anonymous soldier sacrificed his life so that his companions could live. Many soldiers—and others—have done the same, of course. It's often called "the supreme sacrifice." Just about anyone can recognize that such an act is noble and good. Why? Because there is nothing more precious to give away than one's own life. Jesus said as much (and foreshadowed his own death) when he said, "Greater love has no one than this, that he lay down his life for his friends" (John 15:13, NIV).

That's why we honor Christian martyrs, from Stephen (Acts 7) to modern missionaries who are killed for their efforts to preach Christ in dangerous places. That's why we honor soldiers who have given their lives in defense of their countries. That's even why we revere those, like Mother Teresa and Henri Nouwen, who choose to spend their lives in the service of the poor and the mentally handicapped.

Life is among God's most precious gifts, and respecting and honoring human life includes honoring those who have, by necessity or by choice, given their lives away, either through death (like that anonymous soldier in Burma) or in life (like Mother Teresa and Henri Nouwen).

 REFLECT: Do you think sacrificing one's life for someone else is good or bad, noble or degrading? Why? Do you know someone who has sacrificed his or her life to save or care for someone else? How can you honor that person?

 PRAY: "Jesus, thank you for giving your life for me. And thank you for the martyrs and soldiers who have sacrificed their lives so I can live as I do. Help me to appreciate their sacrifice and honor them by_____."

1 No Catch

Bible Reading: Ezekiel 18:21-23, 30-32

I only want them to turn from their wicked ways and live. Ezekiel 18:23

TWO OLDER GUYS show up on your front porch on Super Bowl Sunday. They introduce themselves as Ed McMahon and Dick Clark. One of them holds balloons. The other points a microphone at your face. A TV camera crew seems to be filming everything. A big van is parked in front of your house with Prize Patrol painted on the side in big letters.

"Congratulations!" one of them says. "You've just won eleven million dollars!"

You roll your eyes. "Yeah, and my mother's the queen of England!"

One of the guys chuckles heartily. He holds a cardboard check about the size of Nebraska. "Here's your winner's check!" He extends it in your direction.

You shake your head and start to close the door. "Look," you say, "halftime's almost over. I gotta get back in the house." You start to close the door.

One of the guys wedges a foot in your door. "This is for real!" he says. "We really want to give you eleven million dollars!"

"Look," you say, "you're wasting my time, all right? Now, go away, before I call the cops!" And you slam the door.

Now, you'd never act so rudely, of course. And you'd at least take that big cardboard check and *try* to cash it, right? You might be a little suspicious, but you wouldn't blow a chance like that, right? Or would you?

In some ways we all do that, day after day. Oh, Ed McMahon and Dick Clark don't appear on our doorsteps every day. But God does. And, like the two guys in the story above, God just wants to give us good things to make our life better and to make our futures secure. Over and over again he tells us that he loves us and just wants to do good to us. Over and over again he pleads with us to trust him, trying to convince us that his aim is not to hurt us but to help us.

But we often close the door in his face. We make choices as if God is trying to spoil our fun. We act as though he's trying to "fake us out," like there's a "catch" to his offer of a better life. We seem to think that wrong choices are more desirable than right choices, as though God were trying to keep us from having fun. But that's not true. In fact, God is not trying to spoil things for us—he wants our life to be good and enjoyable and rewarding. He wants to save us from the disappointment, destruction—and death—that sin causes. "I don't want you to die," he says. "I want you to turn from wrong choices so you can *really* live."

 REFLECT: How is God like the "Prize Patrol" in the story above? How is he different? Do you have trouble believing that God loves you? that obeying his commands will protect you? that wrong choices will hurt you? If you really trust God's love, how should that affect the choices you make?

 PRAY: "God, help me to make right choices and really live today!"

2 Your Wedding Day?

Bible Reading: Genesis 2:18-23

Then the Lord God made a woman from the rib and brought her to Adam.
Genesis 2:22

HOW OLD ARE you? Write your age here: _____

What's your full name? Write it here: _____

Who is your best friend? Write his or her name here: _____

Who is your husband or wife? Write his or her name here: _____

What? You say you're not married? Oh, OK, then, let's change the question:

Who *will be* your husband or wife? Write his or her name here: _____

What? You say you don't know whom you're going to marry? And maybe you won't even *get* married—at least, not until you're, like, a hundred years old?

Well, OK. You aren't married. You may never get married. And even if you do someday get married, who knows who will be your husband or wife.

God does. That's right. God knows the answers to all the questions above. He knows how old you are. He knows your full name. He knows who your best friends are. He even knows—right now—if you're going to get married someday. He knows what day you're getting married. He knows whom you're going to marry.

Pretty spooky, huh? Not really. It *is* kind of cool, though. God knows your future husband or wife. He knows what that person had for breakfast today, just like he knows what *you* had for breakfast. (Cold pizza *again?*) And while you may not even have met your future husband or wife yet, while you may not even be interested in having a boyfriend or girlfriend yet, while you may not plan to get married *(ever!)*, God wants to help you become a good husband or wife someday. He wants to help you make right choices now, because those right choices *may* prepare you to be a good husband or wife later. Not that God's in a hurry. He doesn't have to be. He knows exactly how much time he has to help you before your wedding day arrives!

REFLECT: Which of the following are true of you?
☐ I'm not interested in the opposite sex yet. ☐ I don't know if I'll ever get married.
☐ I don't plan to get married *(ever)*. ☐ I don't know whom I am going to marry.
☐ I hope to get married someday. ☐ God knows whom I am going to marry.

If you believe that God knows whom you will marry, how does that make you feel? (Check any that apply.)
☐ Scared ☐ Great
☐ Worried ☐ Peaceful

PRAY: Ask God to bless and protect the person you will someday marry (if that's in his plans for you) and to help you become a good Christian partner for that person.

The Positive Power of "No"

Bible Reading: John 10:7-10
I have come that they may have life, and have it to the full.
John 10:10, NIV.

EVER FEEL LIKE your parents are always saying no to you?

"Mom, can I go over to Carly's house?"
"Dad, can I watch *Blood, Guts, and Gore* on the Movie Channel?"
"Can I have a computer for Christmas?"
"Can I stay home instead of going to Grandma's house?"
"Can I sell my little sister to the gypsies?"
"Can I bungee jump off the roof of the house?"

It *may* seem like your parents never say anything but *no!* It *may* seem like they're always saying, "Don't do this," and "You can't do that." Not only that, but it seems like God does the same thing (except that he says, "Thou shalt not do this," and "Thou shouldst not do that"). It's all so negative, right?

Well, no. It may sometimes seem like *no* is a negative word, but it can be positive. The things you say no to can make your life better, not worse.

For example, say your friends try to talk you into sneaking out your bedroom window tonight so you can go with them to spray-paint bad words on walls. You say no. Your friends get caught, and they have to spend every Saturday until they're, like, eighty years old scrubbing graffiti off walls. Was saying no a negative thing? No, because the results—in the long run especially—were much better than if you'd said yes.

Or consider one more example. Your older brother asks you to tell your parents that he stayed home with you last night, when you know he was really out at a beer party. You don't want to get your brother mad at you, but you say no to your brother and tell your parents the truth when they ask you. He does get mad because your parents ground him. But a week later, a carload of your brother's friends get into a car accident on the way home from another beer party, and you realize your brother could have been hurt—or killed—if you hadn't told the truth. Was saying no a negative thing? No, because the results—in the long run especially—were good.

Saying no can seem like such a negative thing. You might say no to something you or your friends really want to do. But saying no to wrong or unwise things is a positive thing, not a negative thing. That's the positive power of *no*.

REFLECT: Does it seem that your parents always say no to the things you want to do? Have you said no to a wrong or unwise choice recently? Did that make your life worse or better? Why? The next time your parents say no to something you want to do, try to stop and ask yourself if that no might actually protect you or have another positive effect.

PRAY: "God, help me to trust your wisdom—and the wisdom of my parents— whenever I hear the word *no*."

4 Modesto, California

Bible Reading: Proverbs 27:1-2

Do not boast about tomorrow, for you do not know what a day may bring forth. Let another praise you, and not your own mouth; someone else, and not your own lips. Proverbs 27:1-2, NIV

YOU'VE PROBABLY NEVER heard of him, but William C. Ralston was a very important and successful man. He lived in California in the 1800s. He earned so much money that he was able to buy a villa on a hillside and turn it into a huge, elaborate mansion. What was his house then is now the main building on the campus of the College of Notre Dame in Belmont, California, near San Francisco.

Ralston also became very involved in the railroads and helped to start new communities along the railroad lines, like the one between San Francisco and Carson City, Nevada. This community grew well because of W. C. Ralston, and the people soon wanted to make it into a real city with a real government and a real name. They got together to choose a name.

A number of people in the community wanted to name the town after Ralston, in appreciation for all he'd done for them. But, though Ralston was honored, he refused. He suggested they find another name. The townspeople continued to propose that the town be named for Ralston, but he continued to refuse. What were they going to do?

Finally, someone had an idea. They knew that Ralston's humility prevented them from calling the town "Ralston," or something similar, but he certainly couldn't object to the solution they proposed. So they decided to honor Ralston by naming the town *Modesto,* the Spanish word for "modest."

Ralston had many reasons to be proud. He was a successful businessman, wealthy and respected. But he refused to boast or brag about his abilities or accomplishments. He chose to be humble and even refused the honor of having a town named after him. Today, Modesto, California, is a thriving city of more than one hundred thousand people. Most of the people who live there don't even know who W. C. Ralston was—and that would have been just fine with him.

It's easy to admire someone like W. C. Ralston because in spite of his success, he refused to brag or boast. That's because humility is a godly virtue, something that makes us respect an accomplished person even more. It's like a perfect pearl or diamond—valuable because it's good and also because it's rare.

 REFLECT: Would you act differently than Ralston if someone wanted to name a town after you? Why or why not? Do you ever praise yourself? Why or why not? Do you want to develop the kind of humility W. C. Ralston had? If so, how can you start?

 ACT: See if you can locate the town of Modesto in an atlas. Leave the book open on your desk or bedside table today to remind you to be humble in all you do.

 PRAY: "Lord, I'm not worthy of praise, but you are. I praise you, Lord."

5 Don't Crow Too Loud

Bible Reading: Proverbs 21:2-4

Pride goes before destruction. Proverbs 16:18, NIV

TWO ROOSTERS. One barnyard. Bad news.

The barnyard was deserted. The wooden door to the henhouse banged open and shut. Two roosters faced each other, their eyes cold and their beaks unsmiling.

"This coop ain't big enough for the both of us," snarled Rudy Rooster.

"You got that right, ya no-'count varmint," Renaldo Rooster countered. "I want you on the first stage outta this here chicken coop."

"The only rooster leavin' here today'll be you, Renaldo—in a *KFC box!*"

Suddenly, without warning, Rudy jumped Renaldo, and the battle began, the two roosters scratching and clawing and squawking like World War III had come to their little chicken coop. They rolled and flapped in the dirt until Renaldo broke free. He tucked his wings and ran for shelter under a broken-down wagon.

"Ha!" shouted Rudy. "I am the champion!" he crowed. He jumped to the roof of the henhouse and started crowing at the top of his lungs.

While Rudy boasted of his new superiority over the barnyard, an eagle heard his horrible singing. Fastening an eye on the boastful bantam, the eagle swooped down and carried Rudy off in his mighty talons.

Moments later Renaldo emerged from the shelter of the old wagon and cast an eye toward the heavens. The sky was clear, and the day was bright. Renaldo's position was undisputed. He was the only rooster in the whole chicken coop.

Everybody is tempted at some time or another to get a little conceited. It's a common temptation to want to brag about something good you've done. But being prideful is not only unattractive—it's wrong. The Bible says, "Haughty eyes, a proud heart, and evil actions are all sin" (Proverbs 21:4).

That doesn't mean you shouldn't feel good when you do a really good job. Nor does it mean that you shouldn't feel comfortable with who you are. It does mean, however, that when you begin feeling and acting as if you're better than others, you're making a wrong choice. Confidence is good. Taking pleasure in your achievements is good. But haughty eyes and a proud heart are wrong.

So the next time you're tempted to brag and swagger a little bit, remember Rudy and Renaldo, and pray that you won't fall prey—to pride.

 REFLECT: In Proverbs 21:4, what do you think the phrases "haughty eyes" and "a proud heart" mean? Do you ever take try to be "number one" no matter whom it hurts? Do you ever take too much credit for things? How can you avoid the sins today's Scripture reading talks about?

 PRAY (adapted from Psalm 131): "O Lord, if my heart is proud, if my eyes are haughty, teach me to quiet my soul before you, and to humble myself in your sight and in the sight of others, especially when_____."

6 Donkey King

Bible Reading: Matthew 21:1-11

Do not think of yourself more highly than you ought. Romans 12:3, NIV

IT WAS THE first day of the week, and the young donkey plodded slowly along the dusty road. On his back rode a passenger he had never carried before.

The donkey and his passenger had left Bethany early that morning, accompanied by a small group of men who traveled on foot. Now, a few hours later, they rounded the slope of the Mount of Olives and arrived at the glistening city of Jerusalem.

Suddenly, the animal was surprised to hear the excited calls and cries of people as they neared the city gate. Soon the donkey realized that he was the center of attention. *They are looking at me,* he told himself. He lifted his head and looked at the smiling faces that beamed at him. *They are smiling at me!* he thought.

A man took off his cloak and laid it on the dusty road before the donkey. A woman removed her shawl and spread it on the donkey's path. Soon, children were snatching palm branches and laying them in his path to make a soft, clean carpet for his feet. *They are honoring me as if I were a king!* the young donkey thought. He snorted with pride. *They are singing my praises. Oh, I am great! I am wonderful!*

When the regal procession reached the steps of the great temple, everyone stopped and grew quiet. *Why do you stop?* the donkey wondered. *Let the praises continue!*

It was then the animal realized, with a shock, that the people's shouts were not for him. His passenger slowly dismounted and climbed the steps of the temple. The crowds followed him, leaving the donkey alone on the street, loosely tied to a post. *I should have been honored,* the donkey realized, *to carry on my humble back the one they call Jesus, but I was too puffed up with my own imagined importance to appreciate the honor he had granted me.*

Imagine! A donkey taking the praise and worship that belonged to Jesus! How ridiculous! How foolish! How arrogant!

Of course, we humans often make a similar mistake. We become prideful and think we're so great. We may be prideful about how pretty or popular we are. We may be prideful about how well we can sing or play baseball or about the grades we get in school or the games we win at camp. But when we do that, we're like the donkey who took the credit that belonged to Jesus. How ridiculous! How foolish! How arrogant!

God commands us, "Do not think of yourself more highly than you ought" (Romans 12:3, NIV). Why? Because: (1) He knows we tend to get carried away and will even take credit for things we haven't done. (2) Any prideful attitude we may have keeps us from appreciating what God has given to us. (3) God values humility.

 REFLECT: Have you ever acted like that donkey? How can you follow God's command not to "think of yourself more highly than you ought"?

 PRAY: "Thank you, God, for giving me all I have and for making me all that I am."

Heaven-TV

Bible Reading: Philippians 2:5-11
Your attitude should be the same that Christ Jesus had. Philippians 2:5

IF HEAVEN HAD (or needed) a television station, it would have made the eleven o'clock news. In fact, it would have been the lead story. No, it would have been the only story.

Newscaster peers into the camera, stone-faced.
  "Today, heaven announced shocking plans for the Son of the Highest to leave his heavenly throne and descend to earth. . . . More after these messages!"
  Newscaster waits for red light on camera to go out, then turns and shouts into the darkness behind the studio lights.
  "This can't be right! Are you sure you got the story right, Rafe?"
  Voice flows from speakers above newscaster's head.
  "That's the story," he answers. "He's going to be born as a baby!"
  "A baby! You mean a . . . a . . . a *human* baby?"
  "You got it. He's gonna be born in a stable, grow up in a backwater town. He's gonna have to learn to walk, learn to talk, even eat what they eat."
  "Good heavens!" the newscaster says. "You can't be serious!"
  "I'm afraid I am—even lima beans and brussels sprouts. He'll live there thirty-some years, then he'll suffer and die—an ugly, painful death—and—"
  "*No!*" the newscaster covers his ears with his hands and shouts, "I can't listen! I can't! He's the King of Glory, Rafe! The King of Glory!"
  "I know," the voice in the speakers answers. "It's humiliating."
  Director waves at the newscaster and sticks a hand up.
  "We're back from break in five . . . four . . . three . . . two . . ."
  The newscaster swallows hard, then flashes an angelic smile.
  "Welcome back," he says. "Our top story . . ."

Of course, heaven doesn't have a television station—as far as we know! But for Jesus, who is God, to come to earth, be born a child, become a man and suffer and die a hideous death is the ultimate act of humility. He humbled himself, not once, but many times, in order to save you and me. This act reveals why God would command humility and why he values humility—because he humbled himself! He set aside his power and majesty as God and became a man, giving us the ultimate model of humility.

 REFLECT: Philippians 2:5 says, "Your attitude should be the same that Christ Jesus had." What attitude is that? Is your attitude like Christ's (that is, humble)? Are your actions like Christ's? Are there any attitudes or actions you need God's help in ending or correcting? If so, ask him to help you.

 ACT: How many times does today's Bible reading use a word or phrase that refers to Christ's humbling himself? Underline them in your Bible.

 PRAY: "Father God, give me Christ's humble attitude."

8 Humility Brings Honor

Bible Reading: Proverbs 29:23

Pride ends in humiliation, while humility brings honor. Proverbs 29:23

ALMOST FORTY THOUSAND men had died in the battle of Gettysburg. Now, four months later, the governor of Pennsylvania and many others gathered for the dedication of the cemetery where many of those men were buried.

Thousands of people came to the dedication, not just to honor the dead, but also to see and hear the famous speaker Edward Everett. In those days, people attended speeches like they attend baseball and football games today, and it was not unusual for a speech to last as long as today's rock concerts—two or three hours.

Thousands of people came to hear Everett. Everett, the main speaker, had left early in a carriage. Another participant in the event—President Abraham Lincoln—had to ride a horse to the event. Lincoln, the president of the United States, waited patiently while many dignitaries were escorted to the ceremony.

Everett spoke for two hours, during which time the president waited humbly. Then, following a rousing ovation for Everett and the singing of a hymn, Lincoln stood and gave his "dedicatory remarks," which had been planned as a mere formality, like the ribbon cutting at a store opening. Lincoln spoke for less than three minutes, and it was reported that he sat down to a smattering of applause. To many, it may have seemed that Everett was the star of the show.*

But, of course, Lincoln's Gettysburg Address has become one of the most famous speeches ever given. But perhaps more impressive than the words Lincoln spoke is the fact that he—the president of the United States—did not insist on being the main speaker that day. He had not insisted on riding in a fancy carriage as many other guests did, nor had he insisted on being treated like a great man. Instead, he *spoke* great words and *acted* like a great man, and his humility was part of his greatness.

The Bible says, "Pride ends in humiliation, while humility brings honor" (Proverbs 29:23). One reason Abraham Lincoln is so respected and revered more than one hundred years after his death is his character. He was a man who chose to be humble, even when it may have been difficult. A lesser man might have demanded to be treated like a great man. But Lincoln acted as though he knew that humility invites respect, while pride and self-centeredness invite only scorn.

 REFLECT: Humility means not showing off or trying to be the center of attention. Humility also means allowing other people to receive honor. Do you have trouble in any of those areas? If so, how can you behave more humbly in the future?

 PRAY: "God, help me to be humble, not self-centered and prideful, especially when I _____."

*Garry Wills, prologue to *Lincoln at Gettysburg, The Words That Remade America* (New York: Simon and Schuster, 1992), 19–35.

June
9 Uzziah the Pariah

Bible Reading: 2 Chronicles 26:1, 16–21

Pride leads to disgrace, but with humility comes wisdom. Proverbs 11:2

MOST KIDS WOULD be happy just to have clear skin and a driver's license when they reach the age of sixteen. But Uzziah got to be king. Cool, huh? And he handled it pretty well for a while.

Then one day something got into Uzziah. He knew that burning incense and offering sacrifices to God in the temple could only be done by the priests, but he was king and figured he could pretty much do what he wanted. Maybe he thought he could do a better job than the priests. Or maybe he just thought, *Hey, nobody can tell ME what to do—not even God!*

Anyway, Uzziah decided he was going to break the rules and show those priests who was boss, so he headed to the temple. The priests (about eighty of them) heard he was coming and found out what he intended to do. The Bible says that "they followed him in." Several hundred people clogged the streets, whispering that the king wanted to burn incense in the temple. Priests tried to talk him out of it, guards tried to guard him, advisors tried to advise him, and Uzziah ignored all of them. He picked up the incense burner; the protests of the priests became louder and louder. Uzziah got angry. He turned and started yelling at the priests.

"Who do you think you are to tell me what to do? I should have your heads cut off!" While he raged, the Bible says God got his attention. Suddenly the skin on his forehead started to bubble and flake, and within seconds his face was covered with scaly white patches—the telltale signs of leprosy!

The showdown ended, and the priests rushed Uzziah out of the temple. He returned to the palace a leper. He had to live in a separate house the rest of his life. He never again got to enter the temple, and his son took over his throne. Uzziah had leprosy until the day he died. He was even buried in a separate graveyard from the rest of his family because of his leprosy.

All that happened because, "when [Uzziah] had become powerful, he also became proud" (2 Chronicles 26:16). Pride can make a mess of things. It can really mess up your judgment and make you do stupid things. It can ruin friendships. It can make you look silly. Being prideful never earned honor, respect, or friendship for anyone. In fact, it most often destroys those things—just like it did for Uzziah.

 REFLECT: Do you think Uzziah could have taken pleasure in his accomplishments without being sinful? If not, why not? If so, how? Can you take pleasure in your abilities and accomplishments without being prideful? If not, why not? If so, how?

 PRAY: "God, I don't want to be ruined by pride. Help me to remember that no matter how well I do, I can still be humble and should always be grateful to you for any success I enjoy."

Don't Go Hunting for Honor

Bible Reading: Luke 14:7-11

For the proud will be humbled, but the humble will be honored.
Luke 14:11

THERE'S A STORY told of a famous man called Principal Cairns, who was so humble that he would never even enter a room first. He would always stand aside and say to his companions, "You first. I'll follow."

On one occasion this man was among the honored guests at some public event. As he stepped onto the platform, the audience saw Cairns and erupted in applause. Upon hearing their applause, he stopped in his tracks. He motioned for the man behind him to go first, assuming that the clapping and cheering was for that man. He then stood back and joined the applause. He never dreamed the applause could be for him.

Of course, such sincere humility impressed people and brought even greater honor to Principal Cairns. That's sort of what Jesus meant when he said, "The proud will be humbled, but the humble will be honored" (Luke 14:11). When you act like you think you're big and important, it can be embarrassing to find out that you're not as big or not as important as you thought. But when you're humble enough to let other people get the applause and attention, you may be surprised at how much people appreciate you and honor you.

Hunters will tell you that it's better not to peer into the woods and brush, trying to see a deer (or whatever it is you're hunting); instead, you should keep a wide field of vision, not trying to focus too tightly on anything, because it's easier to see small movements out of the corner of your eye. In other words, the harder you look, the less likely you are to see what you're looking for. It's kind of the same with humility and honor. If you go hunting for compliments or applause, you're less likely to get it; but if you're not looking too hard, you might be surprised at the honor that will come your way.

 REFLECT: Jesus was a guest in a Pharisee's house when he spoke the words found in Luke 14:7-11. To find out a little more about the Pharisees (and Jesus' views on pride and position), see Matthew 23:1-12.

Do you ever "go hunting" for compliments? for attention? for applause? Do you want to be more like the guests at the banquet (in Luke 14), who competed for position, or like Jesus, who "did not demand and cling to his rights as God [but] made himself nothing" and humbled himself (Philippians 2:6-7)? What are some ways you can do that?

 ACT: Try to imitate Principal Cairns today by letting others enter a room before you, perhaps even telling them, "You first. I'll follow."

 PRAY: "Lord, forgive me for the times when I've demanded my rights."

June 11

Go Ask Pharaoh

Bible Reading: James 4:4-10

God sets himself against the proud, but he shows favor to the humble.
James 4:6

PHARAOH WAS THE ruler of Egypt, the most powerful man of his time. When Moses told him that God said to let the Israelites go, Pharaoh said no. So what did God do?

Well, God let proud Pharaoh chase the Hebrew people to the Red Sea, which God parted to let his people cross. God then brought the sea back together to give Pharaoh's mighty armies a permanent—and deadly—bath!

Sennacherib, the king of Assyria (and one really bad dude), surrounded the city of Jerusalem with his armies and sent the people of Jerusalem a nasty message, saying, "Do not let Hezekiah deceive you and mislead you like this. Do not believe him, for no god of any nation or kingdom has been able to deliver his people from my hand or the hand of my fathers. How much less will your god deliver you from my hand!" (2 Chronicles 32:15, NIV). So what did God do?

God watched as proud Sennacherib woke up one morning outside Jerusalem to discover that all his soldiers and officers had come down with a mysterious case of . . . death! An angel of the Lord had killed them all during the night! Sennacherib had to slink out of town. But when he arrived home, his own sons murdered him.

Babylon's King Nebuchadnezzar (back in those days, everybody had weird names) thought he was so great that he had a statue made of himself and commanded that everyone in his kingdom should worship him by bowing down to his statue. So what did God do?

God struck proud Nebuchadnezzar with a form of insanity. The king spent seven years living in the yard of his own palace, braying and eating grass like a donkey!

Pharaoh, Sennacherib, and Nebuchadnezzar were all proud, powerful men who were humbled by God. Of course, God doesn't do such things all the time; he may not make you eat grass and live in your backyard if you are too proud. But it is true, as the Bible says, that "God opposes the proud but gives grace to the humble" (James 4:6, NIV).

Sometimes God opposes the proud actively, like he did with Pharaoh, Sennacherib, and Nebuchadnezzar. But even when he doesn't drown armies in the sea or make somebody eat grass, those who are full of pride miss out on the many blessings and advantages that humble people enjoy. Humble people, because they are more teachable, more sensitive, and usually more likable, tend to experience more of God's grace.

 REFLECT: Do you think you're teachable? sensitive? likable? Why or why not? Why (or how) do you think humility will make you more teachable, sensitive, and likable?

 ACT: Eat a salad sometime today or tomorrow to remind you of Nebuchadnezzar, who spent seven years eating grass. As you eat, ask God to help you be humble.

 PRAY: "God, I really do want to be teachable, sensitive, and likable. I want to enjoy all of the blessings you give to the humble."

12 Our Help and Our Shield

Bible Reading: Psalm 33:13-22

But the Lord watches over those who fear him, those who rely on his unfailing love. He rescues them from death and keeps them alive in times of famine. We depend on the Lord alone to save us. Only he can help us, protecting us like a shield. Psalm 33:18-20

A YOUNG GIRL was baking cookies for her mom and suffered severe burns on her hands because she touched the cookie sheet with her bare hands. She forgot to use the oven mitt that lay on the counter by the stove.

A woman lost her sight in one eye after being hit by a rubber ball during an intense game of racquetball. The protective goggles that would have saved her eyesight had been left lying in the bottom of her gym bag.

A police officer was killed in a shoot-out with drug dealers. His chest wound probably would not have been fatal if he had been wearing a bulletproof vest. He had been issued a vest by the police department but had never taken it out of his locker at the police station.

All of these tragedies could have been avoided. All of these people had something—an oven mitt, protective goggles, a bulletproof vest—that could have protected them from harm. So why were they hurt, even killed? Because they didn't use the protection they possessed.

God is our help and our shield. He has given us commands that are meant to protect us. Moses made it clear that "the Lord's commands and laws" were given "for your own good" (Deuteronomy 10:13). He intends for his commands to be like protective goggles or an oven mitt; they're supposed to protect us—but we have to *use* them.

God cannot be our help and our shield if we don't obey him. His commands can't protect us and enrich our life if we don't follow them. If we ignore or disobey God's loving commands, they're just like a bulletproof vest that's left hanging in a policeman's locker or safety goggles that are left in the bottom of a gym bag. But if we obey God and do what he commands, he will protect us and save us from many troubles.

 REFLECT: God's Word says many times that his commands are meant to protect us from danger and harm. Take time to read Deuteronomy 6:24, Jeremiah 32:39, and James 1:25.

Do you keep God and his commandments "in a locker" or locked away somewhere? Do you treat his commands as if they're not important? Or do you obey him and follow his commandments every day?

 ACT: Next time you see an oven mitt on the kitchen counter or a pair of safety goggles in a science lab, remember that God's commandments are meant to protect us from harm.

 PRAY: "Thank you, Lord, for being my help and my shield."

13 The Blind Men and the Elephant

Bible Reading: Deuteronomy 10:12-14

And now, O Israel, what does the Lord your God ask of you but . . . to observe the Lord's commands and decrees? Deuteronomy 10:12-13, NIV

THERE'S AN OLD story about four blind men who encountered an elephant.

One man placed his hands on the elephant's thick leg. "An elephant is like a tree," he announced, "thick and strong."

Another man gripped one of the elephant's ears in his hands. "No, my friend," he said. "An elephant is like a great palm leaf, thin and flexible."

A third man grabbed the animal by the tail. "You are both wrong," he said. "An elephant is like a rope, long and lean."

The fourth blind man leaned against the elephant's massive body. "You are all as stupid as you are blind," he said. "An elephant is none of those things. It is strong and hard, like a mighty wall."

Those four blind men are like you and me in our efforts to learn right from wrong. You may have already discovered that no two people have the same ideas of right and wrong. No one can seem to agree on what's good and what's evil. Some people say, "It's wrong to do that," and others respond, "No, it's wrong to say that's wrong; it's really right."

That's because we're all like those blind men. Each of us can only see a small part of the picture. We can't see the future. We can't even see very well right now. We don't know all the effects our words and actions can have. It would be much easier for a blind man to describe an elephant than it would be for any one of us to see good and evil clearly. But that's OK.

Imagine if someone with perfect sight were to come along and discover those blind men arguing about what an elephant looks like. That person could tell them what an elephant *really* looks like. They might not believe him, but if they listened, his description would make sense out of their different experiences and perspectives.

That's what God's Word does for us. He tells us what things are right and what things are wrong. And he can do that, of course, because (unlike us) he sees everything clearly and knows everything completely. We may choose not to believe him, but if we will listen to him and obey what he says, we'll discover that we can trust God's view of right and wrong—because it's right!

 REFLECT: Do you usually act as if you know more than God or as if God knows more than you do? How does a person act if he or she trusts God's view of right and wrong?

 PRAY: "God, I know that you see everything clearly and know everything completely. Help me remember to trust you to tell me what's right and wrong and to obey what you say."

14 The Right Response

Bible Reading: Leviticus 19:1-3

Each of you must show respect for your mother and father . . . for I, the Lord, am your God. Leviticus 19:3

WHICH DO YOU think would be the right reaction to the following situations?

1. Your mom reminds you that you haven't finished your chores today. You answer:

   a. "Don't have a cow! I'll do it when I feel like it!"
   b. "OK, Mom. I'll do it in a minute."

2. Your dad wears a pair of shorts with black socks and sandals to the store. You:

   a. Tell him he looks stupid and you never want to be seen with him.
   b. Keep your mouth shut and hope he asks you for fashion advice.

3. Your parents drop you and a friend off at a youth group meeting. As they pull away, you turn to your friend and say:

   a. "Finally! I thought we'd never get away from Dad and his corny jokes! He's so pathetic!"
   b. "Parents can be corny sometimes, but Mom and Dad really do a lot of cool stuff for me."

OK, so maybe you wouldn't *quite* do or say any of those things, but at least your reactions would be closer to (b) than to (a) in each case, right?

Chances are, you recognized that the (a) answer to each question was inappropriate, even wrong. Why? Because you know that respect is right and being *dis*respectful is wrong.

God commands us, "You must be holy because I, the Lord your God, am holy." Then he says, "Each of you must show respect for your mother and father . . . for I, the Lord, am your God" (Leviticus 19:2-3). That means that respect isn't a favor you do for your parents, as if you were offering to shovel the sidewalk or shine their shoes; it's more than that. Respect is right. Anything less is wrong.

 REFLECT: How do you know that being respectful is the right way to be? If you got a grade (A, B, C, D, F) for respecting your parents, what do you think your grade would be right now? (Be honest!) Can you bring your "grade" up? If so, how?

ACT: Make a list of five practical ways you can show respect to your parents (such as "opening the door for Mom or Dad," "not talking back to Mom or Dad," etc.) and try to do everything on the list before the end of the next week.

 PRAY: "God, I don't always show respect for_____ when_____. Help me to do what's right."

15 Isaiah's Excellent Adventure

Bible Reading: Isaiah 6:1-7
Therefore stand in awe of God. Ecclesiastes 5:7, NIV

IF THE PROPHET Isaiah were alive today, he might tell the story a little differently than the first time he recorded it (in Isaiah 6:1-7). He might say something like:

"It went down like this: See, I was in the temple, minding my own business, worshiping God, you know, like I always did.

"All of a sudden the place lit up like New York City or Las Vegas or something! I looked up, and it was like the roof had come off the temple. I could see a throne hovering in the sky. On the throne was God, man, God himself, and he was wearing this long robe that hung all the way down and, like, filled the temple. And there were angels—weird-looking, scary-looking angels—flying all around him, and they were singing, 'Holy, holy, holy is the Lord Almighty. The whole earth is filled with his glory!' Man, it was like 'SurroundSound'—know what I'm saying? It shook the whole temple like an earthquake, and the place was filled with smoke!

"Aw, man, I couldn't take it! I fell on my face, and I said to myself, 'O man, O man, I'm done for! I'm dead meat! I'm history, man, my goose is cooked! Here I am, a sinner, man, a sinner, and I've seen the King, the Lord Almighty! Aw, man, I just know I'm gonna be fried any minute!'"

That's a paraphrase, of course, but you get the idea. The whole story is in the sixth chapter of the Old Testament book of Isaiah, but here's the main idea: Isaiah saw the Lord, and his vision of God was so overwhelming that he was filled with awe and respect (so much awe and respect that he nearly had a heart attack right on the spot!).

Why mention it here? Because that kind of awe and respect is the first step in respecting others. You cannot truly respect your parents, your teachers, your friends—even yourself—unless you have a healthy respect for God. Because when you respect God, you can begin to truly respect others. But if you don't respect God, you'll never really respect anyone—including yourself.

 REFLECT: When Isaiah saw God's glory in the temple, he fell on his face in fear and awe. The apostle John had a similar reaction to a vision of Jesus (check out Revelation 1:9-19). Why do you think they had such extreme reactions to God's glory? (Hint: Exodus 33:12-23 might also offer a clue.)

Why do you think respect for others begins with respect for God? How do you show respect for God? Do you think you can develop a deeper respect for God? If not, why not? If so, how?

 ACT: Make a list of five practical ways you can show respect for God (such as "taking off my hat in church," "not talking during the worship service," "kneeling when I pray," etc.), and try to do everything on the list before the end of the next week.

 PRAY: "God, you are so awesome! I praise you, God."

16 Command Performance

Bible Reading: 1 Peter 2:13-17
Show proper respect to everyone. 1 Peter 2:17, NIV

LISTED BELOW ARE a bunch of commands from the Bible. Unfortunately, some commands that aren't in the Bible have gotten mixed in with them. See if you can recognize and cross out those commands that aren't found in the Bible.

1. "Honor your father and mother."
2. "Never give a sucker an even break."
3. "Show respect for the elderly."
4. "Give to dogs what is sacred; throw your pearls to pigs."
5. "Put your right foot in, put your right foot out, put your right foot in, and shake it all about."
6. "Honor [the king], for he is your lord."
7. "Don't cry over spilled milk."
8. "The elders who direct the affairs of the church are worthy of double honor."
9. "Honor one another above yourselves."
10. "Show proper respect to everyone."
11. "Stay tuned for these messages."
12. "Obey the government."

So, how many did you cross out? You should have crossed out five of the twelve commands on the list. If you crossed out more (or less), look back over the list.

If you crossed out numbers 2, 4, 5, 7, and 11, you are exactly right! None of those commands are found in the Bible (though number 4 is the opposite of a command found in Matthew 7:6). The other seven statements are biblical commands. They are, in order, Exodus 20:12, Leviticus 19:32 (NIV), Psalm 45:11, 1 Timothy 5:17, Romans 12:10 (NIV), 1 Peter 2:17 (NIV), and Romans 13:1.

Not only that, but each of those Bible verses is a command to show respect, in one form or another, for someone else. Those verses should make it clear to anyone that God commands us to respect other people. He wants us to respect our parents. He tells us to show respect for the elderly. He wants us to respect church and government officials. He even commands us to respect *everyone*. Can he make it any clearer than that?

 REFLECT: God commands us to respect others. How many different kinds of people does he command respect for? Look back at the various kinds of respect God commands. Do you show proper respect in all those areas? Do you need to try harder in some areas?

 ACT: Make a list of five practical ways you can show respect for others (such as "pushing Mrs. Klein's wheelchair," "not making fun of Mr. Porter," etc.), and try to do everything on the list before the end of the next week.

 PRAY: "There are a lot of people you want me to respect, God. Please give me the help I need to do it."

17 The Hen and the Jewel

Bible Reading: 1 Timothy 5:1-4

Rise in the presence of the aged, show respect for the elderly and revere your God. I am the Lord. Leviticus 19:32, NIV

A HEN WAS once scratching in the barnyard, searching for food. She spied a lump in the ground and pecked at it until she had overturned a bright, shiny diamond!

The hen cocked her head (as chickens will do) and studied the sparkling jewel. Finally, however, she kicked it away with her foot, saying, "If my master had found such a jewel, he would be happy, for he likes such baubles. But I would much rather have a single barleycorn than all the gems in the world!"

That diamond was worth far more than a kernel of corn, of course, but the hen didn't care. Although the farmer would have jumped for joy to have found a diamond, it meant nothing to her.

We often do the same thing. We value things that our Master cares nothing about and ignore things that he thinks are really valuable.

For example, God's Word tells us, "Rise in the presence of the aged, show respect for the elderly and revere your God. I am the Lord" (Leviticus 19:32, NIV). That Bible verse commands us to show respect to people who are old. In the same sentence it tells us to revere (or respect) our God. Why? Because showing respect for elderly people and showing respect for God are related.

You see, God commands respect because he values respect. If we act like that hen in the barnyard and ignore or throw away what our Master values, we're showing that we don't really respect him or worship him. But if we really respect our God, we'll value the same things or the same people he thinks are important. And God values the elderly.

It's easy to believe that elderly people serve no useful purpose in society. After all, some move very slowly. Others may act crabby at times. But, believe it or not, the elderly can be storehouses of information and wisdom. (Check out your grandparents or your great-aunt Bea!)

Since God thinks respect for older people is valuable, we should think so, too. Otherwise, we're just like that silly hen in the barnyard, kicking away diamonds while scratching for corn!

 REFLECT: God commands us to respect others because he values respect. Do you show respect for the elderly? If not, why not? If so, how? Think of some specific older people you know. How can you start making it a habit to show respect for them?

 ACT: Ask your parents if they could serve corn at your next dinner together to remind you of the story of the hen and the jewel. (If that's not possible—or if you hate corn!—buy a small bag of birdseed and feed the birds for the next few days—just make sure there are no diamonds in the bag of birdseed!)

PRAY: "Father God, I thank you for the older people at church, especially_____. Thank you for the older people in my family, too, especially_____."

18 Boy Meets Janitor

Bible Reading: James 2:1-9

It is good when you truly obey our Lord's royal command found in the Scriptures: "Love your neighbor as yourself." James 2:8

AN EPISODE OF the ABC television series *Boy Meets World* once depicted the horror of Shawn (one of the main characters, played by Rider Strong) when his father got a new job—as the school janitor! Shawn was horrified that his father would be mopping up spills and cleaning toilets in front of Shawn's friends and classmates! He became upset with his father for taking the job. He was angry at the principal, Mr. Feeney, for hiring his father. The whole thing seemed to be an adult conspiracy meant to embarrass Shawn and shame him in front of the whole school.

How would you feel if your father was your school's janitor? (Maybe he is.) How would you feel if your mom cleaned for a living? (Maybe she does.) What if your family were poor compared to everyone else on the block? (Maybe they are.)

You know what the Bible's answer would be to those questions?

Big deal.

That's right, big deal. So what if your dad's a janitor or your mom's a cleaning lady? So what if your family is the poorest in your neighborhood? Big deal. "My dear brothers and sisters," the Bible says, "how can you claim that you have faith in our glorious Lord Jesus Christ if you favor some people more than others?" (James 2:1).

The Bible makes it clear that everyone—rich or poor, janitor or principal, cleaning lady or movie star, native or foreigner—deserves to be treated with respect. It doesn't matter what color a person is. It doesn't matter what job a person has. It doesn't matter whether a person is a man or a woman, a boy or a girl. It doesn't matter how much money a person has or what kind of house he or she may live in. It doesn't matter how much a person may weigh or how far he or she can hit a baseball. According to God, we should respect all people because all people were created in God's image. God values all his children, rich and poor, male and female, black and white, short and tall, young and old and in between. And you know what else? We should too.

 REFLECT: Why does God command us to respect everyone, not just certain people? Have you ever favored some people more than others? Have you treated certain people (rich, "important," and so on) with respect while ignoring others? How can you do better at treating everyone with respect?

 ACT: Make a special effort today to show respect to everyone— including school janitors, bus drivers, butchers, bakers, and candlestick makers!

 PRAY: "Lord, I'm really sorry about the time when I wasn't very respectful to _____. Help me to show your love and kindness to all of your children."

19 You Are Somebody

Bible Reading: Ephesians 2:8-10

For we are God's masterpiece. Ephesians 2:10

WAY BACK IN the 1970s (before your parents were even your parents!) there was a special effort aimed at developing the abilities of students in the inner cities. The program was called Excel and was led by the Reverend Jesse Jackson.

Jesse Jackson traveled across the country speaking to students in many inner-city schools. He came from Chicago, where he had begun the program, and traveled to places like Los Angeles; Washington, D.C.; Detroit; and New York. His message was based on the way many children in poor sections of the city (especially poor, African-American children) felt about themselves. They felt that, because of where they lived and what they owned and what they heard others say about them, they weren't worth much. Many young people feel the same way today.

Jesse Jackson brought a simple message into those areas. At a graduation ceremony at Calvin Coolidge High School in Washington, D.C., he started his speech by saying, "I am somebody!" The students repeated the phrase: "I am somebody!" Then he continued: "I am somebody! My mind is a pearl! I can learn anything in the world! I . . . am . . . somebody!"

As he traveled across the country, Jesse Jackson repeated the phrase, "I am somebody," and young people across the nation echoed, "I am somebody." He realized that no one can respect others unless he respects himself. He realized that no one can achieve true greatness unless she respects herself. He realized that people can never become all that God wants them to be unless they first respect themselves.

The apostle Paul once delivered a similar message to early Christians in a city called Ephesus. He wrote, "We are God's masterpiece. He has created us anew in Christ Jesus, so that we can do the good things he planned for us long ago. . . . So now you . . . are no longer strangers and foreigners. You are citizens along with all of God's holy people. You are members of God's family. We are his house, built on the foundation of the apostles and the prophets. And the cornerstone is Christ Jesus himself" (Ephesians 2:10, 19-20).

You are God's masterpiece! *You are somebody!*

 REFLECT: Do you respect yourself? If not, why not? Do you ever treat yourself disrespectfully? If so, why? How do you think respecting yourself helps you respect others?

 ACT: Write the following phrases on separate index cards: "I am God's masterpiece!" "I am a citizen along with all of God's holy people!" "I am a member of God's family!" "I am becoming a holy temple for the Lord." "I am somebody!" Place one card each day at the bottom of your bedroom or bathroom mirror to serve as a "caption" every time you look into the mirror.

 PRAY: Say these words (Psalm 139:14) with the psalmist: "Thank you for making me so wonderfully complex! Your workmanship is marvelous—and how well I know it."

20 A Fable

Bible Reading: Romans 13:1-7

Give respect and honor to all to whom it is due. Romans 13:7

Obey your leaders and submit to their authority. Hebrews 13:17, NIV

A YOUNG STUDENT was reading the Bible one day. He read the words the apostle Paul wrote to the Christians who lived in Rome: "Obey the government, for God is the one who put it there" (Romans 13:1).

"That's easy for you to say," the student said, as if Paul were standing in the room, "but the government where I live is cruel and corrupt."

Suddenly, a robed and bearded figure of Paul appeared beside him. "Young friend," said Paul, "I wrote those words to Christians living under a Roman government that persecuted and often killed Christians."

"But," the student blurted out after a moment of amazed silence, "you say that if we refuse to obey people in authority, we are refusing to obey God." The shadowy figure nodded.

The student continued, "But you don't understand—my language arts teacher isn't even a Christian!"

The figure smiled. "The Roman emperors were not Christians, either, but even they were placed in power by God."

Frustration showed on the young student's face. "But you say to give respect and honor to whom it is due! Well, a lot of the people who are in charge of me—like my teachers and my school bus driver—don't deserve too much respect."

"The Word of God doesn't say to give respect to those you *think* deserve it," Paul said. "It says to give respect and honor to whom it is due—and respect is due those who are in authority over you: police, teachers, even school bus drivers!"

"OK," the student said with a sigh. "I guess you're right. If the authorities are established by God, like the Bible says, I guess I should respect them. Right?"

The student looked up to see that the figure of the apostle Paul had disappeared. Then the youth looked back at the pages of the Bible. The apostle's words were still there, though they seemed much clearer than before.

REFLECT: Does it affect your understanding of Romans 13:1-7 to know that Paul, who wrote those words, was often imprisoned and beaten (and eventually executed) by various religious and civil authorities? Reread that passage and see if knowing that makes a difference.

Do you respect the people who are in authority over you (government officials, church leaders, teachers, school bus drivers)? Do you think that showing respect is always easy? Why or why not? Do you think you should show respect even if it's not easy? Why or why not?

PRAY: "God, help me to obey you. Help me to show respect to people who have authority over me, even when it's not easy. Please help me especially to show respect to_____."

A Tale of Two Criminals

Bible Reading: Luke 23:32-43

One of the criminals hanging beside him scoffed. . . . But the other criminal protested, "Don't you fear God even when you are dying?" Luke 23:39-40

HAVE YOU READ today's Bible reading? If not, you will probably want to read it at least once before you try to tackle the following quiz:

1. Where was Jesus crucified?

   (a) A place called Gomorrah, meaning "The Plain"
   (b) A place called Golgotha, meaning "The Skull"
   (c) A place called Goliath, meaning "The Giant"

2. How did the crowd and the leaders treat Jesus?

   (a) They felt sorry for him.
   (b) They ignored him.
   (c) They made fun of him.

3. How did the thieves treat Jesus?

   (a) One mocked him; the other was respectful.
   (b) Both mocked him.
   (c) Neither one paid any attention to him.

Done? Now check the answers below to see how well you did: 1(b); 2(c); 3(a).

Of the two thieves crucified with Jesus, one treated Jesus with honor and respect. That thief went to paradise that day because he repented and received the forgiveness of his sins through Jesus' sacrifice. His action has been admired for two thousand years as an example of righteous conduct.

Treating others with respect is right. It's also the better way to behave because it produces good results more often than not. Treating other people with respect also protects you from offense and makes you more attractive in many people's eyes. In other words, who would you rather be like: the thief who cursed Jesus or the one who treated him with respect?

REFLECT: The two thieves who were crucified with Jesus illustrate how ugly and offensive disrespectful behavior is, and how attractive and admirable respectful people appear. How does the crowd's behavior compare to the thieves' behavior? Why is respect right? Why is it also better? Whom do you most often act like: the thief who cursed Jesus, or the one who treated him with respect? Do you think acting respectfully can make you more attractive and admirable to other people? In what ways?

PRAY: "God, remind me that obeying you has benefits. Help me to be respectful because it is right and because it is the best way to treat others."

22 Good Feelings, Bad Feelings

Bible Reading: Titus 3:1-2

Do what is good, and you will have praise. Romans 13:3, NASB

SOME DAY YOU may find yourself in one of the following situations. Some of these situations would probably cause you to feel good. Others would more likely make you feel bad. Place a check mark in the appropriate column to indicate whether you think your action would have good results or bad results for you:

Good Results		Bad Results
	Your parents fill your Christmas stocking with straw as a little joke. You decide to fling the straw in their faces, screaming, "I want my presents *now!*"	
	Your teacher gives you a "zero" on a homework assignment because you forgot to put your name on it. You call her "fat and ugly."	
	An elderly woman with a cane is standing in front of a revolving door, hesitant to go in. You stop and help her through the door.	
	A policeman stops you for jaywalking and threatens to give you a ticket. You answer, "Whatcha gonna do, throw me in jail for jaywalking, you big turkey?"	
	The head lifeguard at the city pool calls you over to his chair and tells you that you're not allowed to wear cutoff shorts to swim. You answer, "OK. I'll go home and change right away."	

As you might guess, the point of this exercise is that treating other people respectfully will more often result in good results and good feelings. Treating other people rudely and disrespectfully will often bring some pretty bad consequences—like getting thrown in jail for jaywalking just because you smarted off to a policeman!

The Bible says that if you refuse to give people (especially people in authority) the proper respect, you shouldn't be surprised if you receive condemnation and other bad results. But if you "do what is good" and treat people politely and respectfully, you'll receive praise and other good things. And whatever you do, don't dare a policeman to throw you in jail!

REFLECT: How would you complete this sentence: Respect protects from_____ and provides for_____?

ACT: Conduct an experiment for the next two days: Make a special effort to treat everyone you meet or talk to politely and respectfully. Keep track of any good or bad results you experience (perhaps by writing them down in a journal or notebook).

PRAY: "Thank you, God, for the good things that happen when I show respect to people. Thanks for helping me feel good when I_____."

23 A Soldier's Story

Bible Reading: 2 Samuel 9:1-13
I want to show God's kindness to them in any way I can. 2 Samuel 9:3

DAVID KING, a successful American businessman, waited in the lobby of a Hanoi hotel. Over twenty years had passed since he had been in Vietnam as a soldier fighting the North Vietnamese in a war that cost him one of his legs.

Since that time, he had become rich and had learned to walk without crutches, using a prosthetic leg that enabled him to walk with only a slight limp.

A man wearing an American-made business suit entered the hotel lobby from the street and approached King. "I think I have good news for you," the man said.

"I'm glad to hear that, Ziba," King said, fastening his eyes on his assistant, Jack Ziba.

"I've located one of Lo Dong's sons," Ziba said. "He lives in Haiphong."

"Excellent!" King said. "Let's go!"

Ziba hesitated. "Do you mind if I ask you a question?" When King shrugged, Ziba asked, "Why all this trouble to locate the family of a Vietnamese man you haven't seen in twenty years?"

King inhaled deeply and let out a long sigh. "Because Lo Dong saved my life. If he hadn't dragged me into a hut during a firefight, I would have bled to death. Now that I'm richer than I ever thought possible, I plan to show God's kindness to his family in any way I can, out of respect for Lo Dong."

King and Ziba drove the fifty miles from Hanoi to Haiphong and, after three days of searching, found the son of Lo Dong, the man who had saved King's life. The Vietnamese man bowed to the American, and King bowed back. Then King explained in broken Vietnamese why he had come to Haiphong. The eyes of Lo Dong's son filled with tears; he bowed again when he understood.

Eventually, Lo Dong's son became an executive in King's multinational company, and the two men became close friends—so close, in fact, that King was once quoted in a magazine article as saying, "If I had never made that trip to Hanoi, I would never have known my best friend in the world—the son of the man who saved my life."

 REFLECT: The story of David King and Lo Dong's son didn't really happen. But it is based on a true story. How is it like the events described in 2 Samuel 9:1-13? How is it different?

Do you think treating people with respect will give you more friends or more enemies? Will it make your friendships better? If not, why not? If so, how?

 ACT: Remember the experiment you began yesterday in which you were going to make a special effort to treat *everyone* you met or talked to respectfully? Make today the second day of that experiment. At the end of the day, review the results. Have you had more good results than bad results? You may want to consider extending the experiment indefinitely!

 PRAY: "Thank you, God, for the friends I gain when I'm kind, patient, and respectful."

24 The Daniel Diet

Bible Reading: Daniel 1:3-16
Daniel made up his mind not to defile himself. Daniel 1:8

"WELCOME TO *Babylon Today,* the daily magazine of news, culture, and entertainment for the entire Babylonian Empire!" A blonde female announcer sits in front of a backdrop of a painted sunrise, smiling through thick makeup.

"Our first guest today," the woman says, "is the creator of the popular 'Daniel Diet,' a new health craze that is sweeping the empire." She turns in her seat, and the camera angle widens to show a young man, dressed in finely embroidered robes, sitting next to her. "Tell us," she says, "how this new diet craze came about."

He shrugs and squints against the bright studio lights. "I, uh, never planned to start any diet craze," he says. "I was just training for the service of the king—"

"Of our king, the mighty Nebuchadnezzar—may he live forever!" the woman says, smiling broadly and gazing nervously at the camera.

"Uh, yeah," Daniel answers. "Anyway, when we started training, we were given really big meals with lots of meat and fat and wine and stuff. But, see, I'm Jewish, and Jews have kinda strict requirements about what we eat. To make a long story short, I asked the official in charge of our training for permission to eat healthy things."

"You refused the king's food?" the woman asks. "Weren't you afraid?"

Daniel nods and shrugs. "Yeah, I guess so. But I'd already made up my mind not to defile myself." He turns and faces the camera. "You see, it's a lot easier to do the right thing when you make up your mind ahead of time. I decided when I was first brought to this country that I would not forget my God and the commands he has given. When I first started training for the king's service, I knew the food would be a problem. So I decided ahead of time what I would do when temptation came. That made it easier to send the food back and ask for vegetables and water."

"You—you sent food back to the king's kitchen?" the woman says, staring at Daniel as if he had just sprouted a second head. She clears her throat and giggles nervously. "Uh, th-thank you for t-telling us your story. . . . Uh, we'll be right back after these messages."

REFLECT: For the whole story of "the Daniel Diet," look again at Daniel 1:3-16. If you had been in that situation, how would you have reacted? What made Daniel's choice to do the right thing (as a Jew) and stand up to the king a little easier? How have you made up your mind to avoid wrong choices?

ACT: Decide now that you will do the right thing when you are faced with temptations. Be as specific as you can in completing the following sentences:
When I am tempted to _____, I will _____.
When I am tempted to _____, I will _____.

PRAY: Let the words of Psalm 119:12 (NIV) be your prayer: "My heart is set on keeping your decrees to the very end."

The Snow Hare

Bible Reading: 1 Peter 4:1-5, 19

Of course, your former friends are very surprised when you no longer join them in the wicked things they do. 1 Peter 4:4

A YOUNG SNOW hare was once playing happily outside the snowy hole in the yard where his family lived. His white fur made him almost invisible against the snow, protecting him from the hawks that sometimes flew overhead.

Suddenly, a little mouse appeared. The snow hare invited the mouse to play, and they became friends as they played in the snow near the snow hare's home. The mouse returned the next day and the next, and the new friends played together each day.

Then one day the mouse said, "Hey, let's play at my house!"

The snow hare looked around. "Where *is* your house?"

"I live in a big house, where people live," the mouse answered. "My family and I live in the coal cellar. We can play in the coal and have a lot of fun."

"I-I don't know," the snow hare answered. "I'm supposed to stay close to our hole. My mom doesn't like me to go where she can't hear me." He looked skyward. "There are hawks up there, you know."

"Oh, don't be a wimp," the mouse answered. "The hawks aren't gonna get you. You'll be playing inside a big house, in the cellar! No big bad bird's gonna see you there."

"Well," the young hare answered, "I guess it won't hurt just this once." Besides, he didn't want his friend to think he was a wimp.

So the snow hare and the mouse scampered off to the coal cellar, where the mouse's family lived. They climbed and played and rolled in the coal until it started to get dark, and the snow hare knew he'd better get home. He said good-bye to his mouse friend and ran from the coal cellar as fast as his legs could carry him.

High in the sky a hawk circled, scanning the landscape for his next meal. Suddenly, something caught his eye. It was the snow hare, whose white fur had become almost black from the coal, racing across the snowy white ground toward his home. The hawk dove to the ground and, in a flash, had snatched the snow hare in his talons and carried him off. To this day, snow hare families tell the story of the young snow hare who came to a sad end because he let a friend talk him into a wrong choice.

REFLECT: Do your friends ever talk you into wrong or harmful behaviors? What do you usually do? Do you think friends who try to get you to do wrong are good for you or bad for you? Why? Who usually gets hurt or in trouble when you let your friends talk you into doing wrong—you or your friends?

PRAY: "God, it can be really hard to do the right thing when my friends are trying to talk me into doing wrong things. Help me to keep on doing what is right, and help me to be an example to my friends instead of letting them get me into trouble."

26 Tongue of Pig

Bible Reading: James 3:2-12

We all make many mistakes, but those who control their tongues can also control themselves in every other way. James 3:2

A WEALTHY WOMAN once called her cook in and said, "Tonight, the man I love is coming to visit. I would like you to serve us the most pleasant dish you can create."

That night, the cook served the woman and her love many delicious appetizers. Then he announced, "Tonight's main course is tongue of pig!"

"Tongue of pig!" the woman echoed. "I told you to serve us the most pleasant dish you could think of!"

The cook nodded. "When two people love each other, as you do, their tongues say the most pleasant and loving things. So shouldn't tongue be the most pleasant dish in the world?"

The woman smiled. "That is true," she said. "You are not only a fine cook, you are a wise man." The cook bowed, and the woman and her guest enjoyed the delicious meal. Later, however, they got into a bitter argument and parted angrily.

The next morning the woman approached the cook again. "Tonight," she said, "I would like you to serve the most unpleasant dish you can create."

That night, when the couple sat down to eat dinner, the cook served them many delicious appetizers. Then he announced, "Tonight's main course is tongue of pig!"

"What!" the woman screamed. "Yesterday I told you I wanted the most pleasant dish in the world, and you served tongue of pig. This morning I said I wanted the most *un*pleasant dish in the world, and again you serve tongue of pig."

The cook bowed respectfully. "When two people argue and fight, their tongues say the most unpleasant and hateful things. So is not tongue the most unpleasant dish in the world?"

This folktale from Vietnam illustrates what James wrote in the Bible: "People can tame all kinds of animals and birds and reptiles and fish, but no one can tame the tongue. It is an uncontrollable evil, full of deadly poison. Sometimes it praises our Lord and Father, and sometimes it breaks out into curses against those who have been made in the image of God. And so blessing and cursing come pouring out of the same mouth. Surely, my brothers and sisters, this is not right!" (James 3:7-10).

Your tongue has amazing power for good or evil. In fact, a lot of wrong choices begin with the tongue. But "those who control their tongues can also control themselves in every other way" (James 3:2). If we can learn to talk a little less and listen a little more, we will probably find it a little easier to stay out of trouble.

 REFLECT: Can you think of any wrong choices you've made because you didn't control your tongue? How can you get better at controlling your tongue?

 PRAY: "God, please help me control my tongue today when_____."

27 Good vs. Good

Bible Reading: Genesis 1:1-12

And God saw that it [his creation] was good. Genesis 1:12

PEOPLE USE THE word *good* in a lot of ways. In fact, a lot of commercials and advertisements use the word *good*. See if you can match the slogan with the product it advertises (answers are given below):

1. IT DOES A BODY GOOD
2. GOOD TO THE LAST DROP
3. GREAT TASTE NEVER LOOKED SO GOOD
4. M'M M'M GOOD!
5. THE GOOD STUFF KIDS GO FOR

A. MAXWELL HOUSE COFFEE
B. CAMPBELL'S SOUP
C. SUNNY DELIGHT (CITRUS DRINK)
D. MILK
E. SPECIAL K CEREAL

See? Sometimes *good* can mean "tasty." Sometimes it can mean "healthy" or "nutritious." Sometimes it means "pleasant." And sometimes it means "attractive."

But *good* also means "right" and "moral." That's what a mother means when she says, "Be a good boy at school." That's what people mean when they talk about "do-gooders." That's what the Bible means when it says, "Hate what is evil; cling to what is good" (Romans 12:9, NIV).

It can be confusing, can't it? Sometimes *good* means "tasty" (like "good food") or "pleasant" (like "good music"). But sometimes it means "morally good," the opposite of evil. But you know what makes it even more confusing?

A lot of people think that moral goodness is no different from other kinds of goodness. They think, "Hey, you like chocolate, I like vanilla. You think lying is wrong, I don't." But that's wrong, because they're confusing two different kinds of "good."

People can have different tastes or opinions about what foods are good, what music they enjoy, and what colors they like; but when it comes to what's good and what's evil, what's right and what's wrong, that's not up to you or me to decide. It doesn't matter what we like or don't like. All that matters is what God says is good. He has already told us what's good and what's evil. We can argue. We can disagree. We can ignore what he says. But we can't make up our own version of "good."

 REFLECT: Have your choices today been good, meaning "right" and "moral"? Has your behavior been like God? Pleasing to God? If not, take a few moments to ask God for his forgiveness.

 ACT: Be alert to the various ways you hear people use the word *good*. Ask yourself, "Are they using the word to mean 'tasty,' 'pleasant,' 'attractive,' or 'healthy' (which depend on a person's taste or opinion), or do they mean *moral* goodness (which doesn't depend on taste or opinion)?

 PRAY: "God, thank you for teaching me what is good. Help me to hate what is evil."

THE ANSWERS TO THE MATCHING EXERCISE ABOVE ARE: 1(D); 2(A); 3(E); 4(B); 5(C).

28 God Is Great, God Is Good

Bible Reading: Genesis 1:14-25

You [God] are good and do only good; teach me your principles.
Psalm 119:68

CHECK THE ANSWER you think best fits the meaning of each word.

Do you know what the word *feline* means?

☐ The line where people line up to pay parking fees
☐ Harmless
☐ Like a cat

How about the word *bovine?*

☐ A deep canyon
☐ Like a cow
☐ A vine that grows a rare kind of grape

How about the word *good?*

☐ To do whatever you want as long as it doesn't hurt anybody
☐ To be "one with the universe"
☐ To be like God

Well, you probably get the point. The word *feline* means to be catlike. The word *bovine* refers to a cow or something that resembles a cow. And to be morally *good* means to be like God.

When God created the universe and everything in it, he looked at what he'd created and saw that it was good. That wasn't just an opinion; it was the truth! He was comparing everything he'd made with himself, and because everything was pure and perfect and without sin (like he is), it was "good."

Now, of course, when sin entered the world, it messed up God's "good" creation. But one thing hasn't changed: When something is morally good, it is like God. If it isn't like God, it isn't good.

In fact, you can't go far wrong if you measure everything you think, do, or say against the one standard for what is good—God. If you ask yourself, "Is it like God?" before you make any choice, the difference between good and bad will be a lot easier to see . . . because God is good.

 REFLECT: How many times in Genesis 1 does God call his creation "good"? What was he comparing it to?
Which is easier—to rely on your friends' ideas of what is good or to measure everything you think, do, or say against the one standard for what is good—God himself? Which is right?

 PRAY: "God, I praise you because you are good. You are holy. You are perfect. You are pure. You are righteous in everything you think, do, and say. Help me to remember that you alone are good."

June
29 Reflected Glory

Bible Reading: Genesis 1:26-31

Then God said, "Let us make people in our image, to be like ourselves."
Genesis 1:26

And we . . . are being transformed into his likeness with ever-increasing glory, which comes from the Lord, who is the Spirit.
2 Corinthians 3:18, NIV

YOU'VE SEEN A full moon before, right? Of course you have. A full moon can make the landscape shine almost like daytime. As you walk around you can see great distances, and you can see trees and sidewalks and flowers—all in the middle of the night by moonlight!

But did you know that, in a way, there is no such thing as moonlight?

That's right! Because moonlight doesn't come from the moon—it comes from the sun! The light we see on a moonlit night is actually sunlight that bounces off the moon and shines down onto the earth. Because the earth and moon both revolve around the sun, sometimes we see a full moon, sometimes we see a crescent moon, and sometimes we see no moon at all, when it's a "new moon" so close to the sun that it's invisible.

In a way, we're like the moon. Just as the moon has no light of its own, the Bible says that we have no righteousness of our own. Not one of us is good; we're all sinners. (See Psalm 14:1-3; Mark 10:18; Romans 3:23.)

Just as the moon can only "shine" by reflecting the light of the sun, the only way that we can do good and be good is by reflecting the goodness of God. We are not good, and no matter how hard we try, we can't do good (Romans 7:18-19). But God *is* good, and when we let his Holy Spirit live in us and control us, he can help us make right choices and reflect his goodness.

When we do good with God's help, we're reflecting the image of God just as the moon reflects the light of the sun.

REFLECT: What do you think "being created in God's image" means? Do you think it means we look like God? Do you think it means we can choose between right and wrong? Do you think it means something else? If so, what? How have you reflected God's image this week? yesterday? today? How can you reflect his goodness today and tomorrow?

ACT: Spend a few moments outside after dark tonight. Locate the moon in the night sky, and ask God to help you reflect his image as the moon reflects the light of the sun.

PRAY: "Father God, thank you for creating me in your image. Help me reflect your goodness today when_____."

Bible Reading: Ephesians 5:15-17

So be careful how you live, not as fools but as those who are wise.
Ephesians 5:15

OK, SO YOU ate two beef burritos and a large bowl of spicy chili and topped it all off with a tall glass of eggnog—then threw up all over your Aunt Rita's birthday cake?

And you say you told your dad he couldn't go golfing on Saturday because of the party Mom was planning for him—which no one told you was a *surprise* party?

And then you promised Mrs. Farquard that you'd ask your sister to baby-sit the woman's eighteen children while she had a brain transplant? But you forgot, and Mrs. Farquard had to cancel her surgery, and her doctor gave the brain to someone else?

Wow, rough day, huh? Well, maybe that's never happened to you, but things like that do happen, and they can make you feel awful. But it's important to remember that not every poor choice you make is a wrong choice. For example, take a look at the following pairs of choices: One is clearly a wrong choice. The other—while it may be regrettable, even embarrassing—is not necessarily a wrong choice.

Wrong Choice: Lying to your mother about your trip to the beach
Poor Choice: Lying on the beach until your skin starts to bubble like an egg in
a frying pan

Wrong Choice: Using a bad, bad word when you hit your thumb with a hammer
Poor Choice: Hitting your head with the hammer after you hit your thumb

Wrong Choice: Putting Ex-Lax in the dog's food dish
Poor Choice: Letting the dog sleep in your bed after you put Ex-Lax in his food

Seriously, all of us make mistakes from time to time. Sometimes those mistakes are really wrong choices or sins—we do something God has told us not to do. But sometimes our mistakes are simply poor choices; we may be doing something foolish, but we're not disobeying God or our parents.

The important thing is not to excuse wrong choices and not to feel guilty about poor choices. Accept responsibility for both. Apologize for both. Try as hard as you can to avoid both. But don't confuse the two.

 REFLECT: What's the difference between a wrong choice and a poor choice? Should we feel guilty about both? Should we accept responsibility for both? Apologize for both? Try to avoid both?

 ACT: As you're reading or watching television this week, be alert for choices the characters make. Try to identify which choices are wrong choices and which are simply poor choices.

 PRAY: "Lord, give me the wisdom to avoid wrong choices today. Help me stay away from poor choices too."

A True Measure

Bible Reading: 2 Corinthians 10:12, 18

When they measure themselves by themselves and compare themselves with themselves, they are not wise. 2 Corinthians 10:12, NIV

CAN YOU IMAGINE what the world would be like if there were no standard units of measurement? If what I called "one inch," you called "two inches"? If my "pound" was your "ounce"? If a "mile" to one person was a "hop, skip, or a jump" to another?

So many things in life would be difficult, if not impossible, to do. How could you build a house? How could you weigh food at the store? How could you know how far it was from your house to your aunt Esmerelda's, and how could you know how long it would take you to get there?

Without a set standard to measure these things, life would be full of confusion. It's kind of the same with our spiritual lives.

When the time comes to make a decision, what's your "standard of measure"? Do you go by the decisions your friends make? Following the crowd may be the popular thing to do, but it isn't always smart.

Do you go by a "feeling" you have inside you that tells you what's OK to do and what's not? The problem with following your feelings is that feelings can change from one minute to the next. What may seem like the right thing to do today can seem like the wrong thing to do tomorrow.

Or do you turn to the only true measure there is—God and his Word? God is unchanging, and so is his Word; so you can be sure that you're doing what's right. And you can be sure that it will not only be right that day but also the next and the next and the—well, you get the idea.

When you measure your decisions and your actions against God and his Word, you can be sure that your decisions are good and your actions are right.

REFLECT: Take a few minutes to really think about what your life would be like if there were no standard units of measurement. How would that affect your use of time? your use of money? the clothes you buy and wear? other things? Which of the following standards do you sometimes use to decide whether an action or attitude is right or wrong? (Check all that apply.)

☐ What my parents say   ☐ What I "feel" is right   ☐ What my culture says
☐ What my friends say   ☐ What my horoscope says   ☐ What the law says
☐ What my church says   ☐ What I've been taught   ☐ What God says

Which of the above do you intend to use from now on? (Circle all that apply.)

ACT: Tape a ruler or a tape measure to your bedroom door or mirror today to remind you to measure your actions against God and what he says, instead of using some other standard.

PRAY: "God, you are the standard I choose to live by."

2 Apples and Oranges

Bible Reading: Romans 14:1-4

> *Who are you to condemn God's servants? They are responsible to the Lord, so let him tell them whether they are right or wrong. The Lord's power will help them do as they should. Romans 14:4*

THINK ABOUT THE following questions. How would you answer each one?

- Which of the following is better: Coca-Cola or Pepsi?
- Which color is prettier: blue or green?
- Who's funnier: Donald Duck or Daffy Duck?
- Which fruit is tastier: an apple or an orange?
- Which is more fun: waterskiing or white-water rafting?
- Who's a better singer: Mariah Carey or Celine Dion?

So, did you answer all the questions? Which answers are right? The truth is, either answer for each question may be right. Or neither.

How can that be? Well, you may prefer Coke; your friend may like Pepsi better. You may think Donald Duck is hilarious, while your friend gets hysterical just thinking about Daffy Duck. You may like apples, your friend may like oranges. In fact, you may like them both about the same, or you may hate *both* apples and oranges and go ape over bananas instead!

That's because Coke vs. Pepsi and Donald and Daffy are matters of taste and opinion. There is no right or wrong answer. It's up to you. But that doesn't mean everything is like that. If the question had been, "Which of the following is a Disney character: Donald Duck or Daffy Duck?" the answer would *not* be up to you. There is a right answer—Donald is a Disney character; Daffy is a Warner Brothers/Looney Tunes creation. If the question was, "Which of the following is a primary color: blue or green?" the answer would not be a matter of taste. After all, blue *is* a primary color. Green is a secondary color created by mixing blue and yellow.

Of course, a lot of people get confused and think that right and wrong are just like apples and oranges. "You think it's wrong to do this," they may say, "but I have a different opinion." But God clearly tells us in his Word what things are right (like attending church regularly—see Hebrews 10:25). He also leaves some decisions up to us (like which church we choose to attend). The important thing is not to confuse the two; if God has said something is wrong, we should not say otherwise.

 REFLECT: Do you ever act like the standards of right and wrong are up to you to decide? Why or why not?

 ACT: Eat an apple or orange as a snack or with your lunch today to remind you not to confuse matters of taste with matters of truth.

 PRAY: "God, help me to choose your standards as my standards so that I can maintain a clear conscience before you and everyone else."

3 The Hiding Place

Bible Reading: Psalm 31:19-21

Hide your loved ones in the shelter of your presence, safe beneath your hand, safe from all conspiring men. Psalm 31:20, TLB

DURING WORLD WAR II a family of watchmakers named the ten Booms lived in Holland. While they seemed like a typical family in every way, the ten Booms had a secret: Their home was a hiding place.

The ten Boom home was a place for Jews to stay until they had a chance to leave the Netherlands without fear of being sent to concentration camps. Hidden rooms were built in the home and frequent drills were held to make sure all the "guests" could be quickly hidden and all signs of their presence cleared away.

In spite of all the ten Booms' efforts, this special hiding place was eventually discovered, and everyone, including the ten Boom family, was sent to a concentration camp.

Yet even while imprisoned, Corrie ten Boom didn't lose her faith in God. She was able to smuggle a Bible into the camp—a Bible that became her source of comfort and strength. She found shelter in God's Word. God's commands and promises helped her survive the hardships of being a prisoner of war. And because she taught Bible classes, the women around her also found comfort and hope.

God's loving commands can do the same for us. They can protect us from harm; they can help us rely on his presence; they can remind us of his love; they can help us choose right even when everyone around us is choosing wrong. Of course, God's commands can do none of those things if we don't read them and obey them. But when we read his Word and obey his commands, "his never-failing love protects [us] like the walls of a fort!" (Psalm 31:21, TLB).

REFLECT: If the ten Booms had not taken such risks hiding Jewish families from the Nazis, they might have escaped the concentration camps themselves. Yet they chose to obey God's commands to be merciful and loving toward others even at the risk of their own lives. Are you reading God's Word? Are you obeying his commands? God's Word can be a fortress that surrounds us and gives us strength to do battle each day. What part of God's Word do you need to hide in your heart to help you fight the battles you face this week?

ACT: Have you ever read Corrie ten Boom's thrilling story, *The Hiding Place?* If not, ask your parents or pastor to help you get a copy of her book or the film by the same name.

PRAY: "Lord, sometimes I'm afraid to do what's right. Remind me, Lord, that you are with me each day to help me whenever I face a hard decision."

4 The Right Answer

Bible Reading: Psalm 82:1-8

Rise up, O God, and judge the earth, for all the nations belong to you.
Psalm 82:8

IT MAY BE the middle of summer, but it's time for a quiz. Don't panic! We'll make it a multiple choice quiz. There's only one question—and it's really easy:

1. Today is July 4. If you live in the United States, what are you celebrating?

   a. A day to wear all the red, white, and blue you want without anyone saying you look silly
   b. A day of parades, picnics, and pyrotechnics (OK, OK, fireworks!)
   c. A day of national pride
   d. A day to remember where the right to life, liberty, and the pursuit of happiness really came from—God

OK, time's up. What's your answer?

While none of those answers is wrong, the last answer reminds us of something we too often forget. While the government may honor our basic rights as human beings, it doesn't grant us those rights. God does.

The very basis of the idea of personal rights is the fact that there is a God and he is the one who by his nature defines what is right and wrong. Your rights to live, to be free, and to be treated with respect are not gifts from any government or court; they are gifts from the righteous God, the one from whom all moral judgments—including human rights—are derived. That's true not only for Americans but for all people everywhere.

So in between all those firecrackers and noisemakers, take a few moments to honor God, who has given you rights that no government can give and no government can take away.

 REFLECT: Many documents all over the world have been based on the Declaration of Independence, which refers to our "inalienable rights" of life, liberty, and the pursuit of happiness. *Inalienable* means those rights can't be rightfully canceled or surrendered. Have you ever thanked God for your life? Have you ever thanked him for your freedom or for the other rights you enjoy?

 PRAY: "Lord, thank you for the rights you have given me. Thank you for my life and freedom."

5 White Cane

Bible Reading: Psalm 119:97-101

Your commands make me wiser than my enemies, for your commands are my constant guide. Psalm 119:98

HAVE YOU EVER seen a person who is blind walking down the street? How did that person know where to go, when to stop, and when to turn? Many blind people use a white cane.

A white cane can become an amazing tool in the hands of a man or woman who really knows how to use one. Some people who are blind can walk as well and as quickly as someone with perfect eyesight because they've mastered the use of the white cane. The sight-impaired person can tell by the way the cane bounces whether he's on a sidewalk or grass or a path. The sound of the cane's tapping against the ground changes when the person approaches large objects like a wall or a building. The sound of the cane announces a sudden drop-off, like a curb, or even a small obstacle, like a tricycle or a roller skate.

Using a white cane to find your way is kind of like using God's Word. God's Word warns us of things that can trip us up or hurt us, just as a cane warns a blind person of obstacles in his or her path.

Of course, you don't carry a Bible with you all the time, do you? And sometimes there's just no time to thumb through the Bible looking for answers, right? Most of the time you can't even find what you're looking for, right? *That's* why it's so important to memorize God's Word. When you memorize a verse of the Bible,

- it's always available when you need it;
- you're never caught without the tools you need to make a right choice; and
- it's a lot easier to go the right way without hesitating or stumbling.

So why not start—one verse at a time—to hide God's Word in your heart and mind so that it can guide you, even in the dark? Make the following verse your motto: "Your word is a lamp to my feet and a light for my path" (Psalm 119:105, NIV). After all, a white cane isn't much help if it's left at home, right?

 REFLECT: How is God's Word like a white cane? The above paragraphs mention three reasons why it's important to memorize Bible verses. What are they? You may be surprised at how many Bible verses you already know, such as John 3:16 and Matthew 6:33. How many others can you think of?

 ACT: Read Psalm 119:105 (see above) out loud ten times (including the reference). Then try to say it without reading it. You might be able to repeat it word for word, without looking at the book. If you can, congratulations! You've just memorized Psalm 119:105.

 PRAY: "Help me, Father God, to hide your Word in my heart and to obey it each day."

6 That's Unfair!

Bible Reading: Luke 6:27-31

Treat [others] exactly as you would like them to treat you.
Luke 6:31, Phillips

IT'S NOT ALWAYS easy to tell the difference between what's fair and what's unfair. Telling the difference can be difficult and confusing at times.

But take a look at the following quiz. Don't worry about what you think would be fair or unfair. Just answer each question according to how you would like to be treated. Check one response for each question.

1. You're the captain of one team, and your friend is the captain of the other team. Which way would you rather choose teams?
☐ You and the other captain take turns choosing players.
☐ The other captain picks everyone he wants, and you get whoever's left.

2. You and two friends are bike riding when you get a flat tire about two miles from home. Which would you rather do?
☐ All three of you walk your bikes home together.
☐ Your two friends ride ahead while you walk your bike home alone.

3. You're swimming at the community pool when a friend comes by without a swimming suit. Which would you want your friend to do?
☐ Yell to the lifeguard, "Hey, I saw lightning!" which causes the lifeguard to make you and everyone else get out of the pool.
☐ Say to you, "Hey, I'll go back and get my swimsuit so we can both swim."

4. Your friend's mom bakes a prune and lima bean casserole for dinner and serves liver cookies for dessert. Which would you want your friend to do?
☐ Invite you over for dinner *without* telling you what's on the menu.
☐ Tell you, "If I'm not at school tomorrow, call 9-1-1. I may be dead!"

Well, OK, none of those situations will probably ever happen to you, but you get the idea, right? Your choice in each case is pretty obvious, isn't it? Why? Because it's usually pretty easy to know how you want to be treated in a particular situation. That's what the Bible says: "Do for others as you would like them to do for you" (Luke 6:31).

Guess what—that's often all it takes to figure out what's fair and what's not fair. Usually the first step in treating someone fairly is to ask, How would *I* want to be treated? If you can answer that question, you can answer questions like What would be fair? and What would be unfair? a lot easier.

 REFLECT: When was the last time you felt you were treated unfairly? What would have been fair? Can you recall a time when you were unfair? How would you have acted if you had treated the person the way you like to be treated?

 PRAY: "God, when I'm tempted to be unfair to somebody, help me to remember to treat others exactly as I would want to be treated."

7 This Mud's for You

Bible Reading: Psalm 106:1-3

Happy are those who deal justly with others and always do what is right.
Psalm 106:3

IN THE COMIC strip bearing their names, Calvin and Hobbes are a little boy and his stuffed tiger companion. The strip, created by cartoonist Bill Watterson, is one of the most popular comic strips ever created.

In one series of panels, Calvin and his tiger friend are walking together through the woods. Calvin tells his pal, "I don't believe in ethics anymore. As far as I'm concerned, the ends justify the means." He pounds a fist into his palm and continues, "Get what you can while the getting's good—that's what I say! Might makes right! The winners write the history books! It's a dog-eat-dog world, so I'll do whatever I have to, and let others argue about whether it's 'right' or not."

Suddenly, Hobbes spies a mud puddle. He stops, smiles, and shoves Calvin into the puddle.

"Hey!" Calvin screams. "Why'd you do *that?!*"

Hobbes squats beside his screaming friend. "You were in my way," he answers. "Now you're not. The ends justify the means."

Calvin pulls himself up and starts scraping the mud off his arms. "I didn't mean for *everyone,* you dolt! Just *me!*"

Hobbes may be just a stuffed tiger (although he's real to Calvin), but he's on to something. A lot of people do what Calvin was doing. They try to define right and wrong themselves. They tell themselves that they can do whatever *they* think is right. But they change their tune if someone else acts that way. "Hey!" they'll cry. "You can't do that! It's not fair!"

That's because everybody knows that some things are fair and some things are not fair. And fair isn't whatever *we* say it is; fair is what *God* says it is. And God's Word says this is fair: "Do for others what you would like them to do for you" (Matthew 7:12).

In other words, fairness asks, "How would *I* like to be treated?" Unfairness says, "*This* is different" or "*I'm* special." But if fairness only applies to *other* people but not to you—well, that's not fair, is it?

 REFLECT: What important question will a fair person ask? How would an unfair person answer that question? Who decides what is fair or not fair? Do you ever try to excuse your actions by saying, *"This* is different" or *"I'm* special?" Have you been unfair to anyone today? this week? If so, what could you do to make things fair?

 PRAY: "God, please help me to be fair with others and always do what is right. Help me not to excuse myself by thinking, *This is different* or *I'm special,* but to treat other people the way I would like to be treated."

8 Ether One

Bible Reading: Leviticus 19:13-16

Always judge your neighbors fairly, neither favoring the poor nor showing deference to the rich. Leviticus 19:15

IF YOU'VE EVER been to the dentist to have a cavity filled or a tooth pulled, you've probably been given an anesthetic (that's just a big word for something that numbs pain). The dentist gives you a swab or a shot of something so that when he or she starts poking around in your mouth with picks and drills and other tools of torture, you don't scratch his or her eyeballs out.

The first anesthetic to be used safely was a gas called *ether*. In 1842 a doctor in Georgia used ether to put a patient to sleep during an operation. Three years later he also used ether to deliver a baby. But by the time he wrote about the things he had done, credit for the discovery of ether had already gone to William Morton, a dentist who lived in Massachusetts.

However, when the Massachusetts Historical Society wanted to put up a memorial to honor the man who had discovered ether, many people claimed that another man—Charles Jackson—was the real discoverer. This led to an argument about which name should be on the memorial: William Morton or Charles Jackson?

It was then that a famous doctor named Oliver Wendell Holmes Sr. suggested a humorous solution. He said both names should be inscribed on the memorial with the inscription "To Ether." That way the memorial could honor *either* man!

That seemed to be a fair solution to the problem. It not only brought honor to William Morton and Charles Jackson, it also made Holmes more famous than he already was, because it showed him to be a fair and wise man. (It's not surprising that Holmes's son became a famous Supreme Court justice!)

Oliver Wendell Holmes Sr. was applauded because he was fair. And fairness is good. That's why God commands us to be fair. We should treat other people as fairly as we can. We should look for fair solutions to problems. We should remember that fairness is right and unfairness is wrong. We please God when we obey his command to treat each other fairly.

 REFLECT: Today's Bible reading mentions at least eight ways to be fair to others; how many can you find? Do you like to be treated fairly? Why or why not? Do you treat others the way you like to be treated? Are you obeying God's commands to treat others fairly? If there is anyone you haven't been treating fairly, can you think of a way to correct or change your behavior?

 ACT: Be alert for ways you can be fair (or encourage others to be fair) to everyone you meet today.

 PRAY: "Lord God, help me to keep alert for ways to be fair to others. Remind me to treat others the way I want to be treated."

Three Bills and a Baby

Bible Reading: Genesis 18:18-19

For I have chosen him, so that he will direct his children and his household after him to keep the way of the Lord by doing what is right and just. Genesis 18:19, NIV

TRY THIS EXPERIMENT: Take a one-dollar bill, a five-dollar bill, and a twenty-dollar bill. Place the three bills in front of a baby who is under a year old. (If you don't have a baby brother, sister, or cousin under a year old, try to borrow one from the neighbors!)

Now, watch the baby as you complete the following questionnaire:

Which bill did the child choose first?

☐ The twenty-dollar bill   ☐ The one-dollar bill
☐ The five-dollar bill   ☐ All of the above

What did the child do with the money?

☐ Put it in his or her mouth   ☐ Bought a bag full of candy
☐ Dropped it on the floor   ☐ Invested it in a mutual fund

OK, so you probably don't have to do the experiment to know what the answers would be, right? A little baby wouldn't recognize the difference between a one-dollar bill, a five-dollar bill, and a twenty-dollar bill, so he or she might pick up any one of the three (or all of them). And he or she would probably try to eat it or try to bounce it off the floor!

Why? Because babies don't know that money is valuable. They don't know that money can be exchanged for candy. And they sure don't know that a twenty-dollar bill can buy more candy than a one-dollar bill.

Sometimes older kids—even adults—have sort of the same problem. We don't know what's really valuable. We act like wealth and fame, popularity, or possessions are valuable. But God knows what's really valuable, and he revealed one of those things to Abraham a long time ago. He chose Abraham to be the father of the whole nation of Israel "so that he [would] direct his children and his household after him to keep the way of the Lord by doing what is right and just" (Genesis 18:19, NIV). *That's* what is really valuable: doing what is right and just. That's why God commands us to be just—because he values justice. And he wants us to value it, too. More than one dollar. More than five dollars. Even more than twenty dollars.

 REFLECT: What does it mean to "value" something? How do you know that God values justice (fairness)? What do you value?

 PRAY: "God, since you value fairness, I want to value it, too. I choose to follow justice and justice alone."

10 The Fairest of Them All

Bible Reading: Revelation 15:1-4

Great and marvelous are your actions, Lord God Almighty. Just and true are your ways, O King of the nations. Revelation 15:3

WHAT DO THE following people have in common?

- A black-robed judge
- A baseball umpire
- A police officer
- A football referee in a black-and-white striped shirt
- A schoolteacher

Yes, they all have jobs; what else? OK, so they all have brains. Anything else?

Each of those people is expected to be fair. A judge who isn't fair isn't a very good judge, right? An umpire who treats one team differently from another is going to have to deal with a lot of angry players and fans. A police officer who only arrests people he doesn't like isn't doing a very good job. And nobody likes a referee who calls complete passes incomplete or a teacher who gives bad grades to girls and good grades only to boys!

We expect judges and schoolteachers to be fair, right? Because fairness is right, *right?* That's why a good judge is a fair judge; an unfair teacher is a poor teacher. But *why* is fairness right?

Because God is fair.

Fairness isn't right because you say it's right or because your friend says it's right. It's not right even because your parents and teachers say it's right or because the government has decided it's right. Fairness is right for one reason and one reason only: *God is fair.*

Psalm 9:16 says, "The Lord is known for his justice." Isaiah 30:18 says, "The Lord is a God of justice" (NIV). And the saints in heaven sing a song that says, "Great and marvelous are your actions, Lord God Almighty. Just and true are your ways, O King of the nations" (Revelation 15:3).

God is just; it's part of his nature to be fair. That's why he values justice. And that's why he commands us to be fair. When we're fair with others, we're like our God, who is "just and righteous, whose love is unfailing" (Jeremiah 9:24).

REFLECT: Why does God command justice? Why does God value justice? How do you know that God is fair? How would you complete the following statements?

"When others treat me unfairly, I_____."

"When others treat me fairly, I_____."

"When I treat someone unfairly, I_____."

"When I treat someone fairly, I_____."

PRAY: Pray (or sing) the words of Revelation 15:3-4, the song the saints in heaven sing, as a prayer of praise to God.

The Donkey and the Mule

Bible Reading: Jeremiah 7:5-7

Change your ways and your actions and deal with each other justly.
Jeremiah 7:5, NIV.

A MAN ONCE left home on a long journey. He took with him a donkey and a mule. He placed all his goods and luggage on the donkey's back. Although he walked most of the time, he would occasionally ride the mule.

The donkey carried his load easily. He was accustomed to bearing heavy burdens. But when the three travelers began to climb the side of a steep mountain, his load became too heavy to bear.

The donkey, struggling under his load, asked the mule to help carry some of the load, explaining that he would gladly take the full burden back again after they had climbed the mountain. But the mule refused to help even a little bit.

Before long the donkey slowed and collapsed beneath his load. The man beat him mercilessly, but the donkey was too weak to go any farther.

Not knowing what else to do, the man began unloading the packs from the donkey's back and placed the entire load on the mule. Then, leaving the donkey where he had fallen, the man and the mule continued the journey.

The mule, groaning beneath his heavy burden, said to himself, *If I had only been willing to help the poor donkey, I would now be bearing half the load I carry—and would have a friend besides.*

That's the way it goes. When we deal justly with each other, we not only make things easier on others but usually make things easier for ourselves. Not only that, but treating others fairly will make us far more friends than if we treat people unfairly.

In fact, treating other people fairly usually has at least one of three effects on our friendships: It sometimes *starts* friendships when none had existed before, it often *strengthens* friendships and makes them better than before, and it often *sustains* friendships—it keeps them going when they might otherwise end.

That's a pretty good track record, don't you think? So next time you have the chance to treat someone fairly, don't be mule-headed; do yourself—and the other person—a favor by treating him or her fairly.

 REFLECT: What three effects does fairness usually have on our friendships? Are you more like the mule in the above story (who treated his companion unfairly) or the donkey (who was treated unfairly) or neither? Do you hang around friends who treat you fairly, or do you tend to hang around friends who treat you unfairly? Why?

 ACT: Seize the first chance you have this week to carry someone else's burden (for example, by helping someone carry a grocery bag or offering to run an errand for someone).

 PRAY: "God, thank you for my friends. Thanks for the good things that happen when I'm fair to them."

12 Drive Me Crazy

Bible Reading: Psalm 11:4-5

The Lord is in his holy Temple; the Lord still rules from heaven. He watches everything closely, examining everyone on earth. Psalm 11:4

THE NEXT TIME you're stuck in a traffic jam with your dad or mom or your cousin Elmer, take a few minutes to watch the drivers in the other cars. See if you can identify some of these "animals" (don't look for animals in your own car!):

The Giraffe: This driver is always trying to see ahead. He creeps to the left and then to the right, trying to see around the lanes of traffic to find out what's holding things up. He'll even stick his head as high out of the car as possible in order to see what's happening.

The Frog: This driver seems to think that whatever lane she's in is the slowest lane, so she'll hop from one lane to the other. She may nose her way into your lane before leaping to the next lane. She may even creep by you on one side, then glare as you creep by her on the other side—unless she can get into your lane ahead of you!

The Snake: Sometimes traffic slows or stops because two or more lanes of traffic have to merge into one lane. This species of driver will speed ahead as close to the end of a line of traffic as he or she can, waiting until the last possible second to merge. *Then* the snake will try to nose into traffic ahead of drivers who've been waiting in line since 1963.

Of course, none of those kinds of drivers do themselves (or others) much good. Most traffic would flow a lot better if people would just be fair and polite to each other, taking turns and working together (instead of acting like animals!).

In fact, the whole world would function a lot better if everyone was fair. Your school and church would be much nicer places if everyone acted fairly. And families would get along better if only everyone treated everyone else fairly.

If we just treated each other with fairness, life would be more like God intended it—and less like life in a zoo!

 REFLECT: Today's Bible reading mentions a *big* advantage of doing what is right. What is it? Can you think of other ways life would be better if everyone treated each other fairly? How about in a crowded store? at your school? in church? at home with your family? How can you help your friends (and others) see the benefits of fairness?

 PRAY: "Lord, I want to make my world a better place. Help me to remember to treat others fairly, especially when_____ [I'm at school, I'm at home, I'm in a public place, etc.]."

July 13

Weird Richard's Almanac

Bible Reading: Psalm 37:27-31

For the Lord is righteous, and he loves justice. Those who do what is right will see his face. Psalm 11:7

YOU'VE PROBABLY HEARD old sayings like "He who laughs last laughs best" and "A bird in the hand is worth two in the bush," right? These are examples of sayings that have become famous over the years. Those two were coined by Ben Franklin in his famous *Poor Richard's Almanac.*

A lot of those sayings are out of date, however. For example, take the saying "A penny saved is a penny earned." These days, a penny saved is (after taxes and inflation) about half a penny. Here are some others modernized sayings:

- He who laughs last . . . was slow to get the joke.
- It takes a big man to admit his mistakes . . . and it takes an even bigger man to force the first man to admit them!
- People who live in glass houses . . . better keep their curtains shut!
- Red sky in the morning, sailors take warning; red sky at night . . . sailors better ask, "Isn't it supposed to be *dark* at night?"
- When it rains, it pours . . . and when it doesn't rain, we complain about that, too.
- Laugh, and the world laughs with you; cry . . . and the world laughs at you, too, ya big sissy!

Well, that's enough of that. No, wait, just one more: "The Lord helps those who . . . treat others fairly." OK, so that last one isn't funny like the other ones. But it *is* true.

According to the Bible, "the Lord is righteous, and he loves justice. Those who do what is right will see his face" (Psalm 11:7). That means that when you treat others fairly, you please God. Not only that, when you're fair, you also make it possible for God to bless you in ways that he can't bless you if you're *not* fair.

As with all God's commands, obeying God's command to be fair (Leviticus 19:13-16; Micah 6:8) results in the loving protection and provision of God. For example, when we are fair, others tend to treat us fairly. When we are fair, we develop a good reputation among others. When we are fair, we prompt other people to trust us more. When we are fair, we make friends easier. And when we are fair, we are less likely to lose friends. Those are all blessings from God that come from treating other people fairly.

 REFLECT: Do you think you can please God without being fair? Why or why not? Do you think people who treat others fairly are happier than those who treat people unfairly? Why or why not? Has something good ever happened to you because you were fair with someone else?

 PRAY: "Loving God, show me the many ways you bless people who treat others fairly, and let me be one of those people."

14 Practice Makes Perfect

Bible Reading: Luke 11:5-10

Ask and it will be given to you; seek and you will find; knock and the door will be opened to you. Matthew 7:7, NIV

GYMNASTICS ARE FUN to watch, in person or on television. It's amazing to watch athletes balance and swing on the rings. It's exciting to watch them spin and whirl on the "horse." It's thrilling to watch them turn and twirl on the parallel bars. It's stirring to watch them tumble and spring during the floor exercises.

When you watch the best in the world, like at the Olympics, you'll often see the athletes perform an interesting exercise long *before* their turn in front of the judges and the cameras. You may see it before they get to the arena, before they come out of the dressing room, or while they're on the bench waiting for their turn to compete. But if you look closely, you'll discover that just about all of them do it. You'll see them close their eyes, lean one way and then the other, slightly arch their backs, twist their hips, kick their legs, or move their arms. The movements are almost imperceptible— you have to look closely to even see them.

What are they doing? They're practicing. Not the kind of practice they do for years to get good enough to compete in the Olympics—repeating flips, jumps, and moves hundreds of times until they can do them better than almost everyone else in the world. No, they are practicing their routines or jumps *in their minds*. They rehearse everything they plan to do as if they were actually doing it, remembering all the words of instruction their coaches have given them. They "practice" with their eyes closed so that they will be ready for their time to compete.

We need to do something similar as Christians. We need to spend time with our eyes closed. We need to go through the routine of our day and think about what we may have done wrong in the past that we need to get right today. We need to remember the words of our Coach (God) and prepare ourselves for the obstacles and opportunities we may face today. As we pray, we need to remember that we have an advantage that earthly coaches don't provide: *Our* coach is almighty. He can give us the power to win.

 REFLECT: How many days a week do you spend time with your eyes closed (in prayer)? Two? Three? Four? More? Less? What do you think would happen if you treated every day like an Olympic event by starting with ten or fifteen minutes of prayer to prepare yourself for that day's obstacles and opportunities? Do you think it would be easier or harder to make right choices throughout the day? Explain.

 PRAY: "Lord, help me to start every day with my eyes closed—and my mind turned toward you."

Edison's Failures

Bible Reading: 2 Corinthians 12:6-10

For when I am weak, then I am strong. 2 Corinthians 12:10

YOU MAY KNOW a little about Thomas Edison. He was a great inventor who lived about a hundred years ago. He invented the electric light bulb, the record player, motion pictures, and about a bazillion other things (actually, the number was 1,093 patented inventions).

One of the things he worked long and hard at inventing was a new type of battery. He experimented with different chemicals, metals, and designs, first trying one thing and then another. Some worked better and some worked worse, but for a long time he was unable to come up with the results he needed.

A friend once came to see Edison when he was working on the battery. Edison remarked that after ten thousand experiments he was still not satisfied.

"What?" his friend asked, astonished. "Ten thousand failures?"

"Why, I have not failed," Edison responded. "I've just found ten thousand ways that won't work."

Edison's friend made the mistake of confusing an unfinished experiment with a failure. But Edison knew better.

We make a similar mistake sometimes when we confuse failures and sins. God doesn't expect us to go through life without failing. He knows we're going to try—and fail—many times (maybe even ten thousand times!). You may have failed the first ten times you tried to ride a bike without training wheels, but you didn't give up, did you?

God doesn't mind when we fail, unless our failures are also sins. You see, a *sin* is a choice to do something our own way rather than God's way. *Sinning* means failing to do right when we know what's right; in other words, failing to obey God.

So don't be afraid to fail. All of us do it. Some of us have even failed ten thousand times! Just make sure to choose God's way—the right way—instead of your own way, and he will turn even your failures into something good!

 REFLECT: What's the difference between a sin and a failure? Are sins always failures? Are failures always sins? Can you think of a time when you failed but did not sin? Carry a small battery in your pocket today to remind you that the only failure you need to fear is failing to follow God.

 PRAY: "God, nobody likes to fail, but help me to remember that failing or making a mistake isn't always a sin. And help me not to fail to do right when I know what's right."

16 The Canaan News Network

Bible Reading: Matthew 4:1-11

For we do not have a high priest who is unable to sympathize with our weaknesses, but we have one who has been tempted in every way, just as we are—yet was without sin. Hebrews 4:15, NIV

"WELCOME TO CNN, the Canaan News Network!"

The smiling news anchorman peers into the camera. "This is *Nightly News Tonight.* I'm Dan Beersheba, filling in for the vacationing Peter Jeconiah."

The newsman turns, still smiling, and faces another camera. "Our top story tonight: A scandal is brewing in the wilderness of Judea." A box appears on the screen over the newsman's left shoulder, depicting a map of Israel with a circle around the wilderness of Judea. "Jesus of Nazareth, a man whom some say possesses mysterious powers, was baptized yesterday in the river Jordan by his cousin John, the fiery preacher whom some call a prophet."

A video appears onscreen of a bearded man baptizing another bearded man. "Unidentified sources report that after the brief ceremony, a dove descended from the sky and landed on this Jesus' head, followed by a peal of thunder that some said was the voice of Yahweh, the God of Israel."

The smiling newsman's image appears again. "However," he says, "those same sources report that Jesus of Nazareth has now disappeared into the Judean wilderness, where he will spend the next forty days and nights fasting and . . . *being tempted by the devil!* If these reports are true, the scandal of actually being tempted to sin will certainly destroy Jesus' credibility as a religious and spiritual leader and may even result in—"

The newsman lifts his hand to his earpiece and pauses in midsentence. "What? What's that?" He stares uncertainly at the camera for a moment, apparently listening to his earpiece. He clears his throat. "Uh, it seems that, er, our report is a bit hasty. Our, um, sources tell us there is nothing shameful or scandalous about being tempted." He clears his throat again and chuckles nervously. "It seems that Jesus' credibility as a religious and spiritual leader would only be affected if he were to actually, er, *give in* to temptation. And . . . no reliable source . . . has reported such an event."

He inhales deeply. "In our next story, environmentalists picket the activities of John the Baptist—after these messages."

 REFLECT: Do you think being tempted is a sin? If so, do you think Jesus sinned simply by being tempted? If not, what's the difference between temptation and sin? Are you ever tempted? How? How should you respond when you're tempted?

 PRAY: "God, thank you for showing me the difference between temptation and sin. Help me not to give in to temptation, especially when I'm tempted to _____ [use bad language, do the wrong thing just because my friends are doing it, etc.]."

17 When I Am Weak . . .

Bible Reading: Luke 4:1-4

[F]or forty days [Jesus] was tempted by the devil. He ate nothing during those days, and at the end of them he was hungry. Luke 4:2, NIV

SUPPOSE YOU'RE PLAYING a game of tackle football against three people. If you get a chance to run the ball, would you run in the direction of

- the biggest guy in your neighborhood?
- a guy about the size of a Chihuahua?

Or imagine that your shop teacher at school tells you to saw through a piece of wood balanced between two sawhorses. You notice that the wood is about a foot thick on one end, but it's only three or four inches thick on the other end. Would you

- saw through the thick end?
- saw through the thin end?

Or say you plan to ask your parents for twenty dollars to spend at the mall. Would you

- ask them when their resistance is likely to be strong (like right after they've caught you shaving the dog)?
- ask them when their resistance is likely to be weak (like right after you've just been named "Terrific Kid of the Year" by the United Nations)?

Which answers did you choose? If you're smart, you chose to run the football at the other team's weak spot and saw through the narrow spot in the wood. And, if you're smart, you waited to ask your parents for money at a time when their power of resistance would be weakest (but don't tell your parents we told you that!).

Well, guess what—the devil isn't dumb, either. He isn't going to tempt you much at your strongest points; he's going to tempt you to do wrong when you are weak. That's what he did with Jesus. Jesus was hungry and probably lonely and maybe even tired when the devil came to him in the wilderness (Matthew 4). That's why the devil tempted him with food. And approval. And ease.

So watch out, because he'll do the same thing with you. Temptation to do wrong will usually come when you are weak. So be prepared. Be aware. And be ready to depend even more on God's strength when you're weak.

 REFLECT: Think about recent times when you've made a wrong choice. Did you make that choice at a time of weakness (when you were lonely, tired, disappointed, etc.)? At what times are you "weak"? Do you struggle more with being lonely? tired? hungry? something else? How do you think you can prepare for those weak times so you don't give in to temptation?

 PRAY: "Jesus, you resisted temptation when you were weak. Please help me to remember to be especially careful when I am weak. Please help me depend on your strength when temptation comes."

18 Not like the Book

Bible Reading: Luke 4:5-8

Jesus replied, "The Scriptures say, 'You must worship the Lord your God; serve only him.'" Luke 4:8

BOOK REPORTS ARE no fun, usually. After all, you have to read a book that's a bazillion pages long about somebody who lived a long time ago and said things like, "I wot not what wot I thought I wot." And the whole time you're reading, you're saying, "Huh?"

If you haven't already, someday you'll have to read a book like *David Copperfield*. Now, that wouldn't be so bad if it was about that magician guy who made the Statue of Liberty disappear (don't worry, he put it back). But it's not about *that* David Copperfield. It's about some kid in England and was written by Charles Dickens, the same writer who created such characters as Scrooge, Tiny Tim, and Oliver Twist.

But wait! Several David Copperfield movies have been made. You could just rent one of those movies, watch it, then do your book report. That way you wouldn't have to read the long, boring book, right?

Wrong. That may sound like a good idea, but the problem is that if you do a *book* report on a *movie*, you're lying (you're even putting your lie on paper!), and lying is a sin. And movies based on books always skip a lot of stuff; you'd miss some important things (things that might end up on a test later).

It would be tempting, wouldn't it? But that's just the point. A lot of times temptation to do wrong comes in the form of a "shortcut." You know, *Do it this way; it'll be easier,* or *it'll be quicker,* or *it'll be cheaper.*

That's what the devil tried with Jesus in the wilderness of Judea (Matthew 4:6-8). He offered instant glory and power to Jesus if only Jesus would worship him. But Jesus didn't fall for it. He knew that all glory and power would be given to him after his death and crucifixion. He resisted the temptation to take a shortcut.

In the same way, you will often face the temptation to take a shortcut. You may be tempted to cheat on a test (instead of studying) in order to pass a class. You may be tempted to swipe a few dollars from your mom's purse (instead of saving your allowance) in order to get a new CD.

The devil may whisper, "Come on, it'll be easier" or "It'll be quicker" or "It'll be cheaper." But don't be fooled. Don't take a shortcut if it means making a wrong choice. Because when you do, *you're* the one who ends up on the short end of the stick.

REFLECT: Are you ever tempted to do wrong because it seems easier, quicker, or cheaper? Jesus said, "The highway to hell is broad, and its gate is wide for the many who choose the easy way. But the gateway to life is small, and the road is narrow, and only a few ever find it" (Matthew 7:13-14). In other words, most people choose the easy way—the "shortcut"—but those shortcuts lead to hell. Be alert this week (and always) for temptations to take shortcuts.

PRAY: "God, help me to resist temptation, even when it comes in the form of a shortcut."

19 Bulk Jam

Bible Reading: Luke 4:9-14a

Resist the devil, and he will flee from you. James 4:7, NIV

WHEN WAS THE last time you tried to open a jar and couldn't get it open? When was the last time you tried to lift a heavy item—like the box of trash you have after cleaning your room? Feel weak? Well, there's hope for you.

Charles Atlas was a famous weakling who became a champion bodybuilder. He developed a system for building strength that relied on something called isometric exercises. These exercises are very good for building strength. Even though you can buy exercise machines that work on the principal of isometrics, the greatest thing about isometric exercises is that you can do them with things around the house.

The basic idea is to find something that won't move when you push, pull, or try to lift it. Then you try to push, pull, or lift it. Sounds a little silly, doesn't it? But that's the way it works. For example, say you want to work on your arm strength. The following are two isometric exercises to help you reach that goal.

1. Put your palms together in front of you at about the level of your chest. Push your hands together as hard as you can. (You can do it repeatedly in short spurts or in one long press.)
2. Stand in a doorway. Place your hands at shoulder level on the doorway and press outward. (Again, do it in spurts or one long press.)

If you do these exercises a few times (not very long), you will feel some muscles start to hurt. They are being exercised, even though your hands and arms are not moving.

If you try these exercises for a few days and then try to open that jar again (or get the box of trash out of your room), you'll be surprised at the difference isometric exercises can make. That's because your newfound strength comes from doing exercises that build muscles by using resistance against those muscles.

Well, temptations are kind of like isometric exercises for your spiritual muscles. With every temptation you resist, you become stronger. The resistance is what builds strength, whether the muscles are physical or spiritual. As you build your physical muscles, you'll find that jars are easier to open and boxes are easier to lift. As you build your spiritual muscles, you'll find that temptations also become easier to resist.

So why not get started now? Flex your spiritual muscles; resist temptation whenever it comes your way today, and watch yourself (with God's help) growing stronger and stronger!

 REFLECT: What temptations are hardest for you to resist right now? Do you think you could resist each temptation *once* today? Concentrate on resisting temptation (with God's help) *the first time* it strikes today, then use that success to resist it the second time and so on.

 PRAY: "God, please help me to resist temptation today. And please use every little success, every victory, to make me stronger against the next temptation I may face."

July
20 Just like Samson

Bible Reading: Judges 16:6, 16-21

So Delilah said to Samson, "Please tell me what makes you so strong."
Judges 16:6

YOU'VE HEARD THE story of Samson, right? He was the first muscleman, the first superstar athlete. He had muscles like Sylvester Stallone, a smile like Tom Cruise, and hair like Fabio.

Before Samson was born, an angel appeared to his mother and told her that she would have a son and that "his hair must never be cut," for he would be "dedicated to God" (Judges 13:5). As he grew, Samson learned of his special birth and dedication to God, and the Bible says that "the Spirit of the Lord began to take hold of him" (Judges 13:25). Samson soon became famous among his people for his many feats of physical strength and his many victories against the Philistines (the "bad guys" of the story).

But Samson had a big weakness: beautiful women. One day he fell in love with an enchanting woman named Delilah, whom the Philistines bribed to find out what made Samson powerful so the Philistines could capture him. Well, to make a long story short, Samson ended up telling Delilah, "I was dedicated to God as a Nazirite from birth. If my head were shaved, my strength would leave me, and I would become as weak as anyone else" (Judges 16:17). The next time ol' Sam took a nap, Delilah sneaked a barber into the room and Samson's hair was gone in a minute! Before the day was over, Samson was tied up, blinded, and taken away as a prisoner.

A lot of people read Samson's story and make the mistake of thinking that Samson's power was in his hair. But Samson didn't get his power from his hair; it came from the Lord! His hair was simply a symbol of his dedication to the Lord. He was captured by the Philistines because "he didn't realize the Lord had left him" (Judges 16:20).

You're just like Samson. OK, so you don't have muscles the size of Cleveland, but you are like him in one respect: Your strength comes from the Lord. That means your power to resist temptation comes from God. You'll never find the power to resist temptation *inside yourself.* You can only win over temptation and sin through the power of God and the presence of his Spirit

 REFLECT: The way to resist temptation in the strength of the Lord is through prayer and trust in him. Read the following lines out loud, then seek God's strength by following through on what you've said:
- Before I'm faced with a temptation, I will pray (seeking God's strength through the day).
- When I'm faced with a temptation, I will pray (seeking God's strength for that moment).
- After I've resisted temptation, I will pray (thanking God for victory).

 PRAY: "Lord, I am not strong enough to resist temptation, but I know that you are. Help me to resist the devil's attacks today."

Not the Mama

Bible Reading: Exodus 20:1-7
I am the Lord your God. Exodus 20:2

A TELEVISION SHOW called *Dinosaurs* ran some years ago, featuring the antics of a family of dinosaurs: Mom, Dad, daughter, son, and baby. Occasionally, someone on the show would try to coax the baby into doing something. The baby, however, would usually respond by hitting that dinosaur over the head with a frying pan and chanting, "Not the mama!"

At about the same time that television show was on the air, there was another child—this one a young human girl. The girl had an aunt who tried to offer her some gentle correction such as, "Please don't put the nice little doggie into the oven." Like the dinosaur baby, however, the girl frowned at her relative and sternly announced, "You're not my muffer!"

Maybe you've heard similar responses from other people. Maybe you've tried to point out a better way of doing something or made a simple suggestion like "Don't you think it would be wrong to lock the substitute teacher in the walk-in freezer over the weekend?" and heard the response: "You're not the boss of me!"

The dinosaur baby and the human girl both responded as they did because they questioned another person's authority to tell them what to do; the only "bosses" they recognized were their mothers. And a person who says, "You're not the boss of me!" is doing something similar.

Such phrases are pretty common because most of us don't like it when someone else tells us what to do, especially if that person isn't our "muffer"! We want to make our own decisions.

We even try that when it comes to deciding whether something is right or wrong. We forget (or ignore) what God says and make up our own rules. "It's OK to do this because everyone else does it," we say. Or "it wouldn't be wrong just this once."

But no matter how hard we may try to be our own boss, it won't work. God has said what's right or wrong, and he is the Lord. None of us could do his job. And his job is to be the "boss" of heaven and earth and to help us understand, not decide, what's right and wrong. Our job is to listen and, with his help, obey what he says. And when we do that, we'll discover that God is the best "boss" anyone could ever have!

 REFLECT: How many "bosses" do you have? Do you ever try to be your own boss? Do you ever forget (or ignore) what God says and make up your own rules? Have you ever found yourself saying any of the things above ("Everyone else does it," etc.)? If so, which do you say most often? If you find yourself saying anything like that in the days to come, remind yourself that it's God's job to be the "boss" of heaven and earth and to help you understand what's right and what's wrong.

 PRAY: "Dear God, I admit that sometimes I forget or ignore what you've said about right and wrong. Sometimes I try to make up my own rules. Help me to do better at remembering and obeying what you say is right."

22 A Phone Call for Noah

Bible Reading: Genesis 6:9-22
So Noah did everything exactly as God had commanded him.
Genesis 6:22

NOAH WAS BUSY in his workshop one day when his son Ham handed him a cordless phone. (OK, so they didn't have phones back then, but just play along.)

"Hello?" Noah said. He listened for a few moments. "Who is this? . . . You've got to be kidding! . . . No, no . . . no, Lord, don't hang up! I believe you. . . . It's just . . . well, it's not every day a man gets a call from the Creator, you know."

Noah fell silent again and listened solemnly. "Well, yes, Lord, you're right. Things are pretty bad. I mean, every morning I have to pick up ten or twelve beer cans from my front yard." Noah's eyes widened as he heard God's next words. "Are . . . are you . . ." He swallowed hard and began again. "Are you s-s-sure you want to do that, Lord? I mean, sure everybody's pretty wicked, but I was thinking maybe we could start a home Bible study or something. . . . Oh, that's right, I forgot. The Bible hasn't been written yet."

Suddenly, Noah snatched a pencil and a scrap of paper from his workbench and started scribbling notes in response to the instructions coming through the phone.

"Uh-huh," he said. "OK, 450 feet long . . . right . . . 75 feet wide, and 45 feet high." He looked at the figures in amazement. "That's a pretty big boat, Lord," he said. "In fact, it's huge!"

He stopped writing then and concentrated on listening. He couldn't believe his ears. "Lord," he said, finally, "do you know what you're asking? I mean, people are going to think I'm nuts! Just the lumber alone is going to drain the family bank account—we've been saving for a vacation on the Euphrates River, you know. And how am I going to tell my wife?" He listened for a while. When he spoke again, his voice was quiet and determined.

"No, Lord, you're right. I'll do it. I know it won't be easy, but I'll do it. . . . Right. Thanks for calling." *That was stupid,* he told himself as he hung up. *The Creator of the universe calls and you say, "Thanks for calling"!*

REFLECT: Do you think it was easy for Noah to do "everything exactly as God had commanded him"? Why or why not? Do you think Noah was tempted to give up or change his mind during the years it probably took him to build the ark? Was Noah's choice harder, easier, or about the same as the choices you face? Why is it important to do the right thing even when doing the right thing is difficult?

PRAY: "God, sometimes I don't do the right thing because I'm afraid people will make fun of me. Please help me to keep my eyes on you and do the right thing anyway."

23 A Playground Fence

Bible Reading: Galatians 3:23-24

[The commandments of the Lord] are a warning to those who hear them; there is great reward for those who obey them. Psalm 19:11

IMAGINE A COOL playground filled with happy kids. Some kids are playing on the massive log jungle gym in the center of the playground, climbing in and out of the many openings, tubes, and passages, swinging on bars, playing "fort," and "pirates," and all kinds of other games. Some kids are swinging on the gigantic swing set in one corner of the playground, pumping their legs in rhythm. They smile as the wind blows their hair and giggle as the motion tickles their tummies. Other kids are crawling around the large square sandbox in another corner, digging and shaping the warm sand. Still others are playing on the seesaw, sliding down the slide, or spinning on the merry-go-round.

Now, what if I told you that the playground is surrounded on four sides with a high fence? Would that spoil your picture of the playground? The children can leave the fenced area anytime they want, of course, but if they want to enjoy the playground, they have to play inside the fence.

Does that sound cruel or confining? No? Why not?

"Well," you might say, "some playgrounds have fences because they're right next to a busy street. If there were no fences, the kids might run out into the street and get hurt. Or," you might add, "this playground could be built next to a river or pond, and the fences are there to keep kids from wandering into danger. Or," you might suggest, "maybe this playground has a fence to keep people from coming in and messing up the playground equipment when nobody's there."

And you would be right, of course. We can see that fences around playgrounds are good; they protect the kids and make it easier for them to have fun.

God's commands work the same way. They're not given to us to be cruel or confining. He gave us commands (such as "Don't steal," "Love one another," and "Honor your father and mother") so that we can enjoy as much freedom as possible while still being protected from all sorts of dangers. His commands are meant to be like a playground fence—protecting us and setting us free to have fun.

 REFLECT: In today's Bible reading, what two things did Paul say God's law is like? How are God's commands like a playground fence? Do you think obeying God's commands (such as "Don't steal," "Love one another," and "Honor your father and mother") can protect you from danger? If so, what dangers?

 PRAY: "Lord, thank you for giving me guidance for my life that will keep me from being hurt. Help me to stay inside the loving protection of your commands."

July
24 A Small Act of Kindness

Bible Reading: 1 Thessalonians 5:15-24

Always try to be kind to each other and to everyone else.
1 Thessalonians 5:15, NIV

THE STORY IS told of a man named Martin who lived many centuries ago. He had been born in a place called Pannonia, in what is now Hungary. When he was only fifteen years old, his father (an officer in the army of Rome) insisted that Martin become a soldier.

Five or six years later, Martin was riding through the streets of Amiens, France, with a small band of his fellow soldiers. Their swords and armor glistened in the sunshine, and men and women pressed against the walls of the narrow street to watch the thrilling display of horses and soldiers.

Suddenly, the small procession passed by a beggar, huddled by the side of the road, dressed only in flimsy rags and shivering with cold. When Martin saw the ragged man, he pulled the reins of his horse and stopped. He watched the poor man for a few moments, then looked around uncertainly. Although he had no money, he felt an urgent need to help the beggar.

Then, in a flash, Martin reached a hand to his shoulder and gripped the heavy cloak that hung from his armor. He took it off, then drew his sword. The beggar looked at him with wide, fearful eyes, but Martin did not threaten the beggar with the weapon. Instead, gripping the cloak in one hand and the sword in the other, he sliced through the heavy fabric, cutting it into two pieces. He leaned over and draped one of the pieces over the beggar's trembling shoulders. Then he returned his sword to its place, lifted the other piece of his cloak to his own shoulders, and galloped off after his companions.

Cool, huh? For sixteen centuries, people have admired Martin's act of kindness to that beggar because people recognize that kindness—even a small act of kindness—is good and admirable. In fact, that incident (which occurred over sixteen centuries ago) is one of the reasons Martin was honored as a saint after his death in A.D. 397. Actually, there is really no such thing as a *small* act of kindness, as St. Martin found out the night after he showed kindness to the beggar. He had a dream that night, in which he saw Jesus, surrounded by the angels of heaven. In the dream, Jesus wore one half of a Roman soldier's cloak.

 REFLECT: What do you think St. Martin's dream meant? Do you agree that there is really no such thing as a *small* act of kindness? Why or why not? Can you think of an act of kindness you can do for someone else today?

 PRAY: "Kind and loving Father, thank you for teaching me that kindness is good, no matter how small or simple it may seem. Help me to try to always be kind to others."

25 Who Makes the Calls?

Bible Reading: Luke 6:32-35

Love your enemies, do good to them, and lend to them without expecting to get anything back. Luke 6:35, NIV

YOU PROBABLY KNOW that, in baseball, an umpire decides which pitches are balls and which are strikes, right? But what about other sports? For example, who decides whether a ball is "in bounds" or "out of bounds" in tennis? Who's in charge of deciding whether or not a punch is a "low blow" in boxing? Take a look at the following lists. See if you can match the sport with the official who "makes the calls."

1. Soccer	A. Umpire
2. Diving	B. Line judge
3. Rugby	C. Steward
4. Horse racing	D. Referee
5. Tennis	E. Judge
6. Fencing	F. Touch judge
7. Cricket	G. Chief official

Finished? OK, let's see how you did. Let's begin at the top of the list of sports. In soccer, the referee (aided by linesmen) makes the calls and keeps the game fair. In diving, a panel of judges rate each diver's performance. A touch judge is one of the officials in a rugby match. In horse racing, a steward decides whether to disqualify any horses or jockeys. In tennis, a line judge rules balls "in" or "out." In fencing, a chief official watches carefully to make sure everyone plays by the rules. And in cricket, an umpire is in charge of the game.

Interesting, isn't it? All those different sports have a person (or persons) who decides what's "fair" or "foul," what's "in" or "out," what's "good" or "bad." The athletes themselves don't make those decisions—a referee, judge, umpire, line judge, official, or steward does.

It's the same in life. We're not the ones who decide whether something is true or not. Take kindness, for example. You may say, "Hey, kindness is evil," "Kindness is bad," or "I don't have to be kind." But that doesn't change the fact that kindness is right. Why? Because you don't decide such things—God does. And he makes it pretty clear that kindness—even kindness toward your enemies—is good!

REFLECT: How do you know that showing kindness toward others is right? Do you think showing kindness to your enemies or to someone you don't know is right? Why? (Hint: Look back at today's Bible reading.) Why do you think God wants you to be kind to people who are mean to you?

PRAY: "God, it's not always easy to be kind to others. But help me to always remember that it's right. Help me to be kind, even toward people I don't know or people who aren't very kind to me, like_____."

26 Alien Invasion

Bible Reading: Colossians 3:12-15

Since God chose you to be the holy people whom he loves, you must clothe yourselves with . . . kindness. Colossians 3:12

YOU GROPE YOUR way to the breakfast table, your eyes still closed against the morning light. You sit down in your usual chair and mumble a quick prayer: "Lord, flump this flew to flabbleflubble," or something less clear. When you finally manage to lift your eyelids, you see in front of you a bowl of your favorite cereal, already poured, two slices of toast, and a glass of orange juice. You pinch yourself to make sure you're awake. *Who did that?* you wonder. Then you hear your brother call down the stairs.

"Hope you like the breakfast I made for you!"

You hit the side of your head with your palm. Are you hearing *and* seeing things? He even sprinkled sugar on the cereal. The little squirt didn't miss a thing. What's going on? You turn a few spoonfuls of your cereal just to make sure there's no poison or dead spiders in the bowl. *Maybe he just wants something,* you figure.

When you finish breakfast, you return to your room and find your bed made and your favorite outfit laid out on your bed. You expect to hear spooky music—like the theme to *The X Files.* You begin looking for hidden cameras. Then it dawns on you— aliens have invaded and taken over your brother's body! As soon as you let your guard down, they'll seize you and make you their slave, too!

Things get weirder as the day goes on. You walk into a room, where your brother is watching television, and he offers to change the channel to your favorite show! You get a little thirsty, and the little squirt shows up with a can of pop—*for you!* He even does one of your chores for you, just because (he says) "I felt like doing it!"

That would be pretty cool, wouldn't it? Spooky, but cool. Imagine what life would be like if your little brother or big sister or best friend spent all day being kind to you. It would be great, right?

That's why God commands us to be kind; he knows how great it is when people treat each other kindly. He knows our life would be better if we were all kind to each other. That's why his Word says, "You must clothe yourselves with tenderhearted mercy, kindness, humility, gentleness, and patience" (Colossians 3:12).

So kindness is right because God commands it. Plus, it can be really cool, too.

 REFLECT: How do you think your family life would be different if everyone took every opportunity to be kind to each other? How would your school, church, or neighborhood be different if everyone showed kindness? if *you* took every opportunity to be kind to others?

 PRAY: "Dear God, I know that kindness is right because you command it. Help me to surprise people—even people in my own family—with kindness today as I _____."

27 Putting a Smile on God's Face

Bible Reading: Jeremiah 9:23-24

"I am the Lord, who exercises kindness, justice and righteousness on earth, for in these I delight," declares the Lord. Jeremiah 9:24, NIV

HOW DO YOU picture God? Do you see him as a big, bearded, white-haired man? Do you picture him in white robes? Do you imagine him to be tall?

What about his face? Is it wrinkled? serious? frowning? smiling?

Actually, our pictures of God are likely to be different from someone else's picture of God because those pictures come from our imagination. None of us really knows what God looks like. In fact, he probably doesn't look like anything we've ever seen before.

But I can tell you this—certain things make God smile. Certain things make his face light up. Certain things make his expression brighten like a kid unwrapping presents on Christmas morning.

Want to know what those things are? Do you really want to know what makes God smile? Three of them are mentioned in today's Bible reading: kindness, justice, and righteousness. God says, "In these I delight" (Jeremiah 9:24, NIV). In other words, when God sees kindness, he is delighted. When he sees you being kind to your little brother or sister, his face lights up like a candle. When he sees you comfort a crying baby, the expression on his face reflects delight.

Why? Because God values kindness. He delights in kindness. Kindness is one of his favorite things.

Of course, we knew that already, didn't we? Because God commands us to "always try to be kind to each other and to everyone else" (1 Thessalonians 5:15, NIV). And we know that God's commands reflect God's values.

So next time you have a chance to be kind, take it—and put a smile on God's face.

 REFLECT: What does it mean to "delight" in something? What things delight you? How do you know God delights in kindness? Do you delight in kindness? Do you ever delight in unkindness? How do your actions reflect what you find "delightful"? How do you think God feels when you are kind to someone? How does it make you feel when you are kind to someone? Think of at least two kind things you can do for someone today. Then do each before the day is over.

 PRAY: "Heavenly Father, help me to put a smile on your face today by the way I act toward others and the things I do for them."

28 Desert Discovery

Bible Reading: Psalm 145:17-21

The Lord is righteous in everything he does; he is filled with kindness.
Psalm 145:17

SUPPOSE YOU TURNED on the radio tomorrow morning and heard a news flash that said an ancient document had just been discovered in the desert. Now suppose the newsperson said that this document contained new information about God, with accounts of God's activity on earth. What would you do if you learned

- that God created giraffes just so he could make fun of their long necks?
- that God *really* threw Adam and Eve out of the Garden of Eden because he wanted the Garden all to himself?
- that in 4040 B.C., God saw an old lady crossing a city street in Kish and *tripped* her?
- that God once kicked a dog *for no reason at all?*
- that when David sang Psalm 23 for the first time, God started throwing rotten tomatoes and said, "Aah, get outta here! Your singing stinks! Get some voice lessons"?

How would you respond to such a discovery? Would you say, "Well, whaddya know?" Or would you say, "That's bogus! I don't believe that God would ever do those things!"

Chances are, you wouldn't believe such a document, would you? You would doubt or dismiss its truthfulness, wouldn't you? But why? Because you know better.

After all, you know that God would never trip old ladies or kick dogs. He wouldn't make fun of a giraffe or heckle a church musician, right? Why? Because those things are contrary to God's nature; they would be "out of character" for him because God is kind.

The Bible says, "The Lord is righteous in everything he does; he is *filled with kindness*" (Psalm 145:17, emphasis added). Kindness is part of who he is. Ultimately that's why kindness is right—because God himself is kind. He commands kindness because he values kindness. Because our Father in heaven is kind, we also should be kind.

 REFLECT: Do you think God is kind? How do you know? Has God been kind to you? If so, in what ways? What makes kindness right and unkind attitudes or actions wrong? Name some ways you can reflect God's kindness today.

 PRAY: "Heavenly Father, I praise you because you're filled with kindness, and I thank you because you've been so kind to me. Help me to show your kindness to others today and every day."

29 Mowing Madness

Bible Reading: 2 Samuel 10:1-2

David thought, "I will show kindness to Hanun son of Nahash, just as his father showed kindness to me." 2 Samuel 10:2, NIV

THIS IS THE story of two neighbors, Sam and Jed. One day Jed was mowing his lawn. As he got to the row of small trees that marked the line between his yard and Sam's yard, he decided to mow a little bit of Sam's lawn just to be nice. As he mowed, he thought, *Wouldn't it be nice to keep going?* Before long he had mowed all of Sam's yard!

A few days later Sam was spreading fertilizer on his lawn. He was almost done when he remembered what Jed had done a few days earlier. So when he got to Jed's lawn he kept going, until he had fertilized Jed's yard along with his own.

When Jed arrived home from his tae kwon do lesson, his wife told him what Sam had done. *Hmm,* Jed thought. *That was a really nice thing for Sam to do. After all, mowing Sam's lawn only took a little extra gas. But fertilizer can be downright expensive.*

The next weekend Jed decided it was time to clean out all the leaves and dirt that had collected in his gutters. As he worked, he came up with a plan to repay Sam's "fertilizer kindness." Jed figured that since he had all the cleaning stuff already out, he would just go ahead and clean Sam's gutters.

Later that month Sam was doing some gardening and mulching. When he finished, he still had some mulch left. So he sneaked over to Jed's yard and spread the mulch around his neighbor's trees and flowers.

Over the course of the next several years, Sam and Jed continued their efforts to outdo each other's kindness. They became good friends. And their yards and homes were the best-looking places in their neighborhood.

Before long a funny thing started to happen. Jed's mowing madness had infected the rest of the neighborhood, and people started imitating Sam's and Jed's kindness. And the whole block started to look cleaner and prettier and friendlier.

Sam and Jed are still doing kind things for each other, and they probably will for the rest of their lives. After all, they don't plan to move anywhere else, because they figure they could never find nicer neighbors.

REFLECT: In today's Bible reading, how did Nahash's kindness affect David's relationship with Hanun? Why do you think David reacted that way? How did kindness affect Sam and Jed's friendship? How did it affect their lives? Do you think all neighbors would respond like Sam did? Which do you think kindness is like: a wad of putty thrown against a wall, which sticks where it hits, or a rubber ball thrown against a wall, which bounces back to the person who threw it? Carry a rubber ball in your pocket or purse today to remind you to be kind to those around you.

PRAY: "Lord, help me to see opportunities to be kind to others today, especially as I _____ [go to school, attend band practice, walk through my neighborhood, etc.]."

30 The Little Princess

Bible Reading: Proverbs 11:16-17

A kindhearted woman gains respect, but ruthless men gain only wealth.
A kind man benefits himself, but a cruel man brings trouble on himself.
Proverbs 11:16-17, NIV

ONCE UPON A time there was a little princess. This princess was unhappy because, although she was a princess, she was not very pretty to look at.

One day as the little princess sat crying in the garden of her palace, an old woman came by. The woman's back was crooked, her hair was gray, and her fingers were gnarled with age. She asked the princess why she was crying.

"Because I am homely. I will never be beautiful."

The woman laid a sympathetic hand on the girl's shoulder. "Why don't you go out into your kingdom and find someone who can make you beautiful?" And with those words of advice, the old woman walked away.

The little princess decided to follow the woman's advice and started off to look for someone who could make her beautiful. Before she had gone very far, she saw a boy who had stumbled on the road and was struggling to get up. The princess rushed to his side and helped him up. It was then she realized that he was blind.

"Where are you going?" she asked. When the boy told her that he was trying to find his way home, the princess decided her search could wait. She walked with the blind boy until they had found his home.

The princess started on her way again. Soon she saw a little girl crying by the side of the road. The princess asked what was wrong.

"My mother is sick and has sent me to buy some milk and eggs for her. But because I have no money, I cannot buy any for her," the little girl said, sobbing.

The princess dug in her little purse. She had only two pieces of gold, but she gave one to the girl whose mother was sick. "Here," she said. "Now you can buy your mother some milk and eggs." The girl dried her tears and thanked the princess. She then ran off to the store, laughing and singing.

The princess started on her way again, but soon she saw the old woman again. "I have not found anyone to make me beautiful," she told the woman.

"Oh, but you have!" the woman answered. She lifted a little mirror before the princess's face. "Your kindness has made you beautiful—not only to the children you helped, but to others as well!"

And the little princess saw that her words were true!

 REFLECT: What did the little princess's kindness do for her? Do you think kindness can really make people more attractive? Why or why not? Being kind benefits the person you're kind to, but it also benefits you. What are some other ways being kind can benefit you?

 PRAY: "Kind and loving God, show me the blessings of kindness today as I try to be kind to others."

Little Eva

Bible Reading: Proverbs 14:21, 31

He who despises his neighbor sins, but blessed is he who is kind to the needy. . . . He who oppresses the poor shows contempt for their Maker, but whoever is kind to the needy honors God. Proverbs 14:21, 31, NIV

HARRIET BEECHER STOWE'S famous book, *Uncle Tom's Cabin,* tells the story of Tom and Eliza and other slaves of the South during the years prior to the American Civil War. Part of the book also features a character named Eva, a little girl whose mother complains constantly of sickness and trouble. In one chapter, Eva's mother is complaining about her slave, Mammy, because, she says, "I think it's selfish of her to sleep so sound nights; she knows I need little attentions almost every hour, when my worst turns are on, and yet she's so hard to wake. I absolutely am worse, this very morning, for the efforts I had to make to wake her last night."

Her little daughter, Eva, later asks, "Mamma, couldn't I take care of you one night—just one?"

"Oh, nonsense, child," her mother answers.

"But may I, Mamma? I think," she says in a low voice, "that Mammy isn't well. She told me her head ached all the time lately."

The reader soon learns that Eva seems to be as kind as her mother is thoughtless and selfish. Little Eva even proposes letting the slave Mammy share Eva's bed, "because then it would be handier to take care of her, and because, you know, my bed is better than hers."

What a lovely picture of kindness! And what a reminder that kids are often kinder than adults. And what a perfect description of what the Bible means when it says, "blessed is he who is kind to the needy . . . whoever is kind to the needy honors God" (Proverbs 14:21, 31, NIV). In fact, the word *blessed* in Proverbs 14:21 means "to be honored and made happy by God." So you could say that the person who is kind honors God, and God honors the person who is kind.

 REFLECT: Who are you most like: Eva or her mom? Who are the "needy" people around you? (They don't have to be homeless or poor; they may simply need affection, attention, or comfort.) How can you be kind to the "needy" today?

 PRAY: "God, I believe your Word when it says, 'blessed is he who is kind to the needy' and 'whoever is kind to the needy honors God.' I want to honor you today, especially by being kind to_____. Help me find ways to be kind."

He-Man and You

Bible Reading: Proverbs 3:5-8

Trust in the Lord with all your heart; do not depend on your own understanding. Proverbs 3:5

THE TRADEMARK LINE of the superhero He-Man is "I have the power!" and is delivered as he raises his broadsword above his head.

Of course, people never asked He-Man, "You have the power to do *what?*" He had big muscles, so they probably were afraid he'd beat them up. But it's a fair question, not just for He-Man, but for you as well.

How would you complete He-Man's statement for yourself? Check off any statements in the list below that you think are true:

I have the power to . . .

- ☐ stand on my head.
- ☐ eat whatever I want.
- ☐ leap tall buildings in a single bound.
- ☐ count to one hundred.
- ☐ snap my fingers.
- ☐ make right choices all the time.

- ☐ fly.
- ☐ lift five hundred pounds over my head.
- ☐ get good grades in school.
- ☐ hold my breath for sixty seconds.
- ☐ dump a bucket of mud and earthworms in my sister's bed.

Which ones didn't you check? (If you said you had the power to lift five hundred pounds, write to the International Olympic Committee right now!)

What was your response to the statement "I have the power to make right choices all the time?" Did you check it?

Actually, none of us can honestly check that statement. None of us has the power to make right choices all the time because each of us is sinful. We may want to do good. We may even try to do good. But the secret of doing good and making right choices isn't in trying—it's in trusting God's power.

The key, then, to living a life of obedience to God's commands is knowing God, staying as close to him as you can (through prayer, worship, and Bible reading, for example), then day by day (even moment by moment) trusting him to help you make right choices. And one of those right choices would be deciding *not* to dump a bucket of mud and earthworms in your sister's bed. (Just in case you were thinking about it!)

 REFLECT: Do you think you can trust someone you don't know? How can you get to know God better so you can trust him more? Do you have the power to make right choices all the time? Who does have that power? How can you use that power?

 ACT: Every time you turn a light or appliance on today, try to remember where your power to make right choices comes from.

 PRAY: "God, I trust you for the power to help me do the right thing today and every day."

2 Live from Jericho!

Bible Reading: Joshua 6:1-20

Trust in the Lord with all your heart; do not depend on your own understanding. Proverbs 3:5

NEWSCASTER WITH MICROPHONE appears on screen before the smoking ruins of a city, visible in the background.

"Dan Rathernot here, on location in Canaan, where the mighty city of Jericho has just been conquered by a ragtag band of warriors led by one Joshua ben Nun."

Camera angle widens to reveal a robed man standing beside the newsman.

"Here, for an exclusive interview with us, is the mastermind behind this astonishing military victory." *Dan Rathernot turns, points microphone at Joshua.* "Joshua ben Nun, thank you for agreeing to talk with us."

"Uh, thank you, Dan, but I have to say, I'm not the mastermind of this victory. It was God's strategy."

"Yes, well . . ." *Dan Rathernot clears his throat.* "Rumors are already flying around about your victory." *He laughs nervously.* "Some say that Jericho's city walls were destroyed with a shout."

"That's absolutely true, Dan. God told us to march around the city once every day for six days. Then, on the seventh day, our army marched seven times around Jericho. On the seventh time around, the priests blew their rams' horns, the people shouted, and the walls crumbled into piles of dust."

"That's, uh . . . heh, heh . . . quite a story." *Dan Rathernot's left eyelid starts to twitch.* "Didn't, uh, God's instructions seem kind of—well, er, silly to you?"

"I could see how you might think they were silly, but you've got to understand one thing, Dan. I spent forty years in the wilderness of Sinai with Moses, hearing God speak and watching him work. I learned that it's best to do what God says, even if you don't understand it. If I had depended on my own understanding—" *Joshua turns and points to the pile of rubble that used to be the city of Jericho*—"the walls of Jericho would still be standing."

Dan Rathernot smiles; camera zooms in for a close-up.

"There you have it. An incredible story of one man, one God, one army, and one big mess for Jericho's street crews to clean up."

REFLECT: God's instructions for conquering Jericho are recorded in Joshua 6:2-5. Do you think it was easy for Joshua and the Israelites to follow God's instructions? Why or why not? Do you think they would have conquered Jericho if they had not followed God's instructions? Why or why not? Do you always understand God's commands? Do you think you should follow them even if you don't understand them? Why or why not?

ACT: Walk around your house and make note of the things you use or obey without understanding all about them (electricity, gasoline engines, radio and TV waves).

PRAY: "Lord, help me to trust you, even when your commands seem hard to understand."

3 The Power of a Commitment

Bible Reading: 2 Timothy 1:8-12

Trust in the Lord with all your heart; do not depend on your own under-standing. Seek his will in all you do, and he will direct your paths.
Proverbs 3:5-6

WHAT DO THE following have in common?

- a baseball player's contract
- a dentist appointment
- wedding vows
- a loan agreement

All of the above are commitments of one kind or another. They're promises.

A baseball player commits to play for a particular baseball team for a certain length of time—in exchange for, like, a bazillion dollars.

A bride and groom promise to love each other and be faithful to each other "for better, for worse; for richer, for poorer; in sickness and in health."

A dentist promises to save a certain time of day for a patient whose jaw is swollen to about half the size of Minnesota.

A bank agrees to loan money to someone who agrees to make regular payments.

Why doesn't the bank just loan the money without a loan agreement? Why doesn't the patient just drop in at the dentist's office? Why doesn't the athlete play without a contract? Why do the bride and groom exchange vows? Because commitments are important. There is power in a commitment. When you make a commitment to someone or something, you're not saying, "I'll do this if I feel like it," or "I'll do it if it's easy." Instead, you're saying, "I'll do it whether I feel like it or not." "I'll do it even if it's hard."

That's why it's important to make a commitment to do the right thing. That's why a lot of kids sign pledges not to take drugs. That's why a lot of kids fill out "True Love Waits" commitment cards, promising to stay pure until marriage. That's why a lot of kids sign "Prom Promises" when they're in high school: because it's important to make a commitment to do the right thing.

Making a commitment to do the right thing can help you when you're tempted. You don't have to wonder what to do; you're reminded—by your commitment—that you've already made that decision.

REFLECT: What is a commitment? Why are commitments important? Have you ever committed to making right choices? Have you committed to God and to your parents not to lie? not to steal? not to cheat? not to try drugs? If so, have you told anyone of your commitment(s)?

PRAY: Take a few moments to make a commitment to God in prayer, promising to seek his will in all you do. Be as specific as you can. (For example, you might pray, "God, I want to seek your will in all that I do. I commit to telling the truth, even when it's hard. I commit to obeying my parents, even when I don't feel like it.")

4 The Blindfold Game

Bible Reading: Isaiah 26:3-7

Trust in the Lord with all your heart; do not depend on your own under-standing. Seek his will in all you do, and he will direct your paths.
Proverbs 3:5-6

MAYBE YOU'VE DONE it in school or church youth group or someplace else. You put on a blindfold so that you can't see where you're going. Another person is assigned to you as a companion. It's that person's job to guide you safely away from dangers and get you where you want to go by giving directions such as these:

- "Turn left here."
- "Go straight for about four steps, then turn right."
- "Take hold of the railing and climb three—no, four steps."
- "Watch your head."
- "Step over the rattlesnake."
- "Put your right foot in, put your right foot out, put your right foot in, and shake it all about."

OK, OK, so the last one is part of the hokey pokey. But you get the idea. The key in that game (which is sometimes used in school to help you understand and sympathize with the problems faced by blind people) is to trust your guide and carefully follow his or her instructions. If you don't follow your guide's instructions, you'll bump into walls, fall downstairs—and may even step on a rattlesnake (ouch!).

That's pretty much the key to living the Christian life, too. God has given us some pretty clear instructions. He has shown us the right way to inherit eternal life and to live a life that's pleasing to him and satisfying to us. The key is to obey the instructions God has given us.

Obeying God's commands is like following the instructions of your companion in "the blindfold game." You may choose to "do your own thing," but you'll probably end up with more than a few bumps, bruises, and rattlesnake bites. And worse.

But if you trust in the Lord with all your heart and let him direct your paths, he'll guide you safely away from many dangers and get you where you want to go.

 REFLECT: What kind of guide in "the blindfold game" do you think would be most helpful? Should it be someone you trust? Should it be someone who communicates well? Why or why not? Is God worthy of your trust? Has he given you clear instructions for obtaining eternal life and living a godly life? Have you been following his instructions?

 ACT: Try playing a short round of "the blindfold game" with a friend this week. Take turns wearing the blindfold and acting as guide.

 PRAY: "Dear God, I depend on you to guide me each day. Lead me in the way you would like me to go."

Dumb and Dumber

Bible Reading: Proverbs 13:14-20
*He who walks with the wise grows wise, but a companion of fools
suffers harm. Proverbs 13:20, NIV*

JIM CARREY AND Jeff Daniels starred in the popular movie comedy *Dumb and Dumber*.
Jim Carrey's character was, indeed, dumb. And the guy Jeff Daniels played was even
dumber.

A lot of movies and television shows feature partnerships in which one—or
both—of the characters acts stupid or foolish. See if you can match each character in
the first list below with his or her TV or movie companion on the right.

Wayne	Harry
Bill	Bart
Jafar	Iago
Shenzi	Flit
Lisa	Garth
Lloyd	Ted
Meeko	Ed

How'd you do? You probably knew that Wayne and Garth were the characters in the
Wayne's World movies, and that Bart and Lisa, of TV's *The Simpsons,* are brother and
sister. Bill and Ted were characters played by Alex Winter and Keanu Reeves in *Bill
and Ted's Excellent Adventure* and *Bill and Ted's Bogus Journey.* Meeko and Flit were
the raccoon and hummingbird in *Pocahontas,* and Shenzi and Ed were two of the
hyenas in *The Lion King.* Jafar was the bad guy in *Aladdin* and Iago was his (literally)
flighty companion. And, Lloyd and Harry were *Dumb and Dumber,* respectively.

You may not have a friend like Harry in *Dumb and Dumber* or Garth in *Wayne's
World* (let's hope not!). But even if your friends are smart and cool and fun, they can
still get you into trouble.

The Bible says, "He who walks with the wise grows wise, but a companion of fools
suffers harm" (Proverbs 13:20, NIV). In other words, it's not just important that you
make right choices; it's important to have friends who make right choices, too. A big
part of being wise is choosing your companions wisely.

 REFLECT: Are there any "companions" in the list above that you would like to hang
around with? Any you would try to avoid? Do you have friends who influence you to
make right choices? Any who influence you to make wrong choices? (Be honest about
both!) Have you ever asked God to help you form strong, lasting friendships with wise
companions? If not, why not do so now? Then be alert this week to the ways your
friends influence you . . . *and* to ways *you* influence your friends.

 PRAY: "Lord, I want to be a good influence on my friends, and I want my friends to
be good influences on me. Help me to choose my friends wisely."

6 Amazing Love

Bible Reading: Leviticus 19:16-18

Never seek revenge or bear a grudge against anyone, but love your neighbor as yourself. I am the Lord. Leviticus 19:18

THINK ABOUT WHAT you would do as you read the following situation.

You're standing around with your friends in the cafeteria at school, when all of a sudden a teacher comes up. You see one of your best friends point a finger at you and whisper something to the teacher. The teacher grabs you by the collar.

"What'd I do?" you ask.

"You *know* what you did!" The teacher lifts you by the collar until only your toes are touching the ground and starts dragging you to the principal's office. You look behind you for help from your friends, but they've all disappeared.

When you arrive in the principal's office, you're thrown into a chair. You sit, dazed and unbelieving, while one kid after another—some you don't even know—tell the principal that you broke all the car windows in the school parking lot.

You try to tell the principal that you're innocent, that you would never do such a thing, that you've got witnesses, an alibi. But no one listens. Finally, you're blindfolded and tied to the school flagpole, where everyone in school gathers to laugh at you and call you names. School lets out, and it starts to get dark and cold, and you're left there—alone, shivering, in the dark. And innocent.

How would you respond to such a situation? It would make you pretty mad, wouldn't it? What if it wasn't a teacher but the religious authorities who arrested you? What if your alleged crime wasn't breaking windows but planning a rebellion? What if you weren't taken to the principal's office but were beaten and tortured until you were almost dead? What if you weren't tied to a flagpole but were nailed to a cross? What would you do then?

You know what Jesus did. His friends had betrayed him. He had been unjustly accused. He had been ridiculed and spat upon. He had been treated cruelly, viciously. Yet he responded by praying, "Father, forgive them" (Luke 23:34, NIV).

Why? He had every reason to call down fire from heaven and teach those people a lesson. But he didn't. Even when they betrayed him, he loved them. Even when they treated him cruelly, he loved them. Even when they killed him, he loved them.

Amazing, isn't it? Almost unbelievable. Yet there it is.

That's what love looks like.

 REFLECT: Do you think it's possible to love someone and "get even" with him or her at the same time? Why or why not? Is there anyone you need to forgive right now? If so, why not do it today?

 ACT: The next time you pass a flagpole, remember how Jesus loved and forgave those who hurt him.

 PRAY: If you're dealing with feelings of wanting to get even with someone, ask God to help you love and forgive those who have wronged you.

No Excuses

Bible Reading: Romans 12:17-21
> *Don't just pretend that you love others. Really love them. Romans 12:9*

PEOPLE MAKE ALL kinds of excuses:

- "The dog ate my homework."
- "It was temporary insanity."
- "I didn't realize there was paint in the squirt gun."
- "It just slipped out!"
- "The devil made me do it."
- "I didn't know the gun was loaded."
- "I was pushed."
- "His face hit my fist!"

You've heard 'em all before. Maybe you've even used 'em yourself (admit it, now!).

The making of excuses goes way back to the Garden of Eden when Adam and Eve ate the forbidden fruit: Adam said, "Hey! That woman you put here with me—she gave it to me." And Eve said, "It wasn't my fault! The serpent made me do it!"

Thousands of years later we still haven't learned. We still make excuses for our behavior, especially when our behavior is unloving. "She deserved it," we say. "He had it coming." "He hit me first." "She would've done the same thing to me." "Why should I love him when he doesn't love me?" You get the idea.

But no matter how many excuses we use, there's no excuse for getting even with someone or treating him or her in an unloving way. Oh, sure, so-and-so did this to you. And whatsisname doesn't deserve to be treated nicely. But the Bible says, "Don't just pretend that you love others. Really love them. . . . Never pay back evil for evil to anyone . . . [and] never avenge yourselves. Leave that to God. For it is written, 'I will take vengeance; I will repay those who deserve it,' says the Lord. Instead, do what the Scriptures say: 'If your enemies are hungry, feed them. If they are thirsty, give them something to drink, and they will be ashamed of what they have done to you.' Don't let evil get the best of you, but conquer evil by doing good" (Romans 12:9a, 17-21).

Sure, it's hard. Making excuses would be much easier. But love is what's right. Love is always right.

REFLECT: We all have tried to justify wrong behavior by making excuses. What excuses have you made for not treating someone with love? Are you making excuses to justify wrong behavior now? If so, what should you do instead of making excuses?

PRAY: "Dear God, help me not to make excuses to justify my unloving behavior, like when I _____. Help me instead to do what is right, even when it's hard."

8 Mel, Mariah, and Madden

Bible Reading: 1 Corinthians 13:1-13

Love is patient, love is kind. It does not envy, it does not boast, it is not proud. It is not rude, it is not self-seeking, it is not easily angered, it keeps no record of wrongs. 1 Corinthians 13:4-5, NIV.

IT'S NO SECRET that Shaquille O'Neal likes basketball.

It shouldn't surprise you to find out that Bill Gates likes computers.

Or that Mel Gibson likes to act.

Or that Mariah Carey likes to sing.

Or that John Madden likes football.

Or that Ekaterina Gordeeva likes ice skating.

After all, it's pretty obvious, right? Shaq spends his time playing basketball. Bill Gates made a fortune selling Windows software and other computer-related products. Mel Gibson makes a new movie every year. If Mariah Carey didn't like singing, she'd probably quit her job and do something else.

You can usually tell what people like by what they do or say. In the same way, it's easy to tell that God thinks love is absolutely cool. He talks about it constantly. He says things like "love one another," "love your neighbor," "love the Lord your God," over and over. And he is always loving; the Bible says more than forty times, "his love endures forever." The Bible also says, "And now these three remain: faith, hope and love. But the greatest of these is love" (1 Corinthians 13:13, NIV).

Of course, the greatest indication of how God feels about love is that he commands us to love him, to love each other, and even to love our enemies. His commands make it clear that love is right. To love God is right. To love others is right. To love even our enemies is right—because God says so.

 REFLECT: How does God feel about love? How do you know? How has he shown his love to you? Does your behavior show that you value love? Why or why not? How does your behavior show your beliefs about right and wrong? Are you obeying God's command to love him? to love others? to love your enemies?

 ACT: Write your own version of 1 Corinthians 13:4-5, using your own words to complete these sentences:

- Love is . . .
- Love is . . .
- It does not . . .
- It does not . . .
- It is not . . .
- It is not . . .
- It is not . . .
- It is not . . .

 PRAY: "Loving God, thank you for showing me how to love others. Help me to put your commands into action."

9 The Most Valuable Thing

Bible Reading: 1 John 4:7-11

Dear friends, since God so loved us, we also ought to love one another.
1 John 4:11, NIV

IMAGINE THAT YOUR house is on fire and everyone in your family (pets included) has made it to safety. Next, imagine that an angel tells you that you may return to the house for one thing—*one thing only,* rescue it from the fire, and return to safety with it.

What would you choose?

Would it be your piggy bank? your CD player? Maybe a favorite stuffed animal? a keepsake that a friend or family member gave you, something that has a lot of sentimental value? a photo? a family heirloom?

What would it be? Make sure you've chosen before you continue reading. Have you decided? OK, keep reading.

Why did you choose that object? There can only be one reason: It is the most valuable thing you possess. It may not be the most expensive thing you own. It may not even be worth anything to someone else. But the fact that you would save that possession instead of anything else reveals that to you—for whatever reason—it is the most valuable thing you own.

Now, guess what? If God were faced with the same choice, you know what he would choose? You. In fact, he already has. Ever since the day sin came into the world, everything God created in the universe has been marked for destruction. The rest of the heavens and earth will be destroyed and replaced with a new, improved version. But God sent his Son to save the most valuable part of his creation—you. He had to suffer and die to pull it off, but he did it. And do you know why he did it? Because he loves you. He loved you enough to choose you and to suffer for you and to die for you.

"Dear friends," his Word says, "since God so loved us, we also ought to love one another" (1 John 4:11, NIV). God showed how much he loved you—and how much he values love—when he "sent his one and only Son into the world that we might live through him" (1 John 4:9, NIV).

REFLECT: Can you tell what God values by what he says? Can you tell what God values by what he does? Can you tell what God values by what he saves? If so, how? How did God show how much he loves you? Since God loved you so much, how should you feel about yourself? Since God loved you so much, what should you value? Since God loved you so much, what should you do?

ACT: Keep the item you identified as your most valued possession on your desk or bedside table to remind you how God feels about you, how God feels about love, and how you should act toward others.

PRAY: "Thank you, God, that you value me. I want to show that I value love by_____ [loving others; showing love to my family, etc.]."

10 Critter Quiz

Bible Reading: 1 John 4:16-19

God is love, and . . . as we live in God, our love grows more perfect.
1 John 4:16-17

YOU KNOW WHAT puppies are, right? And you know that kittens come from cats. But can you match the following animals with the kind of young they produce?

1. frog		A. chick
2. beaver		B. fawn
3. goose		C. gosling
4. kangaroo		D. whelp or pup
5. whale		E. calf
6. deer		F. tadpole
7. seal		G. colt
8. ostrich		H. joey
9. zebra		I. cub
10. fox		J. kit

Ready to check your answers? OK, here they are: 1F; 2J; 3C; 4H; 5E; 6B; 7D; 8A; 9G; 10I.

That's right, goslings come from geese, and joeys come from kangaroos. Fawns come from deer, and tadpoles come from frogs.

You know what else? Love comes from God.

You probably already knew that, of course, but it's worth repeating and remembering. Love comes from God. Everyone agrees that love is right and hatred is wrong. But what many people miss is that the *reason* love is right is because God is love. Love is part of his nature; therefore, love is right.

Here's another thing most people miss: The more we "live in God"—praying and reading our Bible and worshiping him, stuff like that—the more loving we will become, even toward those who are hard to love. Even toward those who are *impossible* to love! Because "God is love, and . . . as we live in God, our love grows more perfect" (1 John 4:16-17).

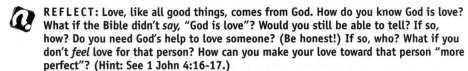

REFLECT: Love, like all good things, comes from God. How do you know God is love? What if the Bible didn't *say*, "God is love"? Would you still be able to tell? If so, how? Do you need God's help to love someone? (Be honest!) If so, who? What if you don't *feel* love for that person? How can you make your love toward that person "more perfect"? (Hint: See 1 John 4:16-17.)

ACT: Be alert this week for any puppies, kittens, or other young animals you may see. When you see them, remind yourself that love comes from God because God is love.

PRAY: "God, I need your help to love_____ [fill in a name]. Because of you, I can love others."

Bible Reading: Hebrews 13:1-3
Continue to love each other with true Christian love. Hebrews 13:1

YOU FLIP ON your radio and turn the dial to 93.5. Guitars wail, and an electric bass throbs while the lead singer sings, "Love me, love me, hug me, hold me. . . ."

You spin the dial again. It lands on WOMY, the "oh, my!" station. A woman's voice shrieks, "All I wanted was love, but all you gave me was sorrow. . . ." *Yuck.*

You turn to another station, WGLD, the "golden oldies" station, and you hear a tinny band singing, "Love, love, love, love, love, love, love . . ." You think, *And Dad says* my *music is monotonous!*

You tune in 104.7, WYBU, the country station, and hear, "I'd paint myself green, / I'd rip out my spleen, / I'd give up my brew, / If that would make you . . . love me. . . ." *Yeah, right!*

Finally, you turn to your favorite station, 107.1, your *"eight million songs in a row"* station! A sultry voice caresses the airwaves, "Your love, baby, your love, baby, your love, baby . . ." *Yeah,* you think, *now that's* real *music!*

Everybody's singing about love, right? Rock songs, country songs, rap songs, even Christian songs are mostly songs about love. Everybody wants love. Everybody wants to receive love. Everybody wants to "fall in love." Why? Because just about everybody knows that love is good. It's not just *good,* it's *great!* It's a gift from God; in fact, all love—not just romantic love—is from him. Love brings satisfaction.

Yet, in spite of all the songs about love and all the people who crave love and talk about love and dream about love, people still get in fights. They argue with each other. They stop talking to each other. They resent each other. They hurt each other. They hate each other.

Doesn't make much sense, does it? No, especially when you consider all the satisfaction and rewards that come from loving others, and all the strife and stress that come from hurting and hating others. If you've ever quieted a crying baby, you know how satisfying it can be to love someone else. If you've ever fallen asleep in your mom or dad's arms, you know how good love feels. If you've ever seen the look on a little kid's face when you give him a piece of candy, you know how much fun love can be.

Love is the right thing to do. It's also a lot more fun than the alternative.

 REFLECT: Here's something to think about. If you give away hatred, you get more and more empty the more you give; if you give love to others, you get more and more full the more you give away.

 ACT: As you listen to the radio today, see how many songs you can count that are about love.

 PRAY: "Dear Jesus, help me to give away real love today."

12 Like a Magnet

Bible Reading: Galatians 5:13-15

> *For you, dear friends, have been called to live in freedom—not freedom to satisfy your sinful nature, but freedom to serve one another in love.*
> *Galatians 5:13*

A LONG TIME ago there was a little boy who worked for a blacksmith in his shop. The blacksmith was a hard man, who kept his shop very clean.

One day the boy's boss gave him a large box of metal shavings. He told the boy to carry the box to the forge, the great fireplace where the man melted and banged out various metal tools and ornaments. The boy obeyed, but on the way he suddenly slipped on the cobblestone floor. The box flew out of his hands and metal shavings spilled onto the floor.

"Oh no!" the boy said. "What am I going to do now?" He had to clean up the mess quickly or the blacksmith would be angry at him for his clumsiness. He fell to his knees and tried to pick up the sharp metal shavings by hand, but they cut his fingers and made them bleed. He ran to get the broom but then realized that the broom would do him no good. Many tiny shavings had fallen between the bricks on the floor and could not be swept up with a broom.

"What am I going to do?" he repeated.

What would you do? You couldn't pick them up by hand. You couldn't sweep them up with a broom. A vacuum cleaner would suck them up into a bag of dust, not into the blacksmith's box. You would probably do the same thing the boy did. He searched and searched until he finally found what he needed—a magnet! The magnet attracted all the tiny shavings that lay on the bricks and between the bricks, lifting them off the floor and into the blacksmith's box.

Did you know that true Christian love has a similar property? Oh, it won't lift metal shavings off a blacksmith's floor. But it will attract loving attitudes and actions like a magnet attracts metal. When you love others, you get love back. True Christian love will act as a magnet, bringing more and more love into your life. The Bible is filled with stories that reveal this property of love, stories of Boaz's love for Ruth, Jesus' love for Lazarus, Paul's love for Timothy.

Hatred and cruelty will repel others and bring misery, but love attracts love the way a magnet attracts metal.

 REFLECT: How is true Christian love like a magnet? Whom have you been loving with true Christian love? Whom have you *not* been loving as you should? What can you do today to show true Christian love to others?

 ACT: If possible, keep a magnet in your pocket or purse this week to remind you that hatred invites hatred, but love attracts love.

 PRAY: "Heavenly Father, help me to see—and experience—the advantages of acting in love toward others."

13 Love Covers All

Bible Reading: Proverbs 10:11-12

Hatred stirs up quarrels, but love covers all offenses. Proverbs 10:12

FOR EACH QUESTION, circle your choice.

Which country do you think is more likely to get into a war:

- a country that tries to steal oil and water from other countries?
- a country that sends food and medical supplies to other countries?

What kind of neighbor do you think is more likely to get reported to the police:
- a neighbor who soaps the windows of the house next door?
- a neighbor who offers a plate of freshly baked cookies to the new family moving in next door?

What kind of kid do you think is more likely to get into a fight at school:
- a kid who calls people names?
- a kid who seems to love everybody (even Walter Wigsniewski!)?

The answers to those questions should be pretty obvious, right? It's easy to figure out that a kid who calls people names is probably going to get into more fights than a kid who seems to love everybody. And a person who soaps his neighbor's windows is more likely to get reported to the police than someone who offers a plate of freshly baked cookies to the new family moving in next door. And any country that tries to steal natural resources, like oil and water, from nearby countries is probably heading for war—much more than a country that sends food and medical supplies to its neighbors!

That's sort of what the Bible means when it says, "Hatred stirs up quarrels, but love covers all offenses" (Proverbs 10:12). Hateful and unloving actions and attitudes cause a lot of conflict and strife—not just for the people who are hated but for the people *doing* the hating! But loving actions and attitudes protect you from a lot of that stuff. Love not only makes it easier for you to get along with other people, it makes them more willing to overlook your faults and forgive your mistakes. Love makes your life more pleasant and peaceful.

Love is another way in which obeying God's commands turns out to be good for us; it protects us from many fights and feuds and provides more peace and happiness in our life, too.

 REFLECT: God's commands are given to us for our own good. Does his command to love one another protect us from anything? If so, what? Does his command to love one another provide us with anything? If so, what?

 PRAY: "God, thank you for loving me. Thank you for giving your loving commands to me. Help me to remember that your commands are given to me for my own good. Help me to love others more and more, especially_____."

14 Boxes Big and Small

Bible Reading: James 2:1, 8-13

My brothers, as believers in our glorious Lord Jesus Christ, don't show favoritism. James 2:1, NIV

HAVE YOU EVER seen a set of nesting boxes? You know, you open a large box, and inside is a slightly smaller box, and inside *that* is an even smaller box, and so on. Sometimes as many as eight or ten boxes can be nested inside each other, each one smaller than the last.

Well, some people's lives are like that. For example, we all make friends from a larger group of people we know—schoolmates, kids who live in our neighborhoods, people who go to our churches, and so on. For some of us, that's a pretty big "box" from which to choose our closest friends.

But some people narrow their choices. "Oh, I could never be friends with her," they might say. "She's weird." So their "box" of potential friends becomes smaller.

Some narrow their choices even more. "I can't sit at *his* lunch table," they say. "He lives in a trailer park!" And their "box" becomes smaller still.

Still others narrow their circle of friends even more. "You can hang out with him if you want," they say, "but I don't hang out with preps."

Others narrow their circle of friends according to skin color or school colors or fingernail colors. Some keep excluding people until their "box" seems impossibly small. *I can't be seen with her,* they may think. *She's not one of the "popular" girls.*

Sometimes when kids do that, they hurt the people they ignore or exclude. But when they act that way, they *always* cheat themselves.

After all, who knows—that "unpopular" girl may be the best friend a person could ever hope to have. That "prep" or "nerd" may be one of the funniest guys you've ever met, once you get to know him. The "poor" kid or the "dumb" kid may have been the kind of friend who would stay after school with you or teach you how to ride a Jet Ski or sit next to you on the school bus when no one else would.

Of course, you'll never know that unless you keep your "box" of potential friends as large as possible. The way to do that is to treat everyone with love—not just the popular kids, or the rich kids, or the cool kids—but *everyone*. Because—who knows?—they might just surprise you someday by becoming a really, really good friend.

 REFLECT: How big is your "box" of potential friends? Have you made it smaller by excluding anyone? How can you keep your "box" of potential friends as large as possible? How can you start doing that today? (Be specific!)

 ACT: Look for the smallest box you can find. Keep it someplace where it will remind you to treat everyone with love today and always.

 PRAY: "Lord, help me to enlarge my 'box' of potential friendships. Give me the courage to love those I would normally ignore or exclude."

15 Facts and Feeling

Bible Reading: 1 Corinthians 13:4-13

Love does not delight in evil but rejoices with the truth.
1 Corinthians 13:6, NIV

IMAGINE A SWEDISH boy going to his mother. "Mama," he says, "I don't vant to be Svedish anymore."

Or imagine a grandfather saying to his granddaughter, "I don't *feel* like being your grandfather today."

Or imagine a poor person saying, "I don't *feel* like being poor this year!"

Imagine a fourth grader saying, "I feel like being in high school!" Or a skydiver saying, "I don't need to wear a parachute because I feel like falling *up* today!"

How would you answer those people?

You'd probably say something like, "It doesn't matter if you don't *feel* like being Swedish; you *are* Swedish!" or "You can *feel* like being in high school all you want, but you're still gonna be a fourth grader!" In other words, a person's feelings have nothing to do with the facts. Feelings don't change the facts, right?

Well, the same sort of thing goes on when people try to make right choices. In fact, maybe you even do it. You know that God says, "Love each other" (1 John 4:11), "Love your neighbor as yourself" (Leviticus 19:18), and even "Love your enemies" (Matthew 5:44). You know he says love is right and hate (or indifference) is wrong.

"But I can't stand that guy," you say.

"But you don't understand how rude and nasty she is," you say.

"But *nobody* likes *him,*" you say.

"But I'm still mad at her," you say.

But a person's feelings have nothing to do with the facts. And you can't change the facts just because of how you feel, right?

Your feelings may be understandable. They may be perfectly normal. They may even be justified. But your feelings don't change what's right and what's wrong. And God has said, "Love each other" (Hebrews 13:1) *That's* what's right—no matter how you feel, no matter how I feel, and no matter how anybody feels. Because our *feelings* don't change the *facts.*

 REFLECT: Do you sometimes act as though your feelings determine what's right and what's wrong? If so, how? What (or who) *does* determine what's right or wrong?

 ACT: You might want to create a motto for yourself based on the following verse: "Lord, let your constant love surround us, for our hopes are in you alone" (Psalm 33:22, TLB).

 PRAY: "God, I admit that I don't always feel like loving other people, so remind me that right and wrong aren't determined by my feelings. Help me to obey you even when I don't feel loving. Help me to even love people who are hard to love."

16 Satan's Strategy

Bible Reading: Jude 1:1-3
Contend for the faith. Jude 1:3, NIV

SUPPOSE YOU WERE the devil. Your job is to tempt people and to keep them from making right choices. You want to make people miserable and eventually to carry off their souls to a really, really bad place. What would you do?

Well, you'd probably want to make them believe there was no such thing as right or wrong, right? If they didn't believe in right or wrong, it would be easier to convince them to do wrong, wouldn't it?

There would probably still be some people who believed that some things were right and some things were wrong. You'd want to keep *them* from learning which choices were right, wouldn't you? If they couldn't figure out which thing was the right thing to do, it would be easier to convince them to do wrong, wouldn't it?

Now suppose there were still some people who had figured out which choices were right and which choices were wrong. Well, if you were the devil, you'd probably try hard to convince them to do the wrong thing anyway, wouldn't you?

Even if there were some people who believed in right and wrong and knew which choices were right and which choices were wrong, yet chose to do the right thing in spite of all your temptations, you'd do everything in your power to keep them from sharing what they knew with other people, wouldn't you?

Aren't those the things you would do if you were in the devil's shoes? Doesn't that sound surprisingly like what the devil really does? He tries to make people think there's no such thing as right or wrong. He works hard to keep people from figuring out what's right to do. He tries to convince people to do the wrong thing, even when they know what the right choice is. And he tries to keep those people who make right choices from sharing what they know with other people.

Unfortunately, the devil's strategy works with a lot of people. But now that you know what he's trying to do, you're not going to let him get away with it, are you? You're going to "contend for the faith" (Jude 1:3, NIV), aren't you? You're going to "give an answer to everyone who asks you to give the reason for the hope that you have" (1 Peter 3:15, NIV), aren't you? You're going to share what you've learned about right and wrong "in a gentle and respectful way" (1 Peter 3:16), aren't you?

Well, of course you are.

REFLECT: What four things does the devil want to do, according to the paragraphs above? Has his strategy ever worked with you?

ACT: Ask your parents or pastor to let you borrow a copy of C. S. Lewis's book *The Screwtape Letters*. It describes Satan's strategy in great detail (read especially the second chapter).

PRAY: "Jesus, help me to share what I've learned about right and wrong in a gentle and respectful way."

17 Laboratory Rat

Bible Reading: Exodus 37:1-3, 10-24

Bezalel made the ark [of the covenant] of acacia wood. . . . He overlaid it with pure gold, both inside and out, and made a gold molding around it. Exodus 37:1-2, NIV

"IT'S RUINED! It's totally ruined!" The scientist pressed his hands against his head as if he were trying to crush his own skull.

"What, master?" hissed his assistant, a stooped man in a lab coat.

"The experiment is ruined! It's all wasted—all my years of research and work!"

The assistant looked back and forth from the scientist's face to the test tubes and dishes that were spread out on the vast table in front of them.

The scientist turned angry eyes on his assistant. "Because *that* . . . ," he said, pointing to a white metal box in the corner, "is not a refrigerator!"

The assistant cast a panicked glance at the box. "It . . . it's n-not?"

"No!" the scientist shouted. "It is . . . or *was* . . . ," he said, struggling to control the emotion in his voice, "a hermetically sealed environment for controlling, perhaps reversing, the human aging process!" He opened the door and pulled out a ham salad sandwich and a Fruit Roll-Up. He held the sandwich in one hand and shook it in his assistant's face. "You . . . you . . . you dirty rat! That box had been sealed for thirteen years, and you ruined thirteen years of work with . . . with a . . . ham sandwich!"

The assistant blinked and cleared his throat. "It . . . it's, uh, ham salad, sir," he said.

So what's the big deal about putting a ham salad sandwich in a hermetically sealed environment? The reason the scientist got so upset was that his experiment had been ruined because *it was no longer pure.* Impurities had ruined his experiment.

That's not only true in scientific experiments; it's true in a lot of things. Pure gold is worth more than gold mixed with other metals or ingredients; that's why Bezalel and the others who helped build the furnishings for God's tabernacle made sure they used pure gold for the ark and all the other stuff. Because purity is good.

That's also why God wants us to be pure. He doesn't want our lives to be made impure because of sin. Of course, we can't make ourselves pure or keep ourselves pure—only God can. He can forgive our sins and purify us from all our guilt and unrighteousness (1 John 1:9). Are you trusting God to help you live a pure life?

 REFLECT: Why do you think using "pure gold" was so important to the people who helped build the furnishings for God's tabernacle? Do you have the power to keep yourself pure (free from sin)? Why do you think God's help is necessary to lead a pure life?

 ACT: Check your kitchen cupboards for something that has the word *pure* on it (a box, a bottle, and so on). Place that item in a place where it can remind you to trust God to help you live a pure life.

 PRAY: "God, remind me that purity is good and right not only in gold but in my life, too."

Bible Reading: Exodus 25:1-9

Make every effort to live a pure and blameless life. 2 Peter 3:14

HOW DO YOU think Moses responded when God told him, "Tell the people of Israel that everyone who wants to may bring me an offering. Here is a list of items you may accept on my behalf: gold, silver, and bronze; blue, purple, and scarlet yarn; fine linen; goat hair for cloth; tanned ram skins and fine goatskin leather; acacia wood; olive oil for the lamps; spices for the anointing oil and the fragrant incense; onyx stones, and other stones to be set in the ephod and the chestpiece" (Exodus 25:2-7)?

You think Moses said: "Hold on a minute, God. The bronze should be no problem, but silver and gold? I don't know. In case you haven't noticed, we're a nation of refugees right now. How about some tin and plastic?"

Or maybe: "Uh, there might be a problem with the yarn. Wal-Mart doesn't carry the scarlet and purple yarns anymore."

If Moses had said any of those things, he would have hit the roof when God started laying down the specifics: pure gold for the ark of the covenant and for the poles used to carry the ark; pure gold for the ark's lid—everything had to be pure! After all, Moses and his friends were living in tents in the desert! They probably had a hundred reasons why pure *anything* would have been too much to ask.

But Moses didn't say any of those things. He didn't protest. Why? Because he knew that God—not Moses and the people—made the rules. And one of the things God said is that purity is good. It's good when you're making a tabernacle, and it's good when you're making a man or a woman.

There may be a hundred reasons why we (or our friends, or teachers, or favorite TV characters) may think purity is too much to ask. But we don't make the rules, God does. It's not up to us to decide what's right or wrong. It is up to us to choose whether we will do right or wrong, whether we will obey God or disobey him. It's up to us to choose whether we will live "pure and blameless" lives (2 Peter 3:14) or not.

What do you choose?

 REFLECT: Do you think purity is too much for God to expect of you? Why or why not? Do you think you need help to live a pure life? If so, what kind of help? From whom? How can you get that help?

 ACT: Go on a scavenger hunt with a friend. Try to locate these items: Something made of gold; blue, purple, and scarlet yarn; something made of linen; something leather; something made of wood; olive oil; spices; gems. As you hunt, let each item remind you that, just as God decided what materials were acceptable for the tabernacle, he decides which behaviors are acceptable (right) and which are not (wrong).

 PRAY: "Only you, Lord, decide what is right. Help me to accept—and obey—your standards in all I do."

19 The Crow and the Canary

Bible Reading: Ephesians 5:1-4

Don't use foul or abusive language. Let everything you say be good and helpful. Ephesians 4:29

ONCE THERE WERE two birds, a crow and a canary, who lived in the same tree. The tree shaded a large old house where a brother and sister lived with their mother.

One day the crow said to the canary, "I will light on the ledge of that open window." He nodded his black beak in the direction of the house. "When the people see me, they will toss me a scrap of bread, and I will sleep with a full stomach tonight."

The canary watched as the crow flew to the window of the house. He craned his neck and began to caw (as crows do). He cawed and cackled, demanding to be noticed in the most shrill tones. Finally his rowdy cawing was rewarded by a woman, who came into the room—and promptly threw an old shoe at him.

The canary laughed so hard he nearly fell off his perch as the crow flapped back to the tree, looking as if the old shoe had bruised his wing.

"I'd like to see you do better," he cawed in response to the canary's musical laughter. "The woman still has at least one shoe left."

Without a word, the canary swooped down to the window. He folded his wings and began to sing his sweet song. The crow watched in amazement as the same woman appeared and let the canary eat tiny morsels of bread from her hand.

When the canary had eaten his fill, he flew back to the tree, where the crow immediately confronted him.

"She fed you," the crow said, "because she thinks you are pretty and I am not."

The canary said, "No, you are wrong."

"Why did she throw a shoe at me, then?"

The canary answered with closed eyes. "Because I sang for her. You only cawed."

The difference, you see, was in what they said and the language they used. Of course, a crow cannot sing like a canary. And a canary doesn't have to practice his song. But you and I can be like the crow or the canary. We can create ugliness with our language or we can create beauty. We can use foul or abusive language, or we can be pure in what we say.

Of course, God commands us to be pure. He makes it clear that "obscene stories, foolish talk, and coarse jokes—these are not for you. Instead, let there be thankfulness to God" (Ephesians 5:4). In other words, God says, "Don't be a crow; be a canary."

REFLECT: Which are you more like—the canary or the crow (be honest!)? Circle any of the following that are problems for you (be honest!):
- foul language
- abusive language (insults, etc.)
- coarse (dirty) jokes
- foolish talk
- obscene stories
- angry words

PRAY: "Dear God, I know that you command purity, even in the things I say. Please help me to obey your commands."

20 What Really Matters

Bible Reading: Philippians 1:9-11

> *I want you to understand what really matters, so that you may live pure and blameless lives until Christ returns. Philippians 1:10*

YOU KNOW WHAT a poll is, right? Somebody calls your house or walks up to you in a mall and says something like, "We're taking a poll of the eating habits of North Americans, and we'd like to ask you a few questions." Then the person asks you things like, "What's your favorite food?" and "Have you ever eaten raw iguana?"

Well, let's take a poll of our own. Just answer the following questions as completely as you can (you'll need a pen or pencil):

What television shows do you watch on a regular basis?

What singers or singing groups do you listen to on a regular basis?

What magazines do you receive or read on a regular basis?

Finally, take a few minutes to think about the TV shows, singers, and magazines listed above. Which of them encourage you to be pure? Which of them encourage you to think, say, or do impure things?

That's an important question because God's commands show us that he values purity. If God values purity, we should value purity, too, don't you think? If we value purity, that will mean we won't feel comfortable watching, reading, or listening to stuff that isn't pure. Whether you get to see the latest episode of *Barbaric Tales* or not doesn't really matter; staying pure in thought, word, and deed *does.*

 REFLECT: In Philippians 1:10, Paul says, "I want you to understand what really matters, so that you may live pure and blameless lives until Christ returns." What do you think really matters? If you're not sure, read Philippians 1:9-11 again. Do you value purity? Why or why not? What really matters most to you?

 ACT: Look back over the TV shows, singers, and magazines you listed. Cross out any that encourage you to think, say, or do impure things and determine to find better ways to spend your time.

 PRAY: "Lord, I know that you command purity because you value purity. Help me to act in ways that show how much purity means to me, too."

21 Dead Man Walking

Bible Reading: Isaiah 6:1-7

Holy, holy, holy is the Lord Almighty; the whole earth is full of his glory.
Isaiah 6:3, NIV

SUPPOSE THAT YOU were a soccer player and your coach told you that you were invited to a big soccer event tomorrow with all the best soccer players in the city.

You get dressed the next day in your soccer shorts, shirt, socks, and cleats. Your clothes are stained with the mud and blood of many tough games, and you wear that ragged, dirt-spattered uniform with pride.

You go to the sports complex, just like your coach told you, but the fields are empty. Then you notice some lights shining in the field house in the middle of the complex. You jog over, open the door, and step in.

Suddenly you're in the field house, and you blink your eyes in disbelief as you see some of your teammates and opponents dressed up, in clean, fancy clothes. It's then you realize that you misunderstood your coach: It's not a game, it's a banquet! You look down at the outfit you put on not long ago with such pride; it's wrinkled and dirty compared to what everyone else is wearing. You're wearing the same clothes you've worn dozens of times around these people. Although you didn't feel dirty during those times, you feel dirty here.

Well, magnify that feeling about a bazillion times, and you know a little bit of how a prophet named Isaiah felt when he had a vision of God in the temple in Jerusalem. Isaiah saw God sitting on a throne, wearing a kingly robe. He saw God's angels flying around calling to each other. He felt the whole room shake, and the place started filling with smoke.

How did Isaiah react? Did he smile and wave at God? No.

Isaiah suddenly became aware that he was dirty compared to God. He saw God in his holiness and purity and said something like, "Oh, man, I'm done for! I'm a dead man! I'm a filthy, sinful man, and I'm standing in the presence of the King, the Lord, who is pure and holy!"

That's not the end of the story, of course, but the point is this: Isaiah saw God and immediately became aware of his own impurity. Why? Because God is pure. He is purely pure. There is nothing impure about him.

That's why God values purity and commands us to be pure. That's why purity is right—because God is pure.

 REFLECT: Isaiah had to go to the temple to learn about God's purity; we can do it simply by reading God's Word. Why does God command purity? Why does God value purity? Why is purity right? How did the angel of God purify Isaiah? Do you think God can purify you? If so, how?

 PRAY: "God, I know that you are pure and I'm not. But I know you can make me pure by forgiving my sins and helping me to obey you every day. Please help me to stay pure in everything I think, say, or do."

22 Committed to Purity

Bible Reading: Psalm 119:9-16

I will study your commandments and reflect on your ways. I will delight in your principles and not forget your word. Psalm 119:15-16

WHY DO PEOPLE make commitments? Why don't they just do what they want to do and not do what they don't want to do? Why do they sign contracts, take pledges, recite wedding vows, and make promises? Earlier this month (August 3), we said that there is power in commitment. Today we want to think about the fact that commitment is a decision *ahead of time* to do (or not do) a certain thing, and making a commitment in front of other people helps you to do the thing you plan to do.

For example, as a Christian you may want to be pure in thought, word, and deed. But what happens when a couple of your friends invite you to smoke cigarettes with them? What happens when you remember a dirty joke that you think will make the most popular kid in your grade think you're cool? What happens when you're invited to watch a video movie at a friend's house that you know contains some impure parts?

Well, it will be a lot easier to do the right thing in cases like those if you've already made a specific commitment to stay pure. For example, if you've committed to God and your family not to use bad language, you won't have to wonder which is the right thing to do when you're tempted to say something wrong. You'll remember that you've made a commitment ahead of time not to do that. Your commitment may help you choose the right thing when the time comes to choose. And, if you're like most of us, you need every bit of help you can get.

 REFLECT: What kind of commitment did the psalmist make in today's Bible reading? How might that commitment help you stay pure? Think about what Psalm 119:9 says: "How can a young person stay pure? By obeying your word and following its rules."

 ACT: Enter into a commitment with God and your family to be pure in thought, word, and deed. Make specific commitments by copying and signing all or part of the pledge below on a separate piece of paper and showing it to your parents, friends, or pastor. (Feel free to add to the pledge or to make it even more specific.)

- I will not use any foul, obscene, or abusive language.
- I will not use any tobacco (cigarettes, snuff, etc.) and will refuse it if anyone offers it to me.
- I will not drink alcohol (beer, wine coolers, etc.) and will refuse it if anyone offers it to me.
- I will not use illegal drugs in any form and will refuse them if anyone offers them to me.
- I will not buy, watch, or look at any movies, magazines, or books that are sexually impure.

I make this commitment today, _____(date).
Signed, _____

 PRAY: "Dear God, I want to commit to following you in a new way. I commit this pledge to you."

Bible Reading: Psalm 24:3-6

Who may climb the mountain of the Lord? Who may stand in his holy place? Only those whose hands and hearts are pure, who do not worship idols and never tell lies. Psalm 24:3-4

UNTIL JOSEPH LISTER came along, if you had an operation—any kind of operation—you had about a 50 percent chance of dying—even if the operation was a great success.

Lister, a British surgeon, studied what happened to patients after their operations. At that time (around 1860), doctors would operate in dirty rooms. The operating table, the rags they used to wipe up blood, and the sheets their patients slept on were probably dirty. Sometimes doctors even used the same dirty instruments to operate on several patients.

Lister changed all that. He insisted that his operating rooms be clean and the instruments be cleaned after every use. He also began to use a chemical called *carbolic acid* to clean instruments, wounds, and dressings.

Lister had discovered the importance of purity. You see, when doctors performed surgery in dirty conditions, germs would get into the patient's body and cause infections. Sometimes those infections killed the patient. But Lister learned that if he could keep the operating room and the instruments clean, he could reduce the number of people who died after surgery. In fact, his efforts were so successful that, if you had an operation in *his* hospital, you had about an 85 percent chance of surviving.

What Lister discovered in operating rooms is also true in other ways. If impurities (like germs) get into your body, they can make you sick; they may even kill you. In kind of the same way, impurities in your heart and soul can also cause problems. That's why God wants you to be pure. He knows that purity protects you from bad things like guilt and shame. He knows that purity can prevent a lot of sadness in your life.

Purity not only protects you from bad things, it also provides good things for you. The psalmist said that people who are pure "will receive the Lord's blessing and have right standing with God their savior. They alone may enter God's presence and worship the God of Israel" (Psalm 24:5-6). Purity produces peace with God and allows him to bless you in ways that he can't bless you if your life isn't pure.

Just as clean operating rooms and instruments made Joseph Lister's patients a lot healthier, a clean heart and life will make you a lot healthier—and happier, too!

 REFLECT: Why is it important to keep your heart and life clean? Is your heart pure? If not, how can you change that? If so, how do you think God helps you to keep it pure?

 ACT: Each time you wash your hands this week, remember the importance of clean hands—and clean hearts.

 PRAY: "God, I know that purity can protect me and provide many good things for me. Help me to experience your loving protection and provision by keeping myself pure."

24 Rotten Fish and You

Bible Reading: Titus 1:15-16

To the pure, all things are pure, but to those who are corrupted and do not believe, nothing is pure. Titus 1:15, NIV

SUPPOSE THERE'S A big old stinking fish in your refrigerator that's been in there for months.

You open the refrigerator and grab a carton of milk and slam the door fast to prevent the terrible smell from escaping. You pour the milk on your breakfast cereal and shovel a spoonful into your mouth. "Mmmph!" you say, spitting the food out. "Tastes like rotten fish!"

So you skip breakfast. But around noon you get really hungry, and you get some bread out. You reach into the refrigerator and quickly pull out some lunch meat. You put a couple of slices on the bread and lift it to your mouth. But before you take a bite, you smell your sandwich. "Ugh!" you say. "Smells like rotten fish!"

So you skip lunch. But by dinnertime that night, you're starving. So you dash to the refrigerator, pull out the leftover pizza from three nights ago, pop it into the microwave, and nuke it for sixty seconds. You open the microwave to pull out the pizza. "Eew!" you say. "Now the microwave smells like rotten fish!"

So you stomp out of the kitchen, determined to issue an ultimatum to your parents: Either they get rid of that rotten fish in the fridge or you're going to enlist in the marines—just to get some decent food!

But wait a minute! What's the big deal? Why should a single fish spoil everything else? Well, if you've ever had a rotten fish in your refrigerator, you wouldn't have to ask that question. Just one bad fish (or rotten egg, for that matter) can spoil everything else in the refrigerator.

The same thing is true with you. No, you don't smell like rotten fish, but if your heart is impure, then just about everything you think about or talk about or experience is going to be affected. Your impure heart will make you suspicious of your friends' motives. Your dirty mind will make everything seem dirty. Your corrupt imagination will take normal, healthy things and make them stink like a rotten fish.

On the other hand, if you're pure inside, you're going to enjoy life a lot more because you'll look at life differently than someone who's not pure. You won't be suspicious of your friends' motives. You won't see filth everywhere you look. You'll be able to enjoy and appreciate normal, healthy things, and they will become beautiful and pure—just like you.

 REFLECT: Do you know anyone to whom "all things are pure"? Do you know anyone to whom "nothing is pure"? Which are you most like?

 PRAY: Is there any impurity in your life? If so, spend a few moments in prayer, confessing that impurity to God, asking his forgiveness, and seeking his purity in place of your impurity.

25 Heart Problems

Bible Reading: Psalm 51:10-12

Create in me a pure heart, O God, and renew a steadfast spirit within me. Psalm 51:10, NIV

TIN MAN HADN'T seen Dorothy, Toto, the Cowardly Lion, and the Scarecrow for years. He didn't know what had happened to them. But he knew what had happened to himself. He'd gotten a heart when he and the others had journeyed to the mystical land of Oz. But now he was pretty upset. His heart wasn't working right.

"There's something wrong with it," he told his tin doctor as he lay on a tin table in the doctor's tin office. "It doesn't work right. It doesn't do right things." Tin Man threw up his hands. His shoulders and elbows creaked like a rusty gate. "Sometimes I'll be talking to my friends, and—" he snapped his tin fingers—"just like that, a bad word will come out. Other times, I'll be watching a TV show, and somebody'll say something naughty, and I'll laugh!" He looked around, as if he were afraid someone might be listening. "And sometimes," he whispered, "I've done even worse."

"I see," said the doctor. "You're right. It *is* a heart problem. But I can't help you."

"You can't?" Tin Man wailed.

Tin Doctor shook his head. "You see, your heart problem can't be fixed. The only solution is to replace it."

Tin Man swallowed loudly. "Replace it?"

The doctor nodded. "You need a new heart. A pure heart. And I'm afraid that's available from only one place."

Tin Doctor was right. The only solution to a problem like Tin Man's is a totally new heart, a pure heart. Trying to fix or reform the old heart won't help. It requires a transplant, a surgery only God can perform.

King David had a similar problem. His heart was messing up, big time! So he fell on his knees and prayed for a transplant. He confessed his terrible sins to God. He admitted that they were wrong. He admitted that he was a sinner and needed God. He asked God for forgiveness. Then he said, "Create in me a pure heart, O God, and renew a steadfast spirit within me" (Psalm 51:10, NIV).

Maybe you feel like the fictional Tin Man, or the real-life David. Maybe your heart isn't working right. You can get rid of an impure heart the same way David did: You can confess your sins and admit that you did wrong. You can admit that you need God and ask him for forgiveness. You can tell God you're willing to give up your own will and surrender to his. If you do that and continue trusting him every day to keep your heart pure, God will take care of your heart problem—in a heartbeat!

 REFLECT: Have you prayed to receive a "heart transplant" from God? If not, why not? If so, do you believe God has forgiven you and given you a pure heart? If so, how can you stay pure?

 PRAY: "Create in me a pure heart, O God, and renew a steadfast spirit within me."

26 Operation: Salvation

Bible Reading: Galatians 3:10-14

No one can ever be right with God by trying to keep the law. For the Scriptures say, "It is through faith that a righteous person has life."
Galatians 3:11

YOU'RE ON THE operating table. You're about to get a heart transplant. The doctors and nurses surround you. Machines blip and bleep softly in the room. Then a man with hairy hands slips a mask over your nose and mouth, and you hear a slight hissing noise.

You rip the mask off your face and push the hairy hand away. "Wait a minute," you say. "What's going on here?"

The doctors and nurses look at you with puzzled expressions.

"You were going to put me to sleep, weren't you?" you accuse.

"Well, uh, yes," the head doctor says. "That's how it's done. We have to put you to sleep while I operate on you."

"While *you* operate on me?" you screech. "No way! I'm doing it myself."

"You?" the doctor says, sounding shocked.

"Yeah," you answer. "Who else?"

He gently places his hand on your shoulder. "Look, I'm the doctor. You're the patient. No matter how much you may want a new heart, you can't do it yourself. You've placed yourself in my care. Now you just have to trust me."

You let out a sigh of relief. "Good. I think I could've handled the inferior vena cava, but I was worried about connecting that superior vena cava in time!"

Of course, you'd never try to perform your own heart transplant, would you? But a lot of us make a similar mistake. We may think we can become Christians and go to heaven by being good and doing the right things. But that's not how it works.

The only way to get to heaven is by believing in Jesus Christ and asking him to forgive our sins. When we do that, his Holy Spirit comes to live in our heart. He then helps us to make right choices. Or, to put it in the doctor's words: When we ask Jesus to "operate" on our heart, we place ourselves in his care and then just have to trust him. That's how the operation works.

 REFLECT: You can never be right with God by just keeping his commands; it is only by trusting Jesus. Does that mean you don't have to worry about making right choices? Why or why not? Does making right choices make you a Christian? Does being a Christian help you to make right choices? What's the difference?

 ACT: Picture faith as an orange tree that stretches to heaven. The oranges are the right choices you make. The oranges won't get you to heaven; only the tree will. But the tree produces the fruit, just as your faith will produce right choices.

 PRAY: If you've never asked Jesus into your life, you can do so now. Pray something like this: "Father God, I admit that I'm a sinner. You sent Jesus to pay the price for my sins. I invite him now into my life. I accept his gift of the Holy Spirit. Thank you, Lord, for giving me eternal life."

27 The Power of Prayer

Bible Reading: 2 Thessalonians 1:3-12

We pray . . . that our God will make you fit for what he's called you to be, pray that he'll fill your good ideas and acts of faith with his own energy so that it all amounts to something. 2 Thessalonians 1:11-12, The Message

YOU'LL NEVER MAKE right choices without prayer. Regular prayer. Real prayer.

Wait! Don't panic. You may think prayer is a real drag. You may think it's hard or boring. Your understanding of prayer may come from your childhood or from listening to grown-ups talk to God in thee's and thou's or six-syllable theological words you never heard of.

Relax. Prayer is simply talking to God about your thoughts, feelings, and concerns. God really does understand modern English (even the bizarre language spoken by your brother or sister). You can be totally confident that God hears you when you pray. In fact, God eagerly waits for you to come to him in prayer. You are his child, and he values every minute you spend with him!

Why is prayer so great?

1. *Prayer helps you to focus on God.* It helps you get to know him better. The psalmist said, "Look to the Lord and his strength; seek his face always" (Psalm 105:4, NIV). When you pray, you "unplug" your mind from the television and CD player and "plug in" to God.

2. *Prayer is intimacy with God.* When you pray, you discover what it means to be intimate with God. The Bible says that when Moses entered the tabernacle, "The Lord would speak to Moses face to face, as a man speaks with his friend" (Exodus 33:11, NIV). That is what happens in prayer. You become friends with God. He becomes a deep, intimate, personal friend who loves you unconditionally.

3. *Prayer is a vital weapon in making right choices.* If you want to stop lying, pray; praying will add God's power to your desire. If you want to be more loving toward your brother, pray; that will add God's help to your good intentions. If you need more patience, more compassion, or more self-control, pray; prayer will add God's energy to your efforts.

When we pray, God takes action! So pray. Pray for yourself. Pray for your family. Pray for your friends. And watch God work.

 REFLECT: How often do you pray (not counting grace at meals)? How often do you think you should pray? When is a good time for you to pray every day? (Morning? After school? Bedtime?) How long do you plan to pray every day? (Five minutes? Ten minutes? Fifteen? More?) Tell someone else about your commitment to pray.

 PRAY: Make a list of four or five kinds of right choices you need to make more often or more consistently (like honesty, compassion, faithfulness, fairness, and so on). Pray for at least one item every day, asking God to help you develop that virtue.

28 Listen and Learn

Bible Reading: Deuteronomy 31:9-13

Listen and learn to fear the Lord your God and carefully obey all the terms of this law. Deuteronomy 31:12

HOW DO YOU learn best?

Some kids learn pretty well just by *listening*. They can listen to a teacher tell a story or explain something and later remember almost everything the teacher said.

Other kids learn better by *reading*. They may listen to a teacher, but they learn a lot better if they can see the words on paper. (That's one reason why kids in high school and college take notes while a teacher's talking; they usually learn the lesson better because they *saw* it as well as *heard* it.)

Some kids have to *talk* in order to learn well. They learn something better if they can talk about it and put it in their own words.

Still other kids learn best by *doing*. They remember things better if they act them out or put them together. Their hands and bodies seem to be always moving, and they can't wait to get started with an experiment or demonstration.

Guess what! No matter how you learn best, God's Word is meant for you. When God gave his commandments to Moses, he told Moses to "read this law to all the people of Israel when they assemble" (Deuteronomy 31:11); that was for the *listeners*. But God also instructed Moses to "write down these words" (Exodus 34:27, NIV); that was for the *readers*. And then, when the Israelites had entered the Promised Land, God told them to gather on the slopes of two mountains and to repeat his commands back and forth in a huge responsive reading (Joshua 8:30-35); that was for the *talkers!* But *all of us*—whether we're listeners, readers, talkers, or doers—are to learn God's laws by *doing*. He tells us that we're supposed to "listen and learn to fear the Lord your God and carefully obey all the terms of this law" (Deuteronomy 31:12).

No matter what our learning style may be, God wants us all to be listeners of his Word. He wants us all to be readers of his Word. He wants us all to be talkers of his Word. But, most important, he wants us all to be *doers* of his Word because we will not only learn best when we do all four but we will also live best when we "listen and learn to fear the Lord [our] God and carefully obey all the terms of this law" (Deuteronomy 31:12). As God promises: "I will make an everlasting covenant with them: I will never stop doing good to them, and I will inspire them to fear me, so that they will never turn away from me" (Jeremiah 32:40, NIV).

REFLECT: Do you *listen* carefully when God's Word is read? Do you *read* his Word on your own? Do you *speak* his Word and memorize important verses? Do you *do* his Word, carefully obeying what he says? How can you listen to God's Word and learn it better?

PRAY: "Lord, I want to be a follower of your Word. Thank you for your guidance."

241

29 Wolf Trap

Bible Reading: James 1:12-16

Temptation comes from the lure of our own evil desires. These evil desires lead to evil actions, and evil actions lead to death. So don't be misled, my dear brothers and sisters. James 1:14-16

DO YOU KNOW how an Eskimo traps a wolf?

First, he takes his hunting knife and hones the blade until it's razor sharp. Then he coats the blade with animal blood and allows the blood to freeze on the knife. He does this several times, layer after layer, until the blade is coated with frozen blood.

Next, he takes the knife to a place where wolves have been spotted or where their droppings have been seen. He buries the knife handle in the frozen ground so the blood-coated blade is sticking up. Then he leaves. That's all there is to it.

You see, a wolf will smell the blood on the knife and follow his sensitive nose to the source of the appetizing scent. Upon finding the knife, the wolf will carefully lick the bloody ice. As he does so, the frozen blood will arouse his animal hunger, and he'll begin licking faster and faster until the ice is licked away, and the sharp blade is exposed. Because of his ravenous hunger, the wolf doesn't notice when the naked blade begins to shred his own tongue and the blood he is licking becomes his own. He continues to lap up the blood from his own tongue until the loss of blood weakens him, and he slumps down in the snow to die.

That is a picture of how temptation traps us. Like the wolf, we think that doing wrong—whether it's lying or cheating, using drugs or smoking cigarettes—is fun and safe. But without realizing it, our evil desires lead to evil actions, which lead to danger and even to death.

Don't be fooled by the temptation to sin. The wrong choice may seem attractive, even delicious—but it will ruin you in the end.

 REFLECT: What four steps to death does today's Bible reading talk about? Does God tempt you to sin? Where does the temptation come from? Do you think temptation to do wrong *ever* has good results? Why or why not? What can you do to resist temptation?

 ACT: Place a butter knife (*not* one with a sharp blade!) in a conspicuous spot today, where it will remind you of the dangerous lure of temptation.

 PRAY: "Lord, I'm trusting you to help me resist temptation and walk away from the lures of sin."

30 The Right Response to Wrong Choices

Bible Reading: 1 John 1:8–2:3

If we say we have no sin, we are only fooling ourselves and refusing to accept the truth. But if we confess our sins to him, he is faithful and just to forgive us and to cleanse us from every wrong. 1 John 1:8-9

NOT TOO LONG ago a teenage boy and his friend were driving around on New Year's Day. They were good friends, and they were having a good time together. Suddenly, the driver noticed the lights of a police car in his rearview mirror. He looked at his speedometer and, for the first time, noticed how fast he was going. He knew he would be in big trouble with his parents for getting a ticket, so instead of stopping and letting the police officer give him a ticket, he drove faster. No matter how fast he drove, the police stayed close. When he rounded a corner and saw another police car waiting for him, he knew he was in even bigger trouble.

After pulling his car to the side of the road beside a wide river, the driver jumped out of the car and ran to the river's edge. His friend followed him. They both dove into the cold water. A few moments later the friend swam back to shore, where the police met him and wrapped him in blankets. The driver, however, disappeared.

For the next three days the police searched the river for the boy. On the fourth day they found his body. One of his aunts, who watched the search efforts every day from the riverbank, said the boy probably panicked because he didn't want his record tarnished. "We always stressed to him to stay out of trouble," she said, because "it could mess his future up. He'd never been in trouble before."

That true story is made sadder by the realization that if the driver had just admitted his wrongdoing and accepted his punishment, he would not have died that New Year's Day.

Sometimes we're tempted to run from our sins. We don't want to admit that we've made a wrong choice, and we're afraid of the punishment we might get. But God wants us to know that when we make a wrong choice, we don't need to run from him. He says, "If we confess our sins to him, he is faithful and just to forgive us and to cleanse us from every wrong" (1 John 1:9).

God will forgive us. He doesn't promise that we'll always escape the consequences of our wrong choices, but he does promise that he'll always forgive us and cleanse us.

When we make a wrong choice, the best way to respond is not to run, but to repent, to admit our sin, and to seek God's forgiveness.

REFLECT: What is the wrong way to respond to wrong choices? What is the right response to wrong choices? Have you ever run from responsibility for a wrong choice you made? If so, what happened?

PRAY: "God, thank you for your promise that, if I confess my sins, you will forgive me and cleanse me from every wrong. Please help me not to do wrong. But if I do, help me to turn to you quickly, admit what I've done, and ask you to forgive me."

31 Word for Word

Bible Reading: Psalm 119:57-64

I have hidden your word in my heart, that I might not sin against you.
Psalm 119:11

"MEMORIZING BIBLE VERSES is such a drag!"

"Totally! It's so boring."

"I know John 3:16, but that's about it."

Have you ever said (or felt) anything like that? It's true, isn't it? Memorizing Scripture is hard. Only "Super Christians" do that, right?

Well, now, hold on a minute. Take the following quiz and see how you do:

1. How many songs do you know all the words to? (Circle your answer.)

    1   2   3   4   more than 5

2. Name all the main characters of your favorite TV show:

3. How many phone numbers do you know by heart? (Circle your answer.)

    1   2   3   4   more than 5

Well, duh! Those questions were easy, right? But why were they easy? Because you know all those things from memory!

It's easier than you think to memorize things. You started memorizing things before you started talking. In fact, every single word you say, you've memorized! You may have memorized one or two storybooks before you even started school.

So why is memorizing Bible verses so hard? It's not, really. You know your friends' phone numbers because you use them every day, right? And you know the words to songs because you sing along with them, right? Well, if you read a single verse every day for a week or two, you'll soon have it memorized. In fact, why not try "singing" today's Bible verse, making up your own melody to help you remember it?

Hiding God's Word in your heart is probably easier than you think it is. It can also be fun. Most important, knowing the Bible can help you know—and choose—what is right. Like the psalmist said, "I have hidden your word in my heart, that I might not sin against you" (Psalm 119:11).

 REFLECT: How many Bible verses do you know from memory? Say them out loud. How can hiding God's Word in your heart help you not to sin? Do you think you could memorize one Bible verse a week? Why not start today?

 ACT: Here's an easy way to memorize today's verse: Write it in bold letters on a sheet of paper. Read it out loud once a day this week, tearing off three words at a time until you can recite the whole verse from memory.

 PRAY: "Lord, I want to honor your Word by hiding it in my heart. Help me to honor that commitment."

1 Adam and Madam Ant

Bible Reading: Proverbs 6:6-11

Take a lesson from the ants, you lazybones. Learn from their ways and be wise! Proverbs 6:6

ONE WINTER DAY, while Adam Ant and his wife, Madam Ant, were busily sorting and stacking their storehouse of corn, kernel by kernel, along came a grasshopper.

"Hello, Mr. and Mrs. Ant," the grasshopper said. He would have doffed his hat, but of course grasshoppers don't wear hats. "I noticed you working so hard this fine winter day, and I wondered if you might be able to spare a few kernels of corn." The grasshopper cleared his throat and added, "I would be most grateful, for I am simply starving."

Adam and Madam Ant, who had been working while the grasshopper addressed them, stopped for a moment.

"Why do you not have a storehouse of corn like ours?" Adam asked.

The grasshopper smiled sheepishly. "Well, you see, I spend my summers singing beautifully in the grass. I have no time to work."

Adam and Madam Ant nodded knowingly.

"I see," said Adam. "If you spend your summers singing, you should not expect to spend your winters eating." And with that, Adam and Madam Ant returned to their work, leaving the grasshopper to regret his laziness.

That story, based on a famous fable, illustrates the fact that work is better than laziness. A willingness to work is a virtue. A person who is not willing to work should not be admired but pitied or despised. As the Bible says, "Take a lesson from the ants, you lazybones. Learn from their ways and be wise! Even though they have no prince, governor, or ruler to make them work, they labor hard all summer, gathering food for the winter. But you, lazybones, how long will you sleep? When will you wake up? I want you to learn this lesson: A little extra sleep, a little more slumber, a little folding of the hands to rest—and poverty will pounce on you like a bandit; scarcity will attack you like an armed robber" (Proverbs 6:6-11).

The person who works hard—whether at school, at home, or at a job—is worthy of respect and admiration, because the Bible makes it clear that working well and working hard is right and good.

 REFLECT: Who is the hardest working person you know? Do you admire him or her? If so, why? If not, why not? Which do you resemble most (in your work habits): an ant, a grasshopper, a snail, or a dead skunk in the middle of the road? Why?

 ACT: Keep your eyes open today for someone who is working hard. Take a moment to thank that person for his or her example of hard work.

 PRAY: "Lord, help me to value hard work instead of giving in to laziness."

2 A Butcher, a Baker, a Candlestick Maker?

Bible Reading: 1 Thessalonians 4:11-12

This should be your ambition: to live a quiet life, minding your own business and working with your hands. 1 Thessalonians 4:11

HAS ANYBODY EVER asked you this question: "What do you wanna be when you grow up?"

You've probably been asked that lots of times, right? You've probably been asked that question so often, you feel like giving a smart-aleck answer every once in a while, like "An adult!" or "About six feet tall!"

But you probably have some idea what career or profession you want to pursue when you get older. Maybe you want to be a doctor or a country-music singing sensation. Maybe you want to be a pilot, a race-car driver, or a steamroller operator. Maybe you hope to become a quarterback in the NFL or a secret agent in the CIA. Maybe you want to be a farmer or a snake charmer. Maybe you want to be a movie star.

However you may answer the question "What do you wanna be when you grow up?" there's an even more important question you might want to think about: *Do you know how to work?*

See, many kids spend a lot of time dreaming and scheming about what they're going to be when they grow up, but they never learn how to work. Oh, they may take the trash out when Mom yells at 'em, but they get through school, and high school, and even college, without learning to work hard and stick to a job until it's done well.

Of course, you may not have to worry about earning a living for a few more years yet. That gives you time to learn—in school, at home, even at church—how to apply yourself to a job and obey God's command to do good, honest work. (See Ephesians 4:28, 1 Thessalonians 4:11, 2 Thessalonians 3:12.) Just keep that in mind the next time there's homework to do or wood to stack or a steamroller to be driven.

 REFLECT: Do any of the careers or occupations mentioned above interest you? If so, which ones? If not, what careers or occupations do interest you? Do you think you need to decide that now or later? Do you believe that "a lazy person is as bad as someone who destroys things" (Proverbs 18:9)? Why or why not? Do you think you know how to work? Why or why not? Do you consider yourself a hard worker? Why or why not? When was the last time you worked really hard? How can you start learning to work hard now?

 ACT: Ask your parents and friends if they think you're a good worker. Then ask for their advice on what you can do to improve.

 PRAY: "Lord, teach me to be the kind of worker you command me to be. If people say that I'm not a hard worker, help me not to get angry. Instead, help me to improve my work habits."

3 Couch-Potato Christians

Bible Reading: 2 Thessalonians 3:6-12

Settle down and get to work. Earn your own living.
2 Thessalonians 3:12

BACK IN THE days when the apostle Paul was still alive, there was a city called Thessalonica (rhymes with Formica). We know that Paul wrote at least two letters to the Christians in that city, because the letters have been preserved in the New Testament as First and Second Thessalonians.

Anyhow, there must have been a bunch of lazy people in that Thessalonian church. Maybe they did nothing but sit on their couches watching *Rosie O'Donnell,* buying things from the Home Shopping Network, and eating Oreo cookies all day. There were probably others who spent their time in cozy rocking chairs on their front porches, sipping cans of Yoohoo! chocolate drink, gossiping about the neighbors, and spitting in the dirt.

"How do you know that?" you may ask. Well, the answer is simple: Read 2 Thessalonians 3:6-12.

Paul wrote those verses to correct a problem that existed in the Thessalonian church. He even went so far as to say, "Stay away from any Christian who lives in idleness and doesn't follow the tradition of hard work we gave you" (v. 6). And then, a few verses later, he suggested to that group of Christians that they live by this rule: "Whoever does not work should not eat" (v. 10). And then he concludes by giving them a clear command: "Settle down and get to work. Earn your own living" (v. 12).

You can "read between the lines," can't you? There were people in that church (Christians, even!) who were being lazy and not working. The Thessalonian church had more than one "couch-potato Christian"! And Paul says, "We'll have none of that!" Why? Because God commands us to work. Why? Because he values good, honest, hard work. And if God values hard work, don't you think we should, too?

 REFLECT: Why do you think Paul kept telling the Thessalonians to get to work? Have you ever been told to "get to work"? Why? If you were one of the Thessalonian Christians being told to "get to work," would you respond positively or negatively? Why?

 PRAY: "Father, I don't want to be like some of the Christians in Thessalonica, who had a reputation for laziness and idleness. I want to be known as someone who knows how to work and who works hard. Teach me to work hard and to value work the way you do."

4 God of Action

Bible Reading: John 5:1-9, 16-17

So the Jewish leaders began harassing Jesus for breaking the Sabbath rules. But Jesus replied, "My Father never stops working, so why should I?" John 5:16-17

WHEN THE RELIGIOUS people of Jesus' day started harassing him because he and his followers didn't obey all their Sabbath rules, Jesus said, "My Father never stops working, so why should I?" (John 5:17).

Now, maybe you've never thought about it, but most people don't picture God *working*. They picture him, oh, floating on a cloud somewhere high up in the sky. Or they imagine him sitting on a throne in a great celestial palace, snapping his fingers whenever he wants something. Or perhaps they see him leisurely looking down on earth from heaven like a city dweller who leans on his or her upper-story windowsill and watches the cars and buses go by on the street below.

After all, why would God work? He doesn't have to; he's got all kinds of angels to do whatever needs to be done. He could go on permanent vacation. He could snap his fingers, create his own island paradise in the Caribbean, and do nothing but eat kiwifruit and sip lemonade for the rest of his life (which, because he's eternal, is a really long time!).

But Jesus said that God *works*. In fact, he said, "My Father never stops working." God is always on duty! He's always "on the job." He never even sleeps (Psalm 121:4).

God works because it's part of his nature. He is a God of action. There's not a lazy bone in his body. (OK, so he doesn't have a physical body, but you get the idea!) And because God is a God of action—a God who works—work is right; honest, hard work is a good thing. It doesn't matter if the work involves building skyscrapers, washing cars, directing traffic, inventing computer software, pumping gas, governing a nation, acting in movies, flipping hamburgers, or writing devotionals! God approves of work because he works, too.

 REFLECT: Did any of the pictures of God mentioned above (floating on a cloud, sitting on a throne, etc.) express how you have imagined God in the past? Has your picture of God changed after reading today's devotional? Why or why not? What kind of work do you think pleases God?

 PRAY: "Father, thank you for always being 'on the job.' Thank you for always being ready to hear and answer my prayers. Thank you for always being 'on duty' to help me. Please help me to do *my* work in a way that pleases you."

5 The Wise Man's Vineyard

Bible Reading: Proverbs 24:30-34

Lazy hands make a man poor, but diligent hands bring wealth.
Proverbs 10:4, NIV

MANY YEARS AGO a very wise man (who also happened to be a farmer), lay on his bed. He knew that he would soon die, so he called his three sons to his bedside.

"My sons," he said, "I will soon die, and I must tell you something." He paused. All three sons craned forward to listen. "Deep in the soil of my vineyard," the wise father whispered, "lies buried a hidden treasure. Dig deep, my sons, and you will find it."

Within a few hours the father died, and the sons took picks and shovels out to their father's vineyard.

"Just imagine what it will be like when we have the treasure!" they told each other. "We can buy whatever we want without working for it and live the rest of our lives in luxury and idleness."

So they began to tear into the soil beneath the farmer's vines. Over and over they turned the soil, digging and digging day after day. But they found no treasure. Finally, they grew disappointed and gave up their search. But the vines, after the sons of the wise farmer had turned the soil so thoroughly, produced so many grapes that the brothers became the wealthy owners of that country's most productive vineyard.

That tale, from Aesop's collection of fables, illustrates today's Bible reading: "I walked by the field of a lazy person, the vineyard of one lacking sense. I saw that it was overgrown with thorns. It was covered with weeds, and its walls were broken down. Then, as I looked and thought about it, I learned this lesson: A little extra sleep, a little more slumber, a little folding of the hands to rest—and poverty will pounce on you like a bandit; scarcity will attack you like an armed robber" (Proverbs 24:30-34).

The sons of that wise farmer learned that treasure was, indeed, hidden in the soil of the vineyard—but it took work to produce that treasure. They also learned that good, hard work produces wealth, not only in money but in character and in satisfaction. You may dream, like those brothers, of "striking it rich" someday and "having it made," but it's far better to work for what you have, to *produce* treasure instead of discovering it.

 REFLECT: Do you think the old farmer was wise in what he said to his sons? Why or why not? Do you think they would have been better off if they had found a chest of buried treasure? Why or why not? According to the paragraphs above, what kinds of wealth does good, hard work produce?

 PRAY: "Lord, like almost everybody else, I do have dreams of 'striking it rich' and 'having it made' someday. Help me to see the wisdom in knowing how to work hard and how to produce treasure instead of just discovering it."

6 Of Shovels, Simba, and Skiing

Bible Reading: Proverbs 14:20-23

All hard work brings a profit, but mere talk leads only to poverty.
Proverbs 14:23, NIV

LET'S RETURN TO *Sesame Street,* the famous children's show that's been on TV since the days when your parents' music was cool. (That was a long, long time ago!) They used to play a game called, "One of these things is not like the others; one of these things just doesn't belong." (If you read the February 23 reading, you've already played this game once.) Players are given a list or a series of items, and they're supposed to pick out which item doesn't belong in the group. Ready? Let's play our own version of that game. For each category, just circle the item that doesn't belong with the others in the group.

One of these things is not like the others; one of these things just doesn't belong:

knife   shovel   fork   spoon

If you answered *shovel,* you're right, because the other three are items you use for eating. Of course, if you use a shovel to eat your lunch, well then, we'll just call you "MegaMouth"! Let's play again!

One of these things is not like the others; one of these things just doesn't belong:

Matthew   Mark   Luke   Simba

If you circled *Simba,* because he's *not* one of the Gospel writers in the Bible, you're really good at this game! Let's play one more time!

One of these things is not like the others; one of these things just doesn't belong:

skiing   swimming   playing basketball   working

How did you answer *that* question? Most people would probably circle *working,* figuring that all the other items on the list are fun, while working isn't. That's one possible way to answer that question. But it's not the only way.

You see, *work* is not the opposite of *play.* Working isn't the opposite of having fun. A lot of people have fun *while* they're working. A lot of people work because they enjoy it. That's one of the reasons the Bible says, "All hard work brings a profit" (Proverbs 14:23a, NIV). That doesn't mean that every job is going to make you rich. However, it does mean that hard work always has some benefit—and one of those benefits is the enjoyment of working! So, if you circled *working* in the list above, you might want to erase your choice and circle something else instead.

 REFLECT: Have you ever done a job that turned out to be kind of fun? What kind of work do you think might be fun to do? How can you make your current jobs or chores more fun?

 PRAY: "God, thank you for teaching me about work. Help me to believe that 'all hard work brings a profit,' and help me please you by the way I do jobs such as_____."

7 Two Necessary Ingredients

Bible Reading: Psalm 32:1-6

Then I acknowledged my sin to you and did not cover up my iniquity. I said, "I will confess my transgressions to the Lord"—and you forgave the guilt of my sin. Psalm 32:5, NIV

SUPPOSE YOU WERE walking down your street and a friend of yours suddenly burst out of his house and deliberately knocked you down on the sidewalk. Now suppose that friend said to you, "Hey, it wasn't my fault. You would've done the same thing if you'd had the chance." How would you feel hearing that sort of thing? You'd be angry, right?

OK, suppose the friend said instead, "I didn't mean anything by it." How would you feel then? Would you be satisfied with that?

More than likely you wouldn't be satisfied, right?

God doesn't want us to say such things when we make a mistake or do something wrong. Why? Because none of those phrases contains the two necessary ingredients of repentance. Do you know what those two necessary ingredients of repentance are? Confession and apology.

In other words, if you do something wrong, you shouldn't try to defend yourself or excuse your actions by saying something like, "It wasn't my fault!" or "She deserved it!" Instead, the best way to respond to a mistake or a sin is with two simple statements:

- "I was wrong."
- "I'm sorry."

That's what David said in Psalm 32 when he told God, "I acknowledged my sin to you and did not cover up my iniquity. I said, 'I will confess my transgressions to the Lord'" (Psalm 32:5, NIV). He didn't try to explain or excuse what he'd done. He didn't try to cover it up. He admitted he was wrong and confessed his sin to God.

That's the path to forgiveness with God—and with anyone. After all, we all make mistakes. We have all sinned. But when you do make a wrong choice, the best way to respond to it is to say, "I was wrong. I'm sorry." When you do that, you open the door to forgiveness.

REFLECT: Do you ever have trouble saying, "I was wrong" and "I'm sorry"? Why or why not? How do you plan to respond the next time you do something wrong?

PRAY: "Father, sometimes I don't like to admit I'm wrong and apologize. Please help me to confess and apologize for my wrongs to you and to anyone I have hurt."

8 Knowing and Doing

Bible Reading: 1 John 1:5-7

If we claim to have fellowship with him yet walk in the darkness, we lie and do not live by the truth. 1 John 1:6, NIV

SO YOU SHOW up the first day of school, and you're assigned a new locker. Your homeroom teacher also gives you a slip of paper with the locker combination written on it: "16 right, 34 left, 16 right," it says. "Oh, no thank you," you say, handing the paper back to the teacher. "I'm just gonna make up my own combination."

Or say you're waiting at a bus stop for the No. 17 bus, the one that will take you across town so you can attend the college football game of the year between Smell U. and Awful State. You ask a woman standing nearby, "Does the number 17 bus stop here?"

"No," she says, pointing across the street. "It stops around the corner at *that* bus stop."

"Thanks," you say, without moving. And you continue to wait for the No. 17 bus at the wrong bus stop.

Or let's say a friend tells you about this cool new website he's discovered. "It's www.CIA.natsecurity.topsecret.wemayhavetokillyou.com," he says. "You wouldn't believe all the cool stuff you can find there! You want me to write down the address for you?" You shake your head. "Nah," you say. "I don't need the address. I'll just look around until I find it."

Well, of course, if you do any of those things, you'd be crazy, right? You'd never get into your locker by making up your own combination. You'd never make it to the football stadium if you wait for the No. 17 bus at the wrong bus stop. And you'll never find a top secret government website by just "looking around." Why? Because truth is of no use unless it's obeyed. It does no good for a teacher to give you a locker combination if you're not going to use it. It's silly to ask people if you're at the right bus stop if you're not going to move when they tell you no. And likewise, it doesn't do any good to know the truth about God and his commands if you don't do anything with that knowledge.

God told us what's right and what's wrong not only so we would *know* the truth but so we would also *obey* it. If you know what's right but don't do it, you're no better off than you were before you knew the truth. (In fact, you're worse off in many ways.) But if you know *and* do what's right, you'll open the door to many of God's blessings in your life.

 REFLECT: Knowing what's right doesn't guarantee we'll *do* right. Can you think of a time when you knew what was right but did the wrong thing anyway? God told us what's right so we would k_____ the truth and o_____ the truth. Knowing the truth is only half the battle; we must also choose to obey the truth.

 PRAY: "Dear God, thank you for helping me to learn right from wrong. Help me not only to know what's right but to do what's right, too."

9 My Way

Bible Reading: Genesis 4:1-7

If you do what is right, will you not be accepted? But if you do not do what is right, sin is crouching at your door; it desires to have you, but you must master it. Genesis 4:7, NIV

SOMETIMES A HIT song becomes so identified with a singer, it becomes that person's "theme song." For example, Elvis Presley had a lot of hits, but "Hound Dog" is probably the song most strongly identified with him.

A generation or two ago, "Thanks for the Memories" was Bob Hope's theme song, and "R-E-S-P-E-C-T" has always been Aretha Franklin's song. These days, Boyz II Men are associated with "Motown Philly" more than any other single song. And say the name Sheryl Crow, and most people will think of the song, "All I Wanna Do."

The song "El Shaddai" is pretty much associated with Amy Grant, who made it a hit. "Awesome God" will always be Rich Mullins's signature song, and "Friends" has become Michael W. Smith's theme song.

Well, one of the most famous singers of all time, Frank Sinatra, had a hit song called "My Way." Even though he'd had many hits before that, "My Way" became his unofficial theme song, maybe because it summed up Sinatra's life: "I did it my way!"

Actually, though, "My Way" could be almost anyone's theme song. We all want to have things our own way and do things our own way. None of us likes taking orders from someone else. We'd rather do it "my way"!

Of course, that's the attitude that got Cain in trouble, way back in Bible times. He wanted to worship God his own way. Then, when Cain got mad because God accepted the sacrifice of his brother, Abel, and not his, God said, "If you do what is right, will you not be accepted? But if you do not do what is right, sin is crouching at your door" (Genesis 4:7, NIV). But even then, Cain refused to listen to God and obey him; he wanted to vent his anger his own way—by killing poor Abel!

Of course, it's easy to see how foolish Cain was for wanting everything his own way. But we do the same thing. When we make wrong choices, it's usually not because we didn't know which way was right; it's usually because we wanted to do things our own way instead of God's way.

"My Way" may have been a hit song for Frank Sinatra, but it's not a very good theme song for a Christian's life.

REFLECT: Think back on a wrong choice you've made. Did you make the wrong choice because you didn't know which way was right or because you wanted to do things your own way? Why? Does doing things your way instead of God's way have bad results? Why or why not? Whose way do you want to follow from now on: your own way or God's way?

PRAY: "Lord, I know you've shown me the right way, but sometimes I choose to go my own way, even when I know it's wrong. Please help me to follow your way from now on, especially when I'm tempted to_____."

10 The President and the Soldier

Bible Reading: Luke 16:10-12

Now it is required that those who have been given a trust must prove faithful. 1 Corinthians 4:2, NIV

IN THE DAYS of the American Civil War, a Union soldier named William Scott was given the responsibility of guarding an important bridge on the Potomac River. Because Confederate troops occupied the hills on the other side of the bridge, the order was given that any guard found sleeping at his post on that bridge would be shot.

William Scott had been on duty one night and the next night had taken the place of a friend who was sick. He was assigned to guard the bridge again—for a third straight night. When another soldier came the next morning to relieve him of his post, William Scott was found asleep and was quickly sentenced to be shot.

A group of that soldier's friends rode the few miles to the White House, where they were granted an audience with President Abraham Lincoln. Lincoln listened to the soldiers' story and to their pleas for him to help their friend. Later that day, the president rode out from the White House and met with Scott.

The president informed William Scott that he was not going to be shot; instead, he would be allowed to return to his regiment. Then, said Abraham Lincoln, "What I want to know is how you are going to pay me back. My bill is a large one, and there is only one man in all the world who can pay it. His name is William Scott. If from this day, you will promise to do your whole duty as a soldier, the debt will be paid."

Scott promised and thanked the president for his pardon. Not long after that event, William Scott's regiment charged into battle against the Confederate army, and Scott was mortally wounded. His friends carried him off the field, bleeding and gasping for breath.

"T-tell the president," he gasped. "I have tried to be a good and faithful soldier." And then he breathed a prayer for Abraham Lincoln as he died.

That story, which was set to verse and read in the United States Senate with Lincoln himself present, shows the gratitude—and faithfulness—of one soldier. But in a much larger way, it shows how good and praiseworthy faithfulness itself is.

It would have made a horrible ending to that story if, after being pardoned by his commander in chief, William Scott had become a lazy, undependable soldier. Why? Because unfaithfulness is a bad thing. But Scott didn't respond that way. We're glad to read of his loyalty and faithfulness because we know faithfulness is good and praiseworthy, whether it's found in a soldier—or in us.

 REFLECT: Do you agree that faithfulness is good and unfaithfulness is bad? Why? Have you ever been given a second chance (like William Scott) to show your faithfulness? If so, did you try harder at being faithful and dependable? Why?

 PRAY: "Father God, thank you for reminding me how important it is to be faithful. Help me to be faithful to you and to those who count on me."

11 Swallowing Camels

Bible Reading: Matthew 23:23-24, 37

You have neglected the more important matters of the law—justice, mercy and faithfulness. Matthew 23:23, NIV

JESUS STOOD LOOKING over the crowds who had gathered to hear him speak. He could see stone-faced men in expensive robes on the fringes of the crowd. Jesus knew these men; they were Pharisees, a group of religious leaders who took great pride in their obedience to all kinds of religious laws and regulations. They even strained their drinking water so they would not accidentally swallow a tiny gnat and so break the Jewish laws about eating "unclean" animals.

But Jesus wasn't impressed by their efforts. In fact, he was angry at the Pharisees because the whole time they were observing all the tiny regulations about washing their hands before eating and how far they could walk on the Sabbath, their lives were filled with cruelty and unkindness and other sins.

"Woe to you," Jesus said, speaking directly to the frowning men on the edges of the crowd. He referred to their habit of giving a tenth of even the tiniest parts of their income to God, while at the same time they treated people unfairly, unmercifully, and unfaithfully. "Woe to you, teachers of the law and Pharisees, you hypocrites! You give a tenth of your spices—mint, dill and cumin. But you have neglected the more important matters of the law—justice, mercy and faithfulness. You should have practiced the latter, without neglecting the former" (Matthew 23:23, NIV). In other words, Jesus was saying, "It's no good to make a point of obeying God in the tiniest detail if at the same time you disobey him in the more important areas of justice, mercy, and faithfulness."

Jesus made it clear that faithfulness is one of the things God desires most from his people. He wants us to be faithful; in fact, he commands it. He wants us to be faithful to him, to our families, to our friends, and to our fellow Christians. He wants us to be faithful to those who depend on us. Why? Because faithfulness, according to Jesus, is one of "the more important matters of the law." That means if we are not faithful, we are not obeying God. Because God commands faithfulness.

REFLECT: Do you think you're a faithful person? Are you faithful to God? to your family? friends? fellow Christians? How do your actions show your faithfulness? If you've been unfaithful or disloyal in some way, have you asked for God's forgiveness and the forgiveness of the person you let down or disappointed?

ACT: Borrow a spice container from your parents' spice rack. Keep it on your dresser or bedside table for the next day or two to remind you of today's Bible reading as well as not to neglect "the more important matters of the law," like faithfulness to your family, friends, and all "who depend on you."

PRAY: "Lord, I know you command faithfulness, but I haven't always been faithful. I ask your forgiveness for those times I've been unfaithful. Help me to be more faithful, with your help, from now on."

12 Faithful Eric

Bible Reading: 1 Samuel 2:27-35

I will raise up a faithful priest who will serve me and do what I tell him to do. 1 Samuel 2:35

ERIC WAS LITTLE, but he loved his grandfather. He especially loved it when Grandpa would let him help around the house. One day, Grandpa and Eric were working together in the garage. They were hanging a piece of Peg-Board on the wall so Grandpa would be able to hang his many tools on it.

As they positioned the Peg-Board against the wall, Grandpa thought of something. "Eric, can you hold this up for just a second?" he asked, nodding at the Peg-Board he held up with his hand. "I left my drill on the kitchen counter."

"Sure, Grandpa," Eric said, smiling. "I can do it."

Grandpa winked at Eric and dashed into the house. He walked through the living room, and snatched his electric drill off the kitchen counter. Then he turned, and the scene on the television—which was running in an empty room—caught his eye. A football game was being played, and Grandpa watched as one of the players caught a kickoff and ran it back. The runner dodged tackler after tackler and finally danced into the opposite end zone—a touchdown! Grandpa smiled and shook his head in amazement at the runner's ability. Suddenly, however, he remembered he had left Eric holding the Peg-Board against the wall!

Grandpa walked to the garage as fast as he could. When the door closed behind him, he saw Eric standing at the wall, his eyes clamped shut. Both hands gripped the Peg-Board as he struggled to hold it up against the wall. Tears streamed from his eyes from the pain in his tired arms.

"Eric!" Grandpa said, easily taking the board out of Eric's arms. "I'm so sorry!"

Eric smiled through his tears. "Oh, that's OK, Grandpa," he said, letting go of the board and rubbing his sore muscles. "I didn't let go, did I? I didn't let go."

"Oh, Eric," Grandpa said, mentally kicking himself for stopping to watch the football game. "You didn't have to keep holding that Peg-Board."

"I didn't want to let you down, Grandpa," Eric said. "And I didn't, did I?"

"No," Grandpa said, setting the Peg-Board down and picking his grandson up into his arms. "No, you didn't."

 REFLECT: What Eric did is admirable, isn't it? Why? Do you think Grandpa valued Eric's faithfulness? Why or why not? Do you think God values faithfulness? Why or why not? Do you think anything in today's Bible reading shows that God values faithfulness? If so, what?

 PRAY: "God, I know you value faithfulness, just like Eric's grandfather valued Eric's faithfulness. Help me to be more like Eric and less like the unfaithful priests mentioned in today's Bible reading."

13 Footprints

Bible Reading: Psalm 146:1-6

> *Blessed is he whose help is the God of Jacob, whose hope is in the Lord his God, the Maker of heaven and earth, the sea, and everything in them—the Lord, who remains faithful forever. Psalm 146:5-6, NIV*

PERHAPS YOU'VE HEARD or read the poem "Footprints." It's been a blessing to thousands and thousands of people, perhaps more than any piece of writing since the Twenty-third Psalm!

"Footprints" is a story told by a man who had a dream about his life. In the dream, he was walking along a sandy beach, making footprints in the sand. He noticed that many times along his path through life there were two sets of footprints. He realized that the second set of footprints belonged to God.

As he looked closer, however, he saw that there were times when only one set of footprints was visible in the sand. He also noticed that this happened at the very lowest and saddest times of his life.

As he stood on the beach looking back over those footprints, he began to feel upset. "Lord," he said, "you promised to always be with me. You said that you would never leave me or forsake me. Yet, I've noticed that during the most difficult times of my life, there was only one set of footprints. I don't understand why you would leave me when I needed you most!"

Then the Lord replied, "My child, I love you, and I would never leave you. During your times of hardship and suffering, when you see only one set of footprints, it was then that I carried you."

What a wonderful picture of God's faithfulness! He is "the Lord, who remains faithful forever" (Psalm 146:6, NIV). He is the one who says, "I will never leave you nor forsake you" (Joshua 1:5, NIV). He is "faithful in all he does" (Psalm 33:4, NIV).

That is why God values faithfulness and commands faithfulness—because he himself is faithful. He is a faithful God. He is a faithful friend. He is a faithful Father because faithfulness is a part of his very nature.

Ultimately, that's why faithfulness is right and unfaithfulness is wrong—because God is faithful. When you are faithful, you do what is right and reflect what is like God.

 REFLECT: Why does God command faithfulness? Why does God value faithfulness? Why is it right for you to be faithful? Hebrews 13:5 gives a promise from God: "I will never fail you. I will never forsake you." What does this promise mean to you?

 ACT: Look up Hebrews 13:5 in your favorite version of the Bible and copy it on an index card. Try to memorize it. Have you ever read the "Footprints" story? If not, look for it (on a greeting card or a laminated wallet-sized card) in bookstores.

 PRAY: "Faithful God, thank you for your promise never to leave me or forsake me. Thank you for your faithfulness. Help me to be faithful like you in everything I do."

14 The Little Hero

Bible Reading: Proverbs 28:14-20

A faithful man will be richly blessed, but one eager to get rich will not go unpunished. Proverbs 28:20, NIV

THERE ONCE WAS a boy named Peter who lived in Holland. Now, Holland is a place where much of the land used to be under water. The people of Holland built great walls called dikes to keep the waters of the North Sea from rushing back in and flooding their fields and homes.

One day Peter's mother sent him to take some cakes to a friend's house. "If you go straight there and don't stop to play along the way, you can get home by dark," she said.

Peter delivered the cakes and turned back toward home. On the way home, however, he saw a sight that struck him with fear: There was a small hole in one of the dikes. A tiny stream of water trickled through the hole. If the water kept flowing, the hole would soon become larger, and before long all their yards and homes would be washed away.

Peter climbed down the side of the dike and poked his finger into the tiny hole. The flow of water stopped. But now what could he do? He couldn't take his finger out, or the water would begin flowing again. He tried calling for help, but no one seemed to hear. It began to get dark, and Peter began to get cold. He tried calling again, but no one answered.

"Mother will come look for me," he told himself, "when I do not come home." But Peter's mother assumed that he had spent the night at his friend's house, and she was preparing to scold him the next morning for not coming straight home as she had said.

It grew colder and colder, and Peter's arm began to ache. He began to cry, but he refused to give up. "I must stand it somehow," he said. "I must save my family and friends. I must keep the water out—if I have to stay here all night."

Peter did stay all night, with his finger stuck in that hole. Early the next morning a man walking to work thought he heard a groan. He leaned over the edge of the dike and called to Peter, "What are you doing?"

"There's a hole in the dike!" Peter said. "Get help, quickly! Please!"

The man sounded the alarm, and soon all of Peter's neighbors showed up with shovels and dirt, and the dike was soon repaired. The whole town thanked Peter for saving them and their homes. All the other kids, who had slept safe and warm in their beds that night, wished that they had done what Peter did. And to this day, Peter is a hero—the little hero of Holland.

 REFLECT: How did Peter's faithfulness benefit his family and friends? Do you think you could be as faithful as Peter? In what ways? Do you think being faithful to God and to others will bring blessings to you? Why or why not?

 PRAY: "Lord, help me to remember that a faithful person will be blessed. Help me to be that kind of person every day."

15 Trust Test

Bible Reading: Nehemiah 13:11-14

Well done, good and faithful servant! You have been faithful with a few things; I will put you in charge of many things. Matthew 25:21, NIV

SUPPOSE YOU ASK your little sister to watch your pet iguana for the weekend while you go to a friend's house. When you return home, the iguana cage is empty, and all your sister can say in answer to your frantic questions is, "I don't know." Would you

(a) ask her to take care of your rare Erobian Mickatoo lizard while you're away for two weeks at summer camp?

(b) never trust her to take care of your animals again as long as you live?

(c) call *America's Most Wanted* and say that your sister is wanted in twelve states?

Or suppose you show a friend your baby picture (the one in which you're *naked!*). Three days later you discover your picture on every bulletin board in school! Would you

(a) show that friend an even more embarrassing photo of yourself?

(b) never ever *ever* show that friend another picture of yourself?

(c) slap a Kick Me sign on your friend's back?

Or suppose you ask a friend to hold ten dollars for you on a school field trip. When it's time for lunch, your friend hands over your money. Would you

(a) never ask that friend to hold money for you again?

(b) trust your friend to hold the change for you?

(c) loudly ask your friend, "Hey! You owe me interest, too!"

If you answered (b) to each question, you know that faithfulness—in a sister, brother, friend, whomever—makes you more likely to trust that person in the future. (If you answered (c) to each question, you should talk to your parents about your mean streak!) And a person who is unfaithful makes you less willing to trust him or her in the future.

That's pretty much common sense, wouldn't you say? When a person is faithful, it's easier to trust that person; unfaithfulness makes it harder to trust someone. That's one of the many ways that God's commands protect us and provide for us. He commands us to be faithful because faithfulness is right; when we are faithful, we enjoy the trust and respect of others. That's just one of many reasons why God's way—the way of faithfulness—is the best way!

 REFLECT: Today's Bible reading (Nehemiah 13:11-14) tells why Nehemiah chose Shelemiah, Zadok, Pedaiah, and Hanan to take charge of the temple storerooms. What was that reason? Have you earned someone's trust because of your faithfulness? If not, why not? If so, name all the people you can think of who trust you because you've been faithful in the past.

 PRAY: "Father in heaven, I want people to trust me and to know that I'm worthy of their trust. Help me to be faithful to you and to others."

16 A Lesson from London

Bible Reading: Psalm 31:21-24

The Lord preserves the faithful, but the proud he pays back in full. Be strong and take heart, all you who hope in the Lord.
Psalm 31:23-24, NIV

ST. PAUL'S CATHEDRAL was completed in London in 1710. It is one of the most beautiful and impressive churches in the world and is the center of the Church of England in London.

During World War II, when Adolph Hitler and the forces of Nazi Germany had conquered most of Europe, the city of London was "a besieged city" (Psalm 31:21, NIV), under almost constant attack from the planes of the Luftwaffe, the German air force. From September of 1940 through May of 1941, Germany's planes bombed London and other British cities almost every night.

Much of London was destroyed during those months, either by the bombs or by the fires the bombs spread through London's buildings. One of the areas that was hardest hit was the section of London called "the City." Near the center of "the City" stood St. Paul's Cathedral.

In the midst of all the destruction caused by Hitler's planes in London, St. Paul's impressive dome stood. While bombs and fires raged all around, St. Paul's (though damaged) was not destroyed. In fact, if you go to London today, proud Londoners will still show you the scars and scorches that yet mark the great cathedral but that never destroyed it.

The preservation of St. Paul's Cathedral through the devastation of the Battle of Britain is a symbol of what God does for those who are faithful to him. Battles may rage around you, even *within* you. The battles may even touch you and scar you. You may go through fires and storms in your life. But "the Lord preserves the faithful," the Bible says, so "be strong and take heart, all you who hope in the Lord" (Psalm 31:23-24, NIV). Be faithful to him because he will always be faithful to you.

 REFLECT: Today's Bible reading says God "will preserve the faithful." Do you think that means you'll never have a problem if you're faithful to him? Do you think it means you'll never be sad? If the answer to both questions is no, what do you think the phrase *does* mean? Does the Lord's faithfulness to you make you want to be faithful to him? Why?

 PRAY: "Lord God, I thank you for your promise to preserve the faithful. Help me to experience the blessings of faithfulness. And please keep me faithful even through all my temptations and problems."

17 Feed the Fire

Bible Reading: 2 Timothy 1:3-6

Fan into flames the spiritual gift God gave you. 2 Timothy 1:6

"SELECT A SPOT on gravel, sand, or bare soil well away from trees, bushes, dry grasses, and anything else that might burn. . . . Clean the fire site down to bare soil, then remove all burnable material from the ground around it. . . .

"You'll need *tinder, kindling,* and *fuelwood.* Tinder catches fire easily and burns fast. Wood shavings, pine needles, dry grasses, shredded bark, and the fluff from some seed pods all make good tinder. . . . Dry, dead twigs no thicker than a pencil are called kindling. Find enough to fill your hat twice. Fuelwood can be as thin as your finger or as thick as your arm. Use dead, dry sticks you find on the ground. . . .

"Gather all the fuel before you light the fire. . . . Place a big, loose handful of tinder in the middle of your fire ring. Lean plenty of small kindling around it. Let the tops of the kindling sticks touch like the poles of a teepee. Arrange larger sticks of fuel around the kindling. Leave an opening in the teepee on the side against which the wind is blowing. This 'door' will let air reach the middle of the fire.

"To light the fire, crouch in front of this door and strike a match. When the match is burning brightly, ease it under the tinder. The flame should spread through the tinder and crackle up into the kindling." (These instructions on building a fire can be found in *The Boy Scout Handbook,* 10th ed., 1990, pp. 83–85.)

That's quite a list of instructions for building a simple campfire, isn't it? But you know what? In building a fire, those first steps are important. If you try to start a fire with a log as big as your arm, you'll probably be disappointed. But if you start the way *The Boy Scout Handbook* teaches, then you'll soon be adding larger and larger pieces of wood to your fire.

It's the same with choosing right instead of wrong. The first steps are important. And the "tinder" and "kindling" for making right choices are prayer and Bible reading. If you try to make right choices without spending time with God in prayer and Bible reading, your efforts probably won't "catch." But if you take time every day to speak to God (through prayer) and let God speak to you (through Bible reading), you will be feeding your soul like you would a fire. Then your life will produce right choices—like a fire produces flames!

 REFLECT: Do you think you can produce right choices without building your relationship with God through prayer and Bible reading? If so, how? If not, why not? Are you ready to begin a daily habit of prayer and Bible reading? If so, what time of the day will you set aside for prayer and Bible reading? Where will you do it? (Choose a quiet, private place where you won't be distracted or interrupted.)

 PRAY: "Righteous God, help me to feed my soul like a woodsman feeds a fire so that with your help I can make right choices and make you happy in everything I do."

18 Tommy's Tactic

Bible Reading: 1 Peter 3:8-12

Finally, all of you, live in harmony with one another; be sympathetic, love as brothers, be compassionate and humble. 1 Peter 3:8, NIV

THERE ONCE WAS a little boy whose name was Tommy. One day in school Tommy's teacher asked him to come to the chalkboard to do a math problem: $2 + 2 = \underline{\quad}$. Tommy strode to the board, picked up a piece of chalk, and wrote the number "5" in the space. When his teacher informed him that his answer was wrong, Tommy thrust out his chest and said, "It may be wrong for you, but not for me. *I* say two plus two equals *five.*"

Later, Tommy was playing at recess. A little girl stood ahead of him in line, waiting to climb the ladder to the giant slide. Tommy pushed her down into the dirt and took her place in line. "Tommy," his teacher said, "you should be more compassionate. Don't you know it's wrong to be so cruel?"

But Tommy stepped onto the ladder and smiled. "Maybe it's wrong for you, but it's not wrong for me. *I* say cruelty is right and being nice to other people is wrong!"

Tommy said such things many times until the last day of school, when his teacher called him aside. "Tommy," she said, "I wanted to show you your report card." She smiled and handed Tommy the piece of paper, which bore a large red F.

Tommy looked shocked. "An F?" he said. "Why are you giving me an F? That's not right!"

The teacher smiled. "An F may not seem right to you, but it's right for me!"

Obviously, Tommy's tactic backfired, didn't it? That's the problem with saying, "Well, it may be wrong for you, but it's not wrong for me!" We all want to be treated fairly, honestly, sympathetically, lovingly, and compassionately. Those things are right whether or not *we* say they're right. Those things are right whether or not *Tommy* says they're right. Those things are right whether or not anyone says they're right. Know why? Because it's not up to any of us to say what's right or what's wrong; that decision belongs to God and God alone. That's a lesson Tommy needed to learn; it's also a lesson we all need to learn.

 REFLECT: Do you ever act like Tommy? Why or why not? Do you ever try to decide what's right or justify what's wrong? Who *really* decides right from wrong? What does today's Bible reading reveal about right and wrong?

 PRAY: "Lord, help me to always remember that it's not up to me to say what's right or what's wrong because that decision belongs only to you. Help me instead to always do what you say is right and stay away from what you say is wrong."

19 Puzzle Me This

Bible Reading: Ephesians 4:32–5:2

Be kind and compassionate to one another. Ephesians 4:32, NIV

GOD GAVE A lot of commands. Everybody knows God told the Israelites, "Do not make idols of any kind" (Exodus 20:4). And most people know that Jesus said, "I am giving you a new commandment: Love each other" (John 13:34). But some commands are less familiar—like the one we're talking about today.

Answer the questions below, printing the letters in the blanks to form the words that are missing in each sentence. Then copy the letters in the numbered spaces below to spell out one of God's commands:

1. The Jordan River runs between the Dead Sea and the __ __ __ of Galilee.
        8 15 7

2. Jesus told the story of the Good __ __ __ __ __ __ __ __ __
    9   5   14   12

3. __ __ __ __ __ __'s father gave him a coat of many colors.
   4   2 6

4. God warned __ __ __ __ of a flood and told him to build an ark.
     11

5. __ __ __ __ __ killed Goliath with a sling and a rock.
  13   10

6. __ __ __ __ __ had a dream of a ladder stretching between heaven and earth.
    3   1

__ __   __ __ __ __ __ __ __ __ __ __ __ __
1 2   3 4 5 6 7 8 9 10 11 12 13 14 15

So how'd you do? If you need help, consult the following Bible verses: (1) John 21:1; (2) Luke 10:25-37; (3) Genesis 37:3; (4) Genesis 6:13-14; (5) 1 Samuel 17:48-49; (6) Genesis 28:10-12.

Today's Bible reading is one of the many instances in which God gives this command to us. He repeated it many times in his Word because he wants us to remember it—and because he wants us to obey it.

 REFLECT: Was the answer to the puzzle above a surprise to you? Why or why not? Did you already know God commanded us to be compassionate to others? Have you obeyed this command today? If so, how? Have you disobeyed this command today? If so, how? What can you do today or tomorrow to show compassion for someone?

 PRAY: "Father, you command me to be compassionate toward others. That's not always easy, but help me to obey you anyway and to be kind and compassionate every day."

20 The Cobbler

Bible Reading: Matthew 25:31-40

When you did it to one of the least of these my brothers and sisters, you were doing it to me! Matthew 25:40

THERE IS AN old tale of a cobbler who felt his faith growing weak one winter morning. So he prayed, "O Lord, please visit me today." He finished praying with the conviction that God would answer his prayer and that Jesus would come to his humble shop that day.

The cobbler opened the shop, where he made shoes, and started looking frequently out the window, expecting the Lord to arrive any moment. As he was watching, he saw one of his neighbors, an old workman, leaning against his shovel, shivering in the cold. The cobbler opened his door and called to the workman, "Come in and warm yourself with a bowl of soup and a cup of tea!" The man returned to his work some time later, warmed by the food and drink—and by the cobbler's kindness.

Later, the cobbler saw a woman pass by his window. In her arms she held a baby, loosely wrapped in a thin blanket. The baby was crying from the cold. The cobbler yanked his door open and called to the woman. "Please come inside. Warm yourself and your child." When the woman came inside, the cobbler found a much thicker blanket than the one she held and gave it to her. The woman left a few moments later, warmed by the cobbler's gift—and by his kindness.

Scenes like that were repeated several times throughout the day, as the cobbler watched and watched for the Lord to come to his humble shop. But night arrived, and still the cobbler watched. Finally, the day came to an end. The cobbler, disappointed, locked his doors and turned down his lamp. "Lord," he said, "I prayed for you to come to my shop today, but you did not."

Suddenly, the cobbler's room blazed with warm light, though the lamp still burned low. He heard a voice and knew immediately that it was the Lord's. "I came, Cobbler," the voice said. "And you fed me. I was thirsty, and you gave me a drink. I was a stranger, and you invited me into your home. I was naked, and you gave me clothing—for when you did it to one of the least of these my brothers and sisters, you were doing it to me!"

The cobbler's story is only a fable, of course. But it beautifully illustrates an important truth: Our Lord views a compassionate act toward another human being as an act of compassion toward him. In fact, that's why he commands us to be compassionate—because he values compassion.

REFLECT: How many different acts of compassion does Jesus mention in today's Bible reading? Can you do any of those things for someone? If so, what? If not, are there other ways you can show compassion to someone today? If so, how?

PRAY: "Lord, remind me today (and every day) that you value compassion. Help me to be kind and compassionate to those around me, especially to_____."

21 Tears in Heaven

Bible Reading: Psalm 103:8-13

The Lord is compassionate and gracious, slow to anger, abounding in love. Psalm 103:8, NIV

TWO ANGELS SAT at a table in the Milky Way Café. They were sipping tea, sharing a piece of angel food cake (they really eat that stuff!), and swapping stories.

"Ooh!" said Kael, almost spilling his tea. "I've got a good one for you. I was on a Terra Class assignment and was given charge of a little kid. She was riding her tricycle down the sidewalk and must have hit a bump or something, because the tricycle stopped, and she went flying over the handlebars." He paused and took a sip of tea.

Ra'Adonoi cocked his head as if he were waiting for the punch line of a joke.

Kael held up a hand to acknowledge that the story wasn't over. "So I'm at the girl's side in a flash of light, and she's all skinned up—her chin, her hands, her knees. And she's crying, and then I felt him."

"The Holy One?"

"The same," Kael said, nodding. "He was there. I mean, it was just a little girl who'd skinned her knees, but he was there."

"Was he checking up on you to make sure you did your job?" Ra'Adonoi asked.

Kael shook his head. "No. He wasn't there for me. He was there for *her*. And you know what else? I saw . . ." Kael stopped for a moment, then continued. "I saw a tear roll down his cheek."

Ra'Adonoi nodded, smiling.

"She was just a little kid on a trike," Kael said, "but I think he cried some of her tears for her."

"Yeah," Ra'Adonoi said after a few moments. "I can believe that because of what happened to me in a place called Passo Fundo, Brazil. . . ."

That story is fiction, of course; it never really happened. But maybe it could have. Because we know, from God's Word, that our God is a God of compassion. We know that he shares our sorrows and bears our burdens. "As a father has compassion on his children," the Bible says, "so the Lord has compassion on those who fear him" (Psalm 103:13, NIV).

And we know that it's right to be compassionate toward others because when we're compassionate, we're doing something that's like God, who is "compassionate and gracious, slow to anger, abounding in love" (Psalm 103:8, NIV).

 REFLECT: *Why* is compassion right (what makes it right)? Did you have any opportunities to be compassionate yesterday or today? How did you respond to those chances to make a right choice? How can you be more compassionate tomorrow?

 PRAY: "Loving and compassionate God, I know it's right to be compassionate because you are compassionate. Please make me like you. Help me to look for chances to be compassionate to others today."

22 Ringing the Chimes

Bible Reading: Exodus 1:8–21

Therefore, as God's chosen people, holy and dearly loved, clothe yourselves with compassion. Colossians 3:12, NIV

ONCE UPON A time in a land far away, the people of a certain town would bring gifts and offerings for the Christ child to their church every Christmas Eve.

Now this particular church had a tall bell tower. The old people in the town said that when the most precious gift of all was laid on the church altar, the chimes would ring a beautiful tune. Some said God himself rang the chimes. Some said the angels stooped toward earth to set them ringing. Nevertheless, the chimes had not rung for many years, so some said the story was just an old fable.

It so happened that one year a boy and his little brother were walking together to the colorful Christmas Eve pageant. As they walked, they talked about the pageant. Everyone in the town would be there, dressed in their finest clothes.

But as they came near to the church, the boy spied an old woman huddled in the snow outside the city gates. She had fallen and had been too sick and too weak to get back up or even cry for help. The boy stooped beside her to help and laid her gray head in his lap. Then he dug into his pocket and drew out a silver coin.

"Take this and place it on the altar for the Christ child for me."

"But you'll miss the celebration!" his brother protested. "You'll miss the choir and the singing and . . . and . . ."

The boy shook his head. "If I don't help her, this poor woman may die out here in the cold. You go." He tried to smile. "I will not miss it so much."

The younger boy hesitated, then left his brother alone with the sick woman. He arrived at the church just as the villagers finished bringing their gifts to the Christ child. Many brought rings of gold and chains of silver. Several gave fine jewels. One woman presented a robe embroidered with the finest stitching. And a great man of the town laid his shining silver sword on the altar. The little brother snuck into the midst of the throng and shyly placed his single silver coin amid the other gifts.

Suddenly the chimes in the bell tower began to ring! A more heavenly sound had never been heard. The minister raised his arms and the congregation stared at the altar to see what gift had made the chimes ring. But all they saw was the little brother of the boy who had stopped to save an old woman's life and the single silver coin he had laid on the altar.

REFLECT: Do you think the boy and his brother's offering pleased God? If so, why? How do you think you would have felt if you had been that little boy? In today's Bible reading, did God reward the Hebrew midwives for their compassion toward the Israelite babies in Egypt? If so, how?

PRAY: "Father, help me to see the many rewards of being compassionate, even when they are invisible."

23 Cool Compassion

Bible Reading: Psalm 112:1-4

When darkness overtakes the godly, light will come bursting in. They are generous, compassionate, and righteous. Psalm 112:4

ERIN WENT TO work with her dad not long ago. A lot of kids do that. But Erin had to travel to India, where her dad was working with the Christian relief organization he had founded.

Erin spent a week in India. She visited a hospital children's ward, where she blew bubbles, made balloon animals, and sang nursery rhymes. She prayed with a teenage girl who had leprosy. She spent hours folding laundry at the Home of the Destitute and Dying. She spoon-fed an elderly blind woman and soon realized that the woman wanted love more than food. So Erin set down the spoon and spent the rest of the afternoon cradling the woman's gray head in her arms.

After a week of depressing sights and backbreaking work, how do you think Erin felt? Do you think she said, "Get me outta here"? Do you think she said, "I can't wait to scarf down a Big Mac and fries"? Do you think she said, "I'm tired; I just wanna veg out in front of the TV"?

She didn't say any of those things. Instead, Erin's response to a week spent showing compassion and working hard among the poor and sick was: "It was cool!"

Cool? Folding laundry is cool? Spoon-feeding a blind woman is cool? Visiting sick and abandoned children is cool?

Yup! It *is* cool, because showing compassion to others can be fun. Showing compassion isn't just good for the *other* person—it's good for you, too. Showing compassion to others can be enjoyable, even in the smelliest and grossest situations.

That's one of the many ways God rewards those who are compassionate. He gives us joy, not in spite of our acts of compassion, but because of them! When you show compassion to a person, you're making *two* people happy—and one of them is *you*.

REFLECT: You don't have to go to India to show compassion to someone else. List the names of three or four people in the left-hand column below who you think may be sad or hurting right now. On the opposite line, list how you might be able to show love and compassion to those people:

_____	_____
_____	_____
_____	_____
_____	_____

PRAY: "Lord, I want to please you by being a compassionate person. I want to help others and experience how much fun being compassionate can be. Help me to show compassion to others in the ways I listed above."

24 The Rich Man's Guest

Bible Reading: Romans 15:1-3

Each one of us needs to look after the good of the people around us, asking ourselves, "How can I help?" Romans 15:2, The Message

THERE'S AN OLD Jewish folktale that tells the story of a famous rabbi who once visited the home of a rich man. The rich man prepared a great feast for his special guest. The banquet table was filled with all sorts of fine food.

Now, the rabbi, like all orthodox Jews, was in the habit of washing his hands thoroughly before eating anything. Sometimes the ceremonial washing of hands could take several minutes.

This time, however, the rabbi poured only a few tiny drops of water from the rich man's pitcher onto his hands.

"Rabbi," the rich man said. "I don't understand. You used so little water, certainly not enough to get your hands clean. The pitcher is full of water! Use as much as you like."

Without speaking a word, the rabbi nodded to a large window in the room. The rich man looked and saw his little servant girl struggling up the hill from the well. She was bent low under a heavy piece of wood that she balanced on her shoulders. From each end of the wooden bar hung a heavy bucket of water.

"How could I wash my hands at the expense of that poor girl?" the rabbi asked his host. "Perhaps the water I saved will prevent one trip to the well for her."

That rabbi knew the meaning of compassion. If the rich man hadn't said anything, no one would have noticed the rabbi's act of compassion. But God would have seen it, of course. And the rabbi would have known that he had done something, however small, to help that servant girl.

That's the kind of thing the apostle Paul suggested when he wrote, "Each one of us needs to look after the good of the people around us, asking ourselves, 'How can I help?'" (Romans 15:2, *The Message*). Helpful actions don't have to be something big or noticeable. In fact, sometimes the smallest acts of compassion are the most beautiful.

 REFLECT: What's the most beautiful act of compassion you've ever seen? What do you think would happen if everyone "looked after the good of the people" and asked, "How can I help?" Have you started to do that? Try doing it today.

 PRAY: "Dear God, help me to see the beauty of compassion and show it to others in all I say and do."

Bible Reading: Psalm 119:65-68

You [Lord] are good and do only good; teach me your principles.
Psalm 119:68

SUPPOSE YOU WANTED to be a pro basketball player someday. Then suppose that you had a choice: You could either have Michael Jordan of the Chicago Bulls teach you everything he knows about basketball, or you could learn basketball from Harvey Klibnitz, who feeds the pigeons at the town square every day. Which would you choose?

Or let's put it like this: Say you wanted to become a famous country singer, and your parents agreed to pay for voice and guitar lessons. Then let's say that your parents said you could take lessons either from LeAnn Rimes, a real country singer who had her first gold record when she was fourteen, or from Katie Sue Ann Bobbi Jo Higgenbottom, who once won the pig-calling contest at the county fair. Which would you choose?

Or suppose you wanted to be a computer whiz when you grew up. Let's say your next-door neighbor on one side is Bill Gates, the multi-bazillionaire who started the Microsoft Corporation (the company that invented Windows) and your neighbor on the other side is Polly Wannacracker, who thinks a monitor is a famous ironclad battleship from the Civil War. Who would you ask for advice?

Or let's just suppose that you want to make right choices in your life. You really care about what's right and what's wrong, and you don't really want to hurt anybody or do anything wrong. Let's also say that you have the word of the Almighty God about what's right or wrong, the God who (the Bible says) is infinitely good and does no wrong. But let's suppose you also have other opinions, like Freddy Finkleheimer, who says it's not so bad to lie as long as you're not hurting anyone. And you have the word of Amanda Lynn String, who says no one can tell you what's right or wrong—you've got to figure that out yourself. Which one would you choose?

If you're smart, of course, you'd choose Michael Jordan to teach you basketball and LeAnn Rimes to give you voice lessons. And you'd ask Bill Gates for computer advice instead of Polly Wannacracker. And you'd certainly believe God, the Maker of heaven and earth and source of everything that's good, about what's right or wrong, wouldn't you? You'd listen to what he says in his Word and do what he says is right, wouldn't you?

Of course you would, because you may not be an expert on right and wrong—but you know who the Expert is, don't you?

 REFLECT: Do you think you have to be an expert on right and wrong in order to make right choices? Why or why not? Do you think it would help to know an expert? Who is the world's Number-One Expert on what's right and what's wrong? How can you seek his advice?

 PRAY: "Lord, you are good and do only good. Please teach me your principles, and help me follow what you say instead of following what others around me are saying."

26 Don't Give Up!

Bible Reading: Galatians 6:7-10
Don't get tired of doing what is good. Galatians 6:9

NO SUPERMARKETS. No pizza delivery. No convenience stores. No drive-throughs. No restaurants.

That's what things were like when the apostle Paul wrote his letter to the churches of Galatia. You see, in those days, most people grew their own food in their own fields.

During the spring they would have to work long, hard days plowing the ground and planting seeds. Then all summer they would take care of what they had planted, which involved weeding, watering, and keeping the wild animals from stealing or destroying their crops. In the fall they would harvest and store their food for the winter.

If a man and his family got tired of planting or weeding or harvesting and decided to quit, they would be in big trouble. The only way they could be assured of having something to eat that winter would be to keep going. They couldn't run down to the grocery store or supermarket for a can of creamed corn. They couldn't order a pizza. If they didn't work hard through the spring, summer, and fall, they would go hungry all winter.

It's the same with us. Fighting temptation and making right choices can be hard. It can be a pain sometimes to be the only one in your family (or class or neighborhood) who's trying to do right. That's why Paul, in today's Bible reading, says, "Don't get tired of doing what is good. Don't get discouraged and give up, for we will reap a harvest of blessing at the appropriate time" (Galatians 6:9).

No matter how hard it gets, don't give up. No matter who makes fun of you, don't get discouraged. No matter how tough it is, don't get tired. Keep leaning on God. Keep asking him to help you. Keep making right choices.

It may not be easy, but it *will* be worth it. God's Word assures us that those who persevere will someday "reap a harvest of blessing at the appropriate time."

 REFLECT: Do you ever get tired of fighting temptation and making right choices? Do you ever get discouraged and feel like giving up? What does God's Word promise to you if you keep following God and obeying his Word?

 PRAY: "Father God, I do get tired of fighting temptation and making right choices sometimes. Thank you for the encouragement to keep following you—and for your promise that I'll 'reap a harvest of blessing at the appropriate time' if I don't give up. Help me to keep going and to please you in everything I do."

27 The Tenth Leper

Bible Reading: Luke 17:11-19

He fell face down on the ground at Jesus' feet, thanking him for what he had done. Luke 17:16

HE'S ONE OF the nameless people in the Bible, one of ten lepers who saw Jesus at a distance and cried, "Jesus, Master, have mercy on us!" He's the one who went back to thank Jesus. Wouldn't it be cool to travel back in time and talk to that leper?

"Yeah," he might say, if he could talk to us, "it was something, all right! Jesus said to show ourselves to the priests. So, even though we didn't feel any different, we started heading that way. All of a sudden I noticed my hand—it wasn't white anymore! The leprosy had disappeared! And then I pinched it—and it hurt! My hand was no longer numb. That was sweet, the sweetest pain I ever felt."

The old man leans forward to hear your next question. "Well, I stopped right then and there. I didn't need any priest to tell me I was healed; I *knew* it! There was no doubt. One minute I was a leper, and the next minute, I wasn't." He snaps his fingers. "Just like that!"

He pokes a stubby finger behind one ear and scratches. "That's when I turned back to find Jesus. I ran back toward the village, and there he was, almost in the same place he was in before. I just pushed my way through the crowd and dropped at his feet. I could hardly speak, I was so happy, but I had to say thank you!"

He shakes his head. "I thought the others would be close behind me," he says. "I didn't know I was the only one until Jesus looked around and said, 'Didn't I heal ten men? Where are the other nine?' That was the first I knew that none of the others had come. But that didn't bother me. I mean, no matter what the others did, I just *had* to say thank you after what he'd done for me, you know? I mean, wouldn't *you* have done the same?"

Ah, that's a pretty good question, isn't it? After all, think of all the Lord has done for you; hasn't he given you many blessings? Hasn't he been good to you in a hundred—a *thousand*—different ways? No matter what others may do, such a good God deserves your thanks and your praise—don't you think so?

 REFLECT: Whom have you been more like in the past: the tenth leper (who showed his gratitude to Jesus) or the other nine (who didn't thank him at all)? If you were to thank the Lord for all the good things he's done for you, how long do you think it would take you? How can you be more like the tenth leper from now on?

 ACT: Take a single sheet of notebook paper. List at least three or four things you thank God for today. Add three or four things to your list every day, until every white space on the sheet is covered with thanks to God.

 PRAY: "Lord, you have done so much for me and given so much to me. I especially thank you today for_____."

28 Standing Alone

Bible Reading: Daniel 3:1–12

They have defied Your Majesty by refusing to serve your gods or to worship the gold statue you have set up. Daniel 3:12

AN OLD FOLKTALE from Africa offers a fanciful explanation for why the thumb stands apart from the other four fingers on the human hand.

It seems that one day the five fingers were lying on a table together, when they noticed a fine gold ring across the table.

"Hey," one of the fingers said, "let's take it!"

"Yeah," said the ring finger, "that sure would look good on me."

They started to reach for the ring when the thumb protested. "Wait a minute, you can't do that," the thumb said.

"Why not?" the fingers shouted, almost in unison.

"Because it would be wrong."

"Oh, come on," said one of the fingers. "No one will see us."

"It would be stealing," insisted the thumb.

"You're nothing but a goody-goody," said the index finger.

"Yeah, you're a party pooper!" added the pinkie.

"Yeah, if you're going to be that way," added another finger, "you can't be a part of our group!"

"Right!" said the other fingers. "Go away! We don't need you anymore."

So the four fingers went off in their own little group and left the thumb standing alone. They thought he would give in and join them in what they wanted to do, but to this day the thumb has stood alone and refused to do what was wrong.

That's what God wants us to do when others try to get us to do something wrong. It may not be easy to stand alone, but it's better to resist our friends than to disappoint God.

 REFLECT: Have you ever acted like the fingers and tried to get a friend to do something wrong with you? Have you ever felt like the thumb in that story? What did you do? How is today's Bible reading like the story of the thumb and four fingers? How can you be more like the thumb the next time someone tempts you to do something wrong?

 ACT: Keep your thumb with you all day long today (!) to remind you of the importance of standing against people who want you to do wrong.

 PRAY: "God, it's hard to do the right thing when everyone's tempting me to do wrong. Please help me to be strong the next time someone tempts me to do wrong, even if I have to stand alone."

29 Message from Dunkirk

Bible Reading: Daniel 3:13-18

Our God whom we serve is able to deliver us from the burning fiery furnace. . . . But if not, be it known unto thee, O king, that we will not serve thy gods, nor worship the golden image which thou hast set up. Daniel 3:17-18, KJV

IN LATE MAY of 1940, during World War II, the German army had overrun the tiny European nation of Belgium. As Hitler's tanks and troops marched across Belgium, they pushed the defenders—British, French, and Belgian troops—toward the sea.

Finally, the Allied forces of Great Britain, France, and Belgium were cornered at a seaport in northern France called Dunkirk. It looked as though all 338,000 of them would be wiped out by Hitler's approaching armies.

Back in Britain, as the British people waited anxiously, a simple three-word message was transmitted from the doomed armies at Dunkirk: "But if not."

Suddenly, the island nation of Great Britain sprang into action. Eight hundred boats of every size and description were called into action. Every battleship, gunboat, fishing boat, motorboat, yacht—even rowboats!—journeyed across the English Channel to help rescue those troops from Dunkirk and return them all safely to Britain.

What was it about that three-word message? How could three short words—only eight letters—start all that?

The Miracle of Dunkirk happened because the British people recognized a phrase from the Bible. They recognized the phrase from the story of Shadrach, Meshach, and Abednego, who trusted in God, even when the king threatened to throw them into a fiery furnace for refusing to worship an idol. And the British people knew that their troops were saying, "We will not give up, even if we die."

You may never be thrown into a fiery furnace. You probably will never be backed into a corner by thousands of tanks and troops. But there will be many times in your life when you'll have to choose between doing the right thing and giving in to sin. You'll face times when doing the right thing will be hard or embarrassing.

At such times remember that doing right is still right even when it's hard or when there seems to be no immediate reward. Doing right is still right even if it might be embarrassing or get you into trouble. God can deliver you, and he may even reward you for doing right—*but if not,* it's still right to do right.

 REFLECT: Have you ever done the right thing and been embarrassed for it? Have you ever done the right thing and gotten into trouble for it? Have you ever done the right thing and not been rewarded for it? If you answered yes to any of those questions, were you sorry you did the right thing? Are you still sorry? Do you think we should do right even when it's hard? Even when there's no reward? Why or why not?

 PRAY: "Lord, I want to be the kind of person who does right even when it's hard. Please help me to make right choices today, even if it's hard or if there's no reward for doing right."

30 Through the Furnace

Bible Reading: Daniel 3:19-27

When you go through deep waters and great trouble, I will be with you.
Isaiah 43:2

A KID ACCIDENTALLY breaks the big picture window in his house and tells his parents the truth. They ground him for the rest of his life.

A teenager refuses to go to a party where she knows there will be alcohol and drugs. Her friends start ignoring her—permanently!

A man sees someone choking in a restaurant. He rushes over, performs the Heimlich maneuver, and dislodges the threatening food from the person's throat. A few days later the man finds out he's being sued for breaking a rib of the person whose life he saved!

These kinds of things really do happen. People do the right thing and get grounded, or even sued!

But how can that be? Aren't we supposed to be better off if we choose right? Won't we enjoy God's protection and provision if we follow him and do right?

Well, yes. You *will* be better off if you choose right. You will enjoy God's protection and provision if you follow him and do right. But God doesn't guarantee that you will always escape pain or hardship if you choose right. He doesn't promise that you'll never be teased or grounded—or even sued—if you choose right. But he does promise to be with you and to help you even if you suffer for doing the right thing.

Remember, Shadrach, Meshach, and Abednego refused to bow down and worship the idol King Nebuchadnezzar had set up. That was the right thing to do. But they were still reported to the king (government officials can be such tattletales!). They were still dragged before the king. They were still thrown into the fiery furnace.

But the next time the king looked into the furnace, he saw Shadrach, Meshach, and Abednego—still alive—and someone else who, the king said, looked "like a divine being" (Daniel 3:25). You see, even though Shadrach, Meshach, and Abednego had to endure the terror of being thrown into the fiery furnace, God was with them all the way! And he even brought them out of the furnace without a single blister!

So don't be afraid to do the right thing. You may be teased or grounded or something else. But God will be with you. God will help you. He'll get you through it one way or another.

 REFLECT: Are you ever afraid to do the right thing? If not, why not? If so, why? Do you think God understands your fear? Do you think that's a good excuse to do the wrong thing? Why or why not? Does God promise you won't ever have problems if you make right choices? What does he promise?

 PRAY: "God, in your Word you say, 'When you go through deep waters and great trouble, I will be with you' (Isaiah 43:2). Thank you for that promise. I don't want to suffer for doing the right thing, but if I do, help me to remember that you are with me and will help me."

1 Doubting the Goodness of God

Bible Reading: Genesis 3:1-6

No good thing will the Lord withhold from those who do what is right.
Psalm 84:11

THE STORY OF the first sin ever committed is recorded in today's Bible reading. The story reports what the serpent said to Eve and what Eve said to the serpent. But have you ever wondered what the Tempter and his victim were *thinking* as they talked? Maybe their thoughts went something like this:

"Really?" the serpent asked the woman. *Let me see; I think I'll start by getting her confused about what God has said!* "Did God really say you must not eat any of the fruit in the garden?"

"Of course we may eat it," the woman told him. *This serpent really bugs me; he acts like he knows so much. Well, I'll show him!* "It's only the fruit from the tree at the center of the garden that we are not allowed to eat." *Let's see; what did God say again? It seems so long ago, now that I think about it.* "God says we must not eat it or even touch it, or we will die." *At least, it was* something *like that.*

OK, let's plant a little doubt in her mind. "You won't die," the serpent hissed. *Come to think of it, a little jealousy wouldn't hurt either.* "God knows that your eyes will be opened when you eat it." *Yeah, that's the ticket; make her think that God's keeping something from her!* "You will become just like God, knowing everything, both good and evil."

The woman was convinced. *Maybe God is trying to hide something from me. Maybe he gave me that command to keep me from having fun!* The fruit looked so fresh and delicious, and it would make her so wise! So she ate some of the fruit.

Now, maybe that's how it happened with Eve, and maybe it's not. But doubting the goodness of God is often the first step toward making the wrong choice.

Many times people act like God gave his commands because he doesn't want them to have any fun. They think that the only way they can have fun or get what they want is by ignoring God's commands. But the Bible says, "No good thing will the Lord withhold from those who do what is right" (Psalm 84:11).

You see, God is good. He wants to give us every good thing there is! The problem is, we often think that God withholds good things from us by commanding us to "do this" and "don't do that." But that's not true. He will withhold no good thing from those who do what is right. If we truly believe that, wrong choices won't be so tempting.

 REFLECT: Have you ever felt like God's commands kept you from getting what you want or kept you from having fun? Do you think it would be easier for you to obey God if you really believed Psalm 84:11? Why or why not?

 PRAY: "God, I know you are good and that you won't withhold any good thing from those who do what is right. Help me, from now on, to really believe in your goodness and to remember that I can't get good things through bad choices."

2 A Clean and Holy Life

Bible Reading: Hebrews 12:14-17

Try to live in peace with everyone, and seek to live a clean and holy life, for those who are not holy will not see the Lord. Hebrews 12:14

IF YOU'VE TRUSTED Christ to forgive your sins and make you a new person inside, you're a Christian. That means your sins are forgiven and you're going to heaven.

But until you get to heaven, you still have a challenge. You're still going to be tempted to sin. And every once in a while, you're going to make a wrong choice. That doesn't mean you're not going to heaven, but it is still a problem. So what should you do? How should you feel about right and wrong choices as a Christian? See if the following True/False quiz helps you to answer those questions:

1. It's OK to sin.	T	F
2. It's OK to sin as long as you plan to ask God's forgiveness later.	T	F
3. A Christian can make right choices or wrong choices; it doesn't really matter in the great scheme of things.	T	F
4. It's impossible for a Christian to live a clean and holy life.	T	F
5. Making right choices is not optional—it's crucial.	T	F
6. If you say you're a Christian but go on sinning, you're not living in the truth.	T	F
7. Being a Christian makes living a clean and holy life possible.	T	F
8. Those who are not holy will not see the Lord.	T	F

How did you do? The first four statements were all false; the final four were all true. Some of those are pretty tough questions, aren't they? They're even tougher when you compare the right answers to your own life.

That's what today's Bible reading is all about. The writer of Hebrews said, "Seek to live a clean and holy life" (Hebrews 12:14). In other words, making right choices is not optional; and if you say you're a Christian but go on sinning, you're not living in the truth (1 John 1:6). Hebrews 12:14 also says that "those who are not holy will not see the Lord." That means if you're a Christian, you will seek to live a clean and holy life by making right choices with God's help.

In fact, being a Christian (and letting God's Holy Spirit control your life) is the only way any of us can live a clean and holy life. It's also the only way we'll ever see the Lord.

REFLECT: Have you ever *acted* like statements 1–4 (in the True/False quiz above) were true? How can you seek to live a clean and holy life from now on? Can you do it on your own? If not, how can you do it? (Hint: reread the last paragraph above.)

PRAY: "Lord, sometimes I act as if it doesn't really matter whether or not I make right choices, but I *do* want to make right choices. I want to live a clean and holy life. I want to see you someday. So please help me to trust you and let your Holy Spirit control my life so I can make right choices."

3 Word Up

Bible Reading: Romans 2:6-8
Never get tired of doing good. 2 Thessalonians 3:13

HAVE YOU EVER been talking to someone when the other person used a word you didn't understand? You probably just nodded and pretended that you used that word every day, didn't you? You also probably wished you could use big words to impress your friends and amaze your family, huh?

Well, wish no more. Here's a quick list of words that ought to do the trick:

- *osculation:* more commonly known as the act of kissing ("Mom and Dad, will you please stop all that *osculation?*")
- *omphaloskepsis:* meditating on your belly button ("I'm sorry, my sister can't come to the phone right now because of her *omphaloskepsis.*")
- *flatulence:* what happens when a person eats too many baked beans ("OK, who filled the car with all that *flatulence?*")
- *ogress:* a female ogre ("My, aren't we acting like an *ogress* this morning?")
- *behemoth:* a really huge or powerful animal ("Wow, that team's forward is a *behemoth!*")

It ought to be fun to try to work *those* words into conversation this week, eh? Oh, by the way, here's one more word:

- *perseverance:* to keep going or to keep doing something even when it's hard or when you are tired ("I really admire your *perseverance!*")

Of all the words we mentioned above, *perseverance* describes what's most useful because it's good to persevere in making right choices—even when making right choices is hard and even when you're tired. That's why Paul told the church at Thessalonica, "Never get tired of doing good" (2 Thessalonians 3:13). He wanted them to persevere, to keep going, to keep doing right no matter how hard it got because God "will give eternal life to those who persist in doing what is good, seeking after the glory and honor and immortality that God offers" (Romans 2:7). When the going gets tough, the tough keep on going!

 REFLECT: What does it mean to persevere? Have you persevered at making right choices, or have you given up? Do you feel like giving up when you get tired or when the going gets tough? How can you keep "doing what is good"? Do you think God can help you persevere? If so, how?

 ACT: Try to use the word *persevere* in conversation at least once today.

 PRAY: "Father, it's not always easy to keep doing what is good. But please help me to persevere even when I'm tired or feel like giving up."

4 Persevering in the Faith

Bible Reading: Acts 4:1-20
We must obey God rather than men! Acts 5:29, NIV

HAVE YOU EVER been . . .

- thrown into jail for talking about God?
- hauled into court for being a Christian?
- whipped and beaten for telling others about Jesus?
- threatened for saying that Jesus rose from the dead?

Maybe you've never had any of those experiences. But Peter and John did.

Peter and John were two of Jesus' disciples. After Jesus died, rose from the dead, and went up to heaven, Peter and John started talking about what had happened. They told people that Jesus had come to save them from their sins and give them forgiveness and eternal life. But a lot of important people in Jerusalem (where Peter and John lived) didn't like what they were saying. So they arrested them and took them to court. They even had them whipped, then told them to stop talking about Jesus.

What would you do if someone said, "If you say another word about Jesus, we'll beat you up"? What would you do if people threatened to put you in jail—or even kill you—for telling others about Jesus?

Well, Peter and John just kept doing exactly what they had always done. They kept preaching about Jesus. They kept talking about how Jesus had died and risen from the dead. They kept telling people how to find salvation by trusting in Christ. They *persevered* even when other people threatened them and caused them a lot of trouble.

That's a great example for us to follow. Peter and John explained their actions by saying, "We must obey God rather than men!" (Acts 5:29, NIV). That's exactly what we should do, too. Even if our friends tease us and call us names, we should obey God. Even if doing the right thing might make us look silly, we should obey God. Even if doing what is right might get us—or a friend—in trouble, we should obey God. And we should keep obeying him, no matter what others say or do. That's perseverance. And that kind of perseverance is right.

 REFLECT: Maybe you've never been in a situation exactly like Peter and John's, but you may have been tempted to give up or give in to pressure from other people. If so, what did you do? Did you persevere in spite of the pressure, or did you give in? What will you do the next time you face pressure to stop doing right (or to start doing wrong)?

 PRAY: "Dear God, help me to be more like Peter and John when people try to get me to give up or to give in to pressure."

5 The Power Source

Bible Reading: Isaiah 40:27-31

> *Don't you know that the Lord is the everlasting God, the Creator of all the earth? He never grows faint or weary. . . . He gives power to those who are tired and worn out. Isaiah 40:28-29*

IF YOU'RE LIKE most people, you eat at least three meals a day, right? Have you ever thought about where the power comes from to chew all that food? Much of it comes from a muscle in your jaw called the *orbicularis oris*. But you already knew that, right?

And you've certainly opened a window at one time or another, haven't you? Where did you get the power to do that? Most of it came from muscles in your arms called *biceps*.

And you've climbed a staircase, haven't you? Well, you got the power to do that mainly from the *rectus femoris* and *biceps femoris* muscles in your upper legs.

You get the power to do sit-ups from the muscles in your belly *(rectus abdominis)*, and you get the power to lift heavy things from a group of muscles *(deltoids, pectoralis majors, biceps)*.

Amazing, isn't it? You've been doing all that stuff for years, but you probably never knew where the power came from, did you?

Well, if you're a Christian, you also have the power to persevere. You have the power to do right, even when it's hard. You have the power to keep going, even when you're tired. You have the power to work hard at something, even when you feel like quitting. But the power to persevere doesn't come from your muscles—it comes only from God.

A prophet named Isaiah once wrote, "Don't you know that the Lord is the everlasting God, the Creator of all the earth? He never grows faint or weary. . . . He gives power to those who are tired and worn out; he offers strength to the weak. Even youths will become exhausted, and young men will give up. But those who wait on the Lord will find new strength. They will fly high on wings like eagles. They will run and not grow weary. They will walk and not faint" (Isaiah 40:28-31).

That's right. When you are tired and worn out, God has the power you need. When you feel weak, God can give you strength to keep going. When you are exhausted and feel like giving up, God can help you to persevere. Just ask him for help. Believe that he is strong even when you're not. And he will help you to persevere—in everything you do.

 REFLECT: According to today's Bible reading, where does the strength to persevere come from? Do you need to persevere in something right now? (For example, persevering in saying no to some of your friends, saying no to a temptation, or in doing a job or a chore.) Talk to God about it, and ask him for help.

 PRAY: "Lord, I know that you never grow faint or weary and that you give power to the tired and strength to the weak. Please help me to find new strength to persevere."

6 Never Give In!

Bible Reading: Hebrews 12:1-3

Let us run with perseverance the race marked out for us.
Hebrews 12:1, NIV

WINSTON CHURCHILL WAS the prime minister of England during World War II. He led the British people through very dark days. When France surrendered to Germany in June 1940, England was left alone to fight the Germans. The air force was badly outnumbered, and the nation was under almost constant attack. But even when defeat seemed certain, Churchill never gave up. Within five years Germany had been defeated, and Europe was once again at peace.

On October 29, 1941, Churchill stood before a gathering of students at Harrow School in England. Every voice in the room was hushed. Every face was turned toward the great leader. Every ear strained to hear every word from the great man's lips.

Churchill banged the podium with his fist. "Never give in!" he said. "Never give in. Never, never, never, never—in nothing, great or small, large or petty—never give in except to convictions of honor and good sense." And with that, he sat down. His speech was over. It was probably the shortest speech that group had ever heard—and one they would remember most.

That short, simple speech expressed the spirit of Winston Churchill. It also expresses God's will for the Christian.

You see, Churchill gave wonderful advice to the students of Harrow School when he said, "Never give in." But God doesn't *advise* us never to give in; he *commands* it! God's Word says that we are to "run with perseverance the race marked out for us" (Hebrews 12:1, NIV). He commands us to "never get tired of doing good" (2 Thessalonians 3:13). He says, "Don't get discouraged and give up" (Galatians 6:9).

Are you getting tired of always being the "good" kid? God says, "Never give in!" Do you feel like you've been tempted so much lately that you're too weak to resist anymore? God says, "Never give in!" Do you feel like giving up trying to make right choices all the time? God says, "Never, never, never, never, never! Never! Never give in."

God commands us to persevere. He wants us to learn how to stick to a job. He wants us to keep trying even when we're tired or discouraged. He wants us to never give up in our efforts to make right choices. "Never give in!" he says. "Never, never, never, never, never! Never! Never give in."

 REFLECT: What do you think might have happened if Sir Winston Churchill (and Great Britain) had given in to the Nazis early in World War II? What do you think might happen if you get into the habit of giving up when you're tired or when a job gets hard? What do you think might happen if you give up trying to make right choices?

 PRAY: "God, I know your Word says I should persevere. I know you want me to learn to stick to a job. I know you want me to know how to keep trying even when I get tired or discouraged. And I know you don't want me to give up trying to make right choices. So please help me to 'never, never, never, never, *never* give in!'"

7 The Picture of Perseverance

Bible Reading: Revelation 2:1-3

You have persevered and have endured hardships for my name, and have not grown weary. Revelation 2:3, NIV

YOU'VE SEEN HIM on TV.

- He never speaks.
- He's pink and furry.
- He has big ears.
- He carries a drum and two drumsticks.
- And he just keeps going . . . and going . . . and going.

Of course, you've already figured out that he's the Energizer Bunny, the battery-operated toy that for years has appeared in the most unexpected places, rolling across the screen and banging his drum everywhere he goes.

That bunny has become famous because he illustrates what everyone wants in a battery: long life, endurance, perseverance.

Well, what people value in batteries, God values in people. That's right. God values perseverance. He thinks it's great when people keep going . . . and going . . . and going in their efforts to make right choices.

That's why God commanded perseverance in the first place. That's why his Word says, "Never get tired of doing good" (2 Thessalonians 3:13) and "Don't get tired of doing what is good. Don't get discouraged and give up" (Galatians 6:9). And that's why God praised the church at Ephesus, saying, "You have persevered and have endured hardships for my name, and have not grown weary" (Revelation 2:3, NIV).

God is disappointed when people quit trying to do right or when they give up instead of persevering. But he likes it when troubles make people try harder and work harder. He likes it when hardships make people more determined. He likes it when people keep going . . . and going . . . and going; when they work hard or choose right no matter how hard it is, no matter how tired they get, no matter how long it takes. Because God values perseverance.

 REFLECT: Does today's Bible reading show you that God values perseverance? If so, how? Do you think you need to persevere right now in spite of some trial or hardship? If so, how can you do that?

 ACT: The next time you see the Energizer Bunny, remember that God values perseverance.

 PRAY: "Dear God, I want to keep going . . . and going . . . and going in my efforts to follow you and to make right choices. Please help me to persevere, no matter how hard it is, no matter how tired I get, and no matter how long it takes."

8 Vacation Cancellation

Bible Reading: Deuteronomy 31:1-6

The Lord your God will go ahead of you. He will neither fail you nor forsake you. Deuteronomy 31:6

A MAN HAD a dream one night. In his dream he stood before the throne of God in heaven. The man crossed his arms on his chest and spoke to God.

"God," he said, "I feel like giving up. Sometimes being a Christian is just too hard, and I don't feel like doing it anymore. It gets discouraging, you know? Isn't there some way for me to just get a 'vacation' from being a Christian?"

God nodded his head. "I see," he said. "And while you're on this vacation, would you like me to still cause the sun to rise every morning? Would you like me to still place a song in the throat of every bird? Would you like me to keep your heart beating? Would you like me to open your eyes from sleep and give you another day of life?

"Would you like me to still listen to your prayers and soothe your hurts? Would you like me to still forgive your sins and keep your soul in the palm of my hand? Would you like me to still send the sun to bed at night and give you the moon and stars to decorate your night sky? Would you like me to close your eyes in sleep and fill your lungs with breath even while you sleep? Or are you suggesting that I go on vacation, too?"

The man swallowed hard before speaking. "Uh, you know," he answered God in his dream, "I . . . I . . . I've ch-changed my mind. I've decided I don't need a 'vacation' after all!"

Most of us feel like that man from time to time. We may be tired of doing our chores. Or tired of doing a certain job. Or tired of making right choices. We may even get tired sometimes of being Christians.

But at times like those, we need to remember that God commands us to persevere. We need to remind ourselves that God commands perseverance because God values perseverance. And we need to understand that God values perseverance because *he* perseveres for us, day after day, moment after moment.

That's why perseverance is right—because God perseveres. He promises never to fail us or forsake us. And because he will always keep going for us, we should learn to persevere in the things we do.

 REFLECT: Do you think God has ever given up on you? Why or why not? Do you think God ever *will* give up on you? Why or why not? How does it make you feel to know that God perseveres for you? Are you glad? uninterested? grateful? sorry? sad? hopeful? something else?

 ACT: On a sheet of paper, make a list of the things God does for you *every day.* (You can start with the things listed in the paragraphs above.) Place that list on your desk or bedside table to remind you of God's perseverance.

 PRAY: "God, thank you for all the things you do for me every day. I know that you'll never give up on me. Please help me to learn to persevere like you."

9 A Tree Grows in Brooklyn

Bible Reading: James 1:2-4, 12

Consider it pure joy, my brothers, whenever you face trials of many kinds, because you know that the testing of your faith develops perseverance. Perseverance must finish its work so that you may be mature and complete, not lacking anything. James 1:2-4, NIV

A TREE GREW in Francie Nolan's yard. Writer Betty Smith told about that tree in the famous book *A Tree Grows in Brooklyn:*

> The tree in Francie's yard was neither a pine nor a hemlock. It had pointed leaves which grew along green switches which radiated from the bough and made a tree which looked like a lot of opened green umbrellas. Some people called it the Tree of Heaven. No matter where its seed fell, it made a tree which struggled to reach the sky. It grew in boarded-up lots and out of neglected rubbish heaps, and it was the only tree that grew out of cement.

That tree wasn't planted by caring hands in a grassy park. No one watered it. No one tied it to a strong stake to help it grow straight. But it grew anyway. It started its life by poking its tender shoots through cracks in cement. It struggled. It searched for sunlight. It stretched its roots underground to find water. But always, always, it kept straining to reach the sky. It kept struggling, until it grew tall.

That picture of a tree growing in Brooklyn is a picture of what perseverance can do. The struggles that tree had to go through to grow made it grow strong and tall. And your struggles can do the same thing for you. The Bible says, "Consider it pure joy, my brothers, whenever you face trials of many kinds, because you know that the testing of your faith develops perseverance. Perseverance must finish its work so that you may be mature and complete, not lacking anything" (James 1:2-4, NIV).

In other words, perseverance can make you like that tree in Brooklyn: strong, tall, mature, complete, not lacking anything. If you learn to persevere even when it's hard, even when you're tired, even when everything seems to stand in your way, you will grow taller and stronger and more mature—if you let perseverance "finish its work."

 REFLECT: According to today's Bible reading, what does the testing of your faith produce? What does perseverance do for you? Has your faith ever been tested? If so, in what ways?

 PRAY: "Heavenly Father, please make me like that tree in Brooklyn. Help me to keep trying and growing so that I can someday be 'mature and complete, not lacking anything.'"

10 Championship Character

Bible Reading: Romans 5:1-5

We also rejoice in our sufferings, because we know that suffering produces perseverance; perseverance, character; and character, hope.
Romans 5:3-4, NIV

EVERYBODY IS GOOD at something. You may not be able to do long division, but maybe you can stand on your head. You may not be able to touch your nose with your tongue, but maybe you can sing better than anyone in your family. Most people are good at several things.

Take a look at the following list and check anything that you can do fairly well.

☐ Throw a football		☐ Imitate your teachers
☐ Eat spaghetti		☐ Play a musical instrument
☐ Play video games		☐ Read
☐ Sing		☐ Listen
☐ Make friends		☐ Follow directions
☐ Make your bed		☐ Run
☐ Get along with others		☐ Remember things
☐ Solve riddles		☐ Do cartwheels
☐ Spell		☐ Say no to wrong things
☐ Draw		☐ Say yes to right things

You're probably good at more things than you thought, aren't you? Did you check those last two things on the list ("Say no to wrong things," "Say yes to right things")? They were the two most important things on the list because if you're pretty good at doing those last two things, you're developing a good character.

Character is the ability to say no to evil and yes to good. And do you know how people develop that ability? Through perseverance.

You see, the Bible says that "suffering produces perseverance," and perseverance produces character (Romans 5:3-4, NIV). In other words, if you learn to keep saying no to wrong things even when it's hard or even when saying no gets you into trouble, you'll get better at saying no to wrong things. And if you learn to keep saying yes to right things even when you don't feel like it, or even when kids make fun of you, you'll get better and better at that, too. And little by little, you'll develop a strong character—until you become a *champion* at saying no to evil and yes to good!

That's one of the things that's so cool about perseverance; it develops champion-ship character. And that's something we could all use.

 REFLECT: Do you need to get better at saying no to wrong things? at saying yes to right things? According to today's Bible reading, how can you do that?

 PRAY: "Lord, I know that perseverance is right. Help me to persevere and to become a *champion* at saying no to evil and yes to good!"

Practice Makes Perfect

Bible Reading: Hebrews 11:24-27

Moses kept right on going because he kept his eyes on the one who is invisible. Hebrews 11:27

WHEN YOUR PARENTS started school, they might have learned to read by reading the Dick and Jane series of books. They read gripping tales about Dick, Jane, and Spot (the dog) like, "See Dick run. See Jane run. See Spot run." Pretty exciting, huh?

Well, your grandparents (or great-grandparents) might have learned to read by using a famous set of books commonly called "McGuffey's Readers." These simple books, published between 1836 and 1857, were used to teach several generations of American schoolchildren to read.

McGuffey's Readers not only taught reading; they taught other important lessons as well. For example, the Readers taught children that perseverance was a good thing:

The fisher who draws in his net too soon
Won't have any fish to sell;
The child who shuts up his book too soon
Won't learn any lesson well.

If you would have your learning stay,
Be patient—don't go too fast;
The man who travels a mile each day
May get round the world at last.

That simple rhyme teaches the truth that perseverance (in fishing, in learning, or in walking) produces success. A person who knows how to stick to a task will usually succeed—maybe sooner, maybe later. If you keep practicing the piano, you'll get better and better. If you keep doing your homework, you'll learn more and more. If you keep exercising, you'll get stronger and stronger.

Perseverance in making right choices produces success, too. If you keep trusting Christ and let him help you make right choices, you'll get better and better at doing so. After all, whether you're practicing the piano or trying to make right choices, practice makes perfect.

 REFLECT: Have you ever finished a job that was really hard or that took a long time? If so, how did it feel when you finally finished? Can you name something you've succeeded at because you kept trying or practicing for a long time (like reading, for example, or playing the piano)? Does that success encourage you to persevere at making right choices? Why or why not?

 PRAY: "Father, it feels really good to succeed, especially when it was really hard or took a long time. Help me to understand and experience the benefits of perseverance."

12 The Grandfather God

Bible Reading: 1 Samuel 12:1, 14–18, 24

*But be sure to fear the Lord and serve him faithfully with all your heart;
consider what great things he has done for you.* 1 Samuel 12:24, NIV

A SIX-YEAR-OLD boy named Aaron described God: "He's old. It's been a long time since he was a kid!"

His seven-year-old sister, Aubrey, offered a more specific portrait of God when she added, "He's like seventy or seventy-two. He's like everybody's grandpa in the whole world." Then she added thoughtfully, "Except he's not our grandpa, he's our Father."

A lot of kids (even older kids) share Aubrey and Aaron's ideas of God as an old man, maybe with white hair and a beard. They think of God as a white-haired old man with rosy cheeks, who pats children on the head and gives them gifts. He's a "Grandfather God" to them. And like most grandparents, this nice old man doesn't discipline or punish anyone; instead, he takes kids to the park or buys them ice cream.

The "Grandfather God" is an understandable idea of God. After all, God has been around a long time. The Old Testament vision of Daniel revealed God as "the Ancient of Days" who, in fact, was described as having hair which was "white like wool." (See Daniel 7:9, NIV.)

He is also loving and kind. The prophet Jeremiah said, "Long ago the Lord said to Israel: 'I have loved you, my people, with an everlasting love. With unfailing love I have drawn you to myself'" (Jeremiah 31:3).

But God is no doddering old man. He doesn't shuffle across heaven's floor in loose-fitting slippers. He doesn't have to put in his false teeth every morning. He is the "eternal, immortal, invisible [King], the only God" (1 Timothy 1:17, NIV).

All this is important because we need to realize that God doesn't wink at his children's sin like a grandfather who pats mischievous kids on the head. He expelled man and woman from the Garden of Eden because of sin. He flooded the world because of sin. He vaporized Sodom and Gomorrah because of sin. He sent his only Son to die on a cruel cross because of sin.

God is loving and kind, but he will not excuse our sin. He went to a lot of trouble to prove that he takes sin seriously

Since he takes sin seriously, we should too. We should not expect him to pat us on the head when we do wrong; instead, we should ask for his forgiveness and for him to help us "sin no more" (John 8:11). We should love God, but we should also respect him. We should "be sure to fear the Lord and serve him faithfully," especially when we "consider what great things he has done for [us]" (1 Samuel 12:24, NIV).

 REFLECT: How do you view God? Is he a "Grandfather God" to you? Why or why not? Do you love and respect God? If so, why? What "great things" has God done for you?

 PRAY: "God, you are the 'eternal, immortal, invisible [King], the only God.' I love you, Lord. I fear and respect you. And I want to serve you faithfully as long as I live."

13 Trust and Obey

Bible Reading: Psalm 78:1-7

Each generation can set its hope anew on God, remembering his glorious miracles and obeying his commands. Psalm 78:7

HAVE YOU EVER entered your family's living room and plopped down on the couch? Sure you have, right? But how did you know the couch would hold you?

Have you ever slapped a stamp on a letter or card and mailed it to someone who lived hundreds of miles away? Of course, you have. But what made you think the letter would actually reach its destination?

Have you ever picked up a telephone, dialed a friend's number, and expected someone at your friend's house to answer the phone? Well, why did you expect to be connected to the phone at your friend's house?

"Don't be dumb," you might say. "I knew the couch would hold me because I've sat on it lots of times before. And I figured the letter would go where I mailed it because I've mailed things before. And I've dialed the same phone number lots of times. Why *wouldn't* it ring at my friend's house, unless they changed their phone number?"

You're absolutely right. You do the same kind of thing every day. You expect the couch to support you because you've sat on it many times, and it's never collapsed, right? The same is true of the letter and the phone call; you expect a certain thing to happen because it's always happened that way before, right? You might say you've learned to *trust* those things, right?

Well, if you can trust a couch because it's never let you down, you should *really* be able to trust God. A couch might get old; it might fall apart. But God never gets old. He never breaks down. He never fails. He is always trustworthy.

And if you can trust God, you can also trust his commands. You can believe that when God says to do something (or not to do something), his command is good because he is good. When God says, "Honor your mother and your father," you can believe that it won't hurt you to honor your mother and your father. When he says, "Do not lie," you can believe that telling the truth is going to help you, not hurt you.

You don't ever have to wonder if this command or that command is worth obeying; you don't ever have to guess which of God's commands is good for you. If you can trust God (and you can), you can also trust his commands.

 REFLECT: Unscramble the following words from today's Bible reading and rewrite them on the blanks to list four reasons why we can trust God.
- sonless   _____ from the past
- urigsloo   the _____ deeds of the Lord
- erowp   his _____
- carmiles   the mighty _____ he did

Answers: lessons; glorious; power; miracles.

 PRAY: "Lord, I know I can trust your commands because I know I can trust you. Help me to remember your glorious miracles and obey your commands every day."

14 The Hitchhiker's Guide to Pride

Bible Reading: Romans 12:14-16

Do not be proud, but be willing to associate with people of low position. Do not be conceited. **Romans 12:16, NIV**

TWO HITCHHIKERS MET on the on-ramp to a major expressway.

"Where ya headed?" the first hitchhiker asked.

"Chicago," the second answered.

"Whaddya know? That's where I'm headed, too."

"Well, isn't that fine!" said his companion. "Which way is it?"

The first hitchhiker pointed to a green-and-white highway sign that loomed over their heads. "That there sign says Chicago's that-a-way." He pointed toward the northbound lanes of the expressway.

The second hitchhiker looked at the sign and nodded. "It sure does," he said. He studied the other hitchhiker's face. "But I'm still wondering. Maybe it's that way," he said, pointing to the southbound lanes of the expressway.

The two watched the traffic flowing south for a few moments. Then the second hitchhiker shrugged and hitched his baggy pants a little higher on his hips. "Sometimes it's just hard to know for sure, ain't it?" And he and his companion sauntered down the ramp toward the traffic that was heading south . . . *away* from Chicago.

That's pretty dumb, isn't it? They stood right under a sign showing them the right way, and they *still* acted as if they didn't know which way was right.

Of course, people do that all the time, especially when it comes to right and wrong. For example, God has made it perfectly clear in his Word that it's wrong to be conceited and prideful; yet people still act as if they're better than other people.

But we don't have to wonder whether pride is right or wrong. In Romans 12:16, God says [through the apostle Paul], "Do not be proud, but be willing to associate with people of low position." And then, just in case you didn't get the message the first time, he repeats it in slightly different words: "Do not be conceited." That's pretty clear—as clear as a road sign.

 REFLECT: What do you think it means to be conceited? (If you don't know, try looking up the word *conceit* in a dictionary.) What does it mean to be humble? Do you have to decide whether being conceited and proud is right or wrong? Why or why not?

 ACT: Using a piece of cardboard or construction paper, make a road sign with the word *conceit* written on it and the international "no" symbol over it (a bold red circle with a diagonal red line through it). Use it as a reminder to "just say no" to pride.

 PRAY: "Dear heavenly Father, I don't want to be like those two hitchhikers in today's reading. Help me to remember and obey your command not to be proud or conceited or to think that I'm better than someone else."

15 Much Ado

Bible Reading: Ephesians 4:1-3
Be humble and gentle. Ephesians 4:2

A LOT OF people confuse the commands of the Bible with other sayings and quotations that *aren't* in the Bible. For example, a lot of people think the phrase "Cleanliness is next to godliness" is found in the Bible. But it's not.

See if you can identify which of the commands or phrases below are really found in the Bible. Place a check mark next to those phrases you think are from the Bible. (If you're not sure, you can use a Bible concordance before looking at the answers.)

1. "Neither a borrower nor a lender be."
2. "Do nothing out of selfish ambition or vain conceit, but in humility consider others better than yourselves."
3. "If anything can go wrong, it will."
4. "We have nothing to fear but fear itself."
5. "Pride goeth before a fall."
6. "Do not be arrogant, but be afraid."
7. "I love you, you love me, we're a happy family."
8. "Don't make much ado about nothing."
9. "Look before you leap."
10. "Be humble and gentle."

Well, was it too easy? Too hard? Or did you already look at the answers? You probably figured out that number one is actually a quote from William Shakespeare's famous play *Hamlet*. Number three is known as Murphy's Law. Number four is a phrase uttered by President Franklin D. Roosevelt. Number seven is a song Barney the dinosaur made famous. And numbers eight and nine are familiar proverbs that date back as far as ancient Greece. The others (2, 5, 6, 10) are Bible verses.

More important, the Bible verses that were included in the list above make it clear that God commands us to be humble, not proud.

It's good advice to "look before you leap" and not to "make much ado about nothing." But it's far more important to obey God's commands to be humble.

 REFLECT: Do you ever brag or act as if you are better than someone else? Do you ever act prideful or conceited about anything? How do you know that humility is good and pridefulness is bad? Do you obey God's command to be humble
    (a) none of the time?
    (b) some of the time?
    (c) most of the time?
    (d) all the time?

 PRAY: "God, your commands tell me that it's right to be humble. Thank you for the way your commands help me to know right from wrong. Thank you for the way your Spirit lives in my heart and helps me choose right instead of wrong."

October

16 MVP

Bible Reading: Isaiah 66:1-2

This is what the Lord says: . . . "This is the one I esteem: he who is humble and contrite in spirit, and trembles at my word."
Isaiah 66:1-2, NIV

AROUND THIS TIME every year, the major league baseball season comes to an end. By that time, each league (the American League and the National League) will have already announced a "most valuable player" for each league.

The very first MVP award was given after the 1911 baseball season. A man named Hugh Chalmers, who owned the Chalmers Motor Company, announced that he would award one of his company's automobiles to one player in each league who "should prove himself as the most important and useful player to his club and to the league at large in point of deportment and value of services rendered." A committee of baseball writers voted, and the first MVP awards were given to Ty Cobb of the Detroit Tigers (who hit .420 that year) and Frank Schulte of the Chicago Cubs (who hit .300 with 21 home runs and 107 runs batted in).

There have been many MVPs since then. Some have had high batting averages. Some have hit a lot of home runs. Some have stolen a lot of bases. Some have been pitchers who won a lot of games. But all have been considered the "Most Valuable Player" on their teams in that particular year.

Well, if God had an MVP award, you know how you could win it? By being humble. At least that would be one of the requirements. In today's Bible reading, God says, "This is the one I esteem: he who is humble and contrite in spirit, and trembles at my word" (Isaiah 66:2, NIV). In other words, God really values humility. He thinks humility is terrific!

Of course, God doesn't give out Most Valuable Person awards; he values all people. But he has announced several Most Valuable *Principle* awards, and the principle of humility is one of his favorites. That's why God commands us to be humble; because humility is something he values—even more than a great batting average or a lot of stolen bases.

 REFLECT: If God gave out MVP awards for humility, would you be nominated? Would you win it? Would you be proud of winning it? OK, so maybe that's a trick question; it's not very humble to be proud of your humility, is it? Do you think it's better to be proud or humble? Why?

 PRAY: "Lord, I know you value humility; you 'esteem' the person who is humble and contrite in spirit. Help me to always be that kind of person toward you and toward others."

17 Coming off Your High Horse

Bible Reading: Hebrews 11:24-27

Take my yoke upon you. Let me teach you, because I am humble and gentle, and you will find rest for your souls. Matthew 11:29

DURING THE AMERICAN War for Independence, a group of soldiers had been assigned to cut down some trees to make a bridge across a creek. The work was very hard, and the men were making slow progress. As they grunted and sweated, a man rode up on a horse and looked over the scene.

The man on the horse spoke to one of the soldiers, who was not working but was telling the others what they should do. "You don't have enough men, do you?" the man on the horse asked.

"No," said the man who had been giving orders.

"Why don't you lend a hand yourself?" the man on the horse asked.

"Me?" the soldier answered in a shocked tone. "Why, sir, I am a corporal!"

"Ah," said the man on the horse, as if the soldier's rank explained everything. He got off his horse and helped the men. When the trees were all cut down and the bridge was built, he got back on his horse and saluted the corporal.

"The next time there's work to be done and you don't have enough men to do it, just call for your commander in chief, and I will come again," he said. The man on the horse was General George Washington.

That story, which is one of many great stories found in William Bennett's book *The Moral Compass,* shows the greatness of George Washington. Although he was a general and the commander in chief of all the American armies in the Revolutionary War (and later the first president), he humbled himself to do the work a corporal wouldn't do!

If that story shows the greatness of George Washington, how much greater is our Lord, Jesus Christ! Although he was God and the one through whom everything in the world was created, he humbled himself and came to earth to live a sinless life and die a horrible death—for all of us!

The example of Jesus reminds us that humility is good and right, because the Almighty God humbled himself for us. If God himself was not "too proud to be humble," we should let him teach us, as today's Bible reading says, to be "humble and gentle" (Matthew 11:29).

 REFLECT: How do you think that army corporal felt when he realized he had been too proud to work beside General George Washington? What do you think Jesus meant when he said, "Let me teach you, because I am humble and gentle"? How can you let Jesus teach you to be humble and gentle today?

 PRAY: "Jesus, thank you for humbling yourself and becoming a man so that you could die for my sins. Please teach me today to be humble and gentle toward everyone I meet."

18 Winning Attitudes

Bible Reading: Deuteronomy 8:6-14

Do not become proud at that time and forget the Lord your God.
Deuteronomy 8:14

NATALIE RACED TOWARD the other team's goal, drew back her foot, and kicked the ball as hard as she could. She watched in amazement as the soccer ball sailed through the air—and past the outstretched form of the goalie! She had scored the winning goal! She started jumping up and down in the air, screaming and laughing. Her teammates soon swarmed around her, and Natalie stood among them, happy and proud.

Lon walked across the stage that had been erected in the middle of the school gym and accepted the Honor Roll award his principal handed to him. He turned his head and looked for his parents in the bleachers. They were clapping for him, and his mom was crying. Lon beamed with pride.

Little Josh dashed from his playroom into the room where his mom sat and showed her the picture he had drawn. She took the page from his tiny hands and praised his work. Josh trotted back to his playroom, smiling proudly.

Do you think Natalie, Lon, and Josh were wrong for feeling proud? Were their reactions wrong?

No. What they felt was not only natural, it was good. Natalie was pleased that her effort had made her teammates happy. Lon felt honored to receive the Honor Roll award and was thrilled that he had pleased his parents. Little Josh was pleased with the results of his drawing "work" and basked in the glow of his mother's praise. They were right to feel proud of what they had done.

There's a difference, you see, between sinful pride and a healthy, godly attitude toward your achievements. To celebrate a winning goal is not sinful pride, but if Natalie had claimed to be "the best player" on her team and made the other players feel bad, *that* would have been prideful behavior. To feel honor at receiving an award isn't sinful pride, but if Lon had strutted across the stage as if he were the smartest kid ever to attend his school, *that* would have been arrogant. To bask in your parents' approval isn't sinful pride, but if Josh started to talk and talk about how well he could draw, *that* would have been boastful.

You see the difference? You can take pleasure in your good qualities or achievements and still be humble. But when you act in a prideful, boastful, or arrogant way, you're not being humble. So enjoy what you like about yourself and what you do well, but make sure you do it with gratitude and humility, and not with pride.

 REFLECT: Do you think a person can be prideful and grateful at the same time? Why or why not? Do you think a person can be humble and grateful at the same time? Why or why not? What's the difference between taking pleasure in your good qualities or achievements and acting in a prideful, boastful, or arrogant way?

 PRAY: "Heavenly Father, help me to have healthy, godly attitudes about what I like about myself and what I do well. Please protect me from sinful pride."

19 The Not-So-Great Wall

Bible Reading: 2 Chronicles 7:11-14

If my people who are called by my name will humble themselves and pray and seek my face and turn from their wicked ways, I will hear from heaven and will forgive their sins and heal their land. 2 Chronicles 7:14

IT'S THE ONLY man-made thing on earth that can be seen from outer space. It's the longest structure ever built entirely by hand, winding for nearly four thousand miles. It's the Great Wall of China.

The Great Wall of China was started about four hundred years before Jesus was born, and it continued to be built off and on for about two thousand years. Although it has collapsed in places, it stretches from the east coast of China all the way into the north-central part of the country. The Chinese people built it to keep other people from attacking and invading their country. To this day, the Great Wall is a great source of pride among the Chinese. Tourists come to see it. Historians study it. And scientists use it to study earthquakes.

But some historians believe the Great Wall (the pride of China) kind of backfired. It may have protected China from some attacks, but it (and the attitudes it symbolized) also isolated the nation from many good things. For centuries, much of the progress and discoveries that benefited people in other parts of the world never reached China. A great nation became a backward nation, partly because the Great Wall kept progress from flowing into China.

That's sort of a picture of what pride does. Some people act prideful because they think it protects them or makes them look better than others around them. But usually what happens is that prideful people obstruct the flow of God's blessings to them. They make it harder for God (and others) to help them and bless them.

On the other hand, humility opens windows of blessing. Humility makes it easier for God to speak to you, help you, and bless you. Humility makes it easier for other people to like you and want to be around you. Pride builds a wall that keeps many good things out of your life; humility opens a window that brings many good things into your life.

 REFLECT: In today's Bible reading, what are the four things God told his people to do if they wanted him to forgive them and heal their land? Do you think God blesses humble people more than proud people? Why or why not? How can you make it easier for God to help you and bless you today?

 PRAY: "God, you've already given me so many blessings and so many things to be thankful for, like_____. Please help me to keep the windows of help and blessing open by being humble instead of proud."

20 Babel Babble

Bible Reading: Genesis 11:1-9

Pride goes before destruction, and haughtiness before a fall.
Proverbs 16:18

IMAGINE WHAT IT would have been like to have been a kid living in the Plain of Shinar thousands of years ago. You wake up in your corner of the family tent and turn on your radio. (OK, so they didn't have radio back then. Just play along, OK?)

"Goood mornin', Plain of Shinar! This is Wolfman Mash, broadcasting live from the site of the Tower of Babel, the greatest real estate development the human race has ever seen!" Wolfman Mash continues. "We've got the latest hits by Dust II Men, The Artist Formerly Known as Arphaxad, and Tupac Shinar—but first, I'm sitting here with Nimrod Trump, one of the builders of this amazing tower. Thanks for joining me and my listeners this morning, Nimrod."

"We are so excited about this project, Wolfman," another voice says. "When it's done it should convince everyone that we don't need any superstitious belief in a god or creator. We are ascending our own ladder to heaven! This tower will shine forever as a monument to the greatness of man—and to the greatness of a Nimrod such as me! And one more thing, Wolfman—razzle frazzle boboli babel!"

You shoot a confused look at the radio. It sounded like that guy just said, "Razzle frazzle boboli babel!" You jiggle the tuning knob just to make sure you're not losing the station. But then you hear Wolfman's familiar voice saying, "Goo, mungu peeekee botahaha goo!"

Suddenly you switch off the radio and shake your mom and dad to wake them up. "Hey, Mom, Dad, I've just decided what I wanna be when I grow up! A translator!"

OK, maybe that's not exactly the way it happened. But the construction of the Tower of Babel came to a halt because of the pride and ambition of its builders (see Genesis 11:1-9). They intended to build a monument to their own name and ability, but their great Tower of Babel soon became a pile of rubble.

That's the way it usually goes. The Bible says, "Pride goes before destruction, and haughtiness before a fall" (Proverbs 16:18). The Bible—and the rest of history—is filled with stories of people whose pride led to their fall (Goliath, Haman, Nebuchadnezzar, Belshazzar, to name a few). That's one of the reasons God wants us to be humble: He wants to protect us from the destruction and disappointment a prideful attitude often invites and fill us with the wisdom and blessing that humility often brings.

And that's a whole lot better than ending up in a pile of rubble.

 REFLECT: Do you agree that pride often invites destruction or disappointment? If so, why? Do you think pride blinds people to some things or makes people less willing to listen to wise advice? Why or why not?

 PRAY: "Wise and loving God, thank you for protecting me from the dangers of pride by teaching me humility. Please keep teaching me to be humble and gentle like your Son, Jesus."

21 Getting Oriented

Bible Reading: John 14:15-17

And I will ask the Father, and he will give you another Counselor, who will never leave you. He is the Holy Spirit, who leads into all truth.
John 14:16-17

HOW MANY DIFFERENT sports can you name? Name as many as you can.

How many can you think of? You probably named baseball, right? And football, basketball, and soccer. Maybe even tennis, hockey, or track. But there's one sport you'd probably never guess in a hundred years. It's called "orienteering."

Orienteering is a sport or pastime that's becoming more and more popular. Participants go out into a wild area (a forest, field, desert, and so on) with almost nothing except a map and a compass. Then, using the map, compass, and their "orienteering" skills, they find their way to some distant destination. People enjoy the sport because it's sort of like solving a puzzle or finding your way through a maze.

Well, all of us are constantly doing something similar. We may not be in a forest or field, but we often find ourselves in areas we've never seen before: "Would it be wrong to tell Mrs. Rotgut that I liked her cake when I really didn't?" "Would it be all right to 'borrow' money out of my brother's piggy bank if I put it back later?" "Is it OK to put shaving cream on my sister's Jell-O and tell her it's whipped cream?"

It can get pretty hard to find our way in such strange territories. Most of the time we feel like we're just guessing. But we don't have to feel that way—not if we have the proper equipment.

When Jesus was telling his disciples that he would soon be leaving them and returning to heaven, he promised them that the Father would "give you another Counselor, who will never leave you. He is the Holy Spirit, who leads into all truth" (John 14:16-17). He knew his followers would sometimes feel lost. He knew that sometimes they wouldn't know what to do. So he told them the Holy Spirit, who would live in their hearts, would lead them into all truth.

One of the keys to orienteering is learning how to use a compass to find out which way to go. One of the keys to making right choices is listening to the Holy Spirit to find out which way to go. We listen to him through prayer and Bible reading and by following his commands. And as we listen to him, we'll find out that the territory we're in becomes less strange as we start to see the way more clearly.

REFLECT: Do you think Christians (who have the Holy Spirit living inside them) should find it easier to know right from wrong than non-Christians do? Why or why not? How is the Holy Spirit's guidance like a map or a compass? How is it different? Do you let the Spirit lead you in making right choices? If not, why not? If so, how?

PRAY: "Dear God, thank you for the gift of your Holy Spirit, who lives inside every Christian. Please help me listen to his voice and follow where he leads me."

22 Thirteen Ways to Say, "I Love You"

Bible Reading: John 14:18-21

Those who obey my commandments are the ones who love me.
John 14:21

THERE ARE MANY, many different ways to tell someone, "I love you." You can

- say, "I love you!"
- mouth the words "I love you";
- send flowers;
- write his or her name in the snow;
- read him or her a story;
- throw a kiss;
- clean his or her room;
- sing a song;
- give him or her a hug;
- send a card or valentine;
- bake him or her a dozen cookies;
- scatter tiny construction paper-hearts in his or her lunch box or lunch bag;
- give that person a command.

Bet that last one surprised you, didn't it? After all, who tells someone else "I love you" by giving that person a command?

A lot of people do. Your parents probably do it all the time. They say, "Don't skateboard in the street"; "Fasten your seat belt"; and "Don't strap a giant firecracker to your back and try to shoot yourself to the moon." They don't give you such commands because they hate you. They don't tell you those things because they've got nothing better to do. They don't give you commands like that because they want to ruin your life. They give you those commands because they love you. For example, they tell you not to skateboard in the street because they don't want you to get run over by a truck. Their "commands" are ways of saying, "I love you."

God does the same thing. He has given us commands like "Don't lie," "Don't cheat," and "Flee sexual immorality" because he loves us. He wants to protect us and provide good things for us. For example, his commands to keep ourselves pure in thought, word, and deed protect us from all kinds of addictions and diseases and other bad things. His commands are ways of saying, "I love you."

And do you know how we can say, "I love you" back? Jesus said, "Those who obey my commandments are the ones who love me" (John 14:21a). If we obey his commands, we're showing Jesus that we love him. So do as much as you can today to say, "I love you, Jesus."

 REFLECT: Can you think of any of God's commands that aren't loving? Why not? Are God's commands the *only* way he expresses his love to us? What are some other ways? Is obeying his commands the *only* way you can express your love for God? What are some other ways? How can you tell Jesus you love him today?

 ACT: Cut out tiny construction paper hearts today and scatter them in someone's lunch box, briefcase, dresser drawer, or book bag to say, "I love you."

 PRAY: "Thank you, God, for showing your love in all your commands. Help me to show my love for you by obeying you in what I think and do and say today."

23 "The Smartest Kid in the World"

Bible Reading: Proverbs 9:9-12

If you become wise, you will be the one to benefit. If you scorn wisdom, you will be the one to suffer. Proverbs 9:12

THREE PEOPLE—a minister and two kids—once went on a short sight-seeing flight in a small, four-passenger plane. One of the kids had just been honored in a national newsmagazine as "the smartest kid in the world."

Suddenly, the pilot shouted to his passengers over the roar of the engine. "We've got a big problem!" he said. "Our gas tank has a leak in it, and we're going to run out of gas in just a couple minutes. We're going to have to jump!"

"That's not so bad," the minister said, forcing a nervous smile. "I've always wanted to learn to skydive!"

The pilot shook his head. "We only have three parachutes. One of us isn't going to make it! I've got a family. I can't leave them alone without a father."

"Well, I'm the smartest kid in the world," said the one kid. "I may be the only person who can discover a cure for cancer or AIDS or something like that! You two will have to fight this out between you." And with that, the kid grabbed one of the parachutes and jumped.

The minister turned to the other kid and the pilot. "You take the other two parachutes," he told them. "I'm not afraid to die."

"Thanks," the other kid said. "But we've got nothing to worry about. The 'smartest kid in the world' just jumped out of the plane with my backpack!"

The "smartest kid in the world" wasn't so smart, was he? He made a foolish decision—not just because he took a backpack instead of a parachute, but also because he made a selfish decision. And he paid for his choice!

You may not be as foolish or as selfish as that kid, but you may discover (if you haven't already) that wrong choices often have a high price. Lying may get you into more trouble. Cheating in school may get you suspended or expelled. Trying to hurt other people may hurt you more than them.

The Bible says, "If you become wise, you will be the one to benefit. If you scorn wisdom, you will be the one to suffer" (Proverbs 9:12). In other words, godly wisdom and right choices pay off—maybe not right away or maybe not for a long time. But if you make a habit of making right choices, you will benefit in many lasting ways. If you don't . . . well, just don't go jumping out of any airplanes.

 REFLECT: Who do you think has more fun: those who are always getting into trouble or those who follow the rules? Have you ever been sorry you made a wrong choice? Have you ever enjoyed any rewards for making right choices? Which are you: a person who is becoming wise or a person who scorns wisdom?

 PRAY: "Lord, I want to be wise in making right choices. Please teach me to be wise and help me to make wise choices today."

24 Guessing Game

Bible Reading: Isaiah 46:3-10

To whom will you compare me? Who is my equal? Isaiah 46:5

IN THE MOOD for a quick guessing game? Let's try it.

You already know that a pattern is a form or a model that's imitated in making something else. For example, you may use a pattern to make a dress. You may use a cookie cutter to make cookies in a certain "pattern." Right? Well, let's play a guessing game about different kinds of patterns. Circle the answers you think are correct.

1. The pattern for the shape of an airplane is
   a. the shape of an ocean vessel.
   b. the human body.
   c. the body of a bird.

2. The pattern for a duck hunter's decoy is
   a. Donald Duck.
   b. Daffy Duck.
   c. a real duck.

3. The pattern for everything that is "good" and "right" is
   a. individual opinion.
   b. human tradition.
   c. the nature and character of God.

You probably don't have to be told that the shape of an airplane is patterned mostly after the body of a bird, and that the pattern for a duck hunter's decoy is the shape and coloring of a real duck. Similarly, the pattern for everything that is "good" and "right" is the nature and character of God.

In other words, we should not compare our behavior to what our friends do to figure out whether we're doing right or wrong. We shouldn't compare our actions to what our government says is OK. God is the only true pattern for what's right and what's wrong. He is the one we should compare our beliefs and behavior to because his goodness and righteousness show us what is good and right.

It's simple. If a thing's like God, it's right. If it's not like God, it's wrong. As long as God is your pattern for right and wrong, you can't go wrong. Right? Right.

 REFLECT: Have you ever tried to figure out right from wrong by using some pattern besides God? Have you ever tried to measure your behavior by your feelings? by what "everyone else" is doing? by what your friends or teachers say? by something else? How do those "patterns" measure up when compared to God?

 PRAY: "Dear God, please help me to remember that you are the only true pattern for what's good and right. Help me to always compare what I think and say and do to *you* and to become more and more like you every day, as your Spirit helps me."

25 "Mister, Are You God?"

Bible Reading: Psalm 145:8-13

The Lord is faithful to all his promises and loving toward all he has made. Psalm 145:13, NIV

CHRISTIAN YOUTH SPEAKER and author Doug Fields has shared a story of an event that happened after World War II.

At the end of that devastating war, much of Europe lay in ruins. Buildings had been bombed and burned out, streets lay under dust and rubble, and many orphaned children wandered the streets, picking among the ruins for clothes and food.

Early one morning an American soldier was driving his jeep through the war-torn streets of London. As he turned a corner, he spied a little boy, dressed in rags. The boy stood with his nose pressed against the steamed window of a pastry shop. Inside, the cook was working a large lump of dough for a fresh batch of doughnuts.

The soldier pulled his jeep to the curb and stopped. He got out, strode into the little shop, and bought a dozen doughnuts. Then he left the store and offered the bag of fresh doughnuts to the boy. "Here," he said. "I bought these for you."

The boy looked at the soldier with wide eyes and took the bag. But as the soldier started to return to his jeep, he felt a hearty tug on his coat. He turned back and faced the boy.

"Mister," the boy asked, his eyes still wide, "are you God?"

What made that boy ask such a question? What could have made him think that an American soldier driving a jeep could be God? That's easy. Something in that soldier's actions reminded the little boy of God. That "something" was love.

That soldier did something very good, something right, when he bought those doughnuts for that boy. It was a loving act, a caring act. And it was right for one reason: It was something God might have done. That boy mistook that soldier for God because love comes from God. That's why love is right (and hatred is wrong)—because God is loving. The Bible says, "The Lord is faithful to all his promises and loving toward all he has made" (Psalm 145:13, NIV). When you are loving, you are doing right, because love is like God.

 REFLECT: Have you treated someone else lovingly today? Have you treated someone else hatefully today? Which is right and which is wrong? Why? Do you need to change the way you've been treating anyone?

 ACT: The next time you eat a doughnut, remember the soldier and the hungry boy, and remind yourself that love is right because God is love.

 PRAY: "God, I know that love is right because you are loving. Help me to love others, just like you do."

26 Jukebox Way

Bible Reading: James 1:19-25

Do not merely listen to the word, and so deceive yourselves. Do what it says. James 1:22, NIV

YOU'RE ON VACATION with your parents. You wanted to go on a two-week tour of the best amusement parks in the world, but your mom and dad overruled you. You're going to the International Jukebox Museum instead.

You've been in the car with your parents and your little sister for four days, and if she sings "If You're Happy and You Know It" one more time, you'll knock yourself unconscious against the window. Your dad has stopped the car only once in those four days, announcing as you poured yourself out of the car, "We leave in three minutes." Lately, however, you've noticed that the scenery seems to be repeating itself.

"Are we lost?" you ask.

"No," Dad says in a voice of exasperation. "We're almost there."

"Daddy, I have to go to the bathroom," your little sister says.

"Why don't you just ask for directions?" your mom suggests.

"I don't need directions. I know where I'm going."

"That must explain," your mom says, pointing out the window, "why we've passed that little park four times now."

"All right, all right," your dad finally says. He jerks the car into a gas station and asks the attendant for directions to the International Jukebox Museum.

"Right at the light," the man answers, popping his chewing gum in his cheek. "Two miles, hang a left at the bottling company. The next left is Jukebox Way." Your dad thanks the man, pulls out of the service station, and turns left at the next light.

"Dear," your mom says, "the man said to turn right at the light."

"I know."

"But you turned left. "You're going the wrong way," Mom says.

"No," your dad answers, "I'll still get there. I'll just go my *own* way."

You slump back in your seat. Your sister starts singing again. You eye the window, wondering how hard you'd have to hit your head to knock yourself unconscious.

That's pretty unrealistic, isn't it? No one would get directions from someone who knows the way and then choose to ignore them.

But we do that all the time. God has given us directions—lots of them! He has told us, point blank, how to live a holy and joyful life. Yet we often choose to go our own way rather than follow directions from someone who knows the way. It's not enough to know right from wrong; you must also *choose* right or your knowledge is useless.

 REFLECT: When was the last time you knew the right thing but did the wrong thing anyway? What made you choose wrong? How can you choose differently the next time?

 PRAY: "Lord, help me not merely to listen to your Word but to do what it says."

27 Bob's Secret

Bible Reading: Psalm 44:1-8

Only by your power can we push back our enemies; only in your name can we trample our foes. Psalm 44:5

THE MOVIE *What about Bob?* starred Bill Murray and Richard Dreyfuss in an odd comedy about a psychologist and one of his patients, a man afraid of almost everything. Bob, the patient, follows the psychologist to his vacation home. The psychologist is angry at Bob, but the doctor's family thinks Bob is fun. In fact, they even take Bob sailing—his first time—and tie him to the mast so he won't chicken out!

When Bob arrives back at the dock, he sees his psychiatrist and begins yelling excitedly, "I sailed! I sailed! I'm a sailor! I actually went sailing!" Later, a calmer Bob explains to the doctor's son (who has a few fears of his own), "I just let the boat do all the work. . . . That's my secret."

Bob's "secret" is actually a lot wiser than it may sound.

You see, a lot of people—people who love God and want to obey him—think it's *their* job to do good things and avoid doing bad things. They imagine that making right choices requires a "grit-your-teeth" struggle against temptation and sin, a struggle in which only the strong survive.

They need to learn Bob's "secret." Trying to make right choices and live a godly life in your own strength is like trying to sail a boat by blowing into the sails. You don't have the strength to do right all by yourself any more than you have enough wind in your lungs to power a sailboat. The only way you can make right choices, time after time, is not by *trying* but by *trusting*. After all, it's "'Not by might nor by power, but by my Spirit,' says the Lord Almighty" (Zechariah 4:6, NIV) that you can live a godly life.

Your job is to pray and to stay as close to God as you can. God's job (through his Holy Spirit) is to help you obey his commands (see Ezekiel 36:26-27). You can make right choices time after time if you let the Holy Spirit be the wind in your sails.

 REFLECT: According to Psalm 44:1-3, who did all the work of conquering the Promised Land for the Israelites? According to Psalm 44:4-8, who "gives us victory"? If your "job" in making right choices is to pray, stay as close to God as you can, and trust him to help you to obey his commands, is there anything you should be doing now that you *haven't* been doing? Is there anything you have been trying to do that you *shouldn't* be trying to do? How can you trust God more and more every day? Can you trust God without being willing to do right? Why or why not?

 PRAY: Reread Psalm 44:1-8, only this time *pray* the verses. Feel free to put them into your own words or to write your own personalized version of those verses in a notebook or prayer journal.

28 Two Towers of Strength

Bible Reading: Jude 1:20-24

But you, dear friends, must continue to build your lives on the foundation of your holy faith. And continue to pray as you are directed by the Holy Spirit. Jude 1:20

THE GOLDEN GATE Bridge stretches across San Francisco Bay in California. This bridge, perhaps the most famous bridge in the whole world, was completed in 1937. It's one of the longest suspension bridges in the world, stretching for 8,891 feet (or one and three-quarter miles—that's almost thirty football fields long!).

Now, the Golden Gate Bridge spans a channel where very strong winds blow. That area has been hit by many earthquakes, some of them strong enough to topple buildings and collapse expressways. Yet the Golden Gate Bridge has withstood those earthquakes and is as strong today as when it was built.

You want to know how the Golden Gate can stand while many other structures all around it have cracked or crumbled?

Part of the secret is in the foundation. You see, the builders of the Golden Gate Bridge knew that the area was subject to earthquakes. (A really bad earthquake destroyed much of San Francisco in 1906, only thirty-one years before the bridge was built.) So they sank the two great towers of the bridge deep into two massive concrete blocks, which had been reinforced with strong steel beams. One of these great blocks, larger than a city block, weighs over 90 million pounds! With that kind of foundation, the Golden Gate Bridge can withstand even severe attacks.

The same is true of you. You may not have to go through any earthquakes, but you may have friends trying to get you to smoke or try drugs. You may sometimes be tempted to lie to your parents or teachers. You will face a lot of temptations to do wrong and may find it hard sometimes to make right choices.

That's why you need to do what the builders of the Golden Gate Bridge did. You need to build a strong foundation for making right choices in your heart and mind. You need to sink two great "towers" of strength into your heart that will help you to make right choices even when your friends try to talk you into wrong choices. What are those two strong towers? *Prayer* and *Bible reading*.

You've probably heard it before, but if you pray faithfully and read your Bible carefully every day, you'll be drilling those two towers deeper and deeper into your heart and mind. So that the next time a really big temptation comes, you'll be ready—to stand strong.

 REFLECT: Do you have trouble making right choices? Do you think spending time with God every day (through prayer and Bible reading) could help you to make right choices? Why or why not? Are you building your faith through prayer and Bible reading? Do you need help to become faithful in prayer and Bible reading?

 PRAY: "God, please help me to be faithful every day in prayer and Bible reading so that I can be strong enough to make right choices."

29 Steer Clear!

Bible Reading: Proverbs 4:14-15

Do not set foot on the path of the wicked or walk in the way of evil men. Avoid it, do not travel on it; turn from it and go on your way.
Proverbs 4:14-15, NIV

A WEALTHY MAN was once searching for a chauffeur to drive his limousine. Many people applied for the job, but the millionaire picked only a few to take a driving test.

The millionaire sat comfortably in the back of the limousine and told the first applicant to begin driving. As they drove along a narrow mountain road, the millionaire called to the driver, "See how close you can steer us to the edge of the cliff without falling off." The driver, eager to show his skill, steered the expensive car within a few feet of the dangerous bluff. When they returned to the mansion, the millionaire said, "Thank you. We'll let you know."

The second driver then slipped behind the steering wheel. Again, the millionaire said, "See how close you can steer us to the edge of the cliff without falling off." The driver, who was determined to outdo the first applicant, steered the long limousine within inches of the cliff! When they returned to the mansion, the millionaire told the second driver, "Thank you. We'll let you know."

Another driver then took the second driver's place and was given the same instructions. But the third driver answered, "No way! I wouldn't go near the edge of that cliff no matter how much money you paid me!" The millionaire smiled and answered, "You're hired!"

The millionaire's request was not intended to test the driver's skill; it was intended to test each man's wisdom. When he found a man who would steer clear of danger even if it meant losing a potential job, he knew he had found a safe driver.

God is looking for young men and women who will steer clear of danger, too, because he knows that making right choices begins with avoiding temptation. He doesn't want his children to see how close they can get to sin without giving in. He wants you and me to look at temptation and say, "No way! I'm not getting near that!"

Many wrong choices can be avoided if we just steer clear of temptation. The Bible says: "Run from all these evil things, and follow what is right and good" (1 Timothy 6:11). If you're tempted to steal cookies, stay out of the kitchen! If your friends are trying to get you to try cigarettes, get some new friends! In other words, if you avoid the temptation before you're tempted, you're less likely to be tempted. And that will make it easier for you to make the right choice.

 REFLECT: Do you usually steer close to temptation or do you tend to steer clear of temptation? Think of your three strongest temptations. How can you steer clear of them?

 PRAY: "Lord, give me the desire to run from all that is evil and to follow all that is right and good."

30 The Disguise of Darkness

Bible Reading: John 3:16-21

Those who do what is right come to the light gladly, so everyone can see that they are doing what God wants. John 3:21

WHEN DO YOU suppose most violent crimes are committed: during daylight hours or at night?

When do you think burglars do their work: during daylight hours or at night?

When do you imagine most vandalism (breaking windows, damaging property, and so on) happens: during daylight hours or at night?

When do you think most arsonists (people who set fire to things on purpose) do their work: during daylight hours or at night?

If you answered "at night" to all those questions, you're correct. But why is that? Why do so many murders or muggings take place at night? Why do people wait until after dark to break windows or set fires?

Because it's dark, of course! People who don't want to be caught doing something wrong will wait until it's dark, so the darkness will disguise their deeds. That's what Jesus meant when he said that people "loved the darkness more than the light, for their actions were evil. They hate the light because they want to sin in the darkness. They stay away from the light for fear their sins will be exposed and they will be punished" (John 3:19-20).

Understanding the truth of Jesus' words can help you to make right choices. If you're doing something that you don't want your parents to know about, guess what—it's probably wrong (unless you're planning a surprise anniversary party for them!). If you have to hide what you're doing, that's a bad sign, because people "want to sin in the darkness. . . . But those who do what is right come to the light gladly, so everyone can see that they are doing what God wants" (John 3:20-21).

So remember—if you have to hide what you're doing, you probably shouldn't do it. Instead, do everything as if God were looking over your shoulder—because he is!

 REFLECT: Have you ever done something you didn't want people to see or know about? If so, what? What should have helped you realize that you might have been doing wrong? If you're doing what God wants, would you probably try to hide it or not try to hide it?

 PRAY: "God of light, help me to be among those who do what is right and not like people who try to hide their deeds under the cover of darkness."

31 Now or Later?

Bible Reading: Hebrews 10:32-36

Do not throw away this confident trust in the Lord, no matter what happens. Remember the great reward it brings you! Patient endurance is what you need now. Hebrews 10:35-36

YOU CAN GET a lot of things instantly these days: instant coffee, instant oatmeal, even "instant winner" lottery tickets. But there are still things that take time. You can't get a high school diploma overnight. You can't grow a sunflower in thirty minutes or less. You can't lose weight instantly (no matter what the infomercials say!). You can't even make instant Jell-O instantly; you have to put it in the refrigerator and let it gel.

The problem is, all those things we can get instantly make it harder for us to wait for other things. We're so used to "fast food" that we can't stand to wait more than a few minutes for dinner in a restaurant (and if we do, we complain about the service!). We're so used to "quick fixes" that we moan and groan when we unwrap a Christmas present that says, "Some assembly required." We're so used to getting things we want *now*, we have trouble saving or planning or waiting for the things we want.

And the devil, our enemy, knows how to use our desire for "instant winners" and fast rewards to get us to make wrong choices. He knows that most of us are used to getting what we want when we want it. So he tempts us to do wrong by promising that the wrong choice will bring instant gratification.

"I know you don't have enough money to see a movie," he'll say, "but all your friends are seeing that new movie *today*. Just take the money from your mom's purse; she'll never miss it."

Or, "Go ahead, make fun of your friend; everybody at your lunch table will laugh and think you're cool *now*. You can always apologize later."

One of the keys to making right choices is learning to say no to the sometimes instant rewards of wrong choices in favor of the greater and more enduring rewards of right choices.

In other words, many temptations to do wrong are like a choice between eating a slice of devil's food cake now and owning your own bakery later. If you can say no now, you can enjoy much greater rewards later. It's often as simple as *now* or *later*.

 REFLECT: Think over recent choices you've made. Did a desire for "instant" gratification cause you to make the wrong choice in any of those instances? If so, how can you make the right choice next time?

 ACT: Buy a pack of the candy called Now & Later. As you eat the candy, remember to "continue to do God's will. Then you will receive all that he has promised" (Hebrews 10:36).

 PRAY: "Lord, help me to say no to the devil's tricks and temptations. Let me see that there are greater and more enduring rewards of doing what is right."

1 Shine

Bible Reading: Philippians 2:12–15

You are to live clean, innocent lives as children of God in a dark world full of crooked and perverse people. Let your lives shine brightly before them. Philippians 2:15

A WEALTHY BUSINESSMAN in India was preparing to retire. He called his two sons into his office and told them of his plans.

"Now, you are both good sons and capable young men," he said. "I can't decide who I should put in charge of my business and all my property. So, I have chosen a test for you." He gave a coin to each son and said, "Take this coin and buy something that will *fill* this house."

Now, the coin he had given each of his sons was of little value and his house was large with many rooms. Each son knew the task would be difficult.

The older son wasted no time. He hurried to the marketplace and began pricing all sorts of bulky materials. He soon decided that the cheapest and bulkiest thing he could buy was straw. So he bought as much straw as his coin would buy and carried great bundles of it into the house. But the straw barely covered half the floors in the house.

The younger son stopped to think about his father's test. He knew that only a most unusual purchase would pass his father's test.

When the younger son returned, he carried only a small package. His brother laughed. "You expect to fill this house with *that?*" he said, pointing to the package.

The younger son said nothing. He opened his little package and took out an assortment of candles. He placed one candle in each room. When he had lighted them all, the entire house was filled . . . with light!

Every day you face the same choice those brothers faced. Every morning a new day stands open before you. You can fill it with wrong choices, selfish choices, choices that bring only darkness and disappointment. Or you can fill your day with right choices with good and decent actions that will shine like a light to everyone around you.

Make it your goal today—and every day—to fill your day with right choices, and let your life shine like a light in a dark world.

 REFLECT: What did you fill your day with yesterday—light or darkness? Right choices or wrong choices? What do you think will happen as people see you making right choices? How can you "shine" like a light to everyone around you today?

 ACT: Ask your parents for permission to light a candle while you eat breakfast tomorrow morning to remind you to fill your day with right choices that will shine like a light to everyone around you.

 PRAY: "Father, please help me to live a clean and innocent life in this dark world. Help me to make right choices that will shine like a light to everyone around me."

2 The Game of Life

Bible Reading: Isaiah 64:4-5

You welcome those who cheerfully do good, who follow godly ways.
Isaiah 64:5

SUPPOSE YOU HAVE the opportunity to make up a game. You design your own playing board. You make playing pieces out of little trinkets you find around the house. You even write down the rules.

Then two of your friends come over. You spread the playing board on the floor. You carefully explain the rules of the game. Then you generously allow someone else to take the first turn.

Everything goes fine for a while. The game is even more fun than you thought. But then one of your friends makes an illegal move.

"You can't do that," you say. "Remember the rules?"

"I don't agree with your rules. I think the game will work better if I get to use my own rules."

"Hey," your other friend says, "if *you* get to make up rules, *I* should get to make up rules."

"But I already told you what the rules are!" you say. But it's too late. Your friends aren't listening. They're playing by their own rules. And they're not even having fun. By the end of the afternoon, they've gotten into several fights. When they finally leave, they're not talking to each other or to you!

How would that make you feel? It would be a bummer, wouldn't it? Well, if you can imagine how that might feel, you can imagine how God feels. After all, he created the universe and everything in it. He placed people on this earth and gave them everything they need to live. He even told them the "rules of the game." But some people don't agree with his rules. They think they should be able to make up their own rules. Others try to convince themselves he never gave any rules in the first place. And some just ignore his rules.

But not only are people wrong when they do that, they also cheat themselves. If they'd just play according to the rules, they'd be a lot better off—and they'd have a lot more fun, too. We all would!

 REFLECT: How do you think God feels when people ignore his commands and try to make up their own "rules" for life? Do you think people would be better off (and have more fun) if they lived according to God's commands? Why or why not?

 ACT: Play a game like Monopoly with your family or friends, and imagine what the game would be like if everyone ignored the rules.

 PRAY: "Lord, you're a wonderful God. You welcome those who cheerfully do good, who follow godly ways. Help me to be like that and not like those who ignore or disobey your loving commands."

3 Bad Influences

Bible Reading: Psalm 1:1-6

Blessed is the man who does not walk in the counsel of the wicked or stand in the way of sinners or sit in the seat of mockers. Psalm 1:1, NIV

THERE ONCE WAS a young woman who was being shown around a large coal-mining camp in West Virginia along with a group of businesspeople. All the others on the tour were dressed in jeans and work shirts, while she wore a sparkling white dress.

As the group prepared to enter the rickety old elevator that would take them down a shaft into the underground coal mine, their guide paused and looked at the woman in the white dress.

"Are you sure you want to go down to the mines, ma'am?" he asked her.

The woman looked slightly offended. "Well, why not?"

The man cleared his throat nervously. "You're wearing a white dress," he said.

"Anyone can see that," the woman answered. "There's nothing to prevent me from wearing a white dress into a coal mine if I want to."

The man nodded and shrugged. "Yes, ma'am," he said as he closed the door to the elevator behind her and the others. "But there's plenty to keep you from wearing a white dress *out* of a coal mine."

That man knew that no matter how white her dress was when she went into the coal mine, it wouldn't be white when she came out. Coal mines tend to rub off on a person, and that's not just true of coal mines. It's also true of other things—like habits.

If you're like most kids, you have friends who don't always make right choices. You may even have some friends who almost *never* make right choices. And you may feel like that woman: "There's nothing to prevent me from hanging around with that person if I want to."

And you may be right. There may be nothing wrong with hanging around with that person. After all, you *should* love everyone, even those who often make wrong choices. But remember, habits—like coal dust—tend to rub off on a person. You may enter such a friendship wearing "a white garment" of pure thoughts and good intentions. But your outfit may not stay "white."

The Bible says you're much better off if you do not "walk in the counsel of the wicked or stand in the way of sinners" (Psalm 1:1, NIV). That doesn't mean you should be rude or unkind to friends who seem to make a lot of wrong choices. It simply means that you should stay away from coal mines and bad influences. Why? Because both tend to rub off.

 REFLECT: Do you have any friends who seem to make a lot of wrong choices? Do you think there's a risk that some of those friends' habits might "rub off" on you? If not, why not? Is there anything you can do to limit their influence on you?

 PRAY: "Father, I want to be like the person described in Psalm 1, who doesn't let others influence him to do wrong. Please help me to delight in your law and stay away from people who might have a bad influence on me."

4 Through the Knothole

Bible Reading: Romans 8:28-30

And we know that God causes everything to work together for the good of those who love God and are called according to his purpose for them.
Romans 8:28

NORMAN ROCKWELL WAS a famous twentieth-century American painter. Many of his paintings were originally created for magazine covers, which made Rockwell one of the most famous artists of his time.

One of Rockwell's paintings depicted a little boy watching a baseball game through a knothole in the ballpark fence. The boy presses his eye tightly against the hole, but he can see only straight ahead. He can't see anything to either side of the field, and he's blind to anything that happens close to the fence. The players and umpires on the field and the spectators in the stands can see the whole game. But the boy looking through the knothole can only see a small part of what's going on.

We are like the boy looking through the knothole. Our view of life is like his view of that baseball game. We don't know what good things might happen if we make right choices. We don't know what bad things might happen if we make wrong choices. And sometimes it seems like a right choice might have unpleasant consequences, while a wrong choice seems to be the easiest and best way to handle a situation. But that's because we can't see everything that is going on.

God sees the whole "game." He can see everything that is happening and everything that's *going* to happen. He tells us we'll be better off in the long run if we make right choices and avoid wrong choices. He has the power to work everything together for the good of those who love him and are called according to his purpose for them (Romans 8:28).

So when the wrong choice looks like it's more fun than the right choice, remember that you're like the boy looking through the knothole. When the wrong choice seems so easy and the right choice seems hard, remember that you can't see the whole playing field. When the wrong choice has immediate benefits and the right choice doesn't, remember that God can see everything that is going on. He says you'll be better off in the long run if you make right choices.

So which view do you think you can trust: the view through the knothole or the view of the whole game inside the park?

REFLECT: Do you ever think a wrong choice seems easy and the right choice seems hard? Does it sometimes seem like the wrong choice has immediate benefits and the right choice doesn't? If so, what do you usually do when that happens? Which view do you think you can trust: the view through the knothole (your view) or the view of the whole game (God's view)? If you trust God's view, which choice will you make?

PRAY: "God, I know you can see everything so much better than I can. Please help me to remember that when the wrong choice looks better or easier or more fun than the right choice. I know I can trust you to help me choose the right thing."

5 The Boy in the Mirror

Bible Reading: Ephesians 4:26-32

Don't sin by letting anger gain control over you. Think about it overnight and remain silent. Psalm 4:4

AN OLD CHINESE folktale tells the story of a young boy who had never seen a mirror before. One day while the boy was playing outside, his father brought home a mirror and hung it on the wall of the house. Sometime later, after his father had gone back out to the fields to work, the boy came home.

He saw the mirror on the wall but didn't understand what it was. He looked with fascination at the boy in the mirror. He thought his reflection was a boy who had come to play with him. He waved, and the boy in the mirror waved back. He smiled, and the boy in the mirror smiled back. He said, "Let's play!" and the boy in the mirror said, "Let's play!" at the same time.

When the boy walked out of the hut, he looked around for his new friend. But the boy in the mirror did not follow him outside. He waited, and the boy in the mirror did not come. Finally, he began to get upset. He walked back into the house and saw the boy in the mirror, just where he had left him!

"Why will you not come and play?" he said, and the boy in the mirror spoke the same words he did. Then he began to get really mad. *He is mocking me!* he thought. *He is copying everything I say!* He frowned in anger, and the boy in the mirror frowned back. He lifted his fist, and the boy in the mirror did the same. Finally, he could not control his anger any longer and threw his fist at the face of the boy in the mirror. Instead of hurting the other boy, though, his punch shattered the mirror and sliced his fist into a bloody mess.

That folktale teaches an important lesson. Our anger often hurts us more than the person at whom we're angry. Bitterness, rage, anger, and harsh words usually bring us more pain and hurt than the people we direct them toward. If you nurse a grudge against someone, you're the one whose happiness is most affected. If you hold bitterness in your heart toward someone, you're more likely to lose sleep or get an upset stomach than the other person.

That's one reason God wants us to learn self-control. It is so much better to control our anger instead of letting our anger control us. That doesn't mean that anger is always wrong (it's right to be angry at evil, for example). But it does mean that self-control is always right.

 REFLECT: Do you have trouble controlling your temper? Does your anger ever get out of control? Have you gotten rid of "all bitterness, rage, anger, harsh words, and slander, as well as all types of malicious behavior" (Ephesians 4:31)? If not, are you ready to ask God to help you develop self-control in this area?

 PRAY: "Dear God, please help me by your Holy Spirit's power to control my anger instead of letting my anger control me. Make me kind, tenderhearted, and forgiving toward others, just like you've been toward me."

6 Horse Sense

Bible Reading: 1 Peter 1:13-16

> *Therefore, prepare your minds for action; be self-controlled; set your hope fully on the grace to be given you when Jesus Christ is revealed.*
> 1 Peter 1:13, NIV

HAVE YOU EVER eaten so much you thought you were going to explode? Most of us have (eaten too much, not exploded!). But did you know that for some animals that is a real danger?

For example, horses love oats. If a horse eats his fill of oats, the dry oats tend to make him thirsty. Then, while his stomach is full of dry oats, the horse will start drinking water. The water causes the oats inside his stomach to expand, like a bowl of oatmeal expands when you add water. Before long the horse "founders," and becomes too sick to walk. He may even die if he doesn't get help.

Pretty gruesome, huh? Tell *that* to your mom the next time she tells you to eat all your oatmeal (just don't tell her you read it here!). Seriously, though, here's the point: An appetite that's out of control is a dangerous thing.

Of course, you'd never eat a whole barrel of oats and then drink yourself sick, would you? But you do have appetites that can hurt you if you don't control them.

"Like what?" you ask.

Well, like the desire to be accepted. Like your desire for approval. Like your desire to be loved. Like your desire to get your own way.

Those appetites and desires are not always bad things, but they sure can get you into a lot of trouble if you don't control them. God wants you to learn self-control because your appetites and desires can hurt you, even destroy you, without it.

Many kids steal things because they can't control their desires. Many kids get hooked on alcohol and drugs because they can't control their desires. A lot of kids get into trouble sexually because they can't control their desires.

So listen to what God says. "Be self-controlled" (1 Peter 1:13, NIV). Practice saying no to your appetites and desires. Learn to control them—instead of letting them control you.

REFLECT: Do you have trouble controlling any of these appetites or desires? (Circle any that apply.)

The desire to be accepted	The desire to get my own way
The desire to be loved	My physical appetite (for food)

How can you practice saying no those desires? Have you asked God to help you develop self-control in any of these areas? If not, why not?

PRAY: "Lord, please help me to learn to control my appetites and desires instead of letting them control me. Please make me holy and self-controlled in all I do by your Holy Spirit's power."

7 Phobiaphobia

Bible Reading: Mark 4:35-41

When I am afraid, I will trust in you. Psalm 56:3, NIV

WHAT ARE YOU afraid of? Some people act like they're not afraid of anything. Some act like they're afraid of everything. In fact, there seems to be a name for almost every kind of fear imaginable. The list below contains just a few:

- *Acrophobia:* the fear of heights
- *Agoraphobia:* the fear of open spaces
- *Arachnophobia:* the fear of spiders
- *Claustrophobia:* the fear of small, closed-in spaces
- *Hydrophobia:* the fear of water
- *Mysophobia:* the fear of dirt or germs
- *Nyctophobia:* the fear of darkness
- *Ochlophobia:* the fear of crowds
- *Schoolphobia:* fear of school
- *Triskaidekaphobia:* the fear of the number 13 (oh no, there it is!)

You probably never knew there were so many things to be afraid of, did you? There's even *phobiaphobia,* the fear of fear itself!

Everybody's afraid sometimes. But being self-controlled means learning to control your worries and fears instead of letting them control you. That's easier said than done, of course, but that's what God desires for us. And that's what he's able to do for us.

Jesus can calm your heart and mind, just as he was able to calm the raging Sea of Galilee (see Mark 4:35-41). He is able to quiet your fears and relieve your worries, just as he soothed the disciples fears that night long ago. The psalmist knew the secret of controlling worry and fear, which is why he wrote, "When I am afraid, I will trust in you" (Psalm 56:3, NIV).

That's the secret. Let the presence of God control your fear . . . instead of letting your fear control you.

 REFLECT: How did Jesus' disciples (in today's Bible reading) respond to their fears? How did they respond after Jesus calmed the sea? Are you ever afraid? If so, when are you most afraid? Which do you think is better: to control your fears or be controlled by your fears? Why? How do you think you can control your fears?

 PRAY: "Lord, sometimes I'm afraid or worried, especially when_____. Please teach me to let your presence and power control my fears instead of letting them control me."

8 Bet You Can't Eat Just One!

Bible Reading: 1 Peter 4:7-11

The end of all things is near. Therefore be clear minded and self-controlled so that you can pray. 1 Peter 4:7, NIV

ONE OF THE most famous advertising slogans of all time was a phrase invented for Lay's Potato Chips: "Bet you can't eat just one!" Six short words. Each word just one syllable.

The idea, of course, was that Lay's Potato Chips were so delicious, so crunchy, so addicting, that once you ate one, you'd have to eat another . . . and another . . . and another. It was a whole ad campaign about self-control.

But there are people in this world who *can* eat just one. There are people who have enough self-control to resist a second Lay's Potato Chip, no matter how tasty it is. Not only that, there are people in this world who have enough self-control to resist even greater temptations. There are people who show self-control in the way they eat, the way they exercise, the way they study, speak, or work. Maybe you even know some of those people. Chances are, if you know them, you also admire them.

You know what else? God feels the same way. God admires self-control. He *values* it. He thinks self-control is pretty cool.

As a matter of fact, that's why God commands self-control. His Word doesn't say, "Be clear minded and self-controlled" because he had a report due for school and had to think of *something* to write. He doesn't command us to control our anger, our appetites, desires, and fears just because he likes the sound of his own voice. No, he commands those things because he *values* self-control. And if God values self-control, shouldn't we?

Shouldn't you?

 REFLECT: Do you admire anyone for his or her self-control? If so, whom? Do you think self-control is a good thing? If not, why not? If so, why? Do you need to develop self- control in any area of your life? If so, what areas? How can you practice self-control in those areas? Have you asked God for help? If not, why not? If so, do you trust him to help you?

 ACT: Share a small bag of Lay's Potato Chips with a friend or family member, and ask that person to pray for and encourage you in your efforts to develop self-control.

 PRAY: "Lord, I do want to be clear minded and self-controlled, especially in the area of_____ [my thought life, my appetites, my desires, etc.]. Please help me to rely every day on the strength you provide."

9 On the Road

Bible Reading: Luke 9:51-56

The Lord is slow to anger and rich in unfailing love, forgiving every kind of sin and rebellion. Numbers 14:18

YOU KNOW HOW you feel when you're really tired.

The disciples had been walking all over the countryside with Jesus, feeding thousands of people, watching Jesus meet Moses and Elijah, healing a demon-possessed boy. It had been a really busy week.

So when the people of a Samaritan village claimed there was no room *anywhere* in the whole village for them to stay, the disciples got kind of huffy.

"Lord, should we call down fire from heaven to burn them up?" James and John suggested. None of them really like the Samaritans anyway. (Samaria High School had been their bitter rival in the state championships for years.)

"Yeah!" someone else agreed. "Let's vap-o-rize them!"

Jesus didn't say anything. The expression on his face made it clear that if he was going to vaporize anyone, his vengeful disciples would be first. Then he turned around again and walked down the road toward the next village.

After a few moments passed, John slapped his brother, James, on the shoulder. "Call down fire!" he said in a disgusted tone of voice. "What a stupid idea."

"Hey!" James answered indignantly. *"You're* the one who said it."

"Did not!" John said.

"Did too!" his brother insisted.

Well, OK, so maybe it didn't happen exactly that way, but it's not that far off. (See today's Bible reading, Luke 9:51-56, for the real story.) This much is true, though: The disciples had an accurate idea of Jesus' power—he *could have* "vaporized" that Samaritan village. But they had an inaccurate understanding of Jesus' self-control—he controlled his power (and maybe even his desire) to destroy that village.

That story illustrates the fact that God not only commands self-control because he values it, but he also values self-control because he *is* self-controlled. God isn't controlled by his emotions. He's not controlled by outside influences. He's not controlled by circumstances. He is *self*-controlled.

You and I should be happy about that. Were it not for the Lord's self-control, *we* might have been vaporized long ago! We should also be grateful because God's self-control helps us to know that self-control is right—even when we're tempted to vaporize a village.

 REFLECT: What makes self-control right? Can you think of any other instances in which God exercised self-control? Do you think he sometimes exercises self-control with you? If so, describe that experience. Do you think he can help you exercise self-control? If so, how?

 PRAY: "God, please help me to become more like you in every way, especially in showing more self-control."

10 Pete's Feats

Bible Reading: 1 Corinthians 9:24-27

All athletes practice strict self-control. They do it to win a prize that will fade away, but we do it for an eternal prize. 1 Corinthians 9:25

PETE WAS SEVEN years old when his dad sat him down for a talk.

"Pete," he said, "if you'll listen to me, if you'll let me teach you the game of basketball, you may be able to get a scholarship someday. If you get a scholarship, you'll be able to get an education. Not only that," his dad continued, "if you're good enough, if you'll listen to me and work and commit yourself to basketball, maybe you'll end up on the pro level. Maybe you could play in the NBA. And Pete, if you play in the NBA, they'll *pay* you to play basketball."

At that time—at the age of seven—Pete had already been playing basketball for three years. But from that moment on, he became serious about the game. He played six to ten hours a day during the summertime. When everyone else was out playing or swimming with friends, Pete was in the gym, shooting baskets by himself. He would get up every morning and jog two miles into Clemson, South Carolina, dribbling a basketball beside him as he ran. At seven o'clock that evening, he'd dribble the basketball all the way home. When he got his first bicycle, he learned how to dribble the ball beside the bike as he rode.

As a result of those years of self-control and dedication, "Pistol" Pete Maravich got a scholarship to college. He became the all-time leading scorer in the history of college basketball, setting sixty records in the NCAA. He also became one of the greatest pro basketball players of all time, a five-time NBA all-star who was elected to the Basketball Hall of Fame in 1987.

Now, not everyone can be a Pete Maravich. But you don't have to be Pete Maravich to discover that self-control has a lot of benefits. It can make you a better athlete. It can make you a better student. It can make you a better listener, a better painter, a better saxophone player. It can make you a better friend. It can make you a better person.

Self-control won't save you from sin; only Jesus can do that. It won't get you to heaven; only Jesus can do that. But learning to be self-controlled *can* help you to resist temptation. It can help you to make right choices. And that can win for you a prize that will never fade away.

 REFLECT: In today's Bible reading, Paul mentions two kinds of prizes people might get when they exercise self-control. What are they? Is one bad and the other good? Or is one good and the other better? Have you enjoyed any benefits of self-control in your life? If so, what benefits have you received?

 PRAY: "Jesus, thank you for your power in my life. Thank you for helping me to become more self-controlled as I trust in you."

11 The Incredible Shrinking Caterpillar

Bible Reading: Proverbs 25:26-28

A person without self-control is as defenseless as a city with broken-down walls. Proverbs 25:28

ANNIE DILLARD, IN her book *Pilgrim at Tinker Creek,* talks about a strange habit some caterpillars have. Now caterpillars do something called "molting." They shed the hard shell-like skin that covers their heads and bodies. After molting, their bodies immediately get bigger, and they grow another outer skin. As they continue to eat and grow, they'll continue to shed their skin as many as twelve times—sometimes even more.

Sometimes, though, when a caterpillar doesn't get enough food, it will go into a "molting frenzy." It begins molting over and over again, changing its skin many times, getting smaller and smaller with every change. This process, says Dillard, "could, in imagination, extend to infinity, as the creature frantically shrinks and shrinks and shrinks to the size of a molecule, then an electron, but never can shrink to absolute nothing and end its terrible hunger."

That doesn't happen, of course. Eventually, the caterpillar stops molting and dies.

That "incredible shrinking caterpillar" is a perfect picture of what can happen without self-control. Caterpillars have to molt. In fact, molting is a good thing for a caterpillar. But when the process gets out of control, it can destroy the little creature.

That's what a lack of self-control can do to people, too. A lack of self-control can turn harmless (even healthy) things into harmful things. For example, you need food in order to stay healthy. But if you constantly eat too much food, it can be harmful.

Or, to use another example, exercise is a good thing. Your body needs exercise. But if your desire to be healthy, strong, and thin gets out of control, you can actually hurt yourself with exercise and dieting.

The Bible puts it like this: "A person without self-control is as defenseless as a city with broken-down walls" (Proverbs 25:28). God desires for us to be self-controlled because he knows that it can make us healthier and happier, safer and stronger. Because he loves us, his commands to "be self-controlled" (1 Peter 1:13; 4:7; 5:8) are intended to help us live a happier, healthier, and more fulfilling life.

 REFLECT: Do you ever feel like an "incredible shrinking caterpillar"? Do you ever feel like something in your life is out of control? If so, do you ever talk to somebody about it? Why or why not? Do you think it would help to talk to somebody when you feel that way? Do you think it would help to talk to God? to your parents? to a friend? to a pastor? If so, why not make plans to do so?

 PRAY: "Lord, sometimes I do feel 'as defenseless as a city with broken-down walls.' But I really want to learn self-control from you so you can make me healthier, happier, safer, and stronger. Please show me the areas where I most need your loving attention."

12 Road to Respect

Bible Reading: Titus 2:11-14

We should live in this evil world with self-control, right conduct, and devotion to God. Titus 2:12

WHICH CHARACTER DO you respect and admire more: Pinky or the Brain? Ren or Stimpy? Roadrunner or Wile E. Coyote? That's kind of a dumb question, isn't it? After all, they're just cartoon characters. Who ever thought of respecting or admiring cartoon characters? OK, then, think about these questions instead:

Which person do you respect and admire more:

- someone who shrugs it off when another kid bumps into him or her in the school hallway?
- someone who starts yelling and screaming, threatening to call the police, the state highway patrol, and the FBI when another kid bumps into him or her in the school hallway?

Which kind of person do you respect and admire more:

- a person who begins crying uncontrollably (and sucking his or her thumb) when he or she gets a C on a test?
- a person who calmly asks the teacher how to do better next time?

Which kid do you respect and admire more:

- the kid who says, "No thanks, I don't drink," when he's offered a can of beer?
- the kid who takes the beer when it's offered and keeps drinking until he's sloppy drunk and silly?

How did you answer those questions? In each case, you probably said you would respect and admire the person who displayed self-control, right? That's only natural. After all, self-control tends to win the esteem and respect of others. People who don't have self-control may sometimes be accepted, feared, or even liked—but they are seldom respected and admired.

That's why God wants us to be self-controlled. He knows what we sometimes forget: Self-control wins the respect and admiration of others.

 REFLECT: Can you think of situations when someone earned your respect by displaying self-control? Can you think of a time when you earned someone else's respect by displaying self-control? Do you think God can produce more self-control in you and in your life? If not, why not? If so, how?

 PRAY: "Father, I know that self-control is right and that you will bless me if I obey you. Help me to live in this evil world with self-control, right conduct, and devotion to you."

13 Hand and Glove

Bible Reading: Romans 8:5-14

But you are not controlled by your sinful nature. You are controlled by the Spirit if you have the Spirit of God living in you. Romans 8:9

A GLOVE IS a wonderful thing. You've probably never thought much about it, but a glove can perform all kinds of tasks. It can turn a doorknob or roll down a car window. It can wave good-bye to a friend or applaud a dazzling football play. It can pat someone on the back or smack someone in the face. It can point. It can give a "thumbs up" sign.

"Wait a minute," you say. "Time out! A glove can't do all that; it's the hand inside the glove that does all those things."

Well, yes. And that's the point. A glove can only perform a task if there's a hand inside it. Otherwise, all it can do is lie there motionless. That's because *the ability the glove possesses comes from whatever fills the glove.*

It is exactly the same with you.

You may really, really want to be more self-controlled. You may want to control your anger, your appetite, your desires, or your fears. But no matter how badly you want self-control, you can't make it happen. Oh, you may improve a little bit, for a while. But no matter how hard you try, you won't develop true self-control by yourself. Because self-control, like all virtues, comes from God.

In other words, your ability to exercise self-control depends on whatever–or whoever–fills you. "That's why," the Bible says, "those who are still under the control of their sinful nature can never please God. But you are not controlled by your sinful nature. You are controlled by the Spirit if you have the Spirit of God living in you" (Romans 8:8-9).

So if you are a Christian, the power to be self-controlled is already living in you–the Holy Spirit. The key, then, is not to grunt and groan and grit your teeth but to surrender to the Spirit's control day by day and moment by moment–just like a glove "surrenders" to the hand that wears it and controls it.

 REFLECT: You already have God's Spirit living in you if you've received forgiveness of your sins and trusted Jesus for salvation. Have you done that? If not, you can do it now by praying this simple prayer: "Lord Jesus, I want to know you personally. Thank you for dying on the cross for my sins. I open the door of my life and receive you as my Savior and Lord. Thank you for forgiving my sins and giving me eternal life. Take control of my life and make me the kind of person you want me to be. Amen."

 PRAY: One way to surrender to the Spirit's control is to sincerely pray a simple prayer every morning, like the following: "God, I want to do right today, but I know I'll need your help. I give up control of the things I do to your Holy Spirit right now, and I ask him to control me all day long. Please help me not to forget or to 'take back' control."

14 Sales Pitch

Bible Reading: Ephesians 5:10-16

Take no part in the worthless deeds of evil and darkness. Ephesians 5:11

YOU'RE MINDING YOUR own business, walking around the mall, when all of a sudden a greasy-haired man in a long coat comes up to you.

"Psst!" he hisses. "Want a great deal?" You try to ignore him and walk by, but he steps in front of you and opens one side of his coat. "I got over seventeen varieties of broken watches here," he says, smiling and wagging his eyebrows.

You look at the watches. "Did you say *broken* watches?" you ask. You see him nod. "Why would I want a broken watch? I want a watch that keeps time!"

You start to step around him, but he quickly shuffles to block your way. "Wait a minute," he says, looking around as if he's letting you in on an even bigger secret than broken watches. "That's not all I've got." He pulls an envelope out of his pocket and shakes an assortment of postage stamps into his open palm. "I got canceled stamps, too. All kinds!"

He shows you the stamps. You think, *This dude's elevator doesn't go to the top floor.*

"Look," you say patiently, "I'm not interested in broken watches or canceled stamps, OK? What you're selling is worthless. So if you'll excuse me . . ." You walk around him, and as you walk away, you notice him approaching somebody new.

That would be a pretty weird experience, wouldn't it? But it's actually pretty common. Oh, you may not meet a guy selling broken watches in the mall, but every day the devil tries to sell you something worthless. He tries to convince you to lie, steal, cheat, or do other things that are even more worthless than broken watches or canceled stamps.

Of course, the devil makes those things look attractive. But no matter how much you shine up a broken watch, it's still broken. And the deeds of evil and darkness may look like they'll bring you fun and fulfillment, but in the end you'll discover—over and over again—that nothing good ever comes of sin. It's always worthless.

So the next time the devil tries to sell you something worthless, remember to "take no part in the worthless deeds of evil and darkness; instead, rebuke and expose them." And "be careful how you live, not as fools but as those who are wise" (Ephesians 5:11, 15).

 REFLECT: Can you think of a time when a wrong choice paid off *and* made you a better person? Can you think of a time when a wrong choice brought you closer to God? Can you think of a time when a wrong choice made you feel good about yourself? What will you plan to do the next time the devil tries to sell you something worthless?

 ACT: Tack a worthless item—a broken watch, a canceled stamp, an empty gum wrapper—to your bulletin board or school locker door to remind you not to take part in "the worthless deeds of evil and darkness."

 PRAY: "God, help me to remember that the deeds of evil and darkness are worthless. Help me not to take part in them but to live 'as those who are wise.'"

15 Right and Wrong in 3-D

Bible Reading: Psalm 119:129-133

> *Guide my steps by your word, so I will not be overcome by any evil.*
> *Psalm 119:133*

HAVE YOU EVER seen a 3-D picture or—better yet—a 3-D movie?

You know that you put on a pair of glasses with plastic or paper frames to watch a 3-D movie. Watching the movie through the glasses makes the movie screen seem three-dimensional, like real life. Not only that, sometimes things seem to "leap out" of the movie screen, right for your face! A train may race across the screen and seem as though it's coming right out of the movie—and into your lap! A bird may be flying around, when suddenly it turns and seems to head straight for your nose! A ball may be thrown by someone in the movie, and it looks as though all you have to do is hold your hands up to catch it!

If you take the 3-D glasses off, of course, all you see is a flat—even slightly blurry—movie screen. The glasses bring the action alive. Without them, you lose the whole effect.

That's sort of how reading God's Word works for those who want to know right from wrong. Reading the Bible brings the action to life.

That's because the Bible acts as a pair of 3-D glasses that make it easier to see and to know right from wrong. If you read the Bible every day, you'll soon start to see things much more clearly than you would otherwise. If you don't read the Bible regularly, you'll probably still struggle to figure out right from wrong.

That's why the psalmist prayed to God, "Your decrees are wonderful. No wonder I obey them! As your words are taught, they give light; even the simple can understand them. . . . Guide my steps by your word, so I will not be overcome by any evil" (Psalm 119:129-130, 133).

If you really want to know right from wrong—if you really want to make right choices—read the Bible. It brings the real action to life.

 REFLECT: Do you think you can make right choices consistently without knowing what's right? Why or why not? Do you think you can know what's right without knowing what the Bible says about right and wrong? Why or why not? Do you think reading the Bible can help you make right choices? If not, why not? If so, how?

 ACT: If you've never developed the habit of reading the Bible every day, you can start by looking up the daily Bible readings in this devotional and reading them through at least once. That's a good start!

 PRAY: "Lord, help me to read your Word. Guide my steps by your Word so that I will not be overcome by any evil."

16 The Vision

Bible Reading: Colossians 3:12-13

Forgive as quickly and completely as the Master forgave you.
Colossians 3:13, The Message

A STORY IS told of a woman who went to her priest. "I keep having this vision," she said. "But I don't know whether it's real or not. I don't know whether to believe it or to have my head examined."

"Tell me about it," the priest suggested.

"Well, in this vision," the woman explained, "Jesus appears to me, just as real as you are right now. And he speaks to me, just like you're speaking to me. He tells me things."

"What things?" the priest asked, his brow wrinkling.

"He tells me that he loves me," she answered. "He tells me that he hears my prayers and that he loves it when I spend time with him."

"I see," the priest said.

"Is there any way to know whether my visions are real?" the woman asked.

"I'll tell you what," the priest answered. "The next time our Lord appears to you in a vision, ask him to tell you what sins I confessed to him that morning. Then when he tells you, come to see me, and we will know whether it is really the Lord."

The woman agreed to the plan and returned to her home. The very next morning she appeared on the priest's doorstep.

The priest seemed surprised to see her. "So," he said, "did you ask our Lord what sins I confessed to him this morning?"

The woman bowed her head and nodded.

"And what did he say?"

The woman raised her eyes to look at the priest. "He said, 'I have forgotten!'"

The priest laid a hand on the woman's shoulder and smiled. "It *is* the Lord!" he said.

That story may or may not be true. But the point of the story is true: Jesus forgives us so completely that, although he knows everything, he forgets our sins once he has forgiven them! And he says *that* is how we ought to forgive each other.

The Bible says, "Forgive as quickly and completely as the Master forgave you" (Colossians 3:13, *The Message*). We know that forgiveness is right not only because God commands us to forgive but also because God has forgiven us. So we should forgive each other—quickly and completely.

REFLECT: Why is it right to forgive others? According to today's Bible reading, *how* should we forgive others? Is there anyone *you* need to forgive today? If so, why not do it now? Is there anyone you need to ask for forgiveness? If so, why not do it now?

PRAY: "Lord, thank you for forgiving and forgetting my sins. Please help me to do what is right and forgive others as quickly and completely as you have forgiven me."

17 The New Kid in School

Bible Reading: Ecclesiastes 12:1, 13-14

Fear God and obey his commands, for this is the duty of every person.
Ecclesiastes 12:13

"HEY," YOUR BEST friend calls to you. "I want you to meet somebody." When you walk over, he says, "This is Jay Hovah. He's new in school." He nods to the person standing beside him.

You smile and nod at the new kid. "How ya doing?" you say. The new kid nods back.

Your friend slaps the new kid on the back. "You should see what this guy can do. He can do five hundred sit-ups—without stopping!"

"Five hundred sit-ups?" you respond. Jay shrugs as if it's no big deal.

"And," your friend continues, "he can bench-press three hundred pounds!"

"Get outta here!" you answer. Jay just smiles and shrugs again. You start to pay less attention to your friend and more attention to this Jay guy.

"He can jump over seven feet in the air from a standing position."

"Oh, come on," you say, "I don't believe tha—" Suddenly the new kid leaps straight up in the air and over your head, landing behind you. You turn around and look at him with undisguised respect.

Your friend leans over and whispers in your ear. "Did I mention he can also control the forces of nature and make dead people come to life?"

Well, of course, that would have been a dead giveaway, right? Only one person could do all those things. The new student at school would have to be God!

That probably won't happen, though. But imagine if you did meet a "new kid" who could do all those things. How would you respond? You'd probably really respect and admire that kid, wouldn't you? After all, anyone who can do five hundred sit-ups and bench-press three hundred pounds is pretty impressive, right?

Well, if that's true, God is much more worthy of your respect. He not only can do all those things but also can control the forces of nature and make dead people come back to life. He can create something out of nothing. He can heal diseases. He can answer prayer. He can destroy nations and create entire solar systems.

But more important, he created you. And, if you're a Christian, he saved you from the punishment your sins deserved. And he is preparing you to live forever in eternity. For those and many, many other reasons, God deserves your respect.

That's why it's right to respect God. In fact, respect for God is the basis of all respect—and of all righteousness. As King Solomon once said, "Fear God and obey his commands, for this is the duty of every person" (Ecclesiastes 12:13).

 REFLECT: Do you think God deserves your respect? Why or why not? Do you respect God? If a private investigator was looking for evidence that you respect God, what evidence would he or she find? How can you show respect for God today?

 PRAY: "God, you are holy and perfect, and you deserve my respect and worship. Please help me to show how much I respect you in everything I do today."

18 Jesus in Jeopardy

Bible Reading: Luke 2:41-52

Jesus returned to Nazareth with [his parents] and was obedient to them.
Luke 2:51

DO YOU THINK Jesus ever got into trouble with his parents? Yup, he sure did. Today's Bible reading (Luke 2:41-52) is a recorded example of how Jesus got into "hot water" with his parents when he was twelve years old.

Did Jesus ever disobey his parents? No, because the Bible says Jesus never did wrong (1 Peter 2:22), and it would have been wrong for him to disobey his parents.

Do you think it was easy for Jesus to obey his parents? After all, think about it. Jesus was God! The whole *universe* had been formed by him (Colossians 1:16). He commanded heaven's angels (Matthew 13:41; 16:27). And he apparently knew, at a very early age, that he had been sent by his Father to do something special (see Luke 2:49). It might have been hard at times for the Lord of the universe to submit to everything his carpenter dad and peasant mom said. Yet, according to the Bible, that's exactly what Jesus did. He always treated his parents with loving obedience and respect (Luke 2:51; John 19:26-27).

That's one of the ways you can know that respect for your parents is right. Of course, it shouldn't be hard to figure out, because the Bible says pretty clearly, "Honor your father and mother" (Exodus 20:12) and "Children, obey your parents because you belong to the Lord, for this is the right thing to do" (Ephesians 6:1). But respect for your parents is not only right because God commands it, it's right because Jesus respected his parents. Being respectful is being like God himself.

It's pretty safe to say that you'll still get in trouble with your parents from time to time; even Jesus did! But make it your goal to obey and respect your parents like Jesus did. That will certainly please God—and might just amaze your parents!

 REFLECT: Is it right to show respect for your parents? Why or why not? Do you think it was hard for Jesus to obey and respect his parents? Why or why not? Do you think it's hard for you to obey and respect your parents? Why or why not? Do you show respect for your parents? If not, why not? If so, how?

 PRAY: "Jesus, help me to please you by showing respect for my parents the way you respected and obeyed your parents."

19 Take a Bow

Bible Reading: 1 Timothy 5:1-2

Show your fear of God by standing up in the presence of elderly people and showing respect for the aged. I am the Lord. Leviticus 19:32

WHEN YOU SEE a friend, you might wave and say, "Hi." Or you might exchange high fives or low fives with a friend or group of friends. If you're meeting someone for the first time, you might shake that person's hand. If you're greeting your grandmother or your Aunt Zelda, you might even exchange hugs.

In Japan, however, people usually greet each other differently. Maybe you've seen several Japanese people meet and greet each other. They don't wave. They don't shake hands. They don't exchange high fives. They don't hug. They bow.

Sometimes they bow once; sometimes they bow several times. Sometimes they bow slightly, and sometimes they bow deeply. How many times they bow and how deeply they bow depend on a lot of things. One of the things that determines how low and how many times a person bows is how much older the other person is. In the Japanese culture, an older person deserves more respect, and so a young man greeting an elderly man will show his respect by the way he bows.

Now you don't have to start bowing to your parents or grandparents. But you could take a few hints from the Japanese. You see, many people in our world don't respect their elders. They think their parents and grandparents don't know anything. They think that only young, pretty people are worthwhile. They think elderly people aren't as smart or as important or as valuable as young people. But the Japanese don't think so. And neither does God.

God commands all of us (not just the Japanese!) to treat older people with respect. He says that we should show respect for him "by standing up in the presence of elderly people and showing respect for the aged" (Leviticus 19:32).

God's Word makes it clear that respect for our elders is right. It's right to treat older people respectfully. Paul told Timothy, "Never speak harshly to an older man, but appeal to him respectfully as though he were your own father." He also said, "Treat the older women as you would your mother" (1 Timothy 5:1-2). Because respect for your elders is right—even if you're not Japanese.

REFLECT: Do you think it's right to show respect for your elders? If so, why? Who are your elders? How can you show respect for them?

ACT: Surprise your parents, guardians, or grandparents today by greeting them with a low bow to show your respect for them. (You might want to have some smelling salts handy; they may faint from the shock!)

PRAY: "Father, I know that respect for my elders is right and that your Word even says that showing respect for the elderly is one way of showing respect for you. So please remind me to obey your Word and show my respect for you by showing respect for my elders."

20 David and the Finkelsteins

Bible Reading: Titus 3:1-8

Remind the people to be subject to rulers and authorities, to be obedient, to be ready to do whatever is good. Titus 3:1, NIV

ANN LANDERS HAS written a newspaper column giving advice and information for over forty years. During that time, readers have often written her to share interesting statements kids and others have made about the Bible, like those listed below:

- "Noah's wife was Joan of Ark."
- "Lot's wife was a pillar of salt by day and a ball of fire by night."
- "Moses went to the top of Mount Cyanide to get the Ten Commandments."
- "Joshua led the Hebrews in the Battle of Geritol."
- "The people who followed Jesus were called the 'Twelve Decibels.'"
- "The epistles were the wives of the apostles."
- "David fought the Finkelsteins, a race of people who lived in biblical times."
- "A Christian should have only one wife. This is called *monotony.*"

As you can see, each of those statements is sort of close to the truth. But each one is wrong because it's based on a misunderstanding. Moses got the Ten Commandments on Mount *Sinai,* not Mount Cyanide. Joshua fought the battle of *Jericho.* David fought the *Philistines,* not the Finkelsteins. Having only one wife is called *monogamy.*

Those kids just got the wrong idea, that's all. And many of us have also gotten a wrong idea when it comes to respecting those who are in positions of authority over us.

You see, a lot of us think that people in authority (police, teachers, presidents, church leaders, and so on) should *earn* our respect. When we get a new teacher, or pastor, or president, we tend to withhold our respect until he or she earns it, until he or she *makes* us respect him or her. But according to the Bible, we should do just the opposite.

The Bible says that we should give respect and obedience to those who are in authority over us. They don't have to earn our respect—we owe it to them; they only have to lose it. There are times when Christians must protest or resist people in authority (see Acts 5:17-42). But unless obeying those authorities would mean disobeying God, God's Word is clear: Respecting and obeying those in authority is right.

REFLECT: In the space below, list ways you can show respect for:

teachers _____

elders _____

police _____

government officials _____

pastors _____

others (specify) _____

PRAY: "Lord, I do want to please you and obey you. Please remind me to show respect for rulers and authorities, to be obedient, and to be ready to do whatever is good."

21 Finger Snappers and Ear Wigglers

Bible Reading: 1 Peter 2:12-17

Show respect for everyone. Love your Christian brothers and sisters. Fear God. Show respect for the king. 1 Peter 2:17

CAN YOU SNAP your fingers? Can you wiggle your ears (without using your hands, of course)? Can you touch your nose with your tongue?

If you can do either of the last two, you're a member of a minority. A recent survey conducted in the United States discovered that 68 percent of people could snap their fingers, but only 13 percent were able to wiggle their ears. And an even smaller group—a mere 10 percent!—could touch their noses with their tongues.

Now, imagine that all those people who could snap their fingers decided to ridicule and disrespect the other 32 percent. Or imagine that "ear wigglers" decided to treat "non-ear wigglers" like second-class citizens. Or imagine that those who could touch their noses with their tongues felt that they could never respect people who couldn't touch their noses with their tongues.

That would be pretty weird, wouldn't it?

But when you think about it, it's not so different from people who disrespect other people because they're a different color. It's not so different from men who don't respect women (or vice versa). It's not so different from people who look down on old people (or kids).

You see, God's Word says, "Show proper respect to everyone" (1 Peter 2:17, NIV). That means that even people who are different from you deserve your respect, whether they're black or white, Asian or Hispanic, male or female, young or old, rich or poor, finger snappers or ear wigglers.

After all, God doesn't say, "Show proper respect to people who are like you." He says, "Show proper respect to *everyone*"—even to people who *can't* touch their noses with their tongues.

 REFLECT: Today's Bible reading says to fear or respect (or accept) several different kinds of people. Can you find at least four? Has anyone ever shown disrespect for you because of your skin color, sex, or age? How about for some other reason? How did it feel? Have you ever shown disrespect to someone for any of those reasons?

 ACT: Take your own poll to see how many of your friends can snap their fingers, wiggle their ears, and touch their noses with their tongues. Compare your findings with the results (68 percent, 13 percent, 10 percent) mentioned above.

 PRAY: "God, sometimes I do only show proper respect to people who are like me. Please help me to show proper respect to everyone, just like you command me to do."

22 A Good Ga-hoo to You

Bible Reading: 1 John 3:1-2

See how very much our heavenly Father loves us, for he allows us to be called his children, and we really are! 1 John 3:1

BACK IN THE 1970s a singing group called the Staples Singers scored a hit with a song written by Luther Ingram and Mack Rice. More recently, the Christian group Big Tent Revival has recorded the song on their debut CD.

The song is called "Respect Yourself," and it contains the message "If you don't respect yourself, / Ain't nobody gonna give a good ga-hoo!"

Now, you may ask, "What is 'a good ga-hoo'?" Good question. Don't know. Don't even know what a *bad* ga-hoo would be. But that's not the point.

The point is, the message of Ingram and Rice's song is a good one. It's even biblical. According to the Bible, respecting yourself is right.

After all, the Bible says, "See how very much our heavenly Father loves us, for he allows us to be called his children, and we really are! But the people who belong to this world don't know God, so they don't understand that we are his children. Yes, dear friends, we are already God's children, and we can't even imagine what we will be like when Christ returns. But we do know that when he comes we will be like him, for we will see him as he really is" (1 John 3:1-2).

Those verses mention several good reasons for respecting yourself. First, in addition to being created by God, you are his child! Not only that, when Christ returns, you will be made like him in ways that will blow your mind! Now, that doesn't mean that you should forget that you're a sinner (like everyone else) or that you should become proud or think you're better than anyone else. It simply means that you should respect yourself, for two reasons: because of *what you are* and because of *what you are becoming!*

So do what songwriters Ingram and Rice say: Respect yourself. But don't do it just because they say so; do it because God's Word says that respect for yourself is right.

 REFLECT: What two reasons does today's Bible reading give for respecting yourself? Do you respect yourself? If so, in what ways? If not, how would your words and behavior change if you started respecting yourself? How can you show more respect for yourself in the future?

 ACT: The next time you're in a Christian bookstore, ask to listen to Big Tent Revival's arrangement of "Respect Yourself" (on their *Big Tent Revival* CD).

 PRAY: "Father, respecting myself might be harder sometimes than respecting others. But I thank you that I'm your child and that when your Son returns, I will be like him. Help me to talk about and treat myself as a child of God who is being changed into the image of your Son."

23 Image Is Everything

Bible Reading: Genesis 1:26-31

So God created people in his own image; God patterned them after himself; male and female he created them. Genesis 1:27

IMAGINE WHAT IT would feel like if your town erected a statue of you in the middle of the town square or in front of city hall, then used your statue as a target, throwing rotten tomatoes and apples at your image!

Imagine what it would feel like to be the president of your own company, with a huge oil painting of yourself hanging in the company's fancy lobby—and then to discover that someone had drawn a silly mustache on your face in the painting!

Imagine what it would feel like if your picture were printed in *People* magazine's annual "Fifty Most Beautiful People" issue; but, when you went to the store to buy as many copies as you could, you discovered that someone had gone through every single issue and written in bold, black marker, "This is an ugly picture!" across your photo.

How would such things make you feel? Sad? Angry? Hurt?

But now, wait a minute. Remember that those people aren't attacking you—they're only attacking *your image*. The statue, the painting, the photo—those were just things that were made in your image, right? But it would still hurt, wouldn't it? When someone attacks, insults, or disrespects something made in your image, it's just like they were doing it to you, right?

Well, then, if you can understand that, imagine how God feels when people attack, insult, or disrespect other people. After all, every human being in the world is made in God's image. Every man and woman has been created in the image of God. So don't you think it makes God sad, angry, or hurt when we don't respect others who bear his image?

You see, that's why respect is right and disrespect is wrong—because we were all made in the image of God. Every human being is made in God's image, whether he or she is old or young, dark-skinned or light-skinned, male or female, able or disabled, sick or well, cool or uncool. Every human being is valuable in God's eyes. And every human being deserves to be respected as a unique and valuable child of God.

 REFLECT: What does today's Bible reading say about human beings? Why is respect for others right? Do you know any person who isn't made in the image of God? Do you know any person who doesn't deserve to be respected as a unique and valuable child of God? Do you think you can respect a person without agreeing with his or her behavior? If so, how? How can you show respect for every human being you meet today?

 PRAY: "God, thank you for reminding me that I am made in your image, just like everybody else in the world. Help me to respect and treat other people the way I should."

24 Chip and Dale

Bible Reading: Romans 12:9-10

Take delight in honoring each other. Romans 12:10

CHIP AND DALE are two cartoon chipmunks.

They're cute, lovable little fellows. They giggle. They scamper. They get into trouble. They get mad at each other. They make up. They're the best of friends.

When you notice how they sometimes behave toward each other, you know why they seem so close.

Have you ever seen them enter a doorway? Chip will stand aside and say something like, "After you."

Dale will smile and answer, "Oh no, I insist. You first."

"Oh no no no no no," Chip will say with a dramatic bow. "You first."

And so it goes, each one seeming to take delight in honoring the other.

We should all be more like Chip and Dale. For several reasons. First, because the Bible says we should be like Chip and Dale. Not in so many words, of course; the Bible was written long before cartoons were invented. But the Bible does say, "Show respect for everyone" (1 Peter 2:17) and "Take delight in honoring each other" (Romans 12:10).

But there's another reason too: Respect encourages healthy relationships. If Chip and Dale weren't so respectful, they probably wouldn't be such lovable creatures. If they didn't treat each other with kindness and respect, they probably wouldn't get along so well.

Think about it. Who would you choose to hang around with: someone who calls you names or someone who is polite to you? Who would you want to spend more time with: someone who treats you like dirt or someone who treats you with respect? Who would you want to be your friend: someone who insists on going first every time or someone who stands aside and says, "After you"?

Most friendships won't last very long without respect because respect is an important ingredient of a good relationship. Respect helps to build strong, healthy relationships; disrespect usually destroys relationships.

So take a lesson from Chip and Dale and from the Bible: "Take delight in honoring each other" (Romans 12:10).

 REFLECT: Do you like being around people who treat you disrespectfully? Why or why not? Do you have any "friends" who treat you disrespectfully? Do you treat any of your friends disrespectfully? Why or why not? Do you want respect to be an ingredient in your friendships? If so, how can you make that happen?

 PRAY: "Lord, I want to treat all my friends and family with respect. Help me to change the way I've been treating_____ and to make respect an ingredient of all my friendships."

25 The Traveler and the Monks

Bible Reading: Matthew 5:14-16

Be careful how you live among your unbelieving neighbors. Even if they accuse you of doing wrong, they will see your honorable behavior, and they will believe and give honor to God. 1 Peter 2:12

THE STORY IS told of a mysterious traveler who once visited an old, run-down monastery. At one time the monastery had thrived; it was known for the devotion of its monks. Young men came from far and wide to join the monastery.

At the time of the traveler's visit, however, all that had changed. Only a handful of monks remained, and they could hardly stand each other. The once-spotless buildings had begun to fall down, and the worship of the monks was uninspired.

The monks told the traveler the dismal story of their monastery. They begged the traveler to stay and help them rebuild, for if something was not done, the monks and monastery would soon die. But he refused. "I cannot help you to rebuild your monastery or restore hope to your order. All I can do is to tell you that one of you is a true apostle of God." And with that, the mysterious traveler left.

The monks were amazed at the traveler's words, and each one began to secretly ponder their meaning. *Could it be?* each thought. *Could one of us actually be a true apostle of God? Could it be the abbot? If not the abbot, who? Perhaps Brother Phillip. Or Brother Thaddeus? Or perhaps . . . perhaps even . . . even me?*

Little by little that old monastery began to change. The monks began to treat each other with new respect, not knowing which of them was a true apostle. In fact, each monk even began to treat himself differently, not knowing if *he* were the one of whom the traveler had spoken. Over the course of time, the monks began to repair the monastery's decaying buildings, to make them suitable as a home of a true apostle of God. Their worship became charged with passion and praise; after all, they knew that a true apostle of God was worshiping among them.

As more time went by, people who passed by and visited the monastery noticed something that had not been there before. Although their number was small, these monks truly seemed to love and respect each other. Before long, people began to visit the monastery to worship with the monks. Younger men began to arrive at the monastery, asking questions. Many chose to stay and join the order. Within a few years, the monastery was thriving once more, and without realizing it, each of the monks had himself become a true apostle of God.

 REFLECT: What effect did the traveler's words have? How does the story relate to today's Bible reading? The story of the traveler and the monks is a nice story, but do you think treating others with respect can change things that much? Why or why not? Do you think it can change you? your family? school? church? If so, how?

 PRAY: "Lord, help me to make a conscious effort today to treat each person— including myself—as if he or she were a true apostle of God."

26 Trust and Obey

Bible Reading: Galatians 3:10-14

Christ has rescued us from the curse pronounced by the law.
Galatians 3:13

"THERE ARE JUST too many rules and commandments to remember. No one can be expected to remember all that stuff!"

Have you ever heard someone say something like that? Have you ever thought it yourself? Have you ever *said* it yourself?

It's true, in a way. There do seem to be a lot of commandments in the Bible: "Do not murder," "Do not steal," Do not covet," "Do not blaspheme God or curse anyone who rules over you." It seems as if it would be impossible for anyone to *remember* all those commands, let alone *obey* them all!

As a matter of fact, it *was* impossible for hundreds of years. Century after century, men and women tried to fulfill God's law, but century after century, they failed. Even the most godly people in the world failed: Abraham, Moses, David. If they couldn't keep all God's commands, who can?

No one—except Jesus. He's the only one who fulfilled all the commands and requirements of the law. He's the only one who never sinned.

So if you're hoping to obey every one of God's commands, give it up. It'll never happen. You can't do it. But Jesus can.

You see, that's one of the wonderful things about Jesus. He not only lived a righteous life two thousand years ago, he's living a righteous life right now. And if you are a Christian, he is living that righteous life in you through his Holy Spirit. You don't have to force yourself to obey all of God's commands. All you have to do is give yourself daily to the control of Jesus Christ. He will live the righteous life you couldn't live.

You can never hope to remember all of God's commands. But you don't have to. Jesus will do it *for* you and *in* you if you just trust him and follow him every day.

 REFLECT: Do you think you could obey God's commands all by yourself? Why or why not? What's the difference between *trying* to obey God's commands and *trusting* Jesus to do it *for* you and *in* you? Which have you been doing? How can you start trusting Jesus every day to live his righteous life in you?

 PRAY: "Lord, thank you for setting me free from sin. Help me to obey your Word every moment today and to keep from sinning."

27 Protective Gear

Bible Reading: Deuteronomy 6:20-25

The Lord our God commanded us to obey all these laws and to fear him for our own prosperity and well-being, as is now the case.
Deuteronomy 6:24

THE BASEBALL COACH dug six shiny new batting helmets out of a cardboard box in the back of his van. Several players stood ready to carry the helmets to the baseball diamond where they practiced. Three players took two helmets apiece and walked away. They turned the helmets around and around in their hands as they walked to the diamond.

Each player noticed that these helmets were different from the helmets they'd always used. They were heavier. They had earflaps on both sides. And a clear piece of plastic curved around the front of each helmet like a football player's face mask.

Every player on the team looked at the new helmets. Every player knew that these helmets were different. Every player inspected the new face mask. But no one complained.

No one said, "Hey, coach, do we *have* to wear these new helmets?"

No one said, "Those face masks are gonna be a real pain!"

No one said, "Why do we have to wear helmets anyway?" No one said, "They're so confining." No one said, "We could have a lot more fun without them."

No one said any of those things because they had all been at the game last summer when their teammate, Tad Rohmer, was hit by a pitch that shattered his jaw, a pitch that would affect his speech and hearing for the rest of his life. No one said anything because they were thinking of Tad and knew that the helmets were intended to protect them.

Those batting helmets are like the commands of God. He tells us to "love one another," "be self-controlled," "flee sexual immorality," and all those other commands because he loves us. His commands aren't intended to confine us or make us miserable; they're intended "for our own prosperity and well-being" (Deuteronomy 6:24).

Just as a batting helmet can protect an athlete from a broken jaw (or worse), God's commands protect us from guilt and shame, from disease and disappointment, from all sorts of problems and pain. Living our life according to God's commands won't guarantee that we'll never get hurt or have problems, but it will bring about prosperity and well-being in many ways.

 REFLECT: Have you ever felt like God's commands were a nuisance or a bother? Why or why not? Do you think God gave us commands to do us good or to do us harm? Do you think living your life according to God's commands helps you? If not, why not? If so, how? Should we be upset with God or thankful to him for giving his commands to us? Why?

 PRAY: "God, I know your commands are meant to protect me and help me. Please help me to obey your commands and always do what is right."

28 Hide-and-Seek

Bible Reading: Isaiah 65:1-2

I revealed myself to those who did not ask for me; I was found by those who did not seek me. Isaiah 65:1, NIV

IT MAY BE a while since you've played a game of hide-and-seek, but can you remember what fun it was? Searching out the perfect place to hide. Not moving a muscle so that you wouldn't give away your hiding place. The rush of adrenaline when you were finally found.

And then there were all those amateur detective skills you had to put into use when it was your turn to be "it." Keeping your ears open for the slightest sound. Figuring out where others thought were the best places to hide. Watching for the slightest clue that would reveal a player's location: a piece of clothing sticking out of a closet door, a pile of laundry piled a little too high, a slight movement behind some drapes.

While most people who play hide-and-seek don't want to be found, if you ever play the game with God, you'll soon discover that he doesn't seem to know the rules. Instead of making himself hard to find, God always seems to give away his "location." Sometimes he makes it almost impossible to miss him!

Although you may not be looking for God, God is constantly looking for you and trying to reveal himself to you. Over and over again, God tells us that he loves us. Over and over again, he tells us in his Word that he wants to do good to us. God's patience with us is infinite. His desire to make us his own will never end.

If your relationship with God has involved a little more hiding than seeking lately, why not decide now to turn that around? The Bible says to "Seek the Lord while you can find him. Call on him now while he is near" (Isaiah 55:6). Seek God through prayer and reading his Word. You'll be sure to find him.

 REFLECT: If God really wanted to hide from us, do you think we could find him? If we tried to hide from him, do you think we could succeed? Are you hiding from God right now or are you looking for him? What are ways you can actively search for God today?

 ACT: Play a short game of hide-and-seek with friends or family as a reminder to seek the Lord and not hide from him.

 PRAY: "Heavenly Father, you are worth more than the effort I make at seeking you. Thank you for the privilege of being able to find you."

29 A Letter to Joan Osborne

Bible Reading: Philippians 2:3-7

Your attitude should be the same that Christ Jesus had. Though he was God . . . he made himself nothing; he took the humble position of a slave and appeared in human form. Philippians 2:5-7

DEAR JOAN OSBORNE,

I know it's been a little while since you wrote your hit song, "What If God Was One of Us?" But I wanted to write you today and share some great news with you.

I know a lot of Christians were upset by that song, particularly by the words of the chorus:

What if God was one of us?
Just a slob like one of us?
Just a stranger on the bus
Trying to make his way home?

Now, I should tell you that I've never been much of a slob. I'm a God of order, not of disorder (1 Corinthians 14:33). But you should be really excited to learn that the words of your song actually came true! God *did* become one of you (John 1:14)! I had the same thought you did, only it was about two thousand years ago. I left my throne in heaven and was born as a human baby. I lived thirty-something years, then I died on a cross so *you* could be forgiven and saved from the punishment your sins deserved.

You see, Joan, God *is* "one of us"! Your wish came true—long before you wished it. And I want to tell you something else, too, Joan: When I humbled myself and left heaven for earth, I showed everyone that humility is a godly trait. I humbled myself, so it's a good thing when humans are able to put aside their pride and become humble. In fact, the biggest problem most people face today isn't believing that God was humble enough to become a man—it's humbling themselves enough to trust me with their lives. That's a problem for them—and for me, because I love them. I love you, too, Joan. I just wanted you to know that.

Love,
Jesus Christ

 REFLECT: Have you ever heard Joan Osborne's song "What If God Was One of Us?" If so, what did you think when you first heard it? How do you think Joan might respond to Jesus' letter? How do *you* respond to Jesus' letter? Why (according to Jesus' letter) is humility right? Do you think you're able to put aside your pride and become humble? How can you show a Christlike humility today?

 PRAY: "Jesus, thank you for humbling yourself and coming to earth as a man so that I could be forgiven and saved from the punishment my sins deserved. Please remind me that humility is right because it's like you. Help me also to be humble like you."

30 Fish Pond

Bible Reading: Philippians 2:5-11
Don't be selfish. . . . Be humble. Philippians 2:3

HAVE YOU EVER been to a carnival or county fair? The games are great, aren't they?

Of course, in most games, you take your chances. You might try throwing balls at a stack of cans or milk bottles, hoping to win a stuffed bear as big as you are. Unfortunately, the only way to knock all the cans or bottles off the platform is to hit a mere one-inch spot on the right side of the middle milk bottle on the bottom row. Miss that spot by a tiny bit, and you lose your money.

Or you might roll a bowling ball in a curving metal frame, trying to make the ball come to rest in the middle of the frame between the two little slopes. Unfortunately, the ball must be rolled at exactly .0178904 miles per hour and be pushed with exactly 1.5829 pounds per square inch of pressure on the exact center of the ball, or you lose your money.

Usually, the only sure way to win at a carnival or county fair is for you to try the fish pond. Using a tiny fishing rod, you try to hook a magnetized fish floating in a canal of water or, in some fish ponds, simply pick a floating fish (or duck) out of the water to reveal a number on the bottom. Either way, you always win a prize: a rubber worm, a plastic ring, a friendship bracelet. It's not much, but at least it's something, right?

There are some people who go through life playing "fish pond," even when they're not at a carnival or fair. And what they're fishing for are compliments and approval.

"Did you see that home run I hit? Knocked it clear into the woods! I don't think anyone else has ever hit a ball that far! *Do you?*"

"When the lady finished cutting my hair and I looked in the mirror, I couldn't believe how good I looked. *Don't you think so?*"

Of course, *you'd* never be guilty of such "fishing expeditions," would you? You'd never fish for compliments. You'd never brag or boast like that, would you?

Actually, almost all of us do it at one time or another. But God is very clear in telling us that we should not fish for compliments or brag about ourselves. He wants us to be humble. He wants us to be like Christ Jesus. Although he was God, Jesus humbled himself in order to become our Savior (Philippians 2:5-8; Hebrews 12:2).

So the next time you find something you're good at, or a new outfit you look wonderful in, leave your fishing pole at home. As the Bible says, "Don't praise yourself; let others do it!" (Proverbs 27:2).

 REFLECT: Do you ever fish for compliments or brag about yourself? Which do you think would be better: to be complimented because you "fished" for a compliment or to be complimented when you weren't "fishing" for a compliment? Why? Think of some ways you can obey the commands in today's Bible reading ("Don't be selfish," "Be humble," "Be interested in others").

 PRAY: "Lord Jesus, help me to avoid fishing for compliments. Instead, help me to look for ways to compliment those around me."

1 The Faith of Ferdinand and Isabella

Bible Reading: James 2:14-20

Faith that does not result in good deeds is useless. James 2:20

CHRISTOPHER COLUMBUS AND his brother, Bartholomew, wanted to find a way to Japan, China, and India by sailing west. In 1482 Christopher went to King John II of Portugal, asking for money and ships, but King John refused Columbus's request. In 1485 the brothers tried to enlist the support of King Henry VII of England, but he also turned them away.

Finally, in 1492, King Ferdinand and Queen Isabella of Spain granted Columbus's request. On August 3, 1492, he sailed from Palos, Spain. On October 12, 1492, Columbus became the first European explorer to set foot in "the New World."

Only Ferdinand and Isabella of Spain had faith in Columbus and his mission. King John of Portugal obviously didn't have much faith in the man or in his mission. King Henry of England didn't have such faith either. How do we know that? *By their works.* Or, in Columbus's case, their lack of works.

It's not hard to see that if the kings of England and Portugal had *believed* in Columbus, they would have *acted* quite differently, right? If they had any faith in Columbus, they would have backed up their faith with money, ships, and titles, like Ferdinand and Isabella did, right?

Faith in Christ works the same way. As James wrote in the Bible, "Dear brothers and sisters, what's the use of saying you have faith if you don't prove it by your actions? That kind of faith can't save anyone. . . . Faith that doesn't show itself by good deeds is no faith at all—it is dead and useless" (James 2:14, 17).

You see, we aren't saved by doing good works, or even by making right choices. We are saved by grace through faith (Ephesians 2:8). A real saving faith in Christ, however, should produce right choices—just as Ferdinand and Isabella's faith in Columbus and his mission produced ships, money, and a whole new world!

REFLECT: Are you a Christian? If so, how did you become a Christian: by doing good deeds or by trusting Christ to save you by his grace? Does being a Christian mean you can do anything you want to? Why or why not? According to today's Bible reading, what kind of "works" should your faith produce?

PRAY: "Heavenly Father, I know that I've been saved by grace, through faith. Please help my faith to grow and produce right choices and good deeds as I follow you every day."

2 Bad News, Good News

Bible Reading: Genesis 40:1-5, 12-23

The unfailing love of the Lord never ends. . . . Great is his faithfulness.
Lamentations 3:22-23

IMAGINE HOW *YOU'D* feel in this situation.

Joseph had been falsely accused and thrown into prison. After he'd been there a while, two other prisoners joined him: Pharaoh's chief cupbearer and chief baker. One night the cupbearer and the baker both had dreams, and they mentioned them to Joseph. When they described their dreams to Joseph, he told them what their dreams meant.

"Good news," he told the cupbearer. "Three days from now Pharaoh will take you out of prison and make you his chief cupbearer again." The cupbearer was overjoyed. "And please have some pity on me," Joseph asked him, "when you're back in Pharaoh's good favor. Mention me to Pharaoh and ask him to let me out of here, too."

Then Joseph turned to Pharaoh's former baker. "Bad news," he said. "Three days from now Pharaoh will cut off your head."

Things happened exactly as Joseph had said. Within three days Pharaoh gave a banquet. He called for his former cupbearer to be released from prison and ordered that his former baker be executed. But the cupbearer quickly forgot Joseph's request, and Joseph remained in prison.

But even though the cupbearer was unfaithful to Joseph, God was faithful. Two years later Pharaoh had a dream, a dream that none of his magicians and wise men could figure out. It was then that the cupbearer remembered Joseph. He told Pharaoh how Joseph had told the meaning of his dream and the baker's dream. Pharaoh took Joseph out of prison and told him his dream. Joseph listened and, with God's help, explained the meaning of the dream to Pharaoh.

Joseph's story (found in Genesis 40-41) shows how unfaithful people can be. It also shows that, no matter how unfaithful your friends or even your family members might be, God is always faithful. The prophet Jeremiah said, "The unfailing love of the Lord never ends. . . . Great is his faithfulness" (Lamentations 3:22-23).

In fact, that's how we know that faithfulness is right—because it's like God. God commands faithfulness, because God is faithful. He never lets us down. He never abandons us. He never ignores us. He never forgets us. He is faithful. And because God is faithful, we should be faithful, too.

 REFLECT: Did the cupbearer do the right thing in today's Bible reading? Why or why not? What makes faithfulness right and unfaithfulness wrong? Have you ever acted like the cupbearer? If so, in what ways? Are you being faithful to God? to your family? to your friends?

 PRAY: "God, your unfailing love never ends. Great is your faithfulness. Please help me to be faithful to you and to my family and friends."

3 In His Steps

Bible Reading: 1 Peter 2:19-25

Christ, who suffered for you, is your example. Follow in his steps.
1 Peter 2:21

IN 1896 THE pastor of a church in Topeka, Kansas, began writing a story, which he read (a chapter at a time) to his church youth group every Sunday evening. The first chapter told the story of a tramp—a jobless, homeless man—who walked into a comfortable church one Sunday morning. The man spoke a few words, then collapsed. Three days later the man died in the pastor's home. But before dying, he spoke to the minister.

"You have been good to me," he said. "Somehow I feel as if it was what Jesus would do."

That tramp's appearance—and his words—prompted a change in the pastor that soon spread through his congregation. That church started measuring everything they did or said by the question "What would Jesus do?" Soon the people of that church were doing amazing things—and seeing amazing results—all because they tried to do only what Jesus would do. In other words, they started following Jesus.

Pastor Charles M. Sheldon's famous book, *In His Steps,* is one of the most successful books ever written. At one point, *In His Steps* had sold more copies than any other book except the Bible.

The apostle Peter once wrote a brief letter that said about the same thing Charles Sheldon's book said. Peter said that "Christ, who suffered for you, is your example. Follow in his steps" (1 Peter 2:21).

Now Peter wasn't saying that the way to become a Christian is to try to imitate Jesus; we can only become Christians by the grace of God and by believing in Jesus Christ. But Peter's letter told Christians that to live as a Christian means to follow in his steps. To make right choices means to follow Jesus' example. To be like Jesus is to be right.

If we compare our actions to Jesus, we'll usually see clearly whether they are right or wrong. If we ask ourselves, What would Jesus do? we will usually know right away what is right. And if we follow in Jesus' steps, we can be sure we're going the right way.

 REFLECT: Today's reading says that "to be like Jesus is to be right." Why is that true? Do you think you would have done anything differently yesterday (or today) if you had first asked yourself, What would Jesus do? Why or why not?

 ACT: If you've never read *In His Steps,* consider reading it now. If your family doesn't own a copy of *In His Steps,* copies may be available in your church or public library.

 PRAY: "God, thank you for sending Jesus to die for my sins. Help me to follow his example in everything I do. Please make me more and more like him every day."

How Low Will You Go?

Bible Reading: Psalm 119:27-29

Keep me from deceitful ways. Psalm 119:29, NIV

THE PRESIDENT OF a company once called in one of his employees, the man responsible for writing the company's checks and paying the company's bills.

"Smithers," he said. "I'm in a tight spot, and I'm thinking you might be the man to help me out."

"Yes sir," Smithers answered. "I hope so, sir."

"Tell me," the president said. "If I gave you a bonus of, say, ten thousand dollars, would you tell a few lies to save me some money on my taxes?"

Smithers didn't answer right away. Ten thousand dollars was a lot of money to him. He thought of all the things he could do with that much money. Finally, he leaned closer to the company president and winked. "I think I could do that," he said, smiling.

The company president smiled slightly. "Thank you, Smithers," he said. "I'll keep that in mind."

As the man turned and started walking to the door, the company president called him back. "Just a moment, Smithers," he said. "Tell me—would you do it for ten dollars?"

"Ten dollars!" Smithers answered. His jaw dropped open. "What kind of a person do you think I am?"

"Oh, you've already told me that," the company president said. "I'm just trying to find out how low you'll go."

Smithers had already shown his boss that he would be dishonest for a price. The company president thought that someone who would be dishonest for ten thousand dollars might also be dishonest for less.

You see, dishonesty is wrong—no matter what the price. It is wrong to be dishonest, no matter how much—or how little—money is involved. There is no dollar amount at which it becomes "right" (or excusable) to be dishonest. Not ten thousand dollars. Not ten million dollars. Not even ten *gazillion* dollars!

 REFLECT: How about you? Is there a high amount of money that would persuade you to be dishonest? Is there a *low* amount that would persuade you to be dishonest ("It's only a quarter, so what's the big deal?")? Do you think honesty is right no matter how much money is involved? Why or why not? Do you think honesty is right even when it's "no big deal"? Why or why not?

 PRAY: "Lord, please keep me from deceitful ways, like today's Bible reading says. Help me to be honest even when it's hard and even when it's 'no big deal.'"

5 Honest Abe

Bible Reading: Leviticus 19:35-37

Do not use dishonest standards. Leviticus 19:35

THE FOLLOWING STORY is told about Abraham Lincoln when he was a young man, before he became known as "Honest Abe."

Abe was working in a store as a clerk. One day a woman came in and bought a few items. Abe jotted down the woman's charges on a scrap of paper, totaled them for her, and then accepted her payment. After she had left the store, though, Abe started wondering whether he had accurately added up the woman's purchases. When he added the numbers again, he found out he had charged her too much. It was only a few cents, but Abe felt bad about his mistake. So, at the end of the day, after closing the store, Abe walked the distance (somewhere between two and three miles) to the woman's house to return the money he had overcharged her.

Another time, he had weighed a half pound of tea for a woman, only to discover the next day that there had been an extra four-ounce weight on the scale. He had given her less than a half pound. As he had done with the few cents, Abe corrected the error by weighing out the missing quantity and delivering it to the woman.

It's not hard to imagine how Lincoln came to be called "Honest Abe." After all, in those two instances (and in many others) he went to a lot of trouble to make sure he didn't cheat anyone and didn't take anything that wasn't his. He didn't try to excuse his mistakes. He didn't try to shrug them off, saying, "Ah, I didn't mean to overcharge the lady." He didn't try to say that taking that extra money would be OK. Instead, he made sure that his behavior was as honest as he could make it.

That's exactly how God wants us to act, too. He doesn't want us to excuse dishonesty or shrug it off. He doesn't want us to say, "Well, in *my* case it wouldn't be dishonest," or "In *this* case it wouldn't be so bad." No, he wants us to remember that he has already told us what is right and what is wrong—and he has made it clear that honesty is right and dishonesty is wrong.

 REFLECT: Do you think Abraham Lincoln did the right thing in the stories above? Do you think he went a little "overboard"? Do you think he deserved to be called "Honest Abe"? Do you ever try to excuse dishonesty or shrug it off? Do you ever try to say something is honest when it's really not? Or do you try to do what God says to do?

 ACT: The next time you buy something in a store, remember Abraham Lincoln's honesty—and count your change carefully!

 PRAY: "Father in heaven, help me always to remember that only you decide what's right and what's wrong. And help me to act honestly, knowing that you have commanded it."

6 The Minister and the Dog

Bible Reading: Leviticus 19:1-2, 11

Do not steal. Do not cheat one another. Do not lie. Leviticus 19:11

A MINISTER ONCE saw a group of boys huddled around a little straggly-haired dog. He watched them for a few moments but couldn't figure out what they were doing. Finally, he walked over to the group of boys and asked what they were doing.

"Telling lies," answered one of the boys.

"Yeah," added another member of the group. "Whoever tells the biggest lie gets to keep the dog."

The minister's jaw dropped open and a look of disapproval appeared on his face. "Why, when I was your age," he said, "I never *thought* of telling lies!"

The boys looked at each other with sad expressions. Finally, the boy who had spoken first shrugged his shoulders.

"You win!" he said. "I guess this here dog is yours!"

Those boys could recognize a lie when they heard one. And so can God.

God commands us to be honest. A long time ago, when the people of Israel had recently escaped from slavery in Egypt, God spoke to them through Moses. And many of the commands he gave them there in the wilderness near Mount Sinai were about honesty. He said, "Do not steal. Do not cheat one another. Do not lie" (Leviticus 19:11).

Those commands are pretty simple, aren't they? They're pretty clear. God tells us to be honest. He doesn't want us to lie; he doesn't want us to cheat; he doesn't want us to steal—because those things are dishonest. And dishonesty is wrong—even for ministers!

REFLECT: According to today's Bible reading, what does God say about lying, cheating, and stealing? Do you have trouble being honest in any of those areas (lying, cheating, stealing)? If so, which area(s)? Do you think being honest in one or two of those areas is enough, or do you think God expects you to be honest in all of those areas? How do you know?

PRAY: "Dear God, I know I've disobeyed you and disappointed you before by being dishonest. Please help me to obey your commands not to lie, not to cheat, and not to steal. Help me to act and speak honestly today and every day."

7 True Value

Bible Reading: Zechariah 8:14-17

"Tell the truth. . . . Don't swear that something is true when it isn't!
How I hate all that sort of thing!" says the Lord. Zechariah 8:16-17, TLB

IF YOU HAD fifty cents to spend, which would you buy (circle one):

a bag of M&M's   *or*   that day's newspaper?

If you had a dollar to spend, which would you buy (circle one):

a bottle of soda   *or*   a six-minute phone call from a pay phone?

If you had a hundred dollars to spend, which would you buy (circle one):

a pair of cool tennis shoes   *or*   a portable CD player?

If you had a hundred *thousand* dollars to spend, which would you buy (circle one):

a house   *or*   a lifetime subscription to *Iguana Owners Monthly?*

OK, so maybe the last one was too easy; after all, *everyone* wants a lifetime subscription to *Iguana Owners Monthly.* But still, take a minute to look back over your choices. Why did you choose *those* items? Why was it really, really easy to choose in some cases?

Because those were things you value. You chose the items you valued. Your choices revealed your values.

Well, the same is true of God. His choices reveal his values. For example, in today's Bible reading, God talks about the things he values and the things he doesn't value! That's not hard to understand. God told the people of Jerusalem, "Tell the truth" because he values honesty. And he told them, "Don't swear that something is true when it isn't" because he actually hates dishonesty (Zechariah 8:16-17, TLB).

And if we love God and want to follow him, our actions should show that we (like him) value honesty.

 REFLECT: Look back over Zechariah 8:14-17. Using the space below, separate what God says to his people into two columns that show what God values and what God hates:

What God values   **What God hates**

_____   _____

_____   _____

How much do *your* values and actions reflect God's values?

 PRAY: "Lord, I know you command honesty because you value honesty. Please help me to show by my actions that I value honesty, too."

8 Two Houses

Bible Reading: Exodus 34:1-6

The Lord, The Lord God, merciful and gracious, longsuffering, and abundant in goodness and truth . . . Exodus 34:6, KJV

TWO HOUSES, BOTH built over a hundred years ago, stand atop a grassy hill in Hartford, Connecticut. The two houses are separated by a single yard.

One of the two houses is one of the most spectacular homes of its day. It is a large and eccentric house. It has gables, cupolas, porches, passageways, garish colors and decorations. Some of the features of this house, like its porches and staircase, resemble a Mississippi River steamboat.

The other house is much smaller, just a cozy little cottage. It has small rooms and a single narrow staircase. It is decorated nicely but not extravagantly. The bookcases throughout the house are filled with Bibles and other books.

If you were to visit these two houses in Hartford, you could probably figure out a lot about the famous person who lived in each house. You could be pretty sure that the person who built and lived in the first house had a vivid and eccentric personality. You might also assume that person loved Mississippi River steamboats. And you would be right, for the first house was the home of Mark Twain (Samuel Clemens), the famous author of *The Adventures of Tom Sawyer* and *The Adventures of Huckleberry Finn.*

You might also think that the second house was owned by a much more modest and quiet person, maybe even someone with a Christian background. And you would be right, because the little cottage on that hill was once owned by Harriet Beecher Stowe, a preacher's daughter who wrote *Uncle Tom's Cabin.*

Interesting, isn't it? You can tell by looking at their houses what kind of people Mark Twain and Harriet Beecher Stowe were. You can see hints that Twain was once a riverboat captain. You can kind of tell that Stowe was a Christian.

It's sort of the same with God and his commandments. His commandments not only show what he values, they show what *he* is like. And his commandments not to lie, not to steal, and not to cheat reveal something about his own nature and character. Moses described the Lord this way after he had received the law: "The Lord, The Lord God, merciful and gracious, longsuffering, and abundant in goodness and truth" (Exodus 34:6, KJV). God values honesty because he is "abundant in . . . truth." He is a God of truth and truthfulness, which is why lying and cheating and stealing are wrong.

REFLECT: How do God's commands not to steal, not to lie, and not to cheat reflect his nature and character? Why is honesty right? Why is dishonesty wrong? Complete the following statements with your beliefs:
- God commands honesty because_____.
- God values honesty because_____.

PRAY: "Lord God, you are abundant in goodness and truth. I know that honesty is right because you are honest and true in your nature. Please help me to be honest, because I know that being honest is being like you."

9 Whom Do You Trust?

Bible Reading: Luke 16:10-12

Kings take pleasure in honest lips; they value a man who speaks the truth. Proverbs 16:13, NIV

WHOM DO YOU trust? Of all the people in the world, there are probably only a few you would trust to hold your lunch money for you, right? And there are probably even fewer you would trust with your deepest secrets. In the space below, jot the names of two or three people that you could trust with your money or your secrets:

Now think about *why* you trust those people. Put a check beside any statement below that expresses why you trust the people you listed above:

- ☐ I trust them because of where they live.
- ☐ I trust them because each of them once lied to me.
- ☐ I trust them because I like them.
- ☐ I trust them because they're kinda good looking.
- ☐ I trust them because I've never seen them steal anything.
- ☐ I trust them because they know all the words to "Louie Louie."
- ☐ I trust them because they like lima beans.
- ☐ I trust them because they've never lied to me or cheated me.
- ☐ I trust them because they pick their noses.

Chances are, you only checked one or two of the statements above, right? Why?

Because you don't trust someone any more or less if he or she knows all the words to "Louie Louie." You don't trust someone simply because he or she picks his or her nose. And you *certainly* don't trust someone because he or she has lied to you before.

If those things don't earn your trust, what does? Simple, right? You trust someone who has been honest. You trust someone who has told you the truth in the past. Because honesty invites trust. That's one of the big advantages to obeying God's commands to be honest. When you're honest, you encourage other people to trust you; when you're dishonest, you make people suspicious and distrustful of you.

One of the proverbs of Solomon says, "Kings take pleasure in honest lips; they value a man who speaks the truth" (Proverbs 16:13, NIV). That's true not only of kings but of everyone. People value—and trust—those who are honest.

 REFLECT: If your friends were to make a list (like the one you made above) of the people they could trust, would they include your name? Why or why not? What about your parents? teachers? other family members? Does your behavior encourage others to trust you or has it been making people distrust you? How do you know?

 PRAY: "Father, I want to be trusted by my friends, parents, teachers, and others. Help me to earn their trust by my honest words and honest behavior."

The Fisherman's Wife

Bible Reading: Proverbs 11:1-6

Good people are guided by their honesty; treacherous people are destroyed by their dishonesty. Proverbs 11:3

AN OLD ARAB fable tells the story of a man who went out fishing early one morning and caught the most beautiful, colorful fish he had ever seen. It weighed six pounds.

He hurried immediately toward home and burst into the house to show his wife. "Isn't it beautiful?" he said. "I've never caught a finer fish! I'm going to cook us all a wonderful meal tonight."

The man left the fish in the corner of the kitchen and went to work. But as the day wore on, his wife began to get hungry. She tried to ignore her hunger (and the large fish in the corner), but she only got hungrier. Just the thought of how delicious that fish would taste made her mouth water. Finally, she couldn't stand it anymore.

She snatched the fish and tossed it into the frying pan, rocking back and forth on her heels and toes as it cooked. When it was cooked, she sat down and ate it until every last bite was gone.

When the man came home, the fish was gone. "Oh!" his wife said, pointing accusingly at the cat. "That wicked cat got into the kitchen this afternoon and ate the whole fish!"

The man seized the cat, and the woman thought he was going to kill it. Instead, the man plopped it down on the kitchen scale. The cat weighed five pounds.

"A cat who ate my fish," the man said, frowning at his lying wife, "would not weigh less than the fish!"

The woman had lied, and her husband knew it.

Dishonesty seems to be an easy way out of some situations, but it's usually a trap. One dishonest act usually leads to another. One lie needs a second lie to cover it up. And the truth has a way of coming out in the end. Usually, the whole mess just leads to discovery—and embarrassment. And shame. And guilt. More often than not, "treacherous people are destroyed by their dishonesty" (Proverbs 11:3).

That's what happened to the wife in the old Arab tale. And it's what could happen to us—unless we "are guided by . . . honesty" (Proverbs 11:3).

 REFLECT: Have you ever been trapped by your own dishonesty? If so, in what ways? Have you ever had to tell a lie to cover up an earlier lie? If so, was it worth it? Which is right: honesty or dishonesty? Which is wiser: honesty or dishonesty? Which protects you and provides for you: honesty or dishonesty?

 PRAY: "Father, I know that dishonesty is a trap. Please deliver me from its dangers and help me to be guided by honesty in everything I do."

11 Fire, Water, and Reputation

Bible Reading: Ephesians 4:17-28

Choose a good reputation over great riches, for being held in high esteem is better than having silver or gold. Proverbs 22:1

ONCE UPON A time three friends went on a long journey together. Their names were Fire, Water, and Reputation.

"My friends," said Fire to his companions, "we have far to go on our journey, and there are many hazards along the way. What should we do if we lose each other?"

"You are wise to think of that," answered Water. "We should agree on a way to find each other if we become separated."

The three friends grew silent for a few moments. Then Fire spoke. "If you should lose me," he said, "simply look up to the sky. Where you see smoke, you will find me."

"If you lose me," suggested Water, "simply look down at the ground. Where you find low, marshy ground, you will find me."

Fire and Water then looked to Reputation for his answer. But his face was sad. "If you lose me," Reputation said, "do not bother looking. For when you lose me, it will be almost impossible to find me again!"

Those words are true. A good reputation is a valuable thing; once it is lost, it is hard (and sometimes impossible) to get it back again. Many people have been ruined or disgraced by dishonesty. Many reputations have been shattered because of one dishonest word or act.

That's one of the reasons why honesty is in your best interests. That's one reason why "honesty is the best policy"—because it's one of the ways God tries to protect you from harm and provide good things for you. Honesty establishes a good reputation; dishonesty can prevent—or ruin—a good reputation.

"Choose a good reputation over great riches," wise King Solomon said, "for being held in high esteem is better than having silver or gold" (Proverbs 22:1). In other words, don't risk losing a good reputation because of a dishonest word or act—you may never get it back again.

 REFLECT: A reputation is what other people think about you. For example, they may think you're honest, or they may think you're dishonest. Which reputation would you rather have? What kind of a reputation do you think you have right now? How can you build (or protect) a good reputation? How can being honest help your reputation?

 PRAY: "Heavenly Father, help me to earn a good reputation by being honest in what I say and do."

12 Headline News

Bible Reading: Leviticus 26:3-12

If you keep my laws and are careful to obey my commands, . . . I will give you peace in the land, and you will be able to sleep without fear. Leviticus 26:3, 6

IMAGINE PICKING UP the newspaper tomorrow morning and seeing these headlines:

- "Crime Rate Plummets"
- "Crack Addict Returns $1,000 Found in Trash Can"
- "Largest Bank in the World Leaves Safe Unlocked—Every Night"
- "Shoplifting Comes to an End As Stores Drop Prices"
- "Gas Stations Now Operating on Honor System"
- "Burglar Alarms, Home Security Systems Become Obsolete"
- "Insurance Companies Stop All Fraud Investigations; Insurance More Affordable Than Ever"
- "Last Metal Detectors at Airport Phased Out; 'Not Needed Anymore,' Says Security Chief"

That would be pretty wild, wouldn't it? But it would be totally predictable—*if* everyone in the world were to suddenly become honest. You wouldn't have to walk through metal detectors at the airport. You could leave the store without asking a clerk to take that white "security clip" thing off when you buy a piece of clothing. You wouldn't have to lock your house, your car, or your school locker.

It would be pretty cool, wouldn't it? That gives you an idea of the wisdom of God's commands. If we all obeyed God, this world would be a totally different—and much better—place. As the Word says, "People with integrity have firm footing, but those who follow crooked paths will slip and fall" (Proverbs 10:9).

But, of course, the world's not going to become honest overnight. It won't even become honest little by little. But you and I can. We can follow God and obey his commands not to lie, not to cheat, and not to steal. That won't change the world, but it sure will change us (and even some of the people around us). And that's pretty cool, too.

 REFLECT: It can be fun to think about how the world would be different if everyone was honest. But take a few minutes to think about this: How might *your* world (your family, your friendships, your school, and so on) be different if *you* were honest every day? if you *and your family* were honest? if you, your family, *and your friends* were honest?

 ACT: Keep a newspaper on your desk, in your book bag, or in your school locker today to remind you of the wisdom and benefits of following God's command to be honest.

 PRAY: "Lord, you say that people of integrity have firm footing. Please help me each day to keep my footing firmly placed in honesty."

13 Ask a Silly Question . . .

Bible Reading: John 14:1-6

Jesus told [Thomas], "I am the way, the truth, and the life. No one can come to the Father except through me." John 14:6

YOU'RE SITTING IN school, listening to your teacher talk. You're listening, but you're not understanding. It's as if the teacher was speaking a foreign language. You feel like raising your hand and saying, "Could you please repeat that? I don't understand a thing you're saying."

But you don't do that, of course. You'd *never* do that. You would sooner smear your hair with bacon grease and jump into the grizzly bear pit at the zoo. After all, nobody wants to ask a silly question in school, right?

Well, no matter how silly your question might be, it wouldn't be the silliest question ever asked. That honor would go to a politician (who else?) named Pilate, who lived nearly two thousand years ago. He stood in an elaborate palace, dressed in regal clothes, and asked, "What is truth?"

"What's so silly about that question?" you might ask. Just this: At that very moment the answer to his question was standing right in front of him! It would have been like walking into class on the first day of school, watching your new teacher write her name on the chalkboard, and then asking her, "What's your name?"

Because, you see, the prisoner who stood before Pilate was Jesus Christ, who said of himself, "I am the way, the truth, and the life" (John 14:6). When Pilate asked, "What is truth?" Jesus could have answered, "He's standing right in front of you."

You see, we generally think of truth as a concept or idea. It exists in our mind as a principle or a quality. But truth isn't just an idea. It is a person, and that person has a name: Jesus Christ.

That's why the only way to really understand truth and apply it to your life is by having a real, live relationship with Jesus Christ—because he is the truth! He doesn't just *speak* the truth. He doesn't just *know* the truth. He *is* the truth!

That means that if you have trusted Jesus Christ for salvation, you have not only become acquainted with truth; you have the Truth himself living inside you! So you see, making right choices isn't really about following a bunch of rules. It's a relationship—a relationship with the Truth himself. And the closer you get to him, the more he—through his Holy Spirit—will help you to learn the truth, know the truth, and live the truth.

REFLECT: Have you trusted Christ for salvation? Are you following the one who said, "I am the way, the truth, and the life"? If not, why not? If so, you have the Truth living inside you. How does knowing Jesus help you to obey his commands?

PRAY: "Lord Jesus, you are 'the way, the truth, and the life.' Thank you for saving me from sin and coming to live inside me. Help me to make right choices, not by following a bunch of rules, but as a natural result of my relationship with you."

14 Fair Game

Bible Reading: Psalm 67:1-5

Tell all the nations that the Lord is king. The world is firmly established and cannot be shaken. He will judge all peoples fairly. Psalm 96:10

THERE'S A NEW arcade game in the lobby of the discount store in your town. It's called Warrior Rage. You scrape together every quarter you can find and walk into the store.

You pop two quarters into the machine, which is bigger than some apartment buildings. A sinister voice says, "Welcome to Warrior Rage. Are you ready to die?"

"Bring it on!" you say, pushing the red and blue buttons on your right.

A grid forms on the screen, introducing six opponents. The game explains that they will all be fighting you at the same time. "Drago" shoots fireballs from his eyes and has five-bladed swords instead of hands. "Nemesis" swings a fifty-pound sledgehammer like a purse, crushing her opponents beneath its solid-steel head. "Malevant" has a powerful thirteen-foot tail that he uses as a weapon and also carries a grenade launcher in his short, dinosaurlike hands. The other three opponents have even more frightening characteristics.

A single bead of sweat appears on your upper lip. You wipe it off. You punch the red button, and a second screen arises. "Choose your weapon," it instructs you. You stare at the screen. You can't believe this. The game gives you only two choices of weapons: a pair of small silver fingernail clippers or ten ordinary rubber bands. You can't even choose both weapons!

"No fair!" you shout, kicking the machine. "This is so wrong!" You decide to play the game anyway, but equipped with only a pair of fingernail clippers you promptly "die." "I want my money back," you whine. "This game isn't even fair!"

That wouldn't be fair, would it? It would be "so wrong," right? Right! Because fairness is right, and unfairness is wrong, right? Right! That's why you would be upset by a game that takes your money and doesn't even give you a fighting chance. But do you know *why* fairness is right and unfairness is wrong?

That's right. Because the God who created us is a just God. He is fair. He is a God who "judge[s] all peoples fairly" (Psalm 96:10). "Everything he does is just and fair," the Bible says (Deuteronomy 32:4).

So you see, fairness is right because God is fair. Unfairness is wrong because it is not like God. We choose right when we are fair to others, because God is always fair.

 REFLECT: Have you ever said, "That's not fair"? If so, can you think of the most recent time you said that? Did you know *why* fairness was right and unfairness was wrong? Have you treated anyone unfairly this week? If so, what should you do about it? If not, how can you continue to be fair to others in the future?

 PRAY: "God, I know that you judge all people fairly. I know that everything you do is just and fair. Help me be more like you: fair to everybody."

15 Animal Tales

Bible Reading: Mark 14:32-38

Keep alert and pray. Otherwise temptation will overpower you.
Mark 14:38

- DID YOU KNOW that an ostrich's eye is larger than its brain?
- Did you know that a cow has two stomachs?
- Did you know that a bird's bones are hollow?
- Did you know that a bee can't hear itself buzz? (It has no ears.)

Some animals can be pretty interesting, can't they? Here's another interesting fact: Did you know that a cat's whiskers are exactly as wide as the widest part of its body? That way, a cat can know if it's trying to squeeze its head through the open end of a pipe or the slats of a fence, whether the rest of its body will fit. If its whiskers brush the pipe or the fence, the cat knows not to try to go through.

Wouldn't it be nice if you and I could know before doing a certain thing whether we're going to get into trouble? Wouldn't it be cool to know, before we even go a certain way, if we're going to be tempted to make a wrong choice?

Well, we may not be equipped with whiskers (though some of us do have a little bit of peach fuzz on our face, don't we?), but that doesn't mean we're helpless. In fact, we have something much better than cat whiskers. It's called *prayer.*

You see, before Jesus faced his trial and crucifixion, he took some of his disciples into the Garden of Gethsemane to pray with him. He knew what was about to happen, but they apparently didn't have a clue. So he tried to warn them. He said, "Keep alert and pray. Otherwise temptation will overpower you" (Mark 14:38). Unfortunately, they didn't listen. They relaxed instead of staying alert and slept instead of praying. If they had prayed, though, they would have been a lot better prepared for the temptations they faced over the next few days. Who knows? Maybe James wouldn't have run away. Maybe Peter wouldn't have denied Jesus. But we'll never know, of course, because they failed to pray and so were overpowered by temptation.

It doesn't matter that we don't have whiskers, but it does matter whether or not we pray. If we pray, "Lead us not into temptation" (Luke 11:4, NIV), the Lord will warn us away from some situations in which we might be tempted to do wrong and bring us through other temptations he knows we're strong enough to face. But we must remember to "keep alert and pray," as Jesus said. Otherwise temptation will overpower us.

 REFLECT: Do you think things might have happened differently if Jesus' disciples had stayed alert and prayed in the garden instead of falling asleep? If not, why not? If so, how? Do you pray every day and ask God to help you resist temptation? When do you think is the best time for you to ask God to deliver you from temptation: during the temptation, after the temptation, or before temptation even strikes?

 PRAY: "Lord, help me to pray every day for strength against temptations to make wrong choices so that I won't be surprised or overpowered when temptation comes."

16 Rotten People

Bible Reading: Psalm 103:1-8

The Lord is merciful and gracious; he is slow to get angry and full of unfailing love. Psalm 103:8

THE BIBLE IS filled with the stories of "rotten people" doing rotten things:

- Sarah laughed at God's promise.
- Jacob made a lifestyle out of cheating people—even his own brother.
- Samson seemed willing to blab the solemn secret of his strength to any pretty woman who came along.
- David stole another man's wife—and then had that man killed!
- Jonah tried to run away instead of taking God's word to people he hated.
- Peter openly denied his Lord with vows and curses.
- John Mark quit the apostle Paul's missionary team and went home, leaving Paul feeling deserted.

And those are just a few of the rotten people whose stories are told in the Bible. Some people did even worse things than those listed above!

Do you know how God responded to those rotten people who did all those rotten things? He could have kicked them out of the Bible, saying, "Just for that, I'm taking your story out and giving Enoch a whole new chapter of his own!" He could have told them to pack their bags and head for jail without passing "Go." He could have totally vaporized them if he wanted to.

But God didn't do any of those things. Instead, he went ahead and gave Sarah the son he had promised her. She named her son Isaac, which means "laughter." He created an entire nation out of Jacob's sons after he renamed him Israel. He forgave David. He restored Peter. He gave John Mark and Jonah a second chance.

God did all those things because he is merciful. As David once wrote in a song, "The Lord is merciful and gracious; he is slow to get angry and full of unfailing love" (Psalm 103:8). God is merciful. He showed his mercy to all the rotten people in the Bible. And he shows his mercy to all kinds of rotten people today.

That's why mercy is right. You see, the reason it's right for you (or anyone) to show mercy to others is because God is merciful. His nature and character make mercy right, because whatever is like God is right, and whatever is not like God is wrong.

 REFLECT: What does today's Bible reading say about the nature and character of God? Who wrote Psalm 103? How do you think David knew that God is merciful? How do you know God is merciful? How do you know it's right to be merciful? Do you think you could be more merciful toward others? If so, how?

 PRAY: "Father God, you are merciful and gracious, slow to get angry and full of unfailing love. You've been merciful toward me in a lot of ways, especially_____. [Fill in a time when God was merciful to you.] Help me not only to remember that it's right to be merciful but also to be merciful toward others."

17 Bad Habits

Bible Reading: Genesis 25:29-34
Follow God's example in everything you do. Ephesians 5:1

DO YOU HAVE any bad habits? Check out the list below. Do you

- ☐ chew your fingernails?
- ☐ chew your toenails?
- ☐ chew carpenters' nails?
- ☐ interrupt when others are talking?
- ☐ pull out your hair?
- ☐ pull out someone else's hair?
- ☐ grind your teeth?
- ☐ insult people?
- ☐ forget to say please or thank you?
- ☐ lose your temper?
- ☐ other?_____

- ☐ put things off until later?
- ☐ eat too much?
- ☐ eat too little?
- ☐ watch too much TV?
- ☐ pick your nose?
- ☐ pick someone else's nose?
- ☐ smoke cigarettes?
- ☐ smoke cigars?
- ☐ smoke old tires?
- ☐ gossip about other people?

Maybe you didn't check any of the items on the list above. Maybe you checked them all! Either way, you probably have at least one bad habit—something you do that is rude or thoughtless or undesirable. Nobody is totally free from bad habits. Sometimes our bad habits are sinful. Sometimes they're just annoying. And sometimes—as Esau found out (in today's Bible reading)—they can really be hurtful and costly.

Whatever bad habit you may have, you don't have to be stuck with it. It may take a lot of self-control, but you can overcome it. In fact, that's one of the reasons God wants you to learn self-control. His Word commands us to "be clear minded and self-controlled" (1 Peter 4:7, NIV).

God wants you to be like him. He is always in control of himself and of the universe he has made. And no matter how strongly rooted your bad habits may be, God is able and willing to help you overcome them. He will help you, through the power of his Spirit, to learn and exercise self-control.

REFLECT: Did you check any of the bad habits in the list above? On the lines below, list three bad habits you'd like to get rid of:

_____

_____

_____

Choose one of the above and start asking God for help to use self-control in overcoming that problem.

PRAY: "Father, you know that I'm weak in the above areas. But you are strong. Please help me to overcome my bad habit_____in your strength."

18 Five Alive

Bible Reading: Matthew 7:24-27

Anyone who listens to my teaching and obeys me is wise, like a person who builds a house on solid rock. Matthew 7:24

SOME PEOPLE DON'T obey God's commands because they don't understand them.

"They don't make sense to me," they may say.

"God can't blame me for not obeying things I don't understand, can he?" they may ask.

"I'll just follow those parts of the Bible that I agree with," they may decide.

But that kind of thinking and acting can be dangerous, as the following true story may illustrate:

There once was a group of five sailors in the British navy who were aboard a small boat. Their boat was towing a much larger ship through rough, choppy waters with a thick wire cable (called a hawser).

Suddenly, through the sound of the howling winds and crashing waves, the five sailors on deck heard their officer shout a single, one-word command: "Down!"

Immediately, those five men flung themselves to the deck of their vessel, a split second before that wire tow cable cracked over their heads and past their ears like a deadly whip. Their commanding officer had seen the cable snap and had issued his order just in time, allowing the five sailors to escape the recoil from the broken hawser. Any man who had been in the path of that cable would have been killed instantly.

Those five sailors survived because they obeyed without hesitating. If they had stopped to wonder why he gave that order, they would have been killed. If they had paused to argue the wisdom of the order, they would have been killed. If they had hesitated to decide whether or not the order made sense to them, they would have been killed. Their immediate obedience saved them from disaster.

Jesus said, "Anyone who listens to my teaching and obeys me is wise, like a person who builds a house on solid rock" (Matthew 7:24). We may not understand all of God's commands. We may not know exactly how his commands will protect us. But if we listen and obey, we will be wise.

 REFLECT: The house Jesus describes in today's Bible reading probably wasn't a house built beside an ocean or lake but a house built in one of the sandy wadis (or dry riverbeds) that were common where Jesus lived. Any house built on the soft ground of such a flat place would be fine during the dry part of the year but would probably be washed away when the rainy season came and the dry bed became a raging river! Are you more like someone who hears the teachings of Jesus and ignores them or like someone who listens and obeys what he said? How does Jesus say (in today's Bible reading) you can build a firm and lasting foundation that will keep you strong when the "storms" of life hit?

 PRAY: "Lord, I want to be a person who listens to your teachings and obeys them. Help me to grow stronger by reading your Word and praying every day."

19 Temper Tantrum

Bible Reading: 1 Timothy 1:15-17

That is why God had mercy on me, so that Christ Jesus could use me as a prime example of his great patience with even the worst sinners.
1 Timothy 1:16

HARVEY COULD HARDLY wait to get out of the music store in the mall. He finally had his own copy of the new Toe Jam CD, *Temper Tantrum.*

As he left the store, he turned the CD case sideways and scratched at the cellophane wrapper. "Come on," he said. "Come on." He kept scratching furiously until a thin strip of cellophane stood apart from the stubborn wrapper. "Finally," he sighed as he gripped the strip between his thumb and forefinger and pulled. A tiny, almost invisible piece of the wrapper came off. The rest of the wrapper remained intact.

Harvey gritted his teeth and turned the CD case over. He applied his thumbnail to the hinge of the CD case, running it up and down the ridge, hoping to break the wrapper. But the cellophane seemed to be unbreakable.

"Come on!" he growled. He stuck the CD case between his teeth and tried to bite the wrapper off. When that didn't work, he pulled a dime out of his pocket and tried to scratch the cellophane open with the side of the dime. Finally, he threw the CD case on the floor and started jumping up and down on it.

When he picked the CD up off the floor, the case was splintered, and the CD was scratched, but the cellophane wrapper was broken. "I DID IT!" he screamed in the crowded mall. He laughed like a maniac. "I DID IT! I OPENED IT! I WIN! I WIN! HA HA HA HA HA!"

Maybe you've never had an experience quite like Harvey's. Maybe you don't get impatient trying to peel the cellophane off a CD case. But you probably do get impatient with something, right? Maybe with waiting in the cafeteria line at school. Maybe with clothes that don't fit right. Maybe with bossy friends or nosy parents.

Regardless of what tries your patience, remember that patience is a virtue. That means it's a good thing. When you choose to be patient, you are choosing to do right.

But *why* is patience right? You probably know the answer already, don't you? (Careful—don't get impatient!)

Patience is right because God is patient. According to the apostle Paul, he has shown "great patience with even the worst sinners" (1 Timothy 1:16). He is patient with you. He's never given up on you. He's never quit loving you and helping you. And because God is patient, you should be patient, too, because patience is a virtue.

 REFLECT: Do you think God has been patient with you? If not, why not? If so, why? What things (or people) try your patience the most? How can you be more patient?

 PRAY: "God, thank you for being patient with me, even when I_____. Help me to be more like you in this area, too. Help me to be more patient when
_____."

Bible Reading: Genesis 4:1-12

People who cover over their sins will not prosper. But if they confess and forsake them, they will receive mercy. Proverbs 28:13

BRAD WAS SUPPOSED to be baby-sitting his little sister, but he had gotten so involved in the television show he was watching that he forgot all about Sissy. When the show ended, he went to look for her. He found her alone in the kitchen, where she had colored one of the walls with crayons!

"Oh no!" he cried, grabbing the crayons out of Sissy's hand. "Mom and Dad are going to kill us both!"

"I'm sorry," Sissy said. Her lower lip shot forward in a pout.

"Don't cry, Sissy," Brad said. "Brad's going to make it better." He gathered together Sissy's crayons and put them away. When he returned to the kitchen, he carried a paint can and brush. "We're going to fix Sissy's mistake," he told his sister. "Mom and Dad won't even know what you did."

He spread newspapers on the floor and started brushing the paint carefully over the crayon marks. The more he worked, though, the worse everything looked. He could still see the crayon marks through the paint. Not only that, the new paint looked darker than the old coat.

"It'll look better when it dries," he told Sissy. But he knew it wouldn't. He stooped over to put the lid back on the paint can and upset the can, spilling paint all over the floor. The newspapers soaked up some of the paint, but even after he had wiped up his mess, paint still showed in the cracks between the floor tiles. By the time his parents got home, the kitchen looked even worse than when he had started—and he was in even bigger trouble than he would have been had he just left Sissy's crayon marks alone!

Have you ever made a mistake or a wrong choice and then tried to cover it up instead of just admitting it and asking for forgiveness? If you have, you're not alone. That's what Adam and Eve did after they ate the forbidden fruit in the Garden of Eden: They tried to hide from God. That's what Cain did after he had killed his brother Abel. When God asked, "Where is your brother?" Cain replied, "I don't know. . . . Am I supposed to keep track of him wherever he goes?"

But trying to hide or deny their sins didn't work for Adam and Eve and Cain. And it won't work for us, either. When you make a wrong choice, it's much better to admit it and ask forgiveness than to try and cover it up. Don't try to hide it. Don't try to deny it. Don't try to explain it. Just confess it and determine to do better the next time.

 REFLECT: How do you usually react when you make a wrong choice? Do you think it's better to admit wrong choices than to try and deny them or cover them up? If not, why not? If so, why?

 PRAY: "Lord, you know that sometimes it's hard to admit it when I make a wrong choice. Please help me, from now on, to quickly 'confess and forsake' my sins instead of trying to cover them up."

Old George

Bible Reading: Numbers 10:29-32

We will share with you all the good things that the Lord does for us.
Numbers 10:32

GEORGE HAD NO home. Most nights he slept at the YMCA. He owned only the clothes he wore: a shirt, a pair of pants, a pair of shoes wrapped with rubber bands to keep the soles from flapping, and a shabby coat. On cold winter mornings George would go to the police station nearby and spend the morning sitting in an old metal chair in the back. At least it was warm inside the police station.

A couple of police officers befriended Old George. They would occasionally slip him a few dollars for a cup of coffee. They found out that Billy, a nearby restaurant owner, gave Old George a hot breakfast every morning at no charge.

The police officers decided to invite George to join their families for Christmas dinner. George agreed. They even gave a few presents to George, which he unwrapped carefully. As they drove their guest back to the YMCA that evening, George asked, "Are these presents really mine . . . to keep?" When the officers nodded, George asked the officers to drive by Billy's restaurant before taking him home.

When they arrived at Billy's restaurant, George had carefully rewrapped all his presents. He tucked them under his arms and walked into the restaurant.

"You've always been real good to me, Billy," he told the man behind the counter. "Now I can be good to you." He plopped the presents down on the counter and slid them toward Billy. "Merry Christmas!" he said. Old George gave all his Christmas presents away.

That story, told by reporter Anne Keegan in the *Chicago Tribune Magazine,* is a true story of one man's generosity. Unfortunately, we are not often like Old George.

Old George received gifts from a couple of generous police officers and promptly chose to share them with someone else. We have received many, many gifts from God and from others, but we don't always show our gratitude by being generous to others.

Really, that's all generosity is: sharing the good things God has given you. That's what Moses offered to Hobab in today's Bible reading. "Come, be our guide," he said, "and we will share with you all the good things that the Lord does for us" (Numbers 10:32). That's what God wants *us* to do—to be generous with all the good things he has given us.

REFLECT: List some of the good things God has done for you or given to you:

Money and Possessions   Talents, Abilities, Blessings

_____   _____

_____   _____

Can you share any of those with others? If not, why not? If so, how?

 PRAY: "Lord, remind me to share with others the many good things you have done for me, especially_____."

22 Man-Eater

Bible Reading: Ephesians 5:3-7

Watch out! Be on your guard against all kinds of greed; a man's life does not consist in the abundance of his possessions. Luke 12:15, NIV

MANY, MANY YEARS ago there was an old man who lived with his son in the forest. The people in the village nearby used to call the old man a miser and say that he kept stacks of money hidden in his house. Some even said that he could rub a silver coin for hour after hour until it would turn to gold!

One day the old man was out chopping wood when a wild tiger appeared and pounced on him. The tiger gripped the old man by the shirt on his back and carried him off, dangling the miser from his mouth the way a kitten might carry a rag doll.

The old man's son saw everything that happened and ran to get his rifle. He soon caught up to the tiger that held his father. The son raised his rifle to shoot the tiger and to save the old man.

"Wait!" cried the old man. "Don't shoot! Aim carefully," he instructed his son. "If you can kill this tiger without spoiling his beautiful hide, we can skin him and get many pieces of silver! Shoot carefully, my son, so that we may get top price for the tiger's skin!"

As the son listened obediently to his father's instruction, he lowered the rifle slightly from his shoulder. The tiger, seeing his opportunity to escape, suddenly bounded into the forest, carrying the old miser with him. The son pursued but could not catch the nimble tiger. He never saw his father again.

That old story illustrates the dangers of greed. By thinking only of money and of his own gain, the old man foolishly lost his life. That's why Jesus said, "Be on your guard against all kinds of greed; a man's life does not consist in the abundance of his possessions" (Luke 12:15, NIV). Greed is sin, and sin never made anyone happy and complete, though it has destroyed many people's lives. So be on your guard against all kinds of greed, and cultivate a spirit of generosity instead.

 REFLECT: Unscramble the scrambled words to complete the following statements, based on today's Bible reading:
- No greedy person will *thineir* the Kingdom of Christ and of God.
- A greedy person is really an *toadiler* who worships the things of this world.
- Don't *rappaticite* in the things these people do.

 PRAY: "Dear God, I know that my life and happiness aren't measured by the abundance of my possessions. But it's easy to forget that and start to be greedy. Remind me how wrong and dangerous greed is and how much better it is to be generous."

Answers: inherit, idolater, participate.

23 Command Performance

Bible Reading: Deuteronomy 24:19-22

Don't forget to do good and to share what you have with those in need, for such sacrifices are very pleasing to God. Hebrews 13:16

SOME OF GOD'S commands are more familiar than others. For example, everyone would be able to complete the famous fifth commandment, "Honor your father and mother." And just about anyone could recite, "Love your neighbor as yourself," right? But others may not be so familiar. Look at the list below, and see if you can change the wrong words in each of the verses so that they read correctly. (The references are given in case you need help; all references are from the NIV.)

- In everything I did, I showed you that by this kind of hard work we must help the weak, remembering the words the Lord Jesus himself said: "It is more blessed to smile than to frown" (Acts 20:35).
- Share with God's people who are in Nebraska (Romans 12:13).
- Therefore, as seen on TV, let us do good to all people (Galatians 6:10).
- Command them to do good, to be rich in milk chocolate, and to be generous and willing to share (1 Timothy 6:18).
- And do not forget to do good and to eat your vegetables, for with such sacrifices God is pleased (Hebrews 13:16).
- If anyone has large eyebrows and sees his brother in need but has no pity on him, how can the love of God be in him? (1 John 3:17).

Of course, by now, you've probably realized that all those Bible verses are commands to be generous, right? To be honest, that was the point of the whole exercise—a way of reminding ourselves that God commands generosity.

A lot of people think that generosity is something nice but not necessary. But God's Word says otherwise. He makes it clear, throughout his Word, that generosity is right and stinginess, or greediness, is wrong. That's why he so often says things like, "Share with God's people who are in need" (Romans 12:13, NIV) and "It is more blessed to give than to receive" (Acts 20:35, NIV).

To put it simply, if you aren't generous, you're disobeying God, because he commands generosity.

 REFLECT: Do you make a habit of being generous? Do you share with others? Are you generous with others in your family? Do you give to people who are in need? Can you name anyone you've been generous to in recent days? Can you think of new ways to be generous to others in the next few days and weeks?

 PRAY: "Father, please help me not to forget to do good and to share what I have with those in need."

24 Are You a Wise Guy?

Bible Reading: Matthew 2:1-12

Then they opened their treasure chests and gave him gifts of gold, frankincense, and myrrh. Matthew 2:11

YOU'VE PROBABLY HEARD the Christmas story many times, right? But how well do you really know it? Take the following quiz, and see if you're truly a "wise guy" (or girl) when it comes to the story of Jesus' birth. (Circle the best answer for each question.)

1. The wise men who journeyed from afar to visit Jesus were
   a. astrologers.   *b.* kings.   *c.* circus performers.

2. How many wise men were there?
   a. Three.   *b.* I don't know.   *c.* I know, but I'm not telling.

3. The wise men found Jesus in Bethlehem and visited him in
   a. a stable.   *b.* a manger.   *c.* a house.

4. The wise men's gifts included
   a. gold.   *b.* Frankenstein.   *c.* fur.

You see, a lot of misunderstanding has arisen about the visit of the wise men to Jesus on that first Christmas long ago. Most of people think the wise men were kings (probably because of the Christmas carol, "We Three Kings"); but they were most likely court astrologers for some city or nation. Most people think there were three wise men, but the Bible doesn't say how many wise men came to visit Jesus. And although your family's manger scene probably shows the wise men visiting Jesus at the stable where the Lord was born, they apparently didn't arrive until Jesus, Joseph, and Mary had moved into a house somewhere (see Matthew 2:11). And, of course, they brought gifts of gold, frankincense (not Frankenstein), and myrrh (not fur). So if your answers were *(a), (b), (c),* and *(a),* you really are a "wise guy" (or girl).

But the story of the wise men visiting Jesus is more than just fun and games. It can remind us that Christmas is more about giving than about getting. The wise men brought generous gifts to the Christ child that first Christmas, but they brought even more than expensive gifts of gold, frankincense, and myrrh. They brought themselves—and their worship.

This Christmas Eve you're probably thinking a lot about what you're getting for Christmas. But a more important question is: What are you *giving?*

 REFLECT: Christmas is exciting, isn't it? It's hard not to think about the gifts you will unwrap this year. But take a few minutes to think about what you're giving for Christmas. Can you think of ways you can be generous tomorrow (with gifts, time, favors, manners, worship, and so on) to your family *and* to Jesus?

 PRAY: "Lord, I know you value generosity. I want to learn about *giving* this Christmas instead of thinking only about *getting.* Please help me to show generosity to others—and to you—this Christmas."

25 The Best Christmas Gift

Bible Reading: Luke 2:1-7

For God so loved the world that he gave his only Son, so that everyone who believes in him will not perish but have eternal life. John 3:16

WHAT'S THE BEST Christmas gift you've ever gotten?

Was it a doll or an action figure? a construction set or a doctor kit? an electronic game or a set of in-line skates? Was it something that cost a lot? Was it homemade? Was it the gift itself or the thoughtfulness behind it that made it special?

What's the best Christmas gift you've ever *given?*

Was it something you made yourself, or did you save up for a long time to buy it? Was it the "perfect gift" for that person? Was it special because of the thought you put into it? Was it special because of the other person's joy at receiving it? Or was it special for some other reason?

Well, believe it or not, the best Christmas gift you've ever been given wasn't a toy or a game or an article of clothing. On the first Christmas morning centuries ago, God gave you a gift that cost more than all the money in the world. He could have gotten off cheaper by wrapping up the stars and the planets and dropping them on your doorstep. He could have economized by sweeping all the gold and silver and diamonds in the world into a big pile in your front yard. But he didn't. He gave you the most generous gift that's ever been given: Jesus, his Son.

God showed you two things by sending his Son as his Christmas gift to you: (1) He showed you that he loves you more than you can imagine (1 John 4:9); and (2) he showed that he is a generous, extravagant God. He will spare no cost to save you. He will endure any pain to give you the gift of eternal life.

And what's the best gift you could give to a God like that? It's yourself. Your love. Your thanks. Your worship. Your devotion. Your life. *That* would be the best Christmas gift you've ever given.

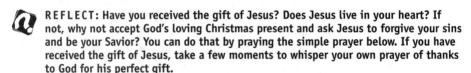

REFLECT: Have you received the gift of Jesus? Does Jesus live in your heart? If not, why not accept God's loving Christmas present and ask Jesus to forgive your sins and be your Savior? You can do that by praying the simple prayer below. If you have received the gift of Jesus, take a few moments to whisper your own prayer of thanks to God for his perfect gift.

PRAY: "Father, thank you for sending your Son to be born and to live and to die for my sake. Thank you for his sacrifice on the cross for my sins. Thank you for forgiving all my sins because of his death. I give myself to you and receive your Son as my Savior and Lord. Please take control of my life from now on and make me the kind of person you want me to be, through your Holy Spirit, who now lives in me."

26 The Two Brothers

Bible Reading: Philemon 1:4-6

Put your generosity to work, for in so doing you will come to an understanding of all the good things we can do for Christ. Philemon 1:6

THERE WERE ONCE two brothers who lived on neighboring farms. One brother lived on one side of the hill with his wife and children. The other brother was not married; he lived alone on the opposite side of the hill.

It happened that one year both brothers had a plentiful harvest. As the married brother's barns started to fill with his abundant crops, he started thinking of his brother. "God is so good," he said to himself. "Why does he bless me more than my brother? I have a loving wife and obedient children, but my brother is all alone." He decided to wait until dark, when his brother was sleeping, to sneak over the hill and carry some of his crops to his brother's fields. *He'll never know the difference,* he figured.

At the same time the unmarried brother sat alone in his house, thinking. "God is so good," he said. "But why has he blessed me so much? My brother has greater needs than I do; he has a wife and children to feed, and I have only myself to take care of." So he decided to wait until dark, then sneak into his brother's fields with as much of his crops as he could carry. *He'll never know the difference,* he reasoned.

So both brothers waited until dark. Then, assuming the other brother to be asleep, each went to his own fields, loaded his shoulders high with grain, and turned toward his brother's farm. Each performed his task and returned to his home. The next day each brother was amazed to discover that he still had as much grain as the night before!

This went on for several nights, until one night they met each other as they carried their gifts over the crest of the hill. Suddenly, each man realized what had been happening—each had been thinking only of his brother and not of himself. And they dropped their loads there on the top of the hill and embraced, crying tears of joy and love.

 REFLECT: The story of the two brothers illustrates the fact that generosity brings joy and blessing into our life. How would the story be different if the two brothers had been stingy with their crops instead of generous? Try writing your own version of "The Two Brothers," depicting how the results would have been different if they had displayed greed instead of generosity.

 PRAY: "God, you are so good, and you have given me so many blessings. Help me to put my generosity to work so I can understand all the good things I can do for Christ."

27 Dewey the Dog

Bible Reading: Ecclesiastes 5:10-14

Whoever loves money never has money enough; whoever loves wealth is never satisfied with his income. This too is meaningless.
Ecclesiastes 5:10, NIV

DEWEY THE DOG trotted away from the butcher shop, humming a little tune in his gruff little dog voice. His teeth gripped a meaty bone, snatched from the floor of the butcher shop.

He trotted down the lanes and streets of the town, snarling occasionally at any animal that eyed his prized bone too long or too hungrily. Finally, he reached the low footbridge that marked the halfway point home. He paused for a moment, artfully shifted the bone's position in his mouth, and peered into the slow-running stream below the bridge.

What he saw shocked him.

There, in the water, was an image of a dog. And that dog, like Dewey, held a bone in his teeth. Dewey's lip curled at the sight; his eyes narrowed. The dog in the stream didn't look tough at all—and the bone in his mouth looked even bigger than Dewey's bone.

Finally, after a few moments of growling and baring his teeth at the dog in the stream, which had returned every growl and every snarl, Dewey made his move. He opened his mouth and snapped at the other dog, attempting to grab his bone. But his attack touched only water, for the other dog was his reflection. And his own bone, which he had carried all the way from the butcher shop in town, slowly sank to the bottom of the stream.

That story, a retelling of one of Aesop's fables, illustrates what greed usually gains: nothing. If Dewey had been content with his prize, instead of greedily fighting for more, he could have gone home and enjoyed a long gnaw on a nice bone. Instead, he lost his own bone because he dropped it in his attempt to get more, and he lost the "other" dog's bone because it was only a reflection in the first place.

Greed gains nothing because the greedy person is never satisfied. But the generous person gains back far more than he gives away, because generosity blesses the giver more than the one receiving the gift. Seems odd, doesn't it? But it's true—it *is* more blessed to give than to receive.

 REFLECT: Today's Bible verse says, "Whoever loves money never has money enough; whoever loves wealth is never satisfied with his income" (Ecclesiastes 5:10, NIV). Do you think that's true? How much money do you think you would need before it would be "enough"? Do you tend to be more generous or greedy with money? with your possessions? with your time? with compliments? In what areas will you try to practice generosity today?

 PRAY: "God, help me to remember that it's better to give than to receive and to show I believe it by the way I handle my money, possessions, time, and compliments."

28 Untold Story

Bible Reading: 2 Corinthians 6:14–7:1

Because we have these promises, dear friends, let us cleanse ourselves from everything that can defile our body or spirit. And let us work toward complete purity because we fear God. 2 Corinthians 7:1

SAMUEL LOGAN BRENGLE was a preacher and writer in the Salvation Army. In one of his books, he told the following story:

> Some time ago, two Salvation Army officers were traveling by train. The railway carriage was crowded and they were separated. One of them sat down by an elderly man, and in a short time they were in conversation with a gentleman in front of them. Soon the elderly man looked about and said, "There are no women near who can hear, are there? I want to tell a story." The officer was at once on guard, and said, "I am a Salvationist, sir. I do not wish to hear a story that would be unfit for ladies to hear." The old man looked ashamed, the gentleman in front looked a look of wonder, and the nasty story was not told. The Salvationist, no doubt, escaped a great temptation.

That Salvationist's answer was surprising to his companions. It was also certainly pleasing to God because that Salvation Army officer made a right choice: purity of heart and mind (and ears!).

Purity is right. It is right because God commands purity (Isaiah 52:11; James 4:8). It is right because God values purity (Matthew 5:8). It is right because God is pure (1 John 3:3).

God wants us to be pure in what we think about. He wants us to be pure in what we say. He wants us to be pure in what we listen to or laugh at. He wants us to be pure in what we put into our body. He wants us to be pure in what we look at. He wants us to be pure in all these areas because he is pure. And to be pure in thought, word, and deed is to be like him.

REFLECT: Think about real, specific ways you can "work toward complete purity" (2 Corinthians 7:1) and then complete the following statements:

- "I want to be pure in what I think about, so I will _____."
- "I want to be pure in what I say, so I will _____."
- "I want to be pure in what I listen to or laugh at, so I will _____."
- "I want to be pure in what I put into my body, so I will _____."
- "I want to be pure in what I look at, so I will _____."

PRAY: "Lord, I want to be pure, as you are pure. Please help me not to _____ [look at impure things, use bad language, etc.], and help me as I cleanse myself from everything that can defile my body or spirit."

29 Man's Vest Friend

Bible Reading: Romans 8:12-18

What we suffer now is nothing compared to the glory he will give us later. Romans 8:18

THE NEW YORK City Police Department uses trained dogs to search buildings before police officers enter. Special video cameras are strapped to the dogs so that police can see if any dangerous people are inside a building before they go in.

But the dogs sometimes get shot. So not long ago someone in the police department came up with an idea. Thirteen police dogs were outfitted with bulletproof vests similar to the vests the police officers wear—except these vests were designed for dogs. Each vest weighs between six and seven pounds. The vests can be very warm and heavy for a dog, but the police officers who train and use the dogs hope the new vests will save the lives of their four-footed friends.

Do you think they might be wondering, *Why do I have to put up with this burden?* [pant, pant] *None of my doggie friends have to wear heavy, hot vests.*

Do you think the dogs might want to say, *Why are you humans always trying to make things harder for us dogs?* [pant, pant, pant] *Why can't we just do what we want? Why do you weigh us down with tight, restrictive things?*

Who knows? Maybe that's what the dogs are thinking. But, of course, *we* know that those bulletproof vests are very light burdens compared to the protection they offer. If those dogs could possibly know that wearing those heavy vests could save their lives, they would certainly choose the vest.

Sometimes Christian kids feel like those dogs. That doesn't mean you pant like a dog or smell like a dog (no matter what your older sister says). It just means that sometimes we feel like God's commands are burdensome. We might think that it would be nicer if we just didn't have to worry about making right choices.

But just as those police officers put heavy, confining vests on their dogs for a reason, God has given his commands for a reason. His commands are given to protect us, not to weigh us down. God's commands work like a bulletproof vest; the good they do *far* outweighs the effort they require. (See Romans 8:17; 2 Corinthians 4:17.)

So if you ever feel like God's commands are sort of a burden, remember that his commands protect you like a bulletproof vest. They will not only protect you from many injuries, they may even save your life.

 REFLECT: Do you ever feel like God's commands are a burden? Do you ever think it might be nicer if you didn't have to worry about making right choices? Why or why not? According to today's Bible reading, what would your sinful nature result in if you didn't obey God's commands? What will turning from your sinful nature and its evil deeds get you? Which choice do you think is better?

 PRAY: "Father, sometimes it does seem hard to follow your commands. But please help me to always remember that whatever I may go through now is nothing compared to the blessings of following you."

30 Don't Be a Quisling

Bible Reading: Psalm 89:1-8

O Lord God Almighty! Where is there anyone as mighty as you, Lord? Faithfulness is your very character. Psalm 89:8

DO YOU KNOW what a *quisling* is? (It's a real word. We didn't make it up.)

If somebody calls you a "quisling," you should be offended. It's the same as calling someone a "Judas" or "Benedict Arnold."

You see, Vidkun Quisling was a politician in Norway when Adolph Hitler became the leader of Germany. When the Nazis invaded Norway in 1940, Quisling cooperated with the Germans, and the Germans rewarded him by making him the "prime minister" of Norway in 1942. He sold out his king and his country to get what he wanted. He also imprisoned and killed people who were still loyal to the king but who had escaped to England after the German invasion. After Germany lost the war, Quisling was arrested, tried, and executed by a Norwegian court. Ever since that time, *quisling* has been another word for traitor.

How would you like for *your* name to become a way to call someone a traitor? That would be a real bummer, wouldn't it? You don't want to be known as a traitor, do you? You want people to think of you as loyal and trustworthy, right?

Of course you do. Most people do. Nobody wants to be known as a quisling, because betraying your friends, family, country, or God is wrong. But *why* is it wrong? Why does almost everyone despise what Quisling did? Why is it wrong to be a quisling? And why is it right to be faithful to your friends, family, country, or God?

Faithfulness is right because God is faithful. Faithfulness is right because being faithful is being like God. The psalmist sang to God, "Young and old will hear of your faithfulness. . . . Your faithfulness is as enduring as the heavens. . . . Faithfulness is your very character" (Psalm 89:1-2, 8). The reason that unfaithfulness is wrong is because that quality is not like God.

So don't be a quisling. Instead, be faithful to your friends, family, country, and God.

 REFLECT: What does it mean to be faithful? Does it mean keeping promises? Does it mean not talking behind someone's back? Does it mean not doing something that would hurt the other person? Does it mean something else? Think about what it means to be faithful by completing the following sentences:
- Being faithful to my friends means _____ .
- Being faithful to my family means _____ .
- Being faithful to my country means _____ .
- Being faithful to my God means _____ .

 PRAY: "God, your faithfulness is as enduring as the heavens. Please help me to be more like you. Make me—and keep me—faithful to you, to my country, to my family, and to my friends."

31 Positive Daydreaming

Bible Reading: Philippians 4:8-9

> *Finally, brothers, whatever is true, whatever is noble, whatever is right, whatever is pure, whatever is lovely, whatever is admirable—if anything is excellent or praiseworthy—think about such things. Philippians 4:8, NIV*

JAMES THURBER WROTE a story called "The Secret Life of Walter Mitty." Thurber's main character in the story was an ordinary man who had a habit of daydreaming. Walter Mitty went through each day imagining himself to be a hero. He imagined that he was flying a navy plane through the worst storm in history when he was actually driving his old car through a drizzle. He fantasized that he was a world-famous surgeon when he was only driving by a hospital on the way to pick up his wife.

You may not quite have Walter Mitty's problem. You may just daydream about falling in love or getting out of school early. But there is a way to daydream that can actually help you make right choices—and become a person of character and integrity.

Paul talked about that kind of "daydreaming" when he wrote to the early church. Paul commanded them to spend their moments concentrating on things that are true, noble, right, and so on. He told them to think about things that are good and right in order to keep their minds from wandering into dangerous or destructive areas. The idea is, if you fill your mind with good things, there will be less room left over for bad things.

So how do you "think about such things"? There are many ways to do that, but let's just mention three:

1. *Memorize Scripture.* If you fill your mind with God's Word (say, by memorizing one verse a week), you'll be better able to resist temptation and make right choices (see Matthew 4:4, 7, 10).

2. *Pray "without ceasing."* Instead of just praying once in the morning, develop a habit of praying all day, even if it's just a few words at a time, such as "Lord, help me say the right thing" or "Thanks for helping me a moment ago, Lord" (see 1 Thessalonians 5:17).

3. *Program your thought life.* If a television show prompts impure thoughts, decide to avoid that show. If a friend tempts you to do things that aren't right, plan to steer clear of that friend. Decide ahead of time to avoid sights, sounds, and places that take your mind off things that are true, noble, right, and pure (see Psalm 101:3).

Those three steps won't guarantee right choices. But *that* kind of daydreaming will help you to make right choices—and become a person of integrity.

 REFLECT: If you'd like to start memorizing Scripture, start with one of the following: John 3:16, John 14:6, Matthew 7:7, 1 John 1:9, or Psalm 119:105. If you want to begin to "pray without ceasing," think of a way you can remind yourself to pray throughout the day. (For example, tie a string to your finger.) If you begin to plan your thought life, what sights, sounds, and places will you avoid?

 PRAY: "Lord, please help me to make a habit of thinking about things that are true, noble, right, pure, lovely, admirable, excellent, and praiseworthy."

Passing On the Truth to Our Next Generation

The Right From Wrong message, available in numerous formats, provides a blueprint for countering the culture and rebuilding the crumbling foundations of our families.

The Right from Wrong Book for Adults

Right from Wrong: What You Need to Know to Help Youth Make Right Choices
by Josh McDowell and Bob Hostetler

Our youth no longer live in a culture that teaches an objective standard of right and wrong. Truth has become a matter of taste. Morality has been replaced by individual preference. And today's youth have been affected. Fifty-seven percent of our churched youth cannot state that an objective standard of right and wrong even exists!

As the centerpiece of the Right From Wrong Campaign, this life-changing book provides you with a biblical, yet practical, blueprint for passing on core Christian values to the next generation.

Right from Wrong, Trade Paper Book
ISBN 0-8499-3604-7

The Truth Slayers Book for Youth

Truth Slayers: The Battle of Right from Wrong
by Josh McDowell and Bob Hostetler

This book, directed to youth, is written in the popular NovelPlus format. It combines the fascinating story of Brittney Marsh, Philip Milford, Jason Withers, and the consequences of their wrong choices with Josh McDowell's insights for young adults in sections called "The Inside Story."

Truth Slayers conveys the critical Right From Wrong message that challenges you to rely on God's Word as the absolute standard of truth in making right choices.

Truth Slayers, Trade Paper Book
ISBN 0-8499-3662-4

103 Questions Book for Children

103 Questions Children Ask about Right from Wrong
Introduction by Josh McDowell

"How does a person really know what is right or wrong?" "How does God decide what's wrong?" "If lying is wrong, why did God let some people in the Bible tell lies?" "What is a conscience and where does it come from?" These and 99 other questions are what kids ages 6 to 10 are asking. The 103 Questions book equips parents to answer the tough questions kids ask about right from wrong. It also provides an easy-to-understand book that a child will read and enjoy.

103 Questions, Trade Paper Book
ISBN 0-8423-4595-7

The Topsy-Turvy Kingdom Picture Book

The Topsy-Turvy Kingdom
by Dottie and Josh McDowell, with David Weiss

This fascinating story from a faraway land is written in delightful rhyme. It enables adults to teach children the importance of believing in and obeying an absolute standard of truth.

The Topsy-Turvy Kingdom, Hardcover Book for Children
ISBN 0-8423-7218-0

The Josh McDowell Family and Youth Devotionals

Josh McDowell's One Year Book of Family Devotions by Bob Hostetler
Josh McDowell's One Year Book of Youth Devotions by Bob Hostetler

These two devotionals may be used alone or together. Youth from ages 10 through 16 will enjoy the youth devotionals on their own. And they'll be able to participate in the family devotionals with their parents and siblings. Both devotionals are packed with fun-filled and inspiring readings. They will challenge you to think—and live—as "children of God without fault in a wicked and depraved generation, in which you shine like stars in the universe" (Philippians 2:15, NIV).

Josh McDowell's One Year Book of Family Devotions
ISBN 0-8423-4302-4
Josh McDowell's One Year Book of Youth Devotions
ISBN 0-8423-4301-6

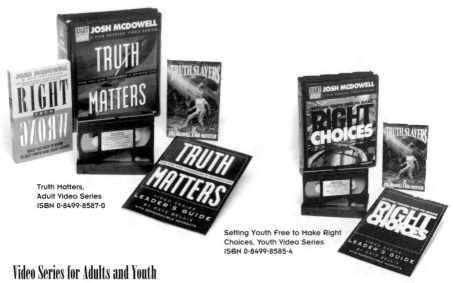

Truth Matters,
Adult Video Series
ISBN 0-8499-8587-0

Setting Youth Free to Make Right
Choices, Youth Video Series
ISBN 0-8499-8585-4

Video Series for Adults and Youth

Truth Matters for You and Tomorrow's Generation Five-part Adult Video Series featuring Josh McDowell
Setting Youth Free to Make Right Choices Five-part Youth Video Series featuring Josh McDowell

These two interactive video series go beyond declaring what is right and wrong. They teach how to make right moral choices based on God's absolute standard of truth.

The adult series includes five video sessions, a comprehensive Leader's Guide with samplers from the five *Right from Wrong* workbooks, the *Right from Wrong* book, the *Truth Slayers* book, and an eight-minute promotional tape that will motivate adults to go through the series.

The youth series contains five video sessions, a Leader's Guide with reproducible handouts that include samplers from the *Right from Wrong* workbooks, and the *Truth Slayers* book.

The Right from Wrong Musicals for Youth

The Truth Works musical by Dennis and Nan Allen
The Truth Slayers musical by Steven V. Taylor and Matt Tullos

The Truth Slayers musical for junior high and high school students is based on the *Truth Slayers* book. *The Truth Works* musical for children is based on the *Truth Works* workbooks. As youth and children perform these musicals for their peers and families, they have a unique opportunity to tell of the life-changing message of Right from Wrong.

Each musical includes complete leader's instructions, a songbook of all music used, dramatic script, and accompanying soundtrack on cassette or compact disc.

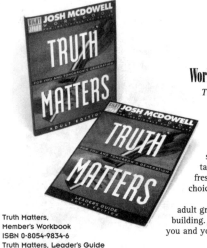

Workbook for Adults

Truth Matters for You and Tomorrow's Generation
Workbook and Leader's Guide
by Josh McDowell

The Truth Matters workbook includes 35 daily activities that help you to instill within your children and youth such biblical values as honesty, love, and sexual purity. By taking just 25 to 30 minutes each day, you will discover a fresh and effective way to teach your family how to make right choices—even in tough situations.

The Truth Matters workbook is designed to be used in 8 adult group sessions that encourage interaction and support building. The 5 daily activities between each group meeting will help you and your family to make right choices a habit.

Truth Matters,
Member's Workbook
ISBN 0-8054-9834-6
Truth Matters, Leader's Guide
ISBN 0-8054-9833-8

Workbook for College Students

Out of the Moral Maze, Workbook with Leader's Instructions
by Josh McDowell

Students entering college face a culture that has lost its belief in absolutes. In today's society, truth is a matter of taste; morality, a matter of individual preference. *Out of the Moral Maze* will provide any truth-seeking collegiate with a sound moral guidance system based on God and his Word as the determining factor for making right moral choices.

Out of the Moral Maze
Member's Workbook and Leader's Instructions
ISBN 0-8054-9832-X